The Art & Craft of College Teaching

A Guide for New Professors
& Graduate Students

The Art & Craft of College Teaching

A Guide for New Professors & Graduate Students

Second Edition

Robert Rotenberg

Left Coast
Press Inc.

WALNUT CREEK, CALIFORNIA

**Left
Coast
Press**
Inc.

LEFT COAST PRESS, INC.
1630 North Main Street, #400
Walnut Creek, CA 94596
http.//www.LCoastPress.com

ISBN 978-1-59874-533-7 hardcover
ISBN 978-1-59874-534-4 paperback

Library of Congress Cataloging-in-Publication Data

Rotenberg, Robert Louis, 1949-
  The art & craft of college teaching : a guide for new professors & graduate students
  / Robert Rotenberg. – 2nd ed.
    p. cm.
  Includes bibliographical references.
  ISBN 978-1-59874-533-7 (hardcover : alk. paper) – ISBN 978-1-59874-534-4
  (pbk. : alk. paper)
  1. College teaching--Handbooks, manuals, etc. I. Title.
  LB2331.R64 2010
  378.1'25--dc22
                              2010007016

Printed in the United States of America

♾™ The paper used in this publication meets the minimum requirements of
American National Standard for Information Sciences—Permanence of Paper
for Printed Library Materials, ANSI/NISO Z39.48–1992.

Contents

Preface

Something new happens every time I go into the classroom. It does not matter what course. It does not matter how many students greet me. If I did not experience this novelty, I would have chosen a different profession. The classroom renews me as a scholar, as a university citizen, and as a colleague. When I first started teaching, I could not believe that they paid me to have so much fun. Now, I am grateful that my school values my contribution to our students' lives with the salary they pay me. I try to share my enthusiasm with my colleagues, especially younger colleagues who discover the secrets of the classroom for the first time.

My university has experienced extraordinary growth in the last decade. This has added dozens of new faculty to our college and doubled the size of my department. As chair, I was the primary mentor for new faculty. I would find myself saying the same things to each new colleague. I decided to write it down. That became the germ of this book. I want to share this approach to college teaching beyond my own institution.

Teaching satisfies many of my needs. One of them is the need to live in a community of citizens who can reason clearly and accurately about the issues we all face. I teach because teaching creates that community one citizen at a time. If I can persuade you to stimulate your students to become the best reasoners they can be, our communities become better places for all of us to live.

Currently you can find a dozen books on college teaching in print and another dozen through libraries. In the first years of teaching, no one has time to read them all. I have read them all and the supporting research literature as well. I have taken the best they have to offer and combined it with my own experience as a teacher, as a mentor, as an administrator, and as a social scientist. The result, I hope, will guide you to a better teaching practice.

Acknowledgments

My model teachers were men and women who established a relationship with me and my fellow students as learners. They put our needs first. I have known such teachers since grade school. I don't even remember all their names. I do remember their classrooms. I remember thinking that being a teacher and working in such a place must be the most satisfying work experience. In high school, the feeling changed. I wanted out. I wanted to skip this stage. With few exceptions, the classrooms were no longer places that had a place for me. Getting into college entailed higher stakes. The teachers kept the gates. They designed their classrooms with opportunities to fail, rather than opportunities to succeed. I looked to college as the chance to return to my own Golden Age of Learning. When I finally arrived, I found the classrooms not that different from high school. Still, the classrooms I sought did exist. I found them; teachers committed to teaching the art of learning. They were men and women of infinite patience. With all the distractions going on in my life at the time, they had to be.

The idea for this book came from my experiences as a fellow at the Internationales Forschungszentrum Kulturwissenschaft in Vienna, Austria, in Fall, 2001. Working with young Ph.D.'s from different European schools made me ever more aware that we continue developing critical thinking skills after graduate school. I am grateful to Gotthart Wunberg and Lutz Musner for creating a superb environment for interaction between senior and junior scholars in cultural studies. I owe a special thanks to the other two senior fellows, Scott Spector and Peter Jelavich, for constructive help in the earliest stages of this project.

This book owes a great deal to my colleagues at DePaul. They helped me sustain a conversation on teaching for over thirty years. It began with an interdisciplinary reading group I joined when I started. With Larry Bennett, James Block, Joanne Devine, Michael Mezey, Charles Strain, Jacqueline Taylor, and Harry Wray, we lowered the disciplinary walls that graduate education had taught us to defend, discovering that we really had a common conversation. While talking about teaching was not our first priority, our classroom experiences found their way in.

The interdisciplinary classroom experiences we developed later emerged from this conversation.

I conducted my first teaching seminar for faculty in 1996. I could not have done so without the support of Jean Knoll of DePaul's School for New Learning and Phyllis Waldron of Morton College. They taught me approaches to the classroom that I might never have encountered otherwise. Jean also introduced me to problem-based learning in 1988. She taught me to teach students to do the same things I did when I set about to learn something new. She changed my teaching radically.

More recently, Charles Suchar, Caryn Chaden, David Jolliffe, Gerry Mulderig, Larry Mayo, Jeffery Carlson, Midge Wilson, Lucy Rinehart, Randell Honold, Sandra Jackson, Beth Kelly, Patrick Callahan, Jody Cressman, and Nancy Hill invigorate my teaching with every conversation we have. Visiting scholars, especially Susan Wolcott and Peter Ewell, have refreshed the ideas from time to time. I am especially grateful to Susan Wolcott for permission to use extensive summaries of her work with the late Cindy Lynch.

Finally, this book could not have been written without the conversations I have had with Michael McIntyre, Heidi Nast, Gil Gott, Sharon Nagy, Jane Baxter-Gordon, Ginger Hofman, Mark Hauser, Robert Adams Anna Agbe-Davies and John Mazzeo during their first five years of teaching. They taught me how to talk about teaching through their questions. They have encouraged me to become a better learner. David Jolliffe, Charles Suchar, Nancy Hill and Beth Kelly read the manuscript at various stages. Each contributed something valuable to its final shape through their comments.

Sonja Rotenberg took an active interest in this project from the beginning. Together we formed a publishing venture to make sure that the book came out in the form we wanted. At the same time, my daughter Ariela was experiencing the extraordinary and sometimes the less than extraordinary teaching of a selective public high school and a selective liberal arts college. She found that selectivity in admissions does not guarantee effective teaching. Without the help of Sonja and Ariela, this book may never have been finished.

I dedicate this book to both of them.

PART 1

Teaching as an Art and Teaching as a Craft

If I have imagined my audience accurately, most of you will spend your careers in institutions that value research above teaching. Personnel committees say that they evaluate our performance according to our accomplishments in teaching, research, and service. In annual reviews and evaluations leading to tenure and promotion, we often treat these as isolated activities, with research the only one that "really counts." The idea that teaching and research would be evaluated for the influence they have on each other is unfathomable in most departments. Some faculty might even consider it offensive. Service and research might influence each other, especially as service is usually defined. That is, as work on university committees. I have been fortunate to work in a college that is among the increasing number nationally that evaluate teaching, research, and service holistically, seeking the connections between them as a measure of a professor's effectiveness. I admit that this experience is unusual. Even if your department, college, or university works from the older, more common tradition, you can profit as a researcher, a teacher, and a community member by increasingly integrating your efforts over time. Doing so provides greater job satisfaction, a coherent research agenda, a more enticing, burnout-free teaching career, and an effective service orientation.

The best way to learn something is to teach it. The most neglected aspect of teaching is the general improvement in the teacher's own reasoning skills. When we teach our students to consistently challenge their thinking habits, developing problem-solving patterns and processes that are ever more effective, we cannot help but reflect on our own habits. As we instruct our students in ferreting out contradictions and fallacies in the work of others, we see how these might creep into our own arguments. As we attempt to model the traits of critical thinking in the classroom, these carry over into our collaborations with graduate students, colleagues, and research partners. In short, teaching with a methodology makes us better methodologists.

One short book is not going to resolve all the issues surrounding university teaching. Urging young professors to think of teaching as part of the realm of scholarship is a first step. I want to convince you, as I have been convinced, that the classroom inspires research. I hope this book will encourage colleagues at all stages of their career to discuss our classroom experience in an informed manner, accurately distinguishing between undergraduate and graduate teaching.

We now know something about how college students learn and what effective teaching looks like. Other than the legitimate complaint about the amount of time it takes to read the research and pull the information together, there is no excuse for college teachers not knowing how to be good at what they do. My aim here is to do a lot of that time-consuming assembling for the new professor or those wanting to become instructors. The perspective I support in forging an effective classroom practice grew out of my reading of this research, especially the idea that intellectual development continues throughout adulthood at different rates for different people, depending on how they are stimulated.

Our students are individuals, each with a unique set of strengths and weaknesses. For some those strengths are prodigious. There are entering students who have the reasoning skills of graduate students. There are graduate students who still reason like the typical entering college student. The differences for all these students between their experiences in high school, in college and in graduate school lie in the expectations that we, their teachers, set for them.

When students come to college, we expect them to struggle with ambiguities of inference and interpretation. At the same time, we expect them to be open to the difference between evidence and opinion in an argument. When students come to graduate school, we expect them to construct well-supported arguments that prioritize among alternative perspectives according to contemporary disciplinary prerogatives and paradigms.

Our few selective colleges and graduate schools admit students with similar levels of preparation. One of my colleagues calls this making a silk purse out of silk. However, the vast majority of university teachers work in schools where the level of preparation for both undergraduate and graduate students is mixed. Here, then, is the compelling intellectual puzzle of post-secondary teaching: how do we deal with the variety of preparations and rates of development in our students while moving all of them toward greater scholarly success?

When we view teaching as a form of scholarship, every classroom presents itself as a new and equal challenge. Each course in the curriculum finds an equal footing with every other course. Faculty judge their worth as teachers not by the proportion of higher-level courses their colleagues entrust to them but by the transformational possibilities of all their classrooms.

The following chapters cull the best ideas from the existing literature on college teaching and offer insights from my own experience. I tell my students that a book is a tool for thinking. I offer this book as a tool to help you think about teaching. It is not merely a how-to manual. It is a program for developing a successful career as a professor.

I expect that this book will stir debate about teaching effectiveness, the assessment of curriculum design, and the mentoring of new professors. At least I hope that the perspective I offer here will breathe new air into these perennial discussions. I do not claim to have all the answers. I have not invented the ultimate evaluation form. Nor have I found the magic words that will help struggling assistant professors find their inner teacher.

Some of the ideas I present here may annoy experienced colleagues as too prescriptive: "That's not how I do it, and I've won teaching awards." I do not intend this work to be exhaustive or encyclopedic. I am sure that I have missed some important questions, research findings, and techniques. I am also certain that readers will discover inadvertent mistakes. I accept responsibility for all these errors, omissions, and oversights and commit myself to correcting them in future editions. I want to thank ahead of time those colleagues who read this book in detail and send me their thoughts on how it can be more useful to them.

The Learning Curve of the College Teacher

Researchers on teaching agree that instructors see their classrooms in one of two ways: as teacher focused or as student focused (Biggs 1999, 57-75; Martin and Balla 1991, 298-304; Prosser and Trigwell 1998; Samuelowicz and Bain 1992, 93-112). Teacher-focused classrooms are ones in which knowledge is transmitted by an expert teacher to a novice student. If the teacher communicates clearly and effectively, the student moves closer to becoming an expert. At the lower levels of the curriculum, this knowledge is primarily definitions of key concepts, elementary algorithms for transforming data, incidents in a historical narrative, and similar lists within categories. At the higher levels of the curriculum, the knowledge takes the form of important concepts necessary for understanding the more subtle research issues in the discipline. The intended outcomes for the student include the ability to reproduce the information and analytical processes.

Student-focused classrooms permanently transform the student's view of the world in a way that leads the student to continuously learn. Student-centered classrooms emphasize independent learning that will shape the student's attitudes and accomplishments throughout life, including their increasing expertise in a discipline. What the student does in the classroom affects this transformation far more directly than what the teacher does in the classroom. Faculty do not set out to specifically create one or the other of these transformations. Rather, the students' experience results from challenges that instructors create for them.

The outcomes of teaching vary. They depend on variables that instructors can never control, as well as ones they can sometimes control. The range of student abilities and the constraints of the curriculum are beyond the instructor's control. Classroom design and assessment are within the instructor's control. Instructors make these choices differently, depending on their experience and reflectiveness. According to Biggs (1999, 57-75), each of these choices determines whether the classroom will end up being student focused or teacher focused.

Beginning instructors realize that there are some students who respond to their efforts and others who resist. They believe that it is the students' responsibility to bring the desire to learn to the class. Teachers in this predicament reason that the best that one can do is to hold the line on standards and allow the variation in the students to emerge as a grade distribution. Biggs calls this practice one that focuses on "what the student is." When students perform poorly, as some of them will in such situations, it is because something in them is deficient: skills, motivation, ability, attitude, or cultural background (Samuelowicz 1987, 121-34).

More experienced faculty will grow tired of this situation. They begin to examine how they might be complicit in their students' achievements. Biggs calls this practice one that focuses on "what the teacher does." They seek out more classroom management skills, collect books on teaching, and cultivate techniques to increase student engagement and motivation to learn. While good management is essential for setting the stage for learning, it does not guarantee student learning. When students continue to perform poorly, as they will even in the most carefully managed of classrooms, it is because something in the teacher is deficient. Teaching becomes a collection of competencies. The more of them that you control, the better teacher you are. This view of teaching often underlies the administrative evaluation of the teaching experience. Departments and colleges make personnel decisions based on claims of teacher effectiveness that essentially measure classroom management skills, rather than student learning.

The most effective teachers realize that they can embody all the possible competencies and some portion of students still will not learn. They begin to ask themselves, "What does it actually mean when students understand a concept? How does it change their thinking or behavior in some demonstrable way? What activities are necessary for this understanding to take place for the student?" These questions begin to shift the focus away from what teachers do and toward what students are doing:

> If students are to learn desired outcomes in a reasonably effective manner, then the teacher's fundamental task is to get students to reengage in learning activities that are likely to result in their achieving those outcomes.... It is helpful to remember that what the student does is actually more important in determining what is learned than what the teacher does. (Shuell 1986, 411-36)

Many faculty will say that they embrace the student-focused classroom, but this is much harder to put into practice than most are willing admit. In general, student-focused classrooms require us to develop three specific areas of the class that are not part of traditional teaching: specific statements about desired outcomes that can be learned in a reasonably effective manner, a set of assessment tasks keyed to these outcomes, and a set of learning (as opposed to teaching) activities where the outcomes have a reasonable chance of being achieved.

If one can skip a stage, it is not really a stage. The same holds for stages in developing teaching. I would not encourage colleagues who have never taught before to jump directly to the student-centered classroom unless that was the basis of the education they received, and they understand its principles. New instructors cannot help but begin with trying to understand the variety of students they meet. This stage can help you learn to articulate the basic principles of your discipline in ways that communicate to the broadest audience. This stage truly acquaints you with the students in your college. You learn how better to manage classrooms. This stage unfolds over at least two years of full-time teaching.

Once you have come to grips with the variation in learners, you begin to search for techniques. There is so much good information out there about classroom design and management that it is almost a malpractice not to seek it out. The administration of your school will expect you to develop ever-greater competencies. Several years of trying out different techniques provides a basis on which student-focused teaching can be built.

The instructor's embrace of student-centered classrooms is not an inevitable one. We all know colleagues who have taught their entire careers in stage 1 and can point to hundreds of students who went on to be successful learners. Stage 2 teachers are the ones who tend to win awards. Their classrooms provide the kind of novelty that holds student interest and generates outstanding evaluations. Their students see them as showing greater concern. These colleagues, too, can point to hundreds of successful learners emerging from their classrooms. Many instructors at this stage hold back from developing further. They do not see their teaching as broken, so why fix it. Stage 3 teachers, therefore, are quite rare at the undergraduate level. Such teaching is more often directed at advanced graduate students. The closer they get to becoming experts, the more they will learn independently. Bringing that attitude into undergraduate practice sets the advanced instructor apart from her peers.

Every school has some faculty who practice these techniques among undergraduates, but it is not a mainstream practice. Each can be effective in meeting some of the desired outcomes. The university will always have classrooms designed by instructors at all three stages of instructor development. I have no illusions that at some point in the future all instructors will embrace student-centered learning the first day they step into the classroom and follow that practice throughout their careers. That being the case, in the chapters that follow I have tried to provide support for faculty at all three stages.

Chapter 2: Plan of the Book

CHAPTER 2

Balancing the expansion the knowledge base of the students with the development of their critical reasoning skills challenges all postsecondary teachers. These two goals cannot be accomplished as addenda to each other. Students do not learn new habits of reasoning by committing lists of items to memory. They do not acquire the knowledge base by drilling on problem sets. The knowledge base must be taught using techniques that are effective for teaching information, and the skill set must be developed using techniques that challenge reasoning. Each moment in the curriculum has its golden proportion of knowledge gained and skills practiced.

Every instructor should know the qualities that students bring to the classroom. There can be at least one generation and sometimes as many as four generations that separate the students from the teacher. You need to understand what these generational experiences are and how they affect performance in the classroom. The current students, born between 1984 and 2000, seem to have something in common with the baby boom and post-boom generations who fill the professoriate. Yet, the differences remain quite large (Howe and Strauss 2000).

More importantly, the vast majority of our students intend to spend their lives outside the university. They have different goals and values than those who chose to work as professors. The professor has always set the standards for classroom performance. Given these generational differences, we must adapt the way we communicate these standards. The failure to do so risks exposing us to charges of irrelevance and ivory-tower-ism.

Our teaching is embedded in a university curriculum. This curriculum makes demands on individual courses that professors cannot ignore. New professors experienced a curriculum as students. When they enter a department, they take on responsibility for holding up their end of a conversation that began before they arrived—namely, what combination of experiences best communicates the important values and accomplishments of the discipline to the students. Having an overview of the curriculum is important for understanding how to implement many of the course design features offered in this book. In the curriculum, the balance changes according to the role the course plays: topical courses are knowledge base heavy; methods sequences emphasize skill sets. How, then, does the department see the courses that lie between?

Course design begins with constructing a syllabus. I understand the syllabus three ways: as a virtual and an actual document of the instructor's complete plan for a course, and as the proffer of a contract with students that outlines everyone's rights and responsibilities in the class. A list of readings, discussion topics, and due dates for assignments and exams is not a syllabus. Add a bibliography and a set of paragraphs about grading and attendance policies, and you still do not have a syllabus, although at least you now have something that begins to define the classroom. The full syllabus is the mechanism through which the entire organization of the course is developed. It is both a working document, in the sense that it evolves with each course, and a scholarly document of the complete teaching effort. Well-constructed syllabi are like journal articles or technical reports. They are complete enough for another teacher to read them and know exactly how the classroom experience was designed, how student learning was assessed, and how the achievement of the goals of the course was evaluated. I will offer a step-by-step plan for developing syllabi.

With the beginning of the actual term, the first order of business is explaining the syllabus. The second is assessment. I have colleagues who see assessment as an unwelcome and silly imposition by an administration cowed by an accreditation agency. They find it busywork that contributes nothing to effective teaching. I begin with it because it is a way of establishing an ongoing conversation with students about classroom learning. There is no more effective aid to teaching than knowing who is sitting in front of you and what their actual knowledge and skill levels are at the beginning of the term. My discussion of assessment here is classroom based and modest in its aims. I see assessment as a stance that you take toward the students, an openness to their actual experience that goes beyond impressions and anecdotes to more solid information sources.

College teachers should be able to design any kind of classroom they wish, moving easily from lecture to discussion or from seminar to field-work. For each of these styles of classroom design, there is more to it than meets the eye. Lecturing is the basic technique of teaching. At a mini-mum, every instructor ought to be able to organize the knowledge they want to communicate and deliver it publicly in an effective and engaging way. There are other ways of transferring knowledge, and in some class-rooms, these alternatives are more effective than lectures. Lecturing to a class of ten, for example, is not the best use of anyone's time.

Most college teachers know how to discuss a topic with students. As their knowledge base expands, they learn how to ask students deeper or more incisive questions. To get students to participate, instructors use some combination of carrot and stick. Nevertheless, most discussions are deadly dull. Effective discussion, as I will show, is a technique that depends on generating conflict between the students' perspectives. This, in turn, requires creating and sustaining an effective, trusting commu-nity among the students.

Seminars differ dramatically from discussion-based classrooms. Discussions can involve the teacher as an active participant and guide. Seminars are usually in the hands of the students. Seminars focus primar-ily on developing reasoning skills. A seminar is more like a laboratory in which the primary technique of discovery is conversation. Seminars are difficult to design well. They require the self-confidence to trust the pro-cess and intervene as little as possible.

Laboratories are the most student-centered classrooms of all. I include every form of cooperative learning environment: scientific laboratory practice, field-based learning, problem-based learning, case-based learning, experiential learning, service learning, and study abroad as kinds of laboratories. These are among the most satisfying teaching experiences because one can observe the greatest amount of transforma-tion in the students.

Advising, like assessment, extends across all classrooms. It is part of the conversation on learning that distinguishes the effective teacher.

The classroom is an important venue for helping a student develop more successful strategies for college. Advising can range from tutoring to mentoring and sometimes even to counseling. The professor has to be prepared to talk to students about more than the class content, or at least to know where to send them for help. Many instructors are unprepared to talk about study habits, career path, or financial difficulties. Advising skills grow as you familiarize yourself with your school's support offices. My aim in discussing it in this book is to lay out the most common issues that arise in the course of ordinary classroom teaching.

The culmination of the class for both instructor and student is the evaluation of student learning and grading. In addition to offering specific advice on how to evaluate students in a timely manner, I discuss grading systems and the construction of essays and exams that will help you to achieve your course goals. This discussion brings us full circle in the design of the course. Seeing teaching as a scholarly activity means using the evaluation of student learning as feedback for the redesign of the course.

Administrative issues surrounding registration and grading can arise in any class. We sometimes face challenges to the grades we assign and instances of cheating or plagiarism. As with the discussion on advising, the goal here is to provide you with resources and information to effectively administer your classes, avoiding misunderstandings of university regulations.

The final section deals with teaching issues that arise at the end of the course. The evaluation of the course and instructor is fraught with anxiety because this information is used in salary, contract tenure, and promotion decisions. If the instructor has done everything he or she can to be an effective teacher, evaluations will improve over time. I am more concerned with making a case that only some kinds of feedback are valuable to helping the instructor improve. While we may ask for specific feedback on readings or projects, the questions I have in mind are relevant in every class. They deal with communication, organization and perceived fairness. The value of course evaluations lies in warning us whenever our students perceive that one or another of these qualities is different from our perceptions.

It is my hope that this extended discussion of the art and craft of college teaching will enable you to develop the answers to the most pressing questions of classroom design and practice. By developing and articulating this philosophy of teaching, you can then explain to your peers and evaluators how you see teaching as an extension of your scholarship. There will always be as many variations in articulating this philosophy as there are teachers. Classroom design will change as your experience grows. Ultimately, your approach to teaching is a statement of your preferences.

For example, one colleague might describe his or her approach as follows: "Given what I can and cannot control in the classroom, I prefer to set challenges for them that are primarily skill based. I therefore gravitate to courses in the curriculum that permit me to construct seminars and laboratories. If you were to ask me what I would like my students to remember a year after they had finished one of my classes, it would be the experience of working through a complex problem that consumed the better part of the term."

Another colleague might offer different but equally compelling choices: "Given what I can and cannot control in the classroom, I prefer to invoke the glorious moment of insight that scholars in my discipline have experienced as they worked through the problems that define our field of inquiry. For that reason, I am attracted to courses that permit me to lecture on these moments, so that I can present them with all the drama and excitement that I experienced when I first encountered them. I am committed to getting students to be excited about our field in every class I teach. If you were to ask me what I would like my students to remember a year after they had finished one of my classes, it would be the experience of this excitement."

Finally, a third colleague might articulate his or her philosophy as follows: "Given what I can and cannot control in the classroom, I prefer to get students involved in debating the great imponderables of our field. I enjoy not knowing what is going to happen next because a student says the unexpected. I call it teaching without a net. It challenges me to be as nimble and as articulate as I can in the moment. For that reason, I am attracted to courses that let me teach ideas through discussion. If you were to ask me what I would like my students to remember a year after they had finished one of my classes, it would be the insights that occurred during some discussion."

I hope these statements call to mind colleagues you know. Each statement comes from a committed teacher-scholar for whom the classroom is a place of creativity and challenge.

Effective teaching requires a committed teacher, but it also requires a group of willing students. In the next chapter, I focus on the students.

PART 2

What Do We Know About Postsecondary Intellectual Development?

Arguments about the effectiveness of university teaching have been raging since the 1960s, when students charged professors with teaching irrelevant courses. In the 1970s, the criticisms shifted to style. Lecturing, in particular, was attacked as alienating to learners who wanted more hands-on engagement with ideas. For example, researchers found that students on average only remember about 42 percent of the material presented in the hour immediately after a lecture (McLeish 1968). They then forget 50 percent of that within two months (Brethower 1977). In another study, a surprise test revealed that only 17 percent of students recalled the important pieces of the material from the previous week's lecture (Cross 1986, 15). With lecturing representing up to 80 percent of the teaching in universities, students were leaving school with only a narrow and fragmentary knowledge base and little experience in applying that knowledge.

The publication of the book *A Nation at Risk* by the National Commission on Excellence in Education (1983) stimulated research in college teaching. Although it focused on the declining quality of high school students, it put universities on notice that they could preserve the quality of their own programs only through assessing their incoming students and providing remedial classes in writing, reading, and computation skills. At the same time, a rapid shift toward information-based economies placed increased pressure on universities to demonstrate higher outcomes in student learning. A flurry of activity in the 1980s attempted to analyze the university classroom experience and put it in a broader economic context (Association of American Colleges 1985; Bennett 1984; Boyer 1987; Education 1984; Newman 1985).

Bloom and Perry on Adult Learners

While the researchers discussed above looked at what the professors were doing, another group looked at how students learn. Adult intellectual development had received very little attention in comparison to child development. Received wisdom held that the learning component of the personality was fully formed by early adolescence, establishing how the individual adapted to all tasks throughout his or her life. The earliest effort to distinguish between children's lower-level learning and the higher-level learning of adults was the taxonomy of cognitive skills developed by Bloom (Bloom, et al. 1956). The taxonomy begins with knowledge acquisition, such as remembering definitions or formulas. The next skill involves comprehension, demonstrating an understanding of the meaning of remembered information by giving an example or by describing a common context. The next skill focuses on application, using knowledge in a new context or applying it to solve a novel problem. The fourth skill is analysis. This involves a varied set of applications, such as breaking knowledge up into its constituent parts and explaining their interrelationships, understanding the boundary conditions of a category, or distinguishing between the relevant and the extraneous in the relationships between elements. The fifth skill is synthesis, which consists of putting the analyzed parts together to form a new and different whole. Synthesis is involved in any reasoning where the results reflect originality and creativity. Bloom's sixth step is evaluation, the fashioning of criteria to arrive at a judgment of value about knowledge. Bloom hypothesized that as children develop into adults they acquire these meta-skills in this order.

Bloom's taxonomy provides a scheme for classifying question sets and problems for classroom discussion or examinations. The revolution that his followers wanted to launch involved getting teachers to go beyond questioning that stopped at the level of remembering and understanding, challenging students to apply, analyze, and evaluate as well. This taxonomy reappears in different forms in several of the learning models that follow.

In 1970 Perry published a study of adult intellectual development that elaborated Bloom's taxonomy to produce nine positions of cognitive development. Perry carefully called them positions rather than stages. He felt that reasoning was subject matter specific. The beginning of the process was a dualistic style of knowing in which people choose between poles, such as right or wrong, good or bad, and beautiful or ugly. Intellectual development, he believed, could not be separated from moral development. As people grew more aware of the ambiguities of knowledge, they integrated their judgments with their social selves, finding personal meaning in knowledge and reasoning. He was particularly interested in relativist judgments and how reasoning could help one act ethically in multicultural communities. He interposed transitional positions that describe, for example, the progression from dualist thinking to styles that embrace a multiplicity of viewpoints. The end of the process was a mind that could make context-relative judgments based on contingencies that allowed for choice, commitment, and the coexistence of opposing viewpoints, all at the same time (Perry 1970).

When most academics are asked to define the qualities of a critical thinker, they usually express some version of Perry's final stage of development. The importance of Perry's work was to point the attention of researchers to the continuing process of intellectual development in late adolescence and adulthood. Many of his distinctions continue to reappear in altered guises in later models. He was the first to suggest that adult learners are not uniform in their learning styles.

Whitkin and Moore followed Perry in the mid-1970s. They emphasized the context for learning over the moral development of the learner. They distinguished between learners who respond best in social contexts with those who learn best on their own. This is known as the field dependency model. Field-dependent learners, as they call social learners, learn well in collaboration with others and in environments that respond to their emotional as well as their intellectual needs. These learners give the impression of being more holistic in their learning style. Field-independent learners are able to focus independent of the environment. They give the impression of being more analytic in their learning style (Whitkin and Moore 1975). The value of Whitkin and Moore's study was to direct attention to students for whom the social context of learning is a crucial variable for success.

CHAPTER
4

Kolb and Experiential Learning

The search for new learning contexts as a way of characterizing adult learning reached a highly sophisticated stage with Kolb's 1984 book on experiential learning. Kolb is often misinterpreted as having identified four different adult learning styles: Divergers (those who learn through feeling and thinking) learn from open-minded, active reflection on concrete experience; Assimilators (those who learn through thinking and watching) learn from building models and testing these models against experience; Convergers (those who learn through thinking and doing) learn by experimenting by applying ideas to experience; and Accommodators (those who learn through feeling and doing) learn by applying feeling to experience. In fact, Kolb does not see these as separate kinds of learners, but rather as separate phases in a developmental process that all adults cycle through when learning from experience. He understands experiential learning contexts in ways that are very similar to Lewin (1951), Dewey (1938), and Piaget (1970)—namely, as an interaction between reflection and concrete experience that is mediated by emotions.

Kolb (1981) believes that by cycling through these phases, individuals develop specific competencies, such as setting goals, building conceptual models, being sensitive to values, or influencing and leading others. In all, he identifies twenty basic competencies, associating five with each of the four phases. The skills of adults as learners derive from the sum total of their competencies. We should design the adult learning environment, in his view, to facilitate the acquisition of the full set of these competencies. Kolb's views have been highly influential in the development of schools and colleges devoted to the education of returning adult students. They also influence the best practices of experiential learning programs, such as study abroad programs, service learning programs, internships, and immersion programs of various kinds.

Gardner and Multiple Intelligences

CHAPTER

5

The focus of research swung back to the qualities of learners themselves with Gardner's work on multiple intelligences (1993). Gardner says there are eight different ways, or channels, to integrate new information. For an individual, the channel that works the best depends on what Gardner calls domains of intelligence. These domains have little to do with each other. They include the linguistic, the logico-mathematical, the musical, the spatial, the bodily-kinesthetic, the interpersonal, the intrapersonal, and the naturalistic. An individual will have a specific mixture of aptitudes divided among all of these different intelligences. Some may have a disproportionate leaning toward the linguistic or the logico-mathematical. Others may lean toward the bodily-kinesthetic or the interpersonal. All of these learners are likely to turn up in our classrooms. That is a problem, says Gardner, because our classroom learning environments favor the linguistic over all other domains. Exceptions to this are mathematics, physical education, music and art studio courses, and experiential education in tutoring, peer counseling, and Outward Bound. It is not that we dismiss or ignore these alternative channels for learning. Rather, we disproportionately privilege the linguistic over all others.

This is a disadvantage for students whose learning strengths lie elsewhere. It is rare for students to be disproportionately gifted in only one of these domains. The channel that school activities consistently exercise is the linguistic. For this reason, it is often co-dominant with the naturally dominant channel in college students. Gardner argues that effective learning operates through multiple channels, stimulating learning through multiple intelligences. Gardner's ideas have been most influential in K–12 education. Currently, these ideas are entering post-secondary education through the principles of universal design.

Baxter-Magolda and Ways of Knowing

CHAPTER

6

Baxter-Magolda extended the learning context model to gender in her 1999 study. She found that learners cluster into four types: absolute knowers, transitional knowers, independent knowers, and contextual knowers. When she questioned people about their perceptions of their knowledge, patterns that often disadvantage women emerged. Among absolute knowers, men tend to view themselves as possessors and generators of authoritative knowledge. Women view themselves disproportionately as the receivers of authoritative knowledge. Among transitional knowers, women are more likely to begin to relativize knowledge based on interpersonal contexts, while men relativize through impersonal contexts. Gender distinctions disappear in those learners with high social or education attainment. This coincides with independent and contextual knowers (Baxter-Magolda 1992).

One can easily imagine that those social groups who are disadvantaged in the same ways that women are disadvantaged face similar disparities. This social mapping of learning patterns alerts us to yet another level of variation within the learning diversity of our classrooms.

King and Kitchener and the Reflective Judgment Model

King and Kitchener (1994) hypothesized that when people are asked to reveal what they think can be known about the world, how that knowledge is gained and how that knowledge is certified, they simultaneously reveal how they come to believe what is unknowable. Their results suggest a seven-stage reflective judgment model that provides an effective restatement of the "higher order learning as an increasing moral independence" process first described by Perry. People in the first positions are operating under pre-reasoning conditions. Those in the middle three positions are emerging as reasoners. The seventh position characterizes people who are in full command of critical reasoning.

In the initial position, thinking is concrete. People know the world through a single category belief system. Perception is privileged over analysis. Knowledge is predetermined. The possibility of alternative facts or interpretations is denied. Beliefs do not require justification. Knowledge and beliefs are the same thing. "If it's on the news, it has to be true, because otherwise they wouldn't put it on" (1994, 47-48).

In the second position, people believe that all knowledge is certain, but that some people do not have access to it. Scientists, teachers and religious leaders know the truth. When facts are uncertain, their habit is to accept authority. Evidence is not a criterion for establishing truthfulness.

In the third position people continue to assert that all knowledge is certain but acknowledge that it is not always apparent at all times. Authority is still the basis of truth in areas of certainty. They retreat to what "feels right" when the facts are ambiguous. Thus, they deflect rather than engage the ambiguities they might encounter while trying to parse complex questions. People in this position cannot distinguish evidence from opinion or belief.

In the fourth position, people insert personal bias to counter uncertainties. If the facts are contradictory, then opinion rises in its rhetorical importance. Bias makes a return to certainty possible. Differences in points of view are the result of upbringing or because of deliberate mischief in distorting information.

In the fifth position, people bracket some portion of knowledge as permanently uncertain, even in the face of personal bias. Interpretation becomes a part of all understanding. This acceptance of uncertainty marks the beginning of higher-order thinking. Some evidence can be evaluated as stronger and more relevant than other evidence.

In the sixth position, people extend their acceptance of uncertainty to knowledge in general. They see facts as context sensitive, and explanatory narratives as historically contingent. Reaching conclusions about anything becomes strenuous and tentative. Subjective interpretation returns, but in the form of context-sensitive questioning that seeks this time to reveal uncertainty rather than to mask it (1994, 250-54).

In the seventh position, in the absence of objectifiable knowledge, people base their beliefs on approximations of reality using the best available evidence. Interpretations of evidence and opinion can be tentatively assigned to problems of limited scope. Through critical inquiry, it becomes possible to evaluate judgments as having greater or lesser truth value, or that one is a more reasonable solution than another (1994, 70-71).

King and Kitchener see knowledge and reasoning skills as having a coherent relationship. A student cannot make progress as a reasoner without an ever increasing, and therefore ever more ambiguous and uncertain, knowledge base. Simultaneously, the knowledge base cannot expand unless and until the student can reason beyond the bounds of certainty.

Following in the research line established by King and Kitchener, Fischer has developed a model that successfully integrates the learner-centered approach and context-centered approach (1980, 477-531; Fischer and Bidell 1998, 467-561). He stresses the collaboration between the development of higher-order reasoning and the test questions, research problems and essay prompts posed to the learner by the instructor. These targeted challenges are called scaffolds. Scaffolds and scaffolding are terms of art for the design of learner-centered classrooms.

In Fischer's model, the skills that the learner acquires in a previous stage support, or scaffold, the performance of tasks in the next stage. When the performance in one position is poor, performance in subsequent steps will suffer. When the instructor inadvertently poses prompts that are more appropriate in a later stage to learners who are not ready for them, performance suffers. For example, if a learner has not yet begun to accept uncertainty and ambiguity, high end prompts, such as open-ended or ill-structured problems, they may misinterpret the problem as having a single correct answer. The learner may understand the open-ended nature of the problem but may not yet be comfortable marshaling different viewpoints necessary to "solve" the problem. They will find it exceedingly difficult to prioritize their observations in a thesis statement or central claim. The result is frustration for both student and instructor.

Learners have a problem solving comfort zone. Faced with a prompt that requires skills they do not yet possess, they retreat into this comfort zone. Only when their habitual patterns are insufficient for dealing with the problem do they begin to take greater risks. Fischer calls these self-scaffolding. All real, permanent change in critical thinking skills is self-directed change. Instructors help this along only when they provide challenges that are keyed to the student's current level of tolerance of ambiguity and then increase the level of ambiguity over time.

What Do We Know About Effective Undergraduate Teaching?

Research has also focused on professors as teachers. The basic question that underlies all scholarship on teaching is "what difference does teaching make to student learning?" Do students learn and grow intellectually because of the teacher, or because of their own efforts? Do they grow as learners because of changes in brain function that would have occurred with or without intellectual stimulation, or because of repeated exposure to lists, plans, procedures, and practices? After all, if teachers play only a small role in the process, then why not just focus on our research agendas and let students fend for themselves with the assistance of more advanced students? Our own experience should remind us that teachers do make a difference in learning. It was a teacher who set us to work on problems, anticipating the intellectual growth that would result from our success and ready to support us if we began to teeter on the brink. It was a teacher who taught us the intellectual standards and modeled for us how those standards should be practiced. It was a teacher who chose the literature that shaped our thinking and inspired our writing. It was a teacher who told us the truth about our accomplishments and helped us set reasonable goals for ourselves.

Research on teaching has resulted in several discipline-based journals on what effective teachers do. Anthologies of these are available. These books cover specific practices that have worked well for college teachers. There is also published research on the cognitive processes that underlie effective teaching. The reference section of this book contains an extensive, though by no means exhaustive, list of this research.

Effective teaching results when instructors pay attention to perfecting three elements of their classroom practice: communication, organization, and fairness. Communication is not merely clear and unambiguous speech. It is also about performance qualities, the use of texts, and student-teacher rapport. Organization is not merely giving students an assignment calendar that indicates when the exams will take place. It is also about knowing how you will grade an essay before you assign it, limiting the content of the course to what you can effectively communicate, and insuring that there is plenty of opportunity for feedback about the learning process. Fairness is not about teaching and grading everyone according to the same criteria—not everyone is the same. Fairness is about teaching and grading students the way they need to be taught and graded, as individuals with unique capabilities and potentials.

Current Approaches to Understanding Growth in Thinking Skills

CHAPTER

8

In the latest research-based model of adult cognitive development, Wolcott and Lynch adapt King and Kitchener's reflective judgment sequence to include transitional phases, while incorporating Fischer's scaffolding scheme. Their approach allows for a more accurate assessment of students' critical thinking skills. Lynch read a large sample of college writing samples and sorted them into groups based on King and Kitchener's sequence. From this sort, she developed a criterion-based rubric for using short writing samples to assess the learner's position in the reflective judgment sequence (Wolcott and Lynch 1997, 59-78). They then devised a set of prompts that provides the appropriate level of challenge for each position.

This model deserves a more detailed description. It represents the best thinking currently available for understanding how we can leverage the variation in student learning in our classrooms into transformative experiences. The discussion of specifics that follow is a summary of Wolcott, Lynch, and Huber's Web publication *Steps for Better Thinking* (2001).

As with previous models, the skill pattern that represents the least complex level of learning looks for the "only" correct answer. These students do not seem to "get it" and complain about this often. They quote inappropriately from textbooks, provide illogical or contradictory arguments, appear unable to read carefully, and insist that the professor, the textbook, or other experts provide them with the "correct" answer, even to open-ended problems. What can be characterized as mixed motivations among general education students in lower-division classes may actually be the higher percentage of these students in those sections. Their motivational problems arise because their reasoning skills do not fit with the demands of the university classroom, even at the introductory level.

At some point in high school or college, self-scaffolding begins to move the student out of this stage into the next one. The key to the transition is the acknowledgment of continuing uncertainty about the nature of facts. King and Kitchener, Fischer, and Wolcott and Lynch agree that this recognition is the way out of the maze of dualistic thinking. Dealing with uncertainty initiates the self-scaffolding process that leads the student to recognize multiple perspectives. This, in turn, is the key to understanding research projects, exam questions, and discussion topics. It also leads the student to use evidence to support arguments, though this is still at a relatively ineffective level.

The position the student is entering with the uncertainty breakthrough is the first stage of what we should recognize, for assessment purposes, as dualistic thinking. Wolcott and Lynch call them Biased Jumpers. Not every form of reasoning, particularly not dualistic thinking, is critical thinking. Students in this position

→ jump to conclusions in discussions or papers.

→ do not recognize their own biases but are quick to accuse others of bias.

→ stack up evidence for their own positions while ignoring counterexamples and contradictions.

→ select evidence based on prejudgment.

→ argue against the counter-position with opinion.

→ equate personal opinion with evidence.

These students can acknowledge multiple viewpoints but cannot adequately address a problem from a viewpoint other than their own. They are likely to be confident enough in their skills to speak up often in class, perhaps even dominating discussion. Many are interested learners and engaged in the material.

Eventually, these students tire of the instructor's comments about unsupported generalizations and unfounded biases and move on. The transition to the second position of critical reasoning involves attempts to control the use of personal bias in papers and discussions. As with the acceptance of uncertainty, controlling personal bias provides the key to the next phase of self-scaffolding. Students begin to

→ identify issues, assumptions, and prejudices associated with perspectives other than their own.

→ evaluate the evidence of these positions logically and qualitatively.

→ struggle with how to organize the information in a meaningful way.

It is a struggle that will generate seriously flawed work for a period of time before the students discover an effective organizational pattern. These students are entering the position of critical thinking where they can begin to acquire solid reasoning skills. However, they are blocked from reaching or adequately defending a solution because of the increased mass of evidence they must sift through. They exhibit strong analytic skills but appear to be wishy-washy and noncommittal, unable to formulate a coherent conclusion. Their papers are long and tend to ramble.

These students do not want to stop analyzing. For this reason, their papers can appear to be less structured than those of the previous stage, even though they are thinking more carefully and systematically. During this transition, student work is more vulnerable to being undervalued by teachers than in other transitions. Wolcott and Lynch (1997) noted a tendency nationally to downgrade the work of students at this stage because they lack a strong thesis or conclusion, while upgrading the students in the previous stage because the formal requirements of good paper structure are met, even if the "evidence" is mostly opinion. The advanced students follow through with the process even though it is evaluated less positively than their previous work. Evaluation rubrics that depend on fulfilling a small number of criteria, like the presence or absence of a well-formed thesis or a conclusion that is more than a summary, can be unduly harsh on students who are attempting to move to a less biased way of thinking.

To succeed in making the transition to the next position, students must avoid getting lost in a sea of perspectives by consciously prioritizing issues and information. This is the key to self-scaffolding for the next position. As with other transitions, the prioritizing will be inadequate or incomplete for some time. Once they have figured out how to prioritize, they will finally be in a position to articulate a well-formed and defensible thesis with appropriate evidence and warrants. Still, these efforts stand out from the larger group of essays written by students at lower skill levels. Successful prioritizers enter the third position of critical thinking where they systematically consider alternatives before reaching conclusions. At this position, students

- → focus on finding pragmatic solutions to research questions and give due consideration to what they can accomplish with the available time and resources.
- → collaborate with others in the process of setting priorities and may consult with experts or fellow students.
- → view the task as finished when they reach the solution.
- → make a real effort to evaluate the limitations, changing conditions, and strategic issues associated with a problem.

Students at this stage can sometimes come across as lower skilled because the written work tends to edit out the process through which they attained the solution. However, a careful reading will reveal a complex pattern of investigation that is not present at lower skill levels.

This skill set is probably the practical limit for what most traditional-aged undergraduates in a four-year program can accomplish. This is not to say that in some future curriculum, with a bar set higher, we might be able to graduate students with even higher reasoning skills. The limitation arises because immersion in a knowledge base becomes increasingly important to further skill development. The undergraduate curriculum, even in the upper division of the major, is too diffuse for this immersion. To do well in graduate school, where immersion in the knowledge base is the curricular objective of the first year, students must make an additional transition to professional forms of problem solving. That means that they must

- → effectively address the priorities and limitations of their work.
- → interpret and reinterpret whole bodies of research findings systematically and over time.

→ forge a strategic, long-term vision for their work.

→ generate new information when confronted with either the unfamiliar or the familiar.

The majority of students entering graduate school are at the stage for this level of reasoning. We perceive them to be ready for graduate school because they have successfully self-scaffolded themselves to be problem oriented. The key to the transition is the recognition that all intellectual effort is limited in both explanatory scope and shelf life. They must accept and be prepared to work with the fact that we actually explain very little about the world in professional studies. To work effectively in this environment, students must develop internal motivational resources and a commitment to long-term planning.

The successful graduate students are those who connect the generalities of the seminar to this process of professional thinking. Students at this position seek continuous improvement in their knowledge base and interpretive skills without prompting from others. These are the students that we often characterize as among "the best students we have taught in twenty of years of teaching." They are true independent learners. They are more likely than others to innovate. They anticipate and are comfortable with paradigm change as an indelible feature of intellectual life. Finally, they work toward constructing knowledge over time. In doing so, they complete the journey begun by the entering college student for whom facts are organic and timeless.

I have incorporated this way of understanding how students learn as often as possible. I am drawn to the model because it is robust; it describes both variation and process. It is falsifiable; more research will strengthen its precision. I can imagine discovering all sorts of exceptions and mixed cases in my students. I would not have known about them unless I first applied this model as a way of describing the people sitting in front of me. Once I know who they are, I can begin to help them find the supports in both the knowledge base and the skill sets that they need to move to the next step in their development as learners.

History and Development of Best Practices Research

CHAPTER

9

One of the professional responses to the movement for greater accountability in teaching was the effort by the Study Group on the Conditions of Excellence in American Higher Education (AAHE) of the U.S. Department of Education (1984) to formulate principles for improving undergraduate education. The American Association for Higher Education Task Force on Best Practices in Higher Education began its work in 1986, at a time when the prominent arguments were about the content of undergraduate education, such as the relation of Western to non-Western studies and the criteria for inclusion in the literary canon, rather than how to teach effectively. The task force included professors from different disciplines and from schools of different sizes, all of whom had published research on teaching effectiveness (Gamson 1991, 5 -12). Their work involved reviewing the major longitudinal studies of college students that had mostly been accomplished in the 1960s (Becker, et al. 1968; Chickering 1969; Feldman and Newcomb 1969; Heath 1968; Katz and Associates 1968; Newcomb, et al. 1967; Perry 1970; Sanford 1962). According to Sorcinelli (1991, 13-26), their findings were also consistent with research on student development that was published more recently (Belenky, et al. 1986; Chickering and Associates 1981; Katachadourian and Boli 1985; Knefelkamp, et al. 1978; Parker and Schmidt 1982; Richardson, et al. 1983; Winter, et al. 1981). The original statement on best practices was published in the AAHE Bulletin in 1987. The AAHE principles have gained a foothold among professors, who otherwise are impatient with "education talk." They provide one of the few statements about university teaching that is nationally recognized and not identified with a single group of researchers. The following sections discuss these best practices.

Encourage Student-Faculty Contact

The task force states, "Frequent student-faculty contact in and out of classes is the most important factor in student motivation and involvement. Faculty concern helps students get through the rough times and keep on working. Knowing a few faculty members well enhances students' intellectual commitment and encourages them to think about their own values and future plans." This point is well documented in the research literature (Cohen 1981, 281-309; Feldman 1976, 243-88; Marsh 1984, 707-54; McKeachie, et al. 1986). Sorcinelli (1991, 13-26) notes that interaction and rapport with students, along with command and organization of subject matter and expressiveness and enthusiasm, are the features that reappear as positives in open-ended student evaluations of good teaching. The pursuit of this level of involvement has sparked the growth of small, seminar-style classes for first-year students and the development of faculty-guided experiential and service learning in undergraduate curricula. The practice also directs our attention to the importance of social context in effective learning.

Faculty must model learning for students in and out of the classroom. The students will really care about learning all the time only when they believe that we do. Wilson and his coauthors (1975) found that relationships developed outside the classroom between faculty and students are the part of teaching that may have the greatest impact. A significant challenge of university teaching is to build a community of lifelong learners. We are all participants in civic communities. Who do you want for neighbors? Who do you want on the city council? What kind of learner do you want the police officer on your beat to be? What kind of learner do you want the elementary school teacher to be who will teach your children to read? University professors are in a position to shape their communities by building a lifelong love of learning into everyone who graduates from their programs. Example and personal contact are the best way to achieve this.

Encourage Cooperation Among Students

The task force states, "Learning is enhanced when it is more like a team effort than a solo race. Good learning, like good work, is collaborative and social, not competitive and isolated. Working with others often increases involvement in learning. Sharing one's ideas and responding to others' actions sharpens thinking and deepens understanding." Study groups, group exercises and research projects, and learning communities that cross disciplinary boundaries are examples of how this principle has begun to influence teaching practice. Research shows cooperative learning groups increase student productivity, develop positive relationships between students, increase the social supports for learning, and enhance self-esteem (Johnson, et al. 1991). In one study of student-centered approaches to teaching, the authors conclude, "the best answer to the question of what is the most effective method of teaching is that it depends on the goal, the student, the content, and the teachers. But the next best answer is 'Students teaching other students'" (McKeachie, et al. 1986). Students and faculty are often reluctant to fully engage cooperative learning models because our culture places so much importance on the evaluation of individual achievement. Fortunately, several techniques have emerged to help us differentiate between cooperation and collaboration on the one hand and individual responsibility and accountability on the other. The discussion of cooperative learning is woven throughout this book.

Encourage Active Learning

The task force states, "Learning is not a spectator sport. Students do not learn much just by sitting in classes and listening to teachers, memorizing pre-packaged assignments, and spitting out answers. They must talk about what they are learning, write about it, relate it to experience, and apply it to their daily lives. They must make what they learn part of themselves." The only effective knowledge base is one that is actively recallable and utilizable. To make knowledge active, one must acquire it through an activity. The more complex the activity is, the more efficient the learning will be. The most active learning is a student pursuing a self-designed learning task independently. Such tasks require the student to be fully engaged in all aspects of the learning, from the delimiting of the problem to completing some report according to a self-imposed schedule. This practice opens up wonderful opportunities for creativity on the part of teachers. We are all successful students because we have developed our own active learning styles. Teaching others by sharing the ways in which we actively learn makes all of us more effective. The least active form of learning is listening to the recitation of facts and then memorizing them for regurgitation on a quiz. This is not what effective lecturers do when they perform. Yet it passes for adequate teaching in large classes despite years of evidence that it puts obstacles in the path of learning. I try to develop techniques for building an active learning environment in every chapter here.

Give Prompt Feedback

The task force states, "Knowing what you know and do not know focuses learning. Students need appropriate feedback on performance to benefit from courses. When getting started, students need help in assessing existing knowledge and competence. In classes, students need frequent opportunities to perform and receive suggestions for improvement. At various points during college, and at the end, students need chances to reflect on what they have learned, what they still need to know, and how to assess themselves." Feedback is not merely an admonition to return graded exams within a reasonable period. It is also about having enough opportunities for evaluation so that students know that their efforts are successful. This feedback should come early and often. We face no greater challenge in the classroom than when we attempt to tell a student what worked and what did not. Many teachers withhold feedback, giving the student as little to argue with as possible. Nothing undermines teaching more than ineffective feedback. Those who are having trouble learning the knowledge base need feedback more often. Occasionally, an office visit to discuss what is going on outside of class is necessary. Students who are not meeting the reasoning standards of the course need feedback that specifically supports their reasoning issues. The chapters on assessment and evaluation specifically address the ways we can make feedback more effective.

Emphasize Time on Task

The task force states, "Time plus energy equals learning. There is no substitute for time on task. Learning to use one's time well is critical for students and professionals alike. Students need help in learning effective time management. Allocating realistic amounts of time means effective learning for students and effective teaching for faculty." Teachers need to support students' efforts to manage their time effectively. There are several techniques for this. They all involve the instructor's recognition of exactly what the time demands of the course actually are. The time spent learning outside of class is distance learning. It may not be effective enough for some students if you merely assign reading a chapter. You may have to give them study questions or procedures that prepare them to discuss the material. You can model techniques for active reading in class. Students can keep a reading journal in which they reflect on the experience of reading the chapter actively. Surveys we have conducted at DePaul show that students rarely spend more than two hours a week in preparation for any one course. This is because the assignments rarely require more than that! Time expectations are part of the institutional culture of the university. If, for example, all instructors agree that students should prepare two hours outside of class for every hour they are in class, then all instructors need to design classes with assignment structures that meet that rule. This does not mean more pages of reading. It means more effective learning from the pages that are assigned.

Communicate High Expectations

The task force states that you should "expect more and you will get more. High expectations are important for everyone—for the poorly prepared, for those unwilling to exert themselves, and for the bright and well intentioned. Expecting students to perform well becomes a self fulfilling prophecy when teachers and institutions hold high expectations of them and make extra efforts." The best reputation a new teacher can have is being demanding but fair. Students will be attracted to the challenge that your classroom presents. They will anticipate the bragging rights to having successfully completed your course. They will come prepared to put in extra effort. They will count on your fairness to not punish them too severely if they can meet only a part of the challenge. Compare this to the teacher with the reputation of low expectations. These classes attract students whose attentions are elsewhere. They count on the information provided to successfully complete the course, rather than what they find through their own efforts. They do not expect the teacher to have anything valuable to contribute to their experience. Even then, attending class itself is irrelevant; they will get the notes from a friend.

Which class do you want to teach? Academic expectations, like time expectations, are part of the institutional culture enshrined in the curriculum. You have to be aware of how your teaching fits into the curriculum to know how demanding you can be. Are you teaching the course that is supposed to excite student interest in the major? Are you teaching the course that graduate schools will look to as the "cut" course? Are you teaching the capstone seminar that will launch the students into the community as lifelong learners? The idea is to be as demanding as possible for the role the course plays in the curriculum. This takes perception, reflection, and risk taking.

Respect Diverse Talents and Ways of Learning

The task force states, "There are many roads to learning. People bring different talents and styles of learning to college. Brilliant students in the seminar room may be all thumbs in the lab or studio. Students rich in hands-on experience may not do well with theory. Students need an opportunity to show their talents and learn in ways that work for them. Then they can be pushed to learning in new ways that do not come as easily." When we look out into that room of students, what do we see? Do we see a mass of essentialized "student" units ranked in terms of grade point averages, credit hours taken, and active registration status that we then "process" through the syllabus? If not, the only alternative is to see individual learners, each with a specific mix of talents, preexisting knowledge, skills, reasoning styles, motivations, and distractions. If we want to teach real people and not units, what do we need to know about them? What is the best way to learn it? How quickly do we need the information? What can we reasonably adjust in our courses to meet the needs of these diverse students? Through the discussion offered here, you will begin to answer these questions for yourself.

PART 4

The Role of the Teacher in the Classroom

Teaching involves creating an environment in which students can learn. The goal of this learning changes, depending on the experience of the student and the position of the course in the curriculum. The teacher's role is to produce the structures that will lead the student toward the goal. Structure is the key variable in teaching. Cronbach and Snow (1977) have shown that students with low prior knowledge of a subject perform better when provided with more structure, while students advanced in the subject matter work best with less structure. More recent research by Veenstra and Elshout (1995, 363-83) has found that the knowledge base of the student is only one variable in how they respond to structure. Other variables are the reasoning and organizational skills of the students. They found that highly structured classrooms did not help or hurt well informed students with critical reasoning skills but did help students who were low skilled and minimally informed. However, structured learning actually impaired students who were minimally informed but who had high-level metacognitive skills. If teaching were just a matter of creating complex and nuanced mazes for students to run through, it would not be an art, and we could hand it over to technicians. When we enter the classroom, we confront a diverse group of learners who are rarely ever all high or low in any category. The environments we create for students must be open to this diversity. Therein lies the art of teaching.

The Real Relationship Between Teacher and Student

I do not know what's on your office wall or on the papers stuck to the edge of your computer monitor, but more likely than not, there are notes you dare not forget. I want to describe the qualities of the relationship between student and college teacher as a set of principles that we dare not forget. These principles are like pre-teaching meditations. They are phrases you can think about in your off moments. Contemplating them in an honest way helps you to adjust your relationship to the students and take the steps to make your classroom a more effective environment for you and your students.

It's About Them—It's Not About You.

A funny thing happens when you land your first teaching job. You have just endured one of the most exhausting, frustrating, intimidating, and sometimes even humiliating selection processes, the candidate side of a university job search. At the end of it, a group of professors have decided that you have that particular set of scholarly strengths they want and that you can now join their department. You are brimming with confidence, but are also uncertain about whether you can live up to these expectations. Then you go into the classroom. Finally, you have a chance to show these students and your colleagues you really do have the right stuff. So, in your first class, you begin to explain to your midlevel class of majors why French Continental philosophy reinvigorated American social science in the 1970s. The next day, every student drops the class. The chair is very upset. What did you do wrong?

This is an extreme example of what is known as the Graduate Seminar Syndrome: new professors bring the voice of the last graduate seminar they attended with them to their undergraduate teaching. Unless new faculty are forewarned about the curse of the Graduate Seminar Syndrome, it takes a year or two for them to adjust their style on their own. There is an appropriate moment to talk about what you know best. Rarely is that moment found in the ordinary courses you are asked to teach. The reason for this is that the course is part of a curriculum. A curriculum is a knowledge base and a learning skill set. Your role is to help students acquire that part of the curriculum in an effective way. Modeling the higher-order graduate versions of the curriculum to less experienced students does not help them learn. It merely marks you as a show-off. The classroom is about their needs, not yours. Put their needs first. Then figure out what you need to do to help them meet those needs.

The students who can best appreciate how valuable we are as scholars are those who are closest to us in achievement—namely, advanced graduate students. Entry-level undergraduates are the furthest from appreciating our worth as scholars. Even though they are more than willing to extend us respect and deference, they do so out of ignorance of what it is exactly that makes our scholarship so valuable. For this reason, most colleagues find the graduate program more compelling to teach. In their view, teaching lower-division classes is best handled by adjuncts and teaching assistants. I suspect this attitude exists because far more personal validation comes from the graduate students. I like to teach graduate students. They challenge me to be especially innovative within my discipline. I love teaching undergraduates. They challenge me to be creative as an intellectual and representative of the university as a valued institution in society. The wide-eyed wonder of the first-year student realizing for the first that the world is full of surprises is a reward that few of us acknowledge.

Teach Students to Value What You Value in Scholarship.

This is a variation on the general principle that one should teach what one knows. In this case, what you need to teach is what you know about how to be an effective student. In every class, you should approach the class as people who struggle with something that comes easily to you and that you value highly. Each class they take is an opportunity to acquire more tools and techniques to make learning easier and more satisfying. If you value the intricacies of the material, teach it in such a way that the students can directly appreciate those intricacies. If you value the give and take of discussion, create a classroom that fully supports the flow of ideas, getting out of the way when necessary. If you value the research side of your discipline, make that experience the core of your classroom. If you value the quiet contemplation of a problem or levels of a text, make journaling and written reflection the basis for your class. If you cherish the quick and easy recitation of facts, give students tools for assimilating facts efficiently. After deciding what you value and how you want to teach it, assess how well you and the students are doing. Finally, use grades to reinforce what you consider important in your class. If that means grading in a nontraditional way or giving emphasis to experiences that others in your department may not value as highly, then so be it (after tenure!). Teach what you value.

It Takes a Long Time to Become an Effective Learner.

We often fall into the trap of seeing our students as inadequately prepared for what we want to teach them. In conversations with colleagues about whether current students are as well prepared as they were in the past, I inevitably hear people say that the preparation appears weaker every year. The opposite is probably closer to the truth. It is our perceptions that need adjustment. We often forget how long it took us to figure out how to be successful students. Your professional education is a good example. Most academics remember those first few years of graduate school as filled with uncertainty about whether they were actually getting it. Think back on your perception of what seemed like an impossible number of books that had to be read in an impossible amount of time. Can you be nostalgic about the quality of the feedback you received from faculty? Our students are going through a similar process. The expectations may not be as high from our point of view, but from their point of view, they are high enough to generate stress. Approach the students respectfully. Acknowledge what they have accomplished. Never make them feel inadequate as learners or unwelcome in your classroom.

Important Learning Is Taking Place Outside Your Classroom.

The classroom is a jumble of information. You are talking. Students are talking. They scribble notes as quickly as possible. Ideas are flying through the air. There is hardly time to think, let alone to reflect or to solidify habits of learning. The classroom acts as a stimulus for students to reflect on their experience outside of class. Aside from the occasional epiphany or the enjoyment of a virtuoso performance by the teacher, the transformative learning experiences happen outside of class: in reading texts, in lab practice, through journaling, in writing essays, in reviewing for exams, in direct experience with a community, through confronting personal growth issues, and during conversations with peers. Using the classroom exclusively to build the students' knowledge base is rarely the most effective use of class time. When you can see class time as the moment in the students' lives when the habits they have acquired outside can be focused, sharpened, assessed, and evaluated, then you have begun to create an effective classroom environment. You can do this in large classrooms or small ones. It is all a matter of what goals you set and the effectiveness of the strategies and tactics you devise to meet these goals.

Set Goals to Challenge Students to Move Ahead as Learners.

If I only set one goal for my students, such as learning the core vocabulary of the discipline, I would probably succeed, but only if vocabulary is the only outcome I measure. Most students in college can memorize textbook material because that was the dominant pedagogy in their high schools. If the goal is easily attained with only a modicum of effort, the students will feel satisfied. They confirm their skills as learners. Push the students out of their comfort zone to learn a new analytic procedure, a real-life application of theory, or group exercises. Focus on a different genre of writing in each course. Practice oral presentations using a variety of formats. The goals statement in a syllabus is the most important piece of information you can provide. It sets the parameters for every other design decision you make.

Students love to hate the tasks we create for them. They complain that courses with sophisticated challenges monopolize their time, crowding out the time they need to spend on other courses or wage work. They claim this in spite of research conducted in my college that indicates that students on average spend less than 25 percent of the time we expect them to spend in course-related learning outside of class. They claim bragging rights over their peers just by completing a well-designed course. Setting goals that push students out of their comfort zone elevates your expectations of student performance. You are saying, "I'll bet you a good grade you can't keep completing all these activities successfully within the allotted time." When you show students in your syllabus and in your feedback that you demand they work above their comfort level, you are offering them the opportunity to grow as learners. You want students to be able to say that your class really helped them do something they could not do before: organize a complex project, gain comfort in group exercises, write a coherent, robust, well-framed argument, use tens of books and articles in a paper instead of three, and so on.

Set Expectations for Individuals, Rather Than for the Class as a Whole.

The reality of college teaching is that some classes are large and attention to the individual occurs when the student initiates it, while other classes are small and the instructor can initiate attention to the individual. Even in large classes, you can act as though you teach individuals. The more you know about these people, the better your classes will be. At a minimum, you should know the student's class year, their major, and, in some universities, their college. This information may be available on the roster, or you can ask students to fill out a 3 x 5 card on the first day of class. While they are filling out the card, you can ask students for contact information, such as a cell phone number and an email address. Some faculty also ask about previous courses in the subject area or the term the student has taken the prerequisite for the class. It is also a good idea to ask students why they took the class and what they hope to get out of it.

The level of challenge you set makes sense only when you know who they are as learners. If you set it too low, you bore them. If you set it too high, you frustrate them. Because of the variety of students, the bored and the frustrated show up in every class. Teachers often choose a portion of the class, such as the majors or the imagined top 33 percent, and teach to them, relegating the others to sink or swim on their own. It is better to work toward making the course expectations individual. To do this effectively, you need to ask more questions and have some way of evaluating the answers. Most of the instructors I know who do this use an initial writing assignment, usually due in the second class meeting. Only then can you know where each student's challenge actually lies. This assessment need not be too finely grained. Who still struggles with the difference between opinion and evidence or who fights her way through competing perspectives instead of making an argument? Students with similar issues can be grouped together. I rarely find more than three or four such groups in a single class.

You begin to set expectations for individuals through the feedback that you provide on assignments. Speak directly to the student's learning issues that you discovered from the initial assessment. Offer suggestions for strategies for the next draft or assignment. Do this in addition to your ordinary evaluative comments. Invite them to meet with to talk you about how they can do better. The difference for students is enormous. They begin to feel that they have a higher stake in the learning goals because you are paying attention to them individually. They have higher motivation to prepare for class, to ask questions, and to consider the subject matter relevant to their lives. A little individual attention, especially at the beginning of the term when the demands on your time are at their lowest, can go a long way.

Be Prepared for Something to Go Wrong.

No matter how carefully you plan your course, something will happen that will force you to make adjustments. No one has arrived prepared for a discussion of a text you consider crucial (require written preparation of some kind for all discussions). Books arrive late or not at all (find library alternatives). The film projector breaks or the computer interface doesn't work (do a learning assessment or partner exercise). Guest speakers fail to arrive or are less than stellar in their performance (convert the presentation into a dialogue with you). Groups that are intended to last the entire term fall apart in acrimony in the fifth week (meet with the group and get them to confront their issues and resolve them). A student becomes particularly disruptive, constantly monopolizing discussion (talk to the student after class to make them aware of their behavior). Experienced teachers have seen each of these scenarios at least once. New teachers can only try to anticipate the disasters.

What you should never do in a disaster is throw a fit. You are the leader of the class. You must exercise leadership in the face of disaster. That means finding an immediate solution. If time allows, the best thing is to consult with colleagues. If you do not have time for that, then reestablish control over the situation by creating an experience that can move students toward the same goal. If all else fails, do a learning assessment or a short in-class writing assignment that can serve as the basis for discussion. If you are a new teacher, do not attempt to do something on the spur of the moment that you have not prepared ahead of time. It rarely works, and you end up spending time later going over the same ground.

Figuring Out What to Teach and How Much of It

CHAPTER

11

In order to reason, one must have facts or ideas at the ready. To decide what facts and ideas are salient to the problem at hand, one must use reason. While it is certainly possible to balance knowledge acquisition and reasoning skills in one course, the most effective balancing of these intellectual necessaries occurs in curriculum planning. There will always be courses that are idea heavy and others that are skill heavy. Yet all courses need to provide students with a strategy for reasoning with the ideas they encounter. The teacher's task is to think through the opportunities for building the reasoning challenges around the course content. Too often teachers feel their job is done after they think through the issues of what topics to cover. Good teachers challenge students to reason with more skill. Good teachers build learning environments that balance the acquisition of a knowledge base with opportunities to reason.

The learning environment is both a physical environment and an intellectual one. Most people take seating plans, blackboards, audiovisual equipment, acoustics, lighting, and privacy for granted. All of these are malleable factors in the service of learning. A seating pattern communicates the location of authority in the classroom, as does the access to chalk or dry markers for writing on the board. Instructor centered classrooms need an environment that focuses the physical environment on the teacher and the teacher's communication tools. Student centered classrooms require flexible seating plans, easy access to chalk and electronic supports, and even different lighting.

We also communicate the learning environment through the syllabus. The syllabus is worth a significant amount of your time. It is your opportunity to work through the details of the course. The syllabus is the blueprint for the learning environment. I always keep a copy in my course file and write notes to myself as the term progresses about what worked and what did not work with my initial design. Over time, the syllabus becomes the history of your experience learning to teach the course.

Humans are social learners. The classroom is a temporary society. Community building often occupies the early meetings. In classrooms where group exercises form the major device for learning, community building can last as long as five class periods! This time is quickly made up once the now more effective groups get up to speed. Community-building exercises are called icebreakers. All of these are variations of students talking to each other about what they know and how they know it. Establishing these baselines for students helps them sort out what is commonsensical for this group. This baseline can also be achieved by conducting a discussion that involves all students. If there is a way to record the notes for the discussion, as with an overhead transparency or whiteboard paper, looking at it again during the last class shows students how their knowledge base has changed. It is important for you to learn their names and for them to learn each other's names. If there are hundreds involved, it ought to be possible for you to learn some of the names. Asking one person whose name you remember to help you find another name in the class is one way to do this. It also gives the other students time to learn each other's names. Taking photos of groups of students, having them introduce themselves and give some relevant information about their background, letting them interview you, and letting them offer something to be put in a class time capsule to be opened in the last class all work to reinforce their sense of being in the class with each other.

Lynch and Wolcott suggest that teachers consider the following in designing their classroom environments:

Collect information about the students early on. Build a baseline of the students' performance on some open-ended task at the beginning of the term. Construct assignments so that the students will have challenges of different skill levels. Use this to understand the variety of learners in the class.

Do not change everything in the course if the students are different than you expected. Make your adjustments slowly over a number of iterations of the course. Begin by changing the wording of assignments, discussions, and other activities to provide students with lower skills opportunities to participate as often as possible, while offering more advanced students greater challenges.

Pay particular attention to helping students identify problems and the relevant information for evaluating those problems. The key for all lower-skilled learners is to begin to appreciate uncertainty. Remember that the development of reasoning skills depends on students changing themselves. All you can do is provide the prompts. The scaffolding that moves them from one stage to another is something that has to happen inside of them. Set realistic expectations. Help them realize the importance of becoming higher-skilled reasoners. Allow them time to experience success. It may not happen in one semester or even in the first year.

Give encouragement. Show them what they are doing that moves them forward and help them identify what they still need to do. Do this in the form of questioning: Why do people disagree here? Why can't we know this for sure?

Keep in mind that they continue learning after they leave your class. Keep the entire curriculum in mind as you design your challenges and understand what kinds of experiences they will have when they register for the next term.

Do not feel that you have to do it all.

Finally, just as you are formulating your first impressions of them, they are formulating one of you. Appearances count. How you look, whether you are on time, whether you are prepared, whether you have something interesting and challenging to offer in the first class, and whether you find ways to get them involved without embarrassing them will cause them to look forward to the next class. It will also buy you a lot of goodwill for the classes down the line that are less than perfect. (Lynch and Wolcott 2001)

CHAPTER
12

Who Are Our Students?

All performers know that the audience is different every night. The same holds for every new class you teach. All effective communication begins with an analysis of who the audience is. You cannot teach effectively if you do not know who your students are—or worse, if you assume they learn one way, when in fact, they learn another. Teaching means creating an environment in which students can learn. When that happens, the students change. This chapter is about what they are like before they change. It is our starting point.

It may be disheartening to think that we do our work for eleven to fifteen weeks, take a few weeks off, and then start over again with the next set of students. Yet that is our work. The heaviest effort occurs with the least experienced students. Teaching in the upper divisions of the curriculum is lighter because of the prior accumulated socialization to intellectual work. We do make progress with our students. We do influence them, even if we seldom see results. Those faculty whose classes work for students begin by knowing them as individuals with specific strengths and weaknesses.

Variations in Motivation

Students go to college for lots of reasons. Very few students are there because they want to live the life of the mind. This is the ultimate goal of postsecondary education, not its starting point. Students' motivations are largely utilitarian. They want to make the transition to adulthood, if they are traditional-aged students, with the capacity to earn a comfortable middle-class income. They know that an undergraduate degree is the key to that transition. They believe that their community will judge their success as an adult primarily by their income. They also believe that what they major in has a direct connection to their opportunities for employment.

For all these reasons, they discount general education courses as not relevant to their goals. They fetishize their majors as a series of courses that will magically land them the big job. When they cannot decide on a major, they need to be reassured that this is not a moral failing on their part. They stand confused in the face of electives, often preferring to give back personal choice in course experiences in favor of double majors or minors that add sauce to their utilitarian steak and potatoes. These people stand in contrast to the culturally and often financially endowed students whose embrace of the liberal arts philosophy represents the ideal participant in our undergraduate curriculums. These are the general traits of the last few generations of North American students. The more specific the groupings of students, the more complex their motivations become: those who hold down a full-time job; those who raise a family, those who hate school and do not know why they let their parents talk them into continuing; those who deal with abuse, homelessness, addiction, disability, illness, or death; and those who commute to school from a community that does not understand the liberating role of university education in society. These students understand what the successful college experience should be different. These students sit in your classroom, deal with your assignments, take your exams, and interpret your comments and grades.

Variations in Core Knowledge

One of the most frustrating experiences for college teachers is the variation in core knowledge among students. One often hears complaints around the faculty dining room about a class that didn't know when World War II ended, what the word "secular" means, or where the United Nations headquarters are located. While these complaints are justified, they are also banal. These variations in core knowledge have to do with a student's situated learning. All such learning is local, with no systemic controls. There is no institution in the United States like the French Lycée. In that system, on any given day at any given hour, the Minister of Education in Paris knows what every teacher of a given subject throughout the country is saying to the class. In the United States, states and large metropolitan systems select textbooks, but teachers vary so much in their use of those textbooks that what students actually learn follows a normal distribution. Even that distribution is distorted by motivational factors, by the informal knowledge of these subject matters that students pick up in their families, and by the presence or absence of knowledge competency testing in their school systems. Entering college students have eighteen years' worth of knowledge about their world, but what they know is different from what their instructors know. It is often different from the student sitting next to them, as well. The university is the solution to the problem of extending common knowledge. To decry the lack of common knowledge in the classroom is to misunderstand the civil function of university education: to give students the tools to learn what is necessary to know about their world so that they base their decisions as community members on an assessment of evidence rather than emotion and opinion.

Certainly, knowing when World War II ended is part of what everyone should know. The university is the place where we fill in such gaps. When doing so, however, it does no good to make students feel inadequate. Their presence in the classroom is itself a commitment to fill these lacunae. Students are present and willing to learn. The buck stops with us. We are responsible for filling in these gaps, while explaining why the missing knowledge is important. Such moments are teachable moments in many ways. They incite curiosity, expand the frame of reference, connect the factoid to its historical and geographic context, and coax the students to want to explore the issue further on their own. Doing so in a supportive and friendly way increases students' willingness to reveal what they do not know.

Variations in Academic Skills

News organizations and the general public rank universities by their admission rates. Selective institutions admit students with demonstrated evidence of academic skills. These students tend to be creative, to write well, and to handle sophisticated mathematical relationships with ease. They are open to challenging intellectual and social challenges. They exhibit reflexivity and value consciousness. They can articulate an intellectual agenda of sorts. They have had leadership experience and enjoy a solid social support network. In short, they have the same personal qualities as their professors. They constitute approximately 15 percent of college students nationwide. These students soon discover that the faculty require them to work harder at honing these skills than they have in past. As a result, variations among even these well-prepared students quickly reveal themselves.

What about the other 85 percent of university students? Faculty are likely to find themselves facing first-year classes whose creativity was beaten down by the numbing high school curriculum. No one asked them ever to write an essay until they arrived at freshman summer orientation. Mathematics is a bore and a chore. School has nothing to do with who they are. Values stir conflict and are best hidden from sight. The only reason to go to college is to get a job. Intellectual goals are an oxymoron.

The university is the place where we fill the gaps in core skills. The traditional solution for most colleges is a series of remedial courses followed by a core skills curriculum. Underprepared students require various services: remediation in rhetoric or computation, English as a second language (ESL) courses, counseling programs for math or test anxiety, or diagnosis and support for learning disabilities. The curriculum then gives students the opportunities to practice long-form and short-form writing and to develop the computation and analytic skills to solve problems in the natural and social sciences. There are enormous benefits to a college that brings all of its students up to the same level of basic academic competence. Building such competence does not end with such programs. One learns to write well over a lifetime of practice, not in two or three courses. Quantitative reasoning is applicable in many areas of knowledge. When designed by experts, supported by the admissions office and the faculty, and taken seriously by the students, these core programs produce a dependable and predictable level of competence that makes teaching easier. I am fortunate to work in such a school. We notice a real skill difference between students who have entered as freshmen and those who transfer from schools that do not vigorously support core skills.

Variations in Privilege

The late French sociologist Pierre Bourdieu (1984) coined the term cultural capital to describe how economic advantage leads to cultural advantage. Because higher levels of disposable income can enlarge the opportunities for situated learning, students from such households know the world in ways that are closer to their professors than do students from households with less disposable income. This is not because all professors come from positions of privilege. Rather, it is because long exposure to the culture of the university has shaped their knowledge in specific ways. They come to possess a firm grasp of the content of literary, artistic, musical, historical, and scientific canons; a specialized but nonetheless extensive understanding of the history of ideas; and an appreciation of how form interacts with content in the experience of art, music and literature. Students who have enjoyed the privilege of higher-income homes are more likely to have experiences that expose them to these patterns of knowledge, albeit nonsystematically. In the eyes of their teachers, they possess cultural capital.

These class patterns often map onto racial, ethnic, gender and class categories. How, then, to avoid the very human tendency to undervalue the knowledge of the underprivileged? This is a much more difficult problem than differences in core knowledge or core skills. It is not necessary or desirable to change people's knowledge patterns to more resemble those of their teachers. What really matters here is for us to realize that elite knowledge does not confer greater wisdom. It does not make it possible to solve life's problems more effectively. It merely confers class or scholarly distinction on the people who possess it. It should be the students' choice as to which knowledge community they want to belong to. It is our responsibility to understand how we respond to differences in privilege, finding ways of treating all students equally as learners. Understanding the priority that we give to evaluating our relationships with others through the performance of elite knowledge is a first step in establishing an atmosphere of civility in our classrooms.

Variations in Ability

What does it mean to be able to perform an academic task, like reading? Does it mean that the performance has to unfold exactly as it does for the professor? I am a fast reader. Does that mean my students are not performing effectively if they read slower than I do? Most people would say that speed does not matter as long as the comprehension is there. Well, what if the process of comprehension requires the student to read very slowly, say, an hour for a single page? I am a reasonably good statistician. Does that mean my students are not performing effectively if they can derive the statistic but it takes them several tries? Most instructors would say that a large number of tries is regrettable. However, once the correct solution is reached, the problem-solving path is established. The student will achieve the results faster the next time. What if it takes just as many tries the next time? I have known students with such qualities who have succeeded in spite of these constraints. These are real issues for a significant minority of university students. They relate to ways the brain establishes connections between experiences. Differently abled learners are likely to stumble in the in-class test or final exam that must be completed in the time allotted, in taking written versus oral examinations, in reading paper-based texts versus recorded texts, and in evaluating mathematical skill by the answer only, rather than the process and the answer.

You do not have to be an expert on such disparate abilities. You do need to be open to the idea that students with such abilities can succeed if given the proper support. At the university level, students usually face difficulties with verbal and mathematical processing, but visual and auditory impairments are also common. Some classes mask the ability; others expose it. I have had students whose abilities hindered them in modern language classes, basic quantitative classes, introductory science classes, research methods, social theory, art history, or music appreciation. Many universities have programs available to support such students, and they usually charge a fee for their services. I have had some students who refuse to pay the fee, thinking that they can overcome their issues on their own. I have had others who participated in the program and found that it did not work as effectively as they had hoped or, in some cases, been led to believe. Following all these students is the stigma of "special education" and the judgment of peers that they are somehow different. There is still a lot to be learned, even by the experts, about how best to support such learners. Visit the program office for student learning disabilities at your school and learn what their staff does. They can tell you what you should know. Being able to describe the program accurately to a student who is having difficulty is a service in itself.

Variation in Attention Practices and the Web-Gen Experience

Still another variation among our students has to do with the increasing importance of technologically mediated communication. A technology gap has emerged in the last twenty years in which access to the Internet coincides with economic privilege. This gap dissipates as smart phones and public access through schools and libraries proliferate. In fact, the technological fix to communication finds a different platform depending on what the consumer can afford. The affluent may be able to afford the iPhones and Blackberries, while low-income students simply text from their standard cell phone plan. The revolution does not reside in how sophisticated a technology one can afford to use. Instead, it lies in the changing expectations and preferences about communication, and especially, attention. This is the variation with which we must be concerned. Students who are accustomed to a specific form of communication technology have developed a rate of attention practices that are different from those of the instructors, even if those instructors use the technology. It is about attention practices, the habits of attending to different sources of information and the amount of time the person gives to one attention focus as opposed to another.

A common conceit of the current literature is to see the Web-Gen students as part of a sub-culture with specific educational prejudices. The following chart is an example of how this dichotomization works. For Brown, the Web-Gen student demands a student-centered approach to classroom design because their involvement with technologically mediated communication, social networking, gaming and entertainment media predisposes them to short attention spanning, highly engaged, and stimulating communication:

Teacher-centered Paradigm	Student-centered Paradigm
"Teaching"	"Learning"
Memorization	Understanding
Recall	Discovery
One size fits all	Tailored; option rich
Talent via weeding out	Talent cultivated and sought out
Repetition	Transfer and construction
Acquisition of facts	Facts + conceptual framework
Isolated facts	Organized conceptual schemas
Transmission	Construction
Teacher = master and commander	Teacher = expert and mentor
Fixed roles	Mobile roles
Fixed classrooms	Mobile, convertible classrooms
Single location	Plurality of locations and space types
Summative assessment	Summative and formative assessment

(Adapted from Brown 2006: 12.6)

The classroom design features advocated under the student-centered paradigm are valuable, but not because of some monolithic relationship to technology. These techniques would have worked just as well with previous generations of students. Brown's use of Web-Gen characteristics as justification for student-centered classrooms masks the real variation that exists among our students with these attention practices. After all, learning to play a multiplayer, multiplatform, role-playing computer game is very time consuming, as is Facebook. Not all of students would have the time or the interest, let alone the Internet access, to develop the practices that are attributed to their generation. Similarly, to be a dexterous text messager, one has to be part of a network of friends who prefer to communicate by text messaging. One is only as competent as one's network of friends as a whole. Disposable income determines who in the network can afford the extra cost of text messaging. Television watching with its thirteen-minute segments interrupted by commercials is often cited as one of the origins of short-attention habits. This argument ignores that over the last forty years, movies have gotten longer. The same sixteen year old who is accustomed to television is also watching two-hour movies without a break. Yes, some of our students have short-attention habits. But many others do not. And those with short attention spans are themselves divisible along a spectrum between those whose short attention spans are habitual, and therefore can be altered, and those for whom the short attention span is chemical, and therefore need accommodation and sometimes medication. Just as we cannot assume that every student with a skill deficit has a learning disability, so, too, we must avoid thinking that every student with a short attention span has an attention deficit. Finally, there are plenty of students with attention spans that are just as indefatigable as their professors. All of them benefit from putting the learning tasks squarely in their hands.

The Virtual Classroom and Hybrid Learning Spaces

CHAPTER

13

The role of the instructor in the college classroom is constantly evolving. Communication technology, for example, has more profound implications for post-secondary teaching than marking some purported generational shift in learning style. These technologies are transforming the university as radically as the printing press did five hundred years ago. Administrators now speak about the design and capabilities of the virtual campus with the enthusiasm often reserved for a new campus building. The virtual campus has benefits for admission, retention, program development, faculty development and campus infrastructure that all result in a healthier bottom line. I believe that this development will better educate our students.

The new instructor must begin to incorporate the communication technology skill set into the teaching practice. This includes mastering at least the basics of course management software, becoming familiar with discussion boards, chat rooms, virtual classrooms, media formats, and the course design features that work best in virtual classrooms. I might add that those instructors of my generation, facing retirement sometime in the next twenty years, would also do well to start redeveloping some of their favorite classes for the virtual classroom. There will always be a market for well-designed classes taught by experienced faculty. There will be a discussion of these skills later in this book.

This new role is not exclusive to the distance learning class. That is, the class that is taught entirely on the Web with no face-to-face interaction. It also pertains to hybrid classes where some portion of the course is face-to-face and some part is on-line. In a sense, all courses are hybrid to some extent. When a student is alone with a book and preparing for class, they are experiencing the same sort of interaction that is envisioned by the on-line portion of a hybrid course. Faculty who have learned how to design a distance learning class discover techniques that they want to immediately incorporate into their traditional face-to-face. You may have the experience if you open yourself to learning this skill set.

The new demands on the instructor are not merely technological. Before one attempts to design an on-line course, one should have the experience of taking one. That is the best way to learn what is expected of the instructor. The best on-line instructors have people-oriented personalities and better than average communication skills. The "Lonely Lecturer" has no place on-line. On-line instructors do not need to be highly technology oriented or on-line twenty four hours a day. Online teaching requires more teaching, rather than less. Instructors need to be organized. Organization is the key element in both student engagement and faculty enthusiasm for the process. The assignments have to be designed with greater elegance than in bricks and mortar classrooms. Expectations need to be clearly communicated. For all these reasons, learning to teach online will greatly improve your traditional teaching skills.

PART 5

Demands on the New Instructor

If you were hired at a teaching institution, you discussed what courses you would teach with the chair. You believed you were filling a gap in a curriculum. When your first year's teaching schedule arrived, you may have been a little shocked that you were responsible for a variety of different classes. If you teach in a large university, the administrator has likely urged you to think about teaching possibilities that you never considered. Programs, departments, colleges, and universities make increasing demands on the creativity, adaptability, and time of all professors, but especially the new professors. You are seen, quite rightly, as still malleable in your teaching portfolio. Your interests and skills can be shaped to better fulfill the various agendas that already exist in the college or department. You may have expected that this would happen to some degree. The surprise is that pushing you to adapt to the agenda continues for the first three or four years. This is the greatest difference between professors' careers in teaching institutions as opposed to research institutions. The trade-off for the professor in a teaching institution is that the research is produced slower. For the professor in a research institution, the teaching skills emerge slower, if at all.

CHAPTER 14

Departmental Demands

Departments have written documents on all kinds of policies. Increasingly, they document the history and development of the curriculum. When I first started teaching, the chair gave me the titles of the courses she wanted me to teach. She also offered to send me the syllabi of other teachers, so I could see how the courses had been taught. That was it. There was no discussion of how those syllabi addressed the knowledge base or the skill set associated with that course title or the classroom environment. When the syllabi arrived, they consisted of the contact information for the instructor, details on the method for computing the final grade, and the schedule of the readings. Were the description of the course content; the course goals; the criteria for grading; the attendance, make-up and style-sheet policies; and descriptions of the test and writing assignments delivered in class or passed out separately? I never found out.

Beginning in the early 1990s, accreditation agencies began to insist that universities institute an assessment of learning outcomes from the course goals to the university's goals. For departments, this meant thinking through the outcomes they expected from students in the major. Faculty resisted this process. Some saw it as a political agenda meant to discredit academia while enshrining the values of business culture in universities. Professors do not need performance measures; they are a self-policing group, like lawyers or doctors. Others saw it as one more burden in an already overburdened work environment. Still others saw it as an encroachment on academic freedom, an effort to limit the kinds of topics that instructors can discuss in the classroom.

I strongly support assessment of learning outcomes. My experience has shown that when departments think through the desirable outcomes of the courses they offer, they begin to assign specific responsibilities to individual courses. They articulate the difference between the separate levels of the curriculum and discover opportunities for the students to build more effectively on prior learning. . When there is department-wide consensus on these matters, the teaching improves and the students benefit. If you find yourself in a department that has paid lip service to assessment while ignoring its fundamentals, you can be sure that teaching is not a top priority. The current department attitude toward assessment would be a good conversation to have during a job interview.

In departments with well-designed curricula, each course contributes to the knowledge and skill base of the students. This process begins with stating learning goals. These statements describe the different emphases of the curriculum. Colleges and universities may have learning goal statements, too. The department statements bring these loftier goals down to the department level, stating how a student majoring in this department fulfills the college's or university's goals. These statements include both knowledge outcomes and skill outcomes. They may also describe other benefits to the student.

Curriculum design assigns appropriate learning tasks to different sets of courses. Are multiple-choice tests permitted in introductory courses or not? Are certain major courses deemed writing intensive? Are others seen as analysis intensive? If there are methodological components in a course, are they reasonable and appropriate for the level of the students and the time available to complete them? Is it up to the individual instructor to decide whether the curricular element will be included, or is it department policy that it must be included? Is there a particular exercise or lab experiment that all students go through in order to gain experience with the method? Are all the forms of writing that characterize a discipline available for students to practice as they fulfill the major requirements? Is the form of writing in a course left to the instructor to decide, or is there an overall plan that the department has agreed to follow? Are students expected to have practice in oral presentations appropriate to the discipline? Are some courses devoted to getting students into the field or the laboratory? All of these features of a well-planned curriculum may be in place and in writing before you join a faculty.

More commonly, the expectations of the curriculum are not articulated. Many of these expectations exist in the heads of your colleagues, but they have never been articulated or discussed. These colleagues assume that their discipline is taught the same way everywhere. Since it is important to know how your courses will fit into the plan, it would be valuable for you to have conversations with colleagues about how they see the whole set of courses fitting together. By initiating the topic you may engender a broader conversation on curriculum within the department.

Some courses in the curriculum require more experience to teach than others. All of us theoretically can reproduce our disciplines in total.

That is why there are oral and sometimes written exams for the doctorate that are discipline focused. But faculty with twenty years of experience have had twenty more years of figuring out how to teach the complexities of the discipline to undergraduates than those fresh out of graduate school. For these reasons, the more difficult courses to teach are usually taught by the older faculty. Similarly, graduate courses are unlikely venues for the newly minted Ph.D. These courses require far more nuance and attention to process than most new professors possess. In graduate education, there is much more attention to the setup of the seminar and far less intrusion by the professor once the seminar gets under way. Pulling back and letting the students develop the class on their own requires a sense of personal and disciplinary confidence that does not have to be demonstrated to the students in order to be felt by them. It is not what you know that counts in leading a graduate seminar, but how well you support students to think independently of you. For all these reasons, the department chair may put you into some courses and not into others. Do not look at this as undervaluing your knowledge or skill. Your time will come. After several years of hearing yourself talk and witnessing the effectiveness of your words on students, you will be ready for the more abstract and challenging courses.

Demands of General Education Courses

CHAPTER

15

You took them as an undergraduate. You taught them as a graduate student. Your new department expects that half of your teaching load will be devoted to them. General education courses are sometimes very large lectures. At other times they are small seminars. Departments often staff them with adjuncts or inexperienced graduate students to fulfill their enrollment demands. Chairs may refer to them as the bread-and-butter courses, the ones that inflate the department averages and enable much lower enrollments in upper-division and graduate courses. Advisors sometimes undermine the curriculum with talk of "getting them out of the way." Students often dismiss them as unimportant and of lower priority than their major curriculum. Yet general education is an enormously successful academic program, the envy of many other national systems, and the largest component in an undergraduate course history. Why don't we talk about it with the same seriousness that we employ with our major curricula?

The general education curriculum developed after World War II as a way of adding a lifelong learning component to a highly professionalized undergraduate experience. By requiring a distribution of courses across the departments, colleges insured that students would have the benefits of exposure to a wider variety of fundamental intellectual questions: What is life? On what does science base its authority to make statements about reality? Is there order in history? Is a just society possible? What is democracy? What is the good life? How do we evaluate public art? What is leadership? Does literature mirror society or only the consciousness of an individual writer? What is the balance between faith and reason? There are several more questions of this ilk. Young people who think through these sorts of questions have greater awareness of their position in the world. I tell first-year students that they come to university with values they have rented from family, friends, and community. Now they can own their values, priorities, and references by examining how they really think about the tough questions—questions that touch on the fundamental issues that underlie our values. General education classes are locations in the curriculum where we address these fundamental questions. I would rather live in a community where all my neighbors had thought about these issues once in their lives, whether they retained the details of that discussion or not, than in a community in which they had not. Being able to solve the challenges presented in subject areas where one does not have the benefit of prior knowledge is daunting. It also marks one's progress in becoming a flexible and efficient learner. For that reason, I take general education very seriously.

The post-World War II development of general education courses was never completely successful. By giving departments the responsibility for constructing these courses, the designers left open the possibility that disciplinary priorities would eventually limit the amount of time that could be devoted to these big-picture issues. The disciplines saw general education courses as a recruitment tool, but only if the general education course could be counted as the first course in the major. As a result, the courses became introductory to the major instead of a general discussion of the fundamental issues on which disciplinary knowledge could shed some light. This actually worked to some extent, although it is not clear what had the larger effect on recruitment, the introductory discourse or the personality of the instructor. At that point, however, the courses became irrelevant to all those not interested in the major. That meant that a significant portion of the class was forced to listen to the disciplinary discourse without any intention of further engaging that discourse. The big questions were pushed to the margins of the course. Students' motivation dropped. Experienced teachers, sensing how difficult it is to teach to the unmotivated, abandoned the courses to the less experienced faculty and the adjuncts. Some teachers, understanding the history and purpose of the curriculum, held their ground and created classes that served the needs of the general student body. They were rewarded with the responsibility of teaching those courses every year in larger and larger lecture halls.

The best general education courses are the ones that are dedicated to addressing those questions the discipline claims as central to its mission. A course designed for a general education audience looks different from the one designed as an introduction to the discipline for majors. The contexts for asking the big questions must be carefully delineated using the students' own life experiences. Teachers can take steps to increase motivation through making the activity of gathering information about the questions more personal. The knowledge base that students bring with them to answer the questions can be validated, examined, critiqued, and rebuilt. When students have a satisfying intellectual experience with someone who is expert in a discipline and who can model how that discipline can shed light on questions important to them, we have laid the basis for effective recruitment in the major. In my opinion, the only way to insure that this approach becomes the norm in college teaching is to remove all general education courses from fulfilling major requirements. Freed from the need to fully engage the disciplinary discourse, these courses will more effectively return to their original purpose. The individual departments are so invested in the existing practices, however, that I hold very little hope of this ever happening.

Individual instructors can make their general education courses more satisfying for themselves and their students by remembering why the course exists in the first place. Try to define what big questions can be addressed in your general education courses. Within the parameters required by the department, provide as much time for addressing the big questions as you can. Most of the information covered is redundant with the knowledge base of the lower division of the major curriculum anyway. If your department has separate courses for majors and nonmajors, you should feel free to make the big questions the course for nonmajors. An even better approach is to work toward department consensus on designing courses especially for the general education program that utilize the talents of the best teachers, the best writers in the field, and the best classroom supports. The department that makes that investment first will also benefit from a surge of new majors. It isn't the ideas of a discipline that recruits students—it is the way they are presented.

Demands of the Undergraduate Major

CHAPTER

16

The major curriculum holds out the promise of teaching a homogeneous, highly motivated group of students with interests similar to those of the instructor. Nothing could be farther from the truth. While the occasional class at the end of a sequence may aspire to this ideal, most major courses are mixtures of students at different levels of skill and knowledge. The culture of the college and the number of competing programs within the department itself determine how mixed those classes will be.

In departments with graduate programs and research agendas, the undergraduate major curriculum is whatever the faculty wants it to be. The lower division of the curriculum is composed primarily of textbook-driven introductory courses. The upper division is a clone of the master's level of the graduate offerings, with many courses hosting both graduate and undergraduate students. Graduate-oriented universities do not have the time, the resources, or the political will to create a major curriculum that provides a nuanced engagement with the discipline at the undergraduate level of knowledge and skill. In these departments, the emphasis must be on the graduate program. This means that the new instructor faces large introductory lectures in the discipline, textbook driven and staffed by graduate assistants. There may be a separate section of such courses for majors, but more often these courses serve both majors and the general education students.

There may also be a second level of introductions to subspecialties before the majors have sufficient knowledge and skill to read the more specialized literature or engage in more sophisticated research. In the second level, the instructor encounters the most homogeneous student group in the curriculum. General education students have gone elsewhere, and graduate students may not receive credit for such courses. Even here, the variety of skills becomes apparent, particularly in reading, writing and reasoning.

At the higher level of the major curriculum, variety returns as master's students and undergrads are mixed together. Here the new instructor faces the challenge of placing the level of difficulty to the benefit of both groups. More often, the level of instruction is directed toward the graduate students, and the undergraduates must scramble a bit to keep up.

In departments without graduate programs, a very different kind of major curriculum emerges. Here the courses offered still depend on the backgrounds and interests of the far fewer faculty that staff these departments, but more time and attention are usually given to learning new approaches and offering students a fuller curriculum. Here, too, one can find the occasional experiments in rethinking how the resources of the college and the major curriculum can better complement each other. Introductory classes tend to be smaller. The number of majors a department can attract has prestige as well as budgetary value. More effort is put into building relationships with undergraduates across the courses of the major. The care and attention that might otherwise be spent on graduate students is here lavished on majors. There are usually two divisions in the curriculum: an introductory, or lower, level with a mixed student group and an advanced, or higher, level with a more homogeneous student group. Still, because the student bodies tend to be smaller, students from other majors register for advanced courses on an elective basis.

These two situations do not exhaust the range of possibilities. There are several other categories of majors in schools that are too large to have the atmosphere of the liberal arts college and too small to sustain graduate programs. There are also schools with combined, multi-discipline departments that offer their own flavor of a major. These contexts increase the mixing of students in classes. Conscientious instructors will design classroom environments with this varied student group in mind and avoid the tedious error of assuming homogeneity simply because the course is in the major.

Demands of Graduate Programs

CHAPTER
17

The graduate curriculum is the most challenging teaching assignment for the new instructor. This sounds counterintuitive. After all, the instructor lived in the graduate environment just recently. Who better to teach other graduate students? The problem is that during the several years it takes to transform a recent college graduate into an independently functioning scholar, the pedagogy must grow increasingly nondirective. Fourth- or fifth-year graduate students do not need instruction. They need guidance from scholars who have had personal experience in completing multiple research projects, not just one project. Even students at the master's level benefit from classrooms that let them take the lead in shaping the dialogue. This means that the skills of the new instructor are in complementary distribution, as the linguists say, to the needs of the students. The new instructor is brimming with knowledge and skills, ready to give it all to students, while the graduate students need freedom from teaching to begin their journey toward independent scholarship. It simply takes time to figure out how much to build in and how much to leave out of a graduate course, how much to say and how much to avoid saying during a discussion.

In previous sections, I have described the importance of creating learning environments that are conducive to balancing skills with knowledge. At the graduate level, the knowledge base is crucial. Hopefully, the admissions committee has selected candidates who are in the top 20 percent of skilled reasoners. The first two years of graduate education must prime them with the core knowledge of the discipline, while not letting their reasoning skills atrophy. In some disciplines, such as the laboratory sciences and the fine arts, this core knowledge is methodological as well as factual. In most of the others, it is primarily factual. In the better graduate programs, this process of examining the factual basis for the discipline is exhaustive. In others, it is more limited but remains a grueling exercise in knowledge acquisition. The pedagogical creativity here lies in how many different ways students can be enjoined to read.

Incoming graduate students have mixed skills and are usually unprepared for the intensity of the knowledge acquisition demands that are placed on them. Do not look for homogeneity here. These students may be good readers, but they are rarely very efficient at retaining arguments. They may be good talkers, but they are not adept at penetrating the author's assumptions. They may have graduated from famous colleges, but they have retained very little of the factual knowledge in their major courses. Most are lacking in the life experiences necessary to contextualize the discipline's knowledge and make it intellectually relevant. The ones who drop out will do so because the learning experience was not what they expected it to be. The pedagogical challenge at this level lies in analyzing individual weaknesses and providing the proper supports to enable students to succeed.

Once the students have survived this concerted effort to see how many books they can read and retain in a week, they pass into a second phase, in which they use their newly won knowledge to expose the weaknesses in the analyses of contemporaries. This application of theory to critique undermines any residual concreteness in the reasoning habits of the students and positions them for the next phase: the application of theory to method. This is where they begin to develop their own research questions and the strategies for competently investigating them. At this point, all that remains is for students to actually mount and complete one such project. At each of the four stages, the instructor steps farther and farther away from the process. The role shifts from an authority figure to a colleague struggling with similar issues. The creativity here lies in giving the student every opportunity for independent action while indirectly guiding him or her toward asking the appropriate questions.

CHAPTER 18

Interdisciplinary Demands

Beginning with the area studies curriculums that bloomed during the Cold War, universities have slowly developed curriculum around interdisciplinary cooperation. These programs can offer a major, but are also likely to serve as minors or substitutes for general education requirements. The vitality and prestige of the interdisciplinary programs at a school are a good indication of the faculty's commitment to work across disciplines to serve the learning of the students.

Honors Programs

Colleges with broad admissions policies sometimes create alternative general education programs for well-prepared students. In these programs students engage the general education program surrounded by peers who are prepared. Unlike high school, they receive no special advantages, like weighting their grades. The requirements are likely to be more complex than in the ordinary program, often including at least a year of laboratory science and two years of foreign language. Some programs involve students only during the first two years. Others are designed to continue over the four years and culminate in a capstone seminar or thesis project.

For the instructor, honors programs can be an opportunity to work with a more homogeneous class in a general education curriculum. Expectations run high in these programs, and there is a tendency to view the students who participate as somehow more like their instructors than the students in the standard courses. There are reasons for well-prepared students to avoid honors programs. These can include honors program fatigue emanating from high school experiences, antisnobbism (whether warranted or not), or scheduling issues that make the honors program inaccessible. Similarly, not all students who are admitted to honors programs—usually based on entering test scores, scholarships, and, sometimes, interviews—are as prepared as they think they are.

As curriculum experiments, honors programs tend to be conservative. They are most often text based, canon driven, and reflective of the instructor's, rather than students', tastes. Instructors who were themselves students of elite undergraduate programs tend to be attracted to teaching honors courses, where they attempt to reproduce their experiences. Under the best of circumstances, the programs are interdisciplinary, forcing instructors to link several different academic traditions in a single course. More often, the courses are simply more pages per week of primary texts, as if reading challenges alone produced a deeper knowledge base or more effective skill base.

All instructors should have a go at honors classes. In the first place, teaching such classes helps younger teachers to calibrate the higher end of their grading scale. The variations that exist among honors students force us to grade with finer discriminations than in the general program. Second, since honors classes tend to be discussion based, younger teachers who otherwise are involved in large lecture classes can gain experience working with the discussion format. Honors students tend to be more flexible and open to classroom innovation. The classes can be opportunities to try out discussion techniques. Finally, honors classes offer the opportunity to teach primary texts, giving the instructor the chance to learn these texts more fully, deepening the instructor's understanding of them, and providing a base of knowledge the instructor can bring to other courses.

Interdisciplinary or Committee Programs

Disciplines are historical artifacts. There is no intrinsic reason why they should be divided as they are. Indeed, the boundaries between them blur more often than not. Part of the reason for this is that the demand for creativity at the doctoral level encourages the harvesting of analytic tools from other disciplines. Thus, over time, disciplines that are highly successful at reproducing themselves will include an increasing number of references to other traditions. This trend produces its own countertendencies where some colleagues see themselves as boundary enforcers, scrutinizing new colleagues for disciplinary purity in their research and teaching. In some colleges, the walls around the disciplines can be very high indeed. This is most often the case where there are expensive research and doctoral programs to defend from predatory administrators. In other colleges, the walls between the disciplines can be almost nonexistent. Here the college's agenda becomes paramount, and the disciplines exist to serve that agenda.

In this complex mix of methodology sharing, turf protection, and competing agendas, cross-disciplinary programs are born. They come in several varieties, depending on the degree of disciplinary identity retained in the classes. At one end are the multidisciplinary programs. In this form, representatives of different disciplines agree to mount a joint curriculum in which the classes retain the theoretical and methodological flavor of the instructor's home discipline. The teaching commitment for the individual instructor is usually a course that can be cross-listed and, hence, continue to serve the needs of the home discipline and the new program. The most common of these is the area studies program.

At the midpoint in the continuum is the interdisciplinary program. Here faculty from different disciplines agree on a curriculum in which the disciplinary identity of the instructor is irrelevant to the course content and skill set. Once in place, the curriculum is driven by its own mission and design principles, and various faculty can cycle in and out of the classes. The most common of these include first-year programs, some general education programs, and some honors programs.

The most extreme form of cross-disciplinary cooperation is the committee curriculum. In this form, faculty agree to design courses that emphasize the shared perspectives of their different disciplines, creating a curriculum that is distinguishable from the home disciplines of the designers. In addition, these faculty are actually released from some teaching responsibilities in the department so that they can serve the needs of the committee curriculum without cross-listing. Although the design effort has a lot in common with the interdisciplinary program, the committee curriculum has a different agenda. It has the resources to actually reform itself into a discipline, especially if it can articulate a preferred methodological strategy, identify a specific research niche, and begin to produce graduate students who are then hired because of their committee experience. Women's and gender studies, international studies, and environmental studies are examples of new disciplines that have emerged from committee-style curricula in recent years.

New disciplines are forming all the time. Some will grow in importance over time; others will collapse back into the primary disciplines that spawned them. Some of the new disciplines that appear to have some potential for continued growth include bioinformatics, environmental studies, new media studies, and gender studies.

Younger faculty working in the forefront of their discipline are often attracted to such programs because of the intellectual flexibility they offer. At the same time, the political issues surrounding the relationship of the program to the traditional department frighten them. The creation of a new department involves a redistribution of limited resources. Departments will fight to maintain their access and prerogatives. For all these reasons, nontenured faculty should probably involve themselves in committee programs only with the blessing of their departments. After tenure, they can take greater risks. In any event, it is a good idea to ask about interdisciplinary programs during the job interview to gauge the level of cooperation between the department and the programs.

Area and Topical Studies

Area studies were born in European and North American institutions to make sense of the world over the last 150 years or so. They were originally a dialogue among specialists who shared a common research language and life experience abroad but practiced different disciplines. The growth of these programs was pushed forward in a dramatic way from generous funding by the Ford Foundation for a decade or so after the start of the Cold War. Eventually, graduate students were brought into the conversation as a way to help them make research contacts and encourage them to write for a wider community of scholars. They took courses offered by area specialists in departments outside their own. Over time, enough of these specialists emerged to create an interdisciplinary curriculum. At this point, undergraduates were admitted to help boost the course enrollments. As the conditions under which people learn languages and live abroad have changed, so have the priorities of area studies programs. The publication of Edward Said's *Orientalism* (1978) set in motion a series of critiques of area studies that culminated in several phases of rethinking their design in the 1990s. Where the areas were previously defined according to ambiguous world regions, like Europe or Latin America, new approaches to creating dialogue among area specialists tries to incorporate around global trends, such as transatlantic studies, open trade communities, Diaspora studies, or borderlands.

No matter how we might define them in the future, multidisciplinary programs insure that the younger instructor has the opportunity to stay abreast with the research in allied fields. They open up new audiences for reporting on research. They provide a community for maintaining foreign language skills. They offer a pool of students in which to test one's ability to articulate the nuances of cultural difference. These programs also present significant teaching challenges. How can we teach students to see qualitative differences that are the effects of the regional or global processes while avoiding the bias that emerges when the effects are reinterpreted as causes? For those faculty with the requisite background, this kind of teaching is a significant contribution to the university community.

First-Year Programs

The general education program can be divided into those courses housed in the departments and those housed in special programs. At a minimum, the college provides remedial courses that departments would rather not have to take responsibility for, such as reading, computation, or ESL. Colleges create a common experience for first-year students to aid in retention. Beginning at the University of South Carolina in the 1970s, first year programs have spread throughout universities, large and small. These are primarily skills-courses in writing, research, and data manipulation. Sometimes an advisory curriculum is attached to the courses, insuring that students learn about the student life resources, as well as the academic ones. Sometimes the program has service components that connect the students with the surrounding community. All of these programs require faculty to design a curriculum for a large number of students, exhausting the capacity of any one department.

Teaching these courses is a challenge because the students are the least experienced. They exhibit the low motivation common to students taking required courses. The instructor does not have the same supports enjoyed when teaching the discipline. The mission of the program may be vague or ambiguous (an artifact of the interdisciplinary dialogue that gave birth to it), leading to confusion over what constitutes a successful course design. Evaluations by students may be unusually harsh. The department's share of the staffing requirements for such programs falls disproportionately on younger faculty. Senior faculty may have no experience teaching in this environment. As a result, they can neither mentor the new faculty effectively for these courses nor appropriately evaluate the teaching outcomes.

Faced with this situation, the instructor should emphasize a skill set. Skill sets readily transfer between disciplines. The skill set appropriate to first-year students is the most generalized of them all. Motivation will increase if they feel they are learning something they can use. The teaching of skill sets can be rationalized within any mission statement. While teaching a skill set, the knowledge base of the course can be as broad or as narrow as the instructor wishes. It can even be disciplinary.

An example from my college may suffice in illustrating how this could work. Here is the description for a first-year course called Quantitative Reasoning:

> Quantitative Reasoning is a course designed to help students become confident and critical users of quantitative information, developing facility in the use of spreadsheets, word processors, email, presentation software, and the internet. They will develop quantitative skills in estimation, percentage change, proportional reasoning, scaling, descriptive statistics, and simple mathematical models (linear and exponential). First year students take this course unless their program of study requires calculus.

The skill set is defined as several computer applications, especially Mathlab and Excel, which are useful across many courses the student will take. It also includes fundamental quantitative manipulations that permit the student to convert mathematical relationships and patterns to evidence in an argument. When one of my mathematics colleagues teaches the course, she chooses the data arbitrarily. When my archaeologist colleague teaches the course, he draws the data from his site surveys. When a computer-aided design colleague teaches the course, he takes the data from rendering problems. Regardless of where the data is drawn, the skill set is the same.

6 Universal Design

I have already discussed the variety of students in our classrooms. To set the stage for this discussion of universal design (UD), allow me to summarize: students with physical differences related to height and weight, students with visual differences, students with hearing difficulties, students with learning difficulties, students with attention difficulties, students with health difficulties and students with communication differences. Every instructor should know and use universal design practices because they are the best solution we have for reaching the diversity in our classrooms.

The ideas that we call universal design today originated with Marc Harrison at the Rhode Island School of Design. He stressed that products should be designed for people of all abilities. Ronald Mace at North Carolina State University used the term in 1970, defining it as the design of products and environments to be usable by all people, to the greatest extend possible, without the need for specialized design (The Center for Universal Design 1997). The principle is put into practice in architecture, product design, information technology and education. The common thread to all the applications is that different users can utilize the space, environment, equipment, or classroom without being singled out for special consideration. All the necessary considerations are already built into the product or environment. Everyone has abilities and disabilities, each of which is located on a continuum between the fully functional expression of the ability and the absence of that ability. UD directs the designer to anticipate this range of abilities and account for it in the design. Instructors are designers of learning environments. Instructors need to know about UD.

Universal Design in Higher Education

CHAPTER 19

UD is comprised of seven principles. These are:

- ► Equitable use: The design is appealing, useful and marketable to people with diverse abilities without segregation or stigma. An example of this might be a course Web page with audio and captioned alternatives to text and pictures.

- ► Flexibility in use: The design accommodates choice, providing a wide range of preferences and abilities, like right-hand or left-hand access. The university gallery, for example, could provide audio guides in addition to descriptions of the contents of displays.

- ► Simple and intuitive use: The design is easy to understand, without prior experience, knowledge, language skills, or special concentration. Buttons on classroom equipment could be labeled with symbols and text students can immediately understand.

- ► Perceptible information: The design communicates all necessary information to the user regardless of the user's environment or sensory abilities. When showing a video presentation in a class, you could enable the captions.

- ► Tolerance of error: The design minimizes adverse consequences of accidental or unintended actions, including fail-safe features. You could include a sheet or Web pop-up with the correct answer and an explanation for each item on a quiz after the student has made their choices.

- ► Low physical effort: The design can be used efficiently, comfortably and with minimum fatigue. All doors to the classroom should have automatic openers.

- ► Size and space of approach and use: Appropriate size and space is provided for approach, reach, manipulation and use regardless of the user's body size, posture or mobility. Science labs could have low benches for seated and wheelchair access. (The Center for Universal Design 1997, with examples from Burgerstahler 2008, 27)

These principles have been adapted to a variety of special environments, including university classrooms. Designs that take these principles into account are accessible and useable for the broadest number of users. They reduce the number of special accommodations, such as those required by the Americans with Disabilities Act of 1990. This act considers a person with a disability to be any individual who is found to

> (1) have a physical or mental impairment that substantially limits one or more major life activities of such individual (including walking, seeing, hearing, speaking, breathing, learning or working), (2) have a record of such impairment, or (3) be regarded as having such an impairment. (1990)

The category of disability includes mobility, hearing, seeing, speaking, learning, and mental health. No otherwise *qualified* person with a disability should be excluded from, denied the benefits of, or subjected to discrimination under programs in an institution of higher education. A qualified individual is

> an individual with a disability who, without reasonable modifications to rules, policies, practices, the removal of architectural, communication, or transportation barriers, or the provision of auxiliary aids and service, meets the essential eligibility requirements for the receipt of services or the participation in programs or activities provided by the public entity.

Those reasonable modifications are also known as accommodations. Examples include sign language interpreters, Braille versions of texts, taking tests in soundproof rooms and wheelchair accessible classrooms. In higher education institutions, students who believe they may qualify for an accommodation must disclose the evidence of their disability, usually in the form of a doctor's letter to an officer of the university who is specially designated and trained to determine the reasonableness of the accommodation. It is this individual who then communicates the necessary information to faculty or staff. With universal design, the instructor may already have anticipated the accommodation and built it into the course. Universal design is the proactive approach to an inclusive educational experience.

CHAPTER 20

Universal Design of Courses

The application of the seven principles to a course may, at first glance, seem oblique. One faculty achieved equitable use by designing the website so that blind students could use text-to-speech software to "read" it.

One of the earliest scholars to anticipate the application of universal design in instruction was Bowe. His simple tip sheet still stands as an efficient way of removing the most obvious hurdles for your students. The eight tips include:

1. Become aware of your own culture's teachings and how these affect you as an educator. What are your expectations of students? How might students with various disabilities challenge those expectations?

2. Provide students with options for demonstrating knowledge and skills. Why must there only be the way you have always done it? Can you imagine other ways that can do the same job?

3. Offer instruction, and accept student work, at a distance. Can your students use the email, learning management software or ordinary mail to learn from you or show you the products of the learning?

4. Alert students to the availability of digitized textbooks. More publishers are offering these and more bookstores are providing them. The increasing possibility of e-book readers makes using e-versions easier.

5. Offer students information in redundant media. Most universities can provide audio and video taping of your course for distribution through the course site.[1]

[1] Faculty will sometimes balk at the idea of recording courses. They believe that students will skip class if recordings are available. There is one study that supports this (Hassiotou and Finnegan 2009) and three that do not. In two out of three sets of comparative attendance counts reported (captured versus noncaptured courses), researchers report a slightly lower attendance rate for captured courses. The third count reported a slightly higher attendance rate, and in all three cases, the results were deemed statistically insignificant (Brotherton and Abowd 2004, 145; Harley et al. 2003, 41; Traphagan 2005, 32).

6. Provide support for students' need to improve accuracy and speed in completing assignments.

7. Translate important materials to other languages as needed by your students. This is time consuming and costly and should be chosen with care.

8. Choose physically accessible locations for your classes. (2000, 5-6)

If some of these actions strike you as beyond the scope of an individual instructor, you are correct. They are ideals. As with the design of doors, furniture and labs, the institution should develop mechanisms that make it easier for instructors to accomplish these ends. Institutions are at different stages in the process.

McGuire, Scott and Shaw's work at the University of Connecticut extends the principles to include two that expressly relate to courses:

9. A community of learners: The instructional environment promotes interaction and communication among students and between students and faculty.

10. Instructional climate: Instruction is designed to be welcoming and inclusive. High expectations are espoused for all students. (2003, 13)

These two points consolidate UD principles with a particular teaching and learning philosophy, one I happen to share. What if you happen to embrace a different philosophy? Burgstahler has found creative instructors who offer multiple ways for students to access materials, numerous ways to participate and diverse forms of assessments covering a multitude of teaching approaches (2008b, 30-31). Burgstahler and Cory's collection of articles has a number of models that analyze the UD possibilities for specific leaning situations in course instruction (2008a).

PART 7

Constructing the Syllabus

The syllabus is your opportunity to describe the learning environment of your classroom. Although it is rarely seen as a scholarly genre, when approached as such, the syllabus provides the basis for documenting effective teaching. As a genre, it fulfills certain administrative functions to be sure, but it also sets the tone of the class. I have seen syllabi that are little more than a schedule of readings and discussion topics. These miss an opportunity to begin developing the relationship with the student. An open, honest, and inviting syllabus tells the students that they can anticipate a positive experience. Some syllabus writers open up the dialogue by including images and cartoons, as well as text. These are meant to stimulate discussion and relieve some of the anxiety students experience when they encounter your high expectations for their performance.

My syllabi would range from six to fifteen pages if they were printed. Since they exist as Web pages, the specific length is not apparent to the student. In spite of the length, I attempt to review the entire syllabus in the first class meeting. If I have taught the class before, I tell the students where I have changed the syllabus to reflect the concerns of previous classes. I invite them to question parts they do not understand and to offer suggestions. This is a good way to begin to generate discussion. I follow through by trying to find something I can change in response to that initial conversation. This helps students to feel that they have a stake in the design of the class.

Nevertheless, the design of the class is the responsibility of the instructor. It is what the art and craft of college teaching is all about. You have a lot of decisions to make in creating the class. This chapter is expressly concerned with the overall design of the course: Where does the course fit in the curriculum? Who are the students? How do you want them to change over the course of the term? The design decisions can be grouped into four sets:

→ The administrative components,

→ The technical components,

→ The selection of materials,

→ The determination of your expectations for the students' achievements.

Administrative components are like being dealt a hand of cards. They are features of the class over which the instructor has little control. They determine what the class experience will be like for you as an instructor. They deal with such questions as the following:

→ How many students are permitted to enroll?

→ How many are actually likely to enroll?

→ When in the day and week is the class scheduled, and what effect does this schedule have on the physical condition of the students (i.e., sleepy, hungry, etc.)?

→ What are the academic levels of students who are likely to enroll?

→ What are the financial and legal limits on what they can read, watch, or listen to?

The answers to these questions may not appear as anything more than a few lines in the initial description of the course. This is where you explain that the course fulfills a general education requirement or has certain prerequisites. But all of these considerations influence how you design the course experience. The most important one is the number of students.

The technical components of the syllabus are the contractual elements. They are what you need to tell students in order for them to understand what the course is and what their experience with the course will be like: attendance policy, evaluation policy, the number and timing of exams and reports, and the outside-of-class requirements for field trips, access to nonlocal libraries, and so forth. This is not merely boilerplate. You may find that the course demands a stricter attendance policy because most of the learning will occur through group work or a seminar. The syllabus for one class may require a more elaborate explanation of how you will grade the students. You might decide that the best place for testing is the end of each unit, rather than the traditional midterm. You may have such a large outside-of-class component that you will need to warn students that the course places an extraordinary burden on their personal time. This is also the most legalistic component of the syllabus. If your college has a grade challenge policy, one of the criteria for a student to challenge a grade is that the faculty member made up or changed the rules throughout the term. Having all of the structural elements described in the syllabus insulates you from this kind of challenge. There is no such thing as a syllabus that is too long.

The selection of materials is your way of making the knowledge base of the course a subset of your discipline. It is the most intellectually demanding aspect of course design and requires you to have knowledge of the available books, articles, and media in excess of what you will actually use. It is also the aspect of course design that you must undertake continuously, not just the week that book orders are due. By continuously, I mean that it is something you should be thinking about whenever you encounter a useful text, idea, approach, or data set that might apply to the course, whether you are teaching it at the time or not.

You need to explain what combination of skills and content you will evaluate. This is the point where you can articulate your goals for the course. Once you can state your goals, you have something to assess in the students' learning, a way to teach them, and accomplishments to evaluate at the end of the process. You can also describe to the students exactly how that assessment, teaching, and evaluation will proceed.

Developing a Course for the First Time

CHAPTER
21

I never use the syllabus categories as the basis for planning a course. Instead, I start with the outcomes that I want the students to achieve. This is called backwards design (Wiggins and McTighe 2005). Since Angelo and Cross (1994) have provided a fairly complete list of possible goals, they make the job a bit easier. Following, for example, are their eight possibilities for connecting the course to disciplinary-specific knowledge and skills, one of several categories of goals they discuss. Unless the course is outside of my discipline, this is where I like to start.

Read through this list and ask yourself which goals you would make your highest priority for a course.

18. Learn terms and facts of this subject.

19. Learn concepts and theories in this subject.

20. Develop skill in using materials, tools, and/or technology central to this subject.

21. Learn to understand perspectives and values of this subject.

22. Prepare for transfer or graduate study.

23. Learn techniques and methods used to gain new knowledge in this subject.

24. Learn to evaluate methods and materials in this subject.

25. Learn to appreciate important contributions to this subject.

Each of these offers a slightly different emphasis: technical vocabulary, conceptual development, technical skills, reflectiveness, professional preparation, research skills, critical skills, or connoisseurship. Which one(s) did you consider the most important for your class. Don't pick more than two goals. If you try to do too much in one course, everything suffers. If you cannot make up your mind between the second and third goals, ask yourself how much time you will actually need to spend on the one as opposed to the other. Orient the course around the one that will take up the most time.

Then, depending on the number of contact hours in the term and the level of the students, decide how many units you want to use for each goal. To illustrate how you might make such a decision, consider an introductory course for a nonmajor student group. The students are seeking to fulfill a distribution requirement in their general education program. The department wants the course to introduce the discipline in such a way as to inspire students to choose it as a major. Which of the goals in the list would you immediately exclude because your objective is to "inspire." The goals numbered 22, 23, and 24 immediately present themselves as inappropriate to this objective. This is an important observation. It means that you can reasonably exclude portions of the disciplinary canon from the course, including not assigning those chapters of the textbook. The process of goal picking is crucial to the entire design of the course.

Of the remaining five goals, 18 caters to the lowest common denominator in the student group, the ones who are mired in concrete reasoning and are the least likely to be engaged by the information. They will certainly be happy that you have couched the course to their comfort zone, but even success in answering your exams on terms and facts will not inspire them to declare the major. Learning the terms and facts of a subject can still be the most appropriate primary goal for a course. This is true when large numbers of keywords begin to dominate the course materials. This scenario is most likely to happen in courses designed to introduce disciplinary or subdisciplinary materials to majors. In the meantime, the students who might have their interests ignited by your discipline's complexities are turned off. They would be most happy with goal 19. However, a high-concept approach to teaching an introductory course means teaching to the top 15 percent of the group. While some faculty do this and even generate new majors as a result, they reinforce the stereotype in the remaining 85 percent that the discipline has nothing important to say to them.

Goals 20, 21, and 25, then, offer a middle ground between pandering to the students who do not want to be challenged and teaching only those students who are the conceptually oriented. Goal 20 has its own issues, since it requires that the materials, tools, and technology be available in sufficient quantities to match the course enrollment. However, if it is possible to do so, introducing the discipline to this audience by letting them handle materials is an effective strategy. Goals 21 and 25 are more easily achieved in larger classes, and appeal to all levels of learners.

For this particular audience, the best choice for a primary goal would be goal 21: "Learn to understand perspectives and values of this subject." You know from your own knowledge of your discipline that there were certain publications, findings, challenges to findings, scandals, and public events through which the perspectives and values of the discipline evolved. One or two of these will frame the goal for the students. If you can find more examples, you can begin to establish goal 25: "Learn to appreciate important contributions to this subject."

The question then becomes, what are the three or four (or five) publications, findings, challenges to findings, scandals, and public events that you want to talk about? What are the historical issues in your discipline that could then lead to a discussion of the important contributions your colleagues have made? More importantly, can you find readings that will supply the students with the context, facts, actions, and effects of these features of the discipline's development? The availability of materials is more likely to drive your choice of unit topics than your own preferences. Because the class time for dealing with these units is very quickly filled up with various activities—your contextualizing lectures, discussions of the readings, breakout sessions for discussing the skill components, assessments, and questions—it is therefore better in this kind of class to choose fewer, pithier topics and spend more time with them than to try to cover a large amount of material superficially

Once you have chosen units and readings, you determine which of the following ways to use the readings:

→ as the text for a close reading

→ as the basis for discussion of perspectives and values

→ as a model of my discipline's analytic style

→ as a source for knowledge that will be utilized in connection with other readings

→ as a demonstration of how treacherous the pitfalls for effective analysis actually are.

Then, you read the book or collections of articles to select the page runs the students will actively read. This allows you to make accurate estimates of how long it will take them to read and discuss the materials. You have already made choices about why you want the materials read. Now the question is how can you support their active reading practice. For a close reading, I write down the prompts I want them to address in their reading journals. As a model of analytic style, you can have them map the author's chain of logic. For each method of reading, there is a corresponding activity that you want the students to complete. These active reading exercises are not graded. They are collected, however, and are part of the class participation grade.

When you have the materials in place, you can then check available sources. You know there are several different ways that scholars have understood the events you want the students to discuss. When I do this, I go through the sources that the students will not be reading to collect relevant quotes that I can use to frame different perspectives as these come up in discussion and, more importantly, to remind me several months from now of the reason I chose this specific unit. In particular, I look for quotes that help me connect the two goals of the course: to understand the perspectives and values of the discipline, and to appreciate its contributions. At this point, you have set the knowledge base of the course and can turn to the skill issues.

In their inventory of potential course goals Angelo and Cross (1994) provide eight goals that help you support specific higher-order reasoning skills in your students. They are:

1. Develop the ability to apply principles and generalizations already learned to new problems and situations.
2. Develop analytic skills.
3. Develop problem-solving skills.
4. Develop the ability to draw reasonable inferences from observations.
5. Develop the ability to synthesize and integrate information and ideas.
6. Develop the ability to think holistically: to see the whole as well as the parts.
7. Develop the ability to think creatively.
8. Develop the ability to distinguish between fact and opinion.

Again, you begin by prioritizing the list for your course. Given the description of the student audience I am using for this demonstration, several of these goals have low priority. Since the students are new to the discipline, the first goal does not apply. Since no data is available, goals 2 and 3 do not apply. Goals 5, 6, and 7 are certainly worthy but would also fall outside the scope of an introductory course. Goals 4 and 8, however, speak directly to the critical reasoning challenges faced by the majority of students in our introductory courses. This is where I would put the skill emphasis of the course. Skills are introduced through specific exercises and reinforced by repetition. As with the knowledge base, you must make choices. You cannot offer every aspect of a skill without confusing the students.

To teach students how to distinguish fact from opinion, you would attach a reading assignment that asks students to select quotes that they feel represent the author's opinion as opposed to the facts presented. In breakout sessions of groups consisting of four to five students (or in the discussion sections of large lectures), the groups talk through the quotes each student brings, noting their agreements and disagreements. Students then write out a report of the results of their discussions, indicating how and why they separated specific quotes as opinion, rather than fact. They repeat this exercise for at least one of the readings in each unit.

Although the students are also drawing reasonable inferences from observations in the previous exercise, you should be more interested in getting them to identify those situations in the readings where unreasonable inferences were drawn from observations. In particular, you want students to read materials that caused controversies because the author utilized a fallacious argument. The most common of these inferential fallacies are:

→ Hasty Generalization. The sample is too small to support a generalization about a population or phenomenon.

→ Unrepresentative Sample: the sample is unrepresentative of the phenomenon or population.

→ False Analogy: the two objects or events being compared are relevantly dissimilar.

→ Slothful Induction: the conclusion of a strong argument is denied despite the evidence to the contrary.

→ Fallacy of Exclusion: the evidence that would change the outcome of an argument is excluded from consideration. (Downes 1995)

Ask students to identify which inferential fallacies are deployed in the service of the conclusion. Students share these observations with fellow students in a breakout discussion, usually toward the end of the unit, and each student submits an individual report on the search for the fallacies. In my practice, neither the report on the opinions nor the one on the fallacies is graded. You merely note that the student turned in the report, and count missing reports as a hit against the class participation grade. I do this because it is the repetition of the skill that I am interested in, rather than consistent accuracy across all three units. If the student doesn't get it until the third iteration, that is fine. They eventually get it. Other instructors may grade skill exercises and count them as a contribution toward the final grade.

You have now defined a knowledge base and skill set and developed readings, responses, and exercises to support them. You could go on to the three remaining groups of Angelo and Cross's goals, but I have found that a well-constructed knowledge base and skill set easily support other goals without having to add anything.

You still have to make two more important choices: How can you be certain that the students are actually learning the elements that will fulfill your goals? How are you going to give students summary feedback on their learning? The first choice is about assessment; the second is about evaluation.

You have already built assessment into the course by having students turn in their reports on the opinionated quotes and the inferential fallacies. These reports will give you a good indication of how the class is proceeding toward your skill goals. To that I would add an initial baseline assessment. This would be a simple take-home assignment, due in the second class meeting. For this assignment, I give the students a paragraph filled with facts and opinions. I then ask a series of questions about the paragraph. From the responses I can immediately ascertain the students' existing awareness of the distinctions. I also schedule very short, one-minute essays for the next-to-last class meeting for each unit that give each student a chance to describe anonymously what he or she finds confusing or ambiguous in the discussion to that point. Doing this in the next-to-last class meeting on the unit gives you one more chance to speak to the confusion. It also forces you to conclude most of what you want them to discuss about the unit while there is still time to clear up any ambiguities.

What you want to evaluate is how well the students understand the primary goals for the course: the perspectives and values of the discipline and how well they appreciate its contributions. You want to evaluate this in a timely fashion because you know from the AAHE Best Practices that prompt feedback helps students to learn more effectively. My practice is to schedule a paper or test on the Monday following the weekend after we conclude each unit, with the assignment on the final unit due during the final exam period. You might choose a different pattern. This should be thought out ahead of time. Give the students the opportunity to adjust to your rhythm.

Since you have already decided what you want to evaluate, put the prompt you want the students to write on or study for (if you give exams) in the syllabus. This connects the evaluation back to the goals of the course. The prompt should include the language of the course goals. For example "Given the facts of the events surround X's publication of book Y, how did the response of the other researchers reflect the specific perspectives and values of this discipline? How have these perspectives and values migrated over time from the discipline's practices to society as a whole?" There will be differences in the students' reflections based on their understanding of the material, their motivation to spend time constructing a strong argument, their skill in using evidence, and their overall cultural literacy.

There will also be variations in the scholarly standards of each essay: clarity, accuracy, precision, relevance, depth, breadth and logical consistency. In other words, putting the final exam question in the syllabus will still result in a distribution of responses, even if they have the entire term to think about their answer. The effect for the student is to see the course as integrated around specific goals from beginning to end and to see you as an organized and effective instructor.

You are now ready to actually write the syllabus. This design process has given you a good handle on what will happen in the different class meetings. You have wrestled with the paper flow between the students and yourself and found a good balance. You have established a rhythm of consistent activities across changing themes that satisfies the need for both structure and variety. Most importantly, you have found a solution to balancing the diverse interests of the students, the department, the curriculum, and your own time. Others might certainly make different choices and produce excellent course experiences as a result. My intentions here are to illustrate the process of integrating the various elements to produce a syllabus.

The Impact of Class Size on a Syllabus

CHAPTER

22

One of our best practices encourages contact between teacher and student. It is easier to maintain contact in smaller classes than in larger classes. The few discussions of class size that exist in the literature see large classes as a significant problem for teachers. The authors want us to cope better with large classes. The approach I take here is that every class size offers both problems and possibilities. You cannot understand the effect of class size if it is isolated from the curriculum as a whole and from the budgetary conditions of a college. Putting class size back into this larger context helps you to decide how you can best serve your students' needs.

In my experience, the most contentious issue in administering a curriculum is class size. Unless a college has a very large endowment, there is a budgetary relationship between course enrollments and the size of a department. Your appointment was probably made possible by the registrations of students in your department's courses. Courses must have enrollments that are appropriate to the level of instruction and the goals of the curriculum. It makes no sense to have a laboratory with twenty seats enrolling forty students, a graduate seminar with sixty students, or an introductory general education course with six students. This latter example may thrill the hearts of experienced teachers, but it is unrealistic in contemporary universities. What administrators are looking for is an average class size that approximates a particular budgetary target. The target will be different in different universities, colleges, and departments, depending on the costs of that unit.

You will face classes that represent the entire range of class sizes in your teaching. For every graduate seminar of eight students, there will be an introductory lecture-style class of sixty or even three or six hundred. This raises several issues regarding effective teaching. Is there room for negotiating class sizes? How does one balance the need to implement the best practices in larger classes? As class sizes grow smaller, are there group dynamics that need to be considered? Finally, is there an ideal class size in undergraduate teaching?

Just as administrators are looking at averages, the individual faculty member should be looking at averages, too. The total number of students you teach in a year should approximate the average number for faculty in your rank in the department. A well-administered department generates parity of student load for faculty within their ranks once release time is factored in. If the chair is not calculating this, you should ask for the numbers and calculate it yourself. Furthermore, the number of students you teach per term can fluctuate wildly. The person doing the scheduling should consider the equity issues of faculty who consistently take on the large classes. Some may enjoy teaching large classes and excel in those teaching challenges. The person teaching a large class makes it possible for many of their colleagues to teach smaller classes. Teaching assistants may reduce the time it takes instructors to grade the exams and papers, but that is only the most visible time demand in teaching a large class.

Consider the differences in implementing various teaching strategies as enrollments increase. Not many colleges can afford to sustain enrollments of fewer than ten undergraduates per class, unless they are capstone-type seminars for seniors or remedial classes for freshmen. I call these micro classes. Some graduate seminars consist of fewer than ten students, but usually at the post-M.A. level only. Such classes are ripe for laboratory- and seminar-style strategies. Individual variations in motivation and learning have the greatest impact on the learning outcomes for a class of this size. Students expose their strengths and weaknesses in greater detail. When the students' skills and background match, the learning process can accelerate dramatically. In these very small classes, the balance between knowledge base acquisition and skill development usually tips toward skill development. You will find yourself talking more about the fine points of reading and preparation for class, rhetorical skills, and research technique.

The typical small class enrolls between ten and twenty students. Seminar-style teaching works if you are prepared to develop the students' independence. This is always easier with seniors and graduates. It is more difficult with freshmen. Laboratory-style teaching is especially effective with this size because it permits you to be more closely involved with the process than you can when the class is forty students. For lower-division classes with small enrollments, discussion with the group as a whole also works well. You can keep better track of the students' preparation. It is easier to establish community. Adjustments in response to assessment are easier to make. This is the ideal environment to mount a process-writing regime; students work through multiple drafts in pursuit of increasing rhetorical skills and critical acumen. Lecturing in a class of this size is less effective than other approaches. Students still present individualized learning styles, although if you use ongoing assessments you can discover how these are grouped. The balance between knowledge base acquisition and skill development still tips toward skill development. This is primarily a feature of the pressure on students to prepare adequately for class.

As enrollments increase above twenty students, seminar strategies become more difficult to implement. The absolute limit on an effective seminar in my experience is twenty-five. Sometimes it is possible to split the class and run two seminars simultaneously. I was once forced to have six groups of ten students engaged in separate, simultaneous seminars in the same room for a term. I do not recommend this. This splitting requires a bit of moving around on your part. Most discussion-oriented faculty would say that classes with up to thirty students do not make that big a difference in the quality of the discussion, even if there are more papers to grade.

As the class size approaches thirty, it becomes easier for students to hide. Laboratories can work well for up to thirty students, if space permits. This would result in five groups of six, or six groups of five, or three groups of ten, all of which are within the reasonable limits of oversight for a single instructor. Lecturing to classes of this size is probably not a practice I would endorse as the primary design feature of the class. There are too many opportunities in classes under thirty that are otherwise compromised by the lecture format. However, as a break from discussion, students welcome an occasional lecture that frames a unit or summarizes the work that has been done.

A final important restriction that appears as the enrollments approach thirty is the process-writing regime of the class. With thirty students, the routine of reading and returning drafts quickly becomes a serious drain on your time. Process writing begins to give way to product writing. The several short pieces may remain, but the give-and-take between student and instructor in the multiple draft process is now restricted. In a class size of thirty, the single research paper as the primary intellectual challenge of the course begins to appear in the classroom. Variations in students begin to fall into groups. There is a slowdown in development of new critical reasoning habits. The pressure to perform lessens, and with it, the motivation to adopt new techniques and develop new habits.

If we add ten to fifteen more students, does the environment change? The typical medium-sized class has between thirty and forty-five students. Instructors in these classes are always seeking to balance their approach between what works for thirty students and what works for forty-five. A syllabus designed for thirty students overwhelms the instructor in a class of forty-five. The real pressure is in the writing intensive exercises. Even using criteria-based grading rubrics, working through forty-five research papers will exhaust the patience and attention of all but the most dedicated teachers. Discussion utilizing the class as a whole is already unwieldy with thirty students. It is more difficult to create an early and effective sense of community in a class this large. More breakout varieties of discussion do work, such as panels, debates, and birdcage formats.

Socratic discussion (teaching by asking instead of telling) thrives on larger numbers. When you are careful to control the students' participation by using a seating chart, calling on students randomly to respond to your questions is a powerful way of reinforcing the knowledge base. You do not have to lecture. On the other hand, the Socratic method will terrorize students. Remember Professor Kingsfield from the film *The Paper*

Chase? As long as the Socratic probing is done cheerfully and with your recognition of how challenging this technique is for students, they will respond positively. In these medium-size classes, the balance between knowledge base acquisition and skill development begins to tip in favor of knowledge base acquisition.

Differences in individual motivation begin to predominate in performance on tests and essays. "Baseline" learning style variations, the styles that students present at the beginning of the class, define clearer groupings. These form a flattened pyramid, with "concrete" learners at the bottom representing nearly 50 percent of the class, "opinionated" learners on the next rung at about 35 percent, "evidentiary" learners next at 13 percent, and "prioritized evidentiary" learners at the top at 2 percent. These groups seem to persist over the course of the term. This is partly a result of the opportunity for students to hide and not have their performances challenged, and partly the result of the loss of emphasis on skill development. It also is a product of the greater heterogeneity found in classes taught at the lower end of the curriculum.

Adding ten to fifteen students to these forty-five does not change this dynamic. Most faculty would not feel the difference between forty-five and sixty students. A syllabus designed for forty-five students can easily accommodate more. However, the classrooms designed to hold more than forty-five students may look different. Most jurisdictions in which universities are situated have fire codes that require different features in rooms designed for fifty occupants or more. In larger classrooms, desks are fixed and there are multiple entrances and exits. Moving around in these classrooms has more to do with safely than it does with communication. Changing the focus of discussion from the front to the middle of the room is particularly difficult. Managing group exercises is difficult. Discussion techniques that use breakouts, debates, or birdcage discussions also become more difficult to manage. The opportunities for invisibility for any one student increase even further. At these numbers, even the research paper becomes an unwieldy form of evaluating.

The role of writing in the class is reduced to ungraded prewriting exercises of various sorts. Two essays per student are still feasible, but their scope is reduced and they are often paired with shorter questions testing students' control of the knowledge base. The balance between knowledge base acquisition and skill development definitely favors the knowledge base. The use of a single textbook to structure the student's encounter with the course begins to dominate the information sources of the course.

Evaluation relies increasingly on the tests of mastery of the knowledge base. The more students you have, the harder it is to keep track of how each one reasons. It is very difficult to assess and support the variety of reasoners in a class of fifty or more students. Baseline variations in reasoning habits interacting with variations in motivation dominate the learning outcomes. That means that you can almost predict the final grade from the baseline assessment and the attendance record. Classes of sixty or more students shift the course design entirely toward lecture strategies. This does not mean that there must be a wholesale retreat on skills development. It is possible to build skill exercises into large classes. Very few teachers actually do so.

What classes over sixty also mark is the beginning of the need for some kind of assistance. The management of the paperwork, the diminishing number of opportunities to engage students individually or through discussion, and the necessity to use a single text work best with a pair of assistants. As the class size increases, now by fifties rather than tens, there are very few differences in the syllabus or the administration of the course. The scale increases without a concomitant increase in complexity, as long as the number of assistants increases proportionately. I faced classes of 120 students on my own when I first started teaching. Such unassisted management of large classes requires highly entertaining lectures to motivate students to read relatively unchallenging texts, with modest assessments once a term and evaluations that place a premium on arriving at an individual grade in the shortest possible time, such as optical scanning of multiple-choice tests.

CHAPTER

23

Taking the Calendar into Account

The population of students shifts at the beginning of each term. Some students "shop" classes, looking for a fit between their needs and the course demands. Course titles confuse some, while bad advice victimizes others. While you struggle to create a community that will insure effective discussion, the members of that community migrate in and out. You can do little about this. If you attempt to ignore it, the newly arrived students will be only dimly aware of what you are trying to do. You can try to assert a 100 percent attendance policy and block any student who first shows up in the third class. The dean's office will not appreciate the complaints this can generate. If you have a website for the course where you post the syllabus, or if the school provides students' email addresses on the roster, you can attempt to communicate the attendance policy to students early on. If it is really crucial that students be there on the first day of class, you might try adding a note to the course title in the website where students register, alerting them to your policy. Whatever you do, the rules of the college may interfere with your efforts to create an early and effective community.

This is why it helps you to take account of the academic calendar. The date after which students cannot add the course means that new faces will stop appearing. That is when you begin to establish community. There may also be a date after which students cannot change to auditor status. Auditors come and go with impunity. There are various withdrawal dates: one for full reimbursement, one for partial reimbursement, one for no record of having attended the class, and one with a record of having attended the class. Some schools want faculty to check their attendance against the official roster from time to time and report students who have never attended. Some students use course registrations for financial aid and immigration purposes that colleges attempt to control. As the restrictions of students studying in the U.S. on a visa increase, there will be Federal pressure on schools to take attendance in every class. If you are aware of the dates, you can put them in your schedule for the course. To the extent that you can, you might try to schedule quizzes, essays, exams, or other kinds of feedback so that the results are in students' hands before the relevant deadlines for withdrawal.

Some universities require that the last assignment in the course, regardless of whether it is a paper, a presentation, or an exam, occur during the scheduled final exam period instead of the last regular day of the term. The reason for this is to avoid the extra pressure on students to complete several important assignments on the last day of classes. Scheduling the last assignment during the final exam period gives the students more time to organize their efforts. You should always ask about this since the colleagues who follow this rule resent the ones who violate it.

Other elements of the calendar that affect your relationship with students include the college's idea of when midterm exams ought to be given, the date when students can begin registering for the next term, and the date when book orders for the next term are needed by the bookstore. This is more than just an issue of looking ahead. Midterm exam periods are times when students are under greater stress. Even if you are not giving a midterm exam, you will likely see evidence of their stress. Discussions during this week are likely to be less lively than at other times. Students have had less time to prepare.

The period during which students register for the next term means that more students will looking for you in your office for advice on what courses to take. Depending on your department's policy of student advising, you may have to add on additional office hours. If you were planning on reading thirty take-home essays that week, you may be frustrated by the unexpected demands on your time.

Placing a book order means that you have thought out what you are going to do with the class the next term. If you are ordering for a new course, you need to spend time deciding on the books. If you've devoted weeks before writing the syllabus, you are prepared. If not, the time you spend on the courses you are currently teaching must compete now with the time you need to plan the course you will teach next. Keeping track of these dates helps you to be proactive, rather than reactive, in your teaching. That makes you a better teacher.

Ordering Books and Photocopying Material

CHAPTER

24

Book orders are a source of contention between you and your students. They want to read books, but they do not want to waste their time and money. If you have not read the book or thought about how it will work, you are risking the goodwill of your students by ordering it. To say that books should be chosen carefully seems trite. In the rush of preparations to start the new class, "carefully" too often means that you are looking for an opportunity to teach the book, rather than looking for a book from which the students can learn. The craft of teaching lies in always keeping the students' needs ahead of your own.

There are many sources of textbooks. One of the main reasons for attending academic conferences is to visit the book exhibit. Here you can easily compare various textbooks, readers, and monographs. Such exhibits are always crowded because your colleagues are doing the same thing. Publishers grant you a conference discount if you want to bring the book home to look at it more carefully. Fewer publishers every year send free copies. These policies will be clearly stated at the booths. Spending your own money on books you will use in courses makes more sense than buying books that interest you but are outside of your immediate research area. Those in your research area have to be read immediately. Those you are interested in can be borrowed from a library in a few months. Those you will teach from will be used over and over again as you prepare for class. Try to buy the hardcover whenever possible. It saves having to buy a second copy of the paperback in five years. Other sources of textbooks are colleagues' syllabi, websites, book reviews in journals and conversations with colleagues at conferences.

In fields that are changing rapidly or are so new that there are few monographs and no texts available, collections of articles often fill the gap. These are themselves the products of conference panels. When scanning the program, look for panels on topics you are teaching, as well as those in your research area. Catching one of the participants after the panel can often lead to insights in how to pair texts to a course. In short, the texts for courses ought to come from your knowledge of what is being read in similar courses around the country. With more experience and more knowledge about your discipline, you can invent your own approaches.

Students see the cost of textbooks as unfair. It would not matter if they were paying $20 per course or $200 per course. After students pay tuition, the purchase of textbooks appears to them to be one more way that the university has found to separate them from their money. They have a point. University systems in other countries do not consume textbooks in anywhere near the volume that universities in the United States do. Students change their minds about the value of the money they spend on textbooks only after they have read them and learned from them. Unfortunately, they also encounter far too many textbooks that are badly written, beyond their level of comprehension, and/or poorly used in the context of the course. The solution is to choose the best written texts and use them effectively in furthering the goals of the course.

Begin by selecting a book that is a tried-and-true standby for the course. This should be a book that other people who have taught the course have found to be consistently effective. Even if you disagree with the approach and find the ideas old-fashioned, use it anyway. Before selecting the next book, read it. Think about a student in your course reading it for the first time. Is it written at or near the same level as the first book? How will you use it: close reading, basis for discussion, model for analysis, source for the knowledge base, or skill exercise? Make a note of this in your syllabus draft so that when you devise the evaluations, you will remember why you chose the book. If you choose a book as the basis for a discussion about a general principle and then evaluate students on their control of the fine detail in the argument, you have pulled the rug out from under them. They come away with negative feelings toward the book. It is not necessary to dumb down the readings, but it is important to choose books that are accessible, or the students will not read them. You can always build more complexity on top of the reading through framing lectures or Socratic discussion.

Write your own summary of the argument. Is the book organized with a clear outline? If so, students will read it more quickly than they will a disorganized or complex narrative. My test for the strength of a text's outline is to read a chapter backward, beginning with the conclusion and the first and last sentence of every paragraph until I reach the beginning. If I feel I have a sense of what the author did in the chapter, so will my students.

Whenever you assign a book, you are also committing yourself to teaching how the book should be read. Many original texts use archaic language and rhetorical forms. You can give the students more confidence with such texts by going over a difficult passage in class before they begin reading. Consider the need to prepare a study guide that defines obscure words or concepts or that fills in the context for a particular argument before you decide to adopt the book, not the weekend before you begin to teach it.

Repeat this process for each of the books, films, and articles you select. Then, before making your final decision, look at the whole ensemble.

→ Can you make effective transitions between the readings, or have you gerrymandered the readings from several different courses?

→ Will the students see these connections, or are they apparent only to you?

→ Is there an order to the readings, such that each builds on the arguments, information, analysis, or skills of the previous ones?

→ If the course is a survey, do the texts allow you to cover the breadth of material required by the curriculum?

When you are satisfied with your choices, order the books. Your students' experience will be a good one.

Not all classes need books. There is certainly no requirement that students must read books. Scholars write journal articles, chapters of books, Web articles and audio files that often present the same ideas as books in other forms. Course packets including photocopies of shorter writings that focus on the particular course topic are very popular among instructors. To select these articles, you should follow the procedure I discussed a little earlier. The articles must be readable, germane to the topic, and linked to the articles that precede it. As students read through the articles, the direction of the course should always be apparent to them. Bear in mind that reading shorter works requires different skills than reading an entire book. Be prepared to tutor students in these differences. Emphasize the stronger role of argument in articles. Show how arguments can be diagramed. Demonstrate the different parts of the article, including the abstract. Show how each section provides a distinct view of the whole piece. Asking them to write the abstract or conclusion section in their own words is an excellent way to have them prepare for discussion. Make sure they understand the style sheet, how to format the subheads, what to include as the footnotes or endnotes, and what the reader is supposed to learn from the reference list.

Whenever instructors copy the work of others, U.S. copyright laws apply. Do not let anyone tell you differently. You can be prosecuted for ignoring these laws. The university will not protect you. Assuming that your reasons for copying the work are entirely instructional—that is, you are not pocketing a percentage of what the students pay for the course packets as personal income—the fair use principle in the law applies.

The fair use of a copyrighted work for purposes such as criticism, comment, news reporting, teaching (including multiple copies for classroom use), scholarship, or research is allowed under the copyright law and is not an infringement of copyright. In determining whether the use made of a work in any particular case is fair use, the factors to be considered shall include:

- → The purpose and character of the use, including whether such use is of a commercial nature or is for non-profit educational purposes
- → The nature of the copyrighted work
- → The amount and substantiality of the portion used in relation to the copyrighted work as a whole, and
- → The effect of the use upon the potential market for or value of the copyrighted work. (Amended December 1, 1990, Public Law 101-650, Sec 607, 104 Stat. 5132; see http://www.loc.gov/copyright/title17/circ92.pdf)

You must take all four of the bullet points into consideration before determining if you must contact the copyright owner for permission to copy the work, or if you can copy the work without permission. The first point is not an issue because of the teaching context. The second point requires that the works you are copying are themselves scholarly works intended for the dissemination of ideas. Copying relatively new creative work intended for a mass market might create some difficulties, depending on how much you are copying. The third point is the crucial one for course packets. Since the copyrighted work as a whole could either be the article or the journal or the book, the "Substantiality of the portion" can vary. It is not as simple a matter as counting the number of pages. For example, if the copyright pertains to the specific article, you may need permission. If it pertains to the journal, you may be able to use one article without permission but not two or more articles from the same issue. The same would apply to chapters in a book. Finally, in regard to the fourth point, collections of chapters in books are intended for the same market as your course packet. It is unfair to the editors and publishers to undermine the value of their work by photocopying several articles instead of having the students buy the book, unless you ask permission to do so. These permissions involve a fee that is then passed on to the students.

You can freely photocopy anything in the public domain in its entirety. By law, no individual owns these works. The laws governing when a work passes into the public domain are complicated. Different rules apply, depending on when the work was created and what medium was used. Fortunately, there is a website that is kept up-to-date on the changes in the law (http://www.unc.edu/~unclng/public-d.htm). You should consult with the appropriate office of the university if you have any doubts about how to proceed. In many universities, the library is the best source of information in interpreting copyright restrictions on works. Most retail photocopy services will not copy works for you unless you have proof that you have permission to do so from the copyright holder or declare that no such permission is necessary. This moves the liability for being sued for infringement of copyright from the institution to you.

You can obtain permission easily. The owners of the works want to make it as simple as possible for universities to comply with the law. Most universities automatically offer this service to instructors. If so, you must take into consideration that it may add several weeks to the turnaround time on the photocopying of your course packet. Several clearinghouses exist to seek the permissions for you. Your library should be able to tell you the one that has the university's account. Copyright holders will occasionally ask you to pay fees, especially if you are reproducing substantial portions of works that are still active in the market. If you go through the clearinghouse, these fees are paid directly by the university and recouped by adding them to the cost of the packet to the students. The clearinghouses will want to know exactly how many copies you are making. When permission is granted, it applies only to the current term.

You will not get permission to copy the work whenever you like. Also, leftover copies cannot be sold in subsequent terms without asking for additional permission. The owners may stipulate that certain information, like the copyright page from the work, be included in every copy. Very rarely, permission is denied. This can occur when a work has recently been reissued in a new edition and the publisher wants to sell more copies of it. By refusing to permit a copy of substantial portions, the publisher is hoping that you will ask the students to buy the whole work. Permission is almost never refused for journal articles or articles that are copyrighted separately.

This may seem like one more layer of bureaucracy between you and your students. However, the protection of the value of ideas in the marketplace is part of our responsibility as scholars. If we violate the rights of our peers, what kind of example are we setting for our students? Many of us may wish to live in a world in which ideas flow freely through our community without relying on the mechanism of the marketplace. Acting toward published works as if that world exists now creates only personal liability and merely the illusion of greater freedom. By showing respect toward the scholarly works of our peers, we provide the appropriate model for our students, but only when we tell them what we did, how we did it, why we did it, and how little it cost them in the end.

Technical Components of a Syllabus

A complete syllabus has several parts. There is faculty contact information so students will know immediately that we want them to contact us through specific channels. In my case, those are my email address, my office phone number, and my office hours. Then the syllabus should describe the kinds of students who are expected to take the course, whether the course fulfills certain requirements, whether the course has prerequisites and why these are important, and whether the course is a prerequisite for later courses and what the students are expected to carry forward. It then should give a brief overview of the course, including the kinds of books, assignments, and experience students can expect. I describe the kind of learning environment I want to develop in the class, defining what I mean by lecture, discussion, laboratory, or seminar and what specific role I expect the students to play in that environment. In this section, the reading list uses the preferred reference or bibliographic style for the course, and I point that out to students. The syllabus, thus, also serves as the style sheet for the course.

The next important section describes the learning goals for the course. Sometimes I subdivide these under different headings, like reading goals, writing goals, critical thinking goals, creative goals, goals related to the major or program curriculum, professional growth goals, or personal growth goals. Not all of these apply in every course to be sure, but the subdivisions help the students to focus on what expectations they should set for themselves. I always have a personal goals section, and with one exception, I leave it blank for them to fill out. Letting them talk about their goals is a good way to get at their expectation bias (the assumptions they make about who you are, what you believe, and what you secretly want the class to be about) early in the class. This is especially true of general education and other required courses.

Setting the goals of the course is one of the most important decisions you will make in constructing the learning environment. It will determine the form of instruction, the workload, the form of assessment, and the form of evaluation. The teaching goals inventory developed by Angelo and Cross (1994) that I used earlier is a good place to start to help you accomplish your goals and communicate them to your students.

The syllabus should describe the evaluation policies. This includes all the different ways you intend to evaluate student performance, whether the particular evaluation is formative or summative, and what features students need to be aware of before they are evaluated. Because many of my classes have a discussion component, an important part of this section for me is class participation. I try to describe how I evaluate this as clearly as I can. To the extent that the course content and learning goals have coalesced in my mind (and this is a process, not a given), I provide rubrics in the syllabus that show students the differences between the letter grades for each type of assignment and especially how the grades for class participation are defined.

My practice is to stipulate an attendance policy, a lateness policy, and a class disruption policy. This is one of your important design decisions. It defines the primary responsibility of the student to the class: presence. It will come up often in the discussion of specific classroom environments. I want the student to understand how their disregard for these policies can impact the final grade. Any policies on makeup exams, incomplete grades, extra-credit registrations, or grade challenges would come next, if they apply to your practice.

I append the college or university's language on academic integrity. I include a short definition of plagiarism and differentiate it from cheating, just to make sure that we start off with the same understanding of what these offenses mean. Most institutions have well-defined policies, and it is only necessary to point students to the appropriate page in the student handbook or web page to cover yourself if you should encounter dishonesty down the line. Much of this is boilerplate. You write it once and copy it into every syllabus.

The next section is the class schedule. The common pattern of structuring a course around a set of texts and evaluating students on what they can reason from the texts produces a straightforward schedule. Where these schedules get complicated is when you design multithreaded course themes with several different projects, assignments, exercises, and readings going on simultaneously, each one of which deserves to have individual attention paid to it periodically. A well-planned and easy-to-read schedule helps students negotiate the complexity of such courses. At the very least, the schedule should describe each individual class meeting and all due dates. I find it easier to write mine into a three- or four-column table, depending on whether the course meets twice a week or three times a week. For classes that meet once a week, even more specificity might be necessary.

The most important part of the schedule is the pattern of when work is due. We want our students to plan their work effectively. That means they must coordinate work that is due in four or five different classes. You defeat their efforts at effective planning if you change the due dates after they have committed to the class.

Finally, for each major assignment, I provide a full description of what the experience of the assignment should be like:

→ What kind of research is involved.

→ What are the core issues or questions surrounding the research, the process I expect students to go through to complete the assignment.

→ What are the questions students should address in their self-assessment (if I choose to use one).

→ What is the style sheet they should use in the written report.

If there is also an oral report, I describe what that should be like. If there is an essay exam, I provide the questions. If there is a knowledge-based exam, I provide a study guide. Doing all this in the syllabus rather than just before the assignment is due lets the student develop more effective study habits. Sometimes a particular assignment will require a departure from or an addition to the general evaluation rubric. It may be necessary to restate the differences between the A, B, and C letter grades in the context of the specific demands of an assignment. The idea is to have as much transparency on the evaluation process as possible, reducing anxiety about it to near zero. This is a judgment on my part of where I want to put the emphasis in my course. I have chosen to put it on the learning process, rather than the evaluation process. It should be noted that in my experience, giving the students all this information about the evaluation does not change the distribution of grades. There is still so much variation in motivation, competing priorities, and reasoning skill, even in the most homogeneous student group, that even with all this extra information, I still find significant amounts of below-average work.

Selecting the Knowledge Base for the Course

CHAPTER

26

An extensive knowledge base is intimidating to students. You can help to reduce some of this anxiety by acknowledging what you yourself do not know. Discuss your own experience of acquiring knowledge. For example, you have the advantage over them of having read the books several times, repeatedly derived the statistics, solved similar problems, or had multiple experiences with the procedure. Control of the knowledge base is a function of repetition. Validate their feelings of inadequacy and tell them where you think they will be in the process at the end of the class and at the end of the program. Explain how the course will help them increase their control of these facts. Realism in the matter of our relative ignorance builds legitimacy.

Some teachers use the strategy of making the students a part of the process of constructing the knowledge base. Let them own some of the knowledge. Reserve some small piece of the course design for them to make a contribution that will be shared with the rest of the class. In small classes, it could be a short presentation. In middle-sized classes, it could be a poster presentation. In large classes, it could be a handout or study guide. Making students a part of the process helps them invest in the knowledge acquisition process.

No course can ever do it all. Keep saying that to yourself. Do not even try to do it all. All courses are built on ideas and facts that are chosen for specific purposes from a larger universe of ideas and facts. In other words, the knowledge base of the course is defined by the goals. A goal of the course could be to acquire everything written about the subject over the last twenty-five years. Who would such a course serve, you or your students? How would that level of knowledge help them to reason better? How would it help them develop as lifelong learners? Such a knowledge base is appropriate at a professional level but not at an undergraduate, or even first-year graduate, level. If it is inappropriate to read everything, then what is an appropriate way of limiting knowledge acquisition in an undergraduate or first-year graduate course?

CHAPTER

27

Selecting Texts

This is the most common way of limiting the knowledge base for a particular course. In the undergraduate curriculum, you can set limits by the number and size of the texts. At the graduate level, because of the difference in learning skill and efficiency, students will usually read everything available in a particular subject without you having to assign it. Selecting texts always involves a trade-off between time spent in acquiring the knowledge through reading and recapitulation during class and time spent using the knowledge in the exercise of reasoning skills in discussion, exposition, and problem solving.

Some courses have textbooks that function much like encyclopedias. That is, commonly accepted knowledge in the discipline is arranged around a traditional rhetorical structure. It is assumed that all of the core knowledge, issues, and values associated with the course are available to students in the textbook. Textbook authors work from previous models. They are often held hostage to a publishing regime that is conservative in its approach to the market. In my discipline, textbooks say the same thing today that they said when I was an undergraduate. They may have added more bells and whistles over the years, but they are oblivious to the fact that the professional conversation has moved elsewhere. So when you choose to let a textbook limit the knowledge base of the course, you have selected a conventional solution. There are good reasons for doing so, and there are good reasons for selecting an alternative approach. The reasons in favor of the textbook are that it works. It does provide a way for students to acquire a coherent knowledge base, which they can then work with to strengthen their reasoning skills, in a subject area where they have no previous exposure. It also reinforces the scope of cultural literacy: they will acquire the same knowledge in this course that students in other universities are acquiring. In choosing this way of limiting the knowledge base, the size, heft, and cost of the textbook dominate the design of the course, often crowding out other activities and other sources of knowledge. To justify the weight and expense of the text, covering it becomes the task of instructor and student alike.

New teachers tend to start with textbooks and then, as they become more fluent in explaining the core knowledge of their discipline, they move on to alternative ways of limiting the knowledge base. If you want to use a textbook, look at as many of them as possible. Find out who has the biggest collection on their office bookshelf and ask to borrow them. When textbook representatives come around, get to know them. They are the best source of information about the variety of texts in the marketplace. No textbook will ever satisfy you completely. You may find one or two that are easier for you to work with than others. All textbooks have a point of view. Is it one you can identify with? Read how the basic definitions are worded. Will you end up contradicting these as you lead the students through the examples you like to use? If so, keep looking. Examine how the issues you are most familiar with are handled. Is the discussion competent? Can you add more recent research findings without confusing the students? How much of the textbook can you realistically cover in the time available without offending the students' sense of value ("I paid $100 for this book, and she only had us read half of it!")? When you have found the right book, it should last you for a few repetitions of the class. It always takes at least one repetition before you feel comfortable with any book. After several more repetitions, you grow bored and start looking for alternatives.

Alternatives to textbooks can include the following:

→ Students research and develop their own text from a set of standard texts that they use as a reference collection.

→ Students work with monographs and develop knowledge based on cases.

→ Students use articles in popular media, films, and television and contrast this knowledge base with that found in professional journals and textbooks.

Each of these approaches will work. I have found that the farther I move away from textbooks in introductory courses, the more I end up having to be the textbook. That means I have to have the definitions, arguments, procedures, critical examples, and exceptions that prove the rule at my fingertips as issues arise. After thirty years of teaching, I can do that easily. In my first few years of teaching, however, it was more difficult. No matter how attractive these alternatives might seem to you, make sure you know how to communicate the basics clearly before abandoning the textbook.

Does the curriculum expect the course to teach the canon? The canon is often the way that the discipline communicates its history to the next generation. Canons develop historically to support a particular research paradigm. When this research paradigm is fundamental for introducing specific analytic procedures or habits, elements of the canon must be introduced. Canons are also the conversational database on disciplines. One cannot "talk the talk" without exposure to the canon. Canons have come under fire for the criteria underlying what they exclude as much as for the relevance of what they include. If a canon is important to the department you are teaching in, the curriculum will feature it through a sequence or set of required courses. Curriculum meetings should include discussion of what portion of the canon should be offered in nonmajor courses. Depending on the freedom of choice available to you, you might choose a wider variety of texts for nonmajors. When teaching the canon, you must decide how much of the critical tradition that develops around the canon to include. If there are groups of critics, students can be assigned to research each position on a particular text. After the class has had a chance to voice their own opinions, a course meeting can be devoted to a review of the critics' positions.

Fitting the Course into the Curriculum

CHAPTER

28

In the sciences and the arts, linear sequences of courses structure the curriculum. Instructors teaching upper division courses can confidently build on the knowledge base, technical skill, and reasoning or creative skills of the course that precedes it. In the social sciences and the humanities, a linear curriculum is rare. There may be recognition that students need a year or two of seasoning in the discipline before taking a particular historical or methodological sequence, but exceptions are often made. The underlying principle behind these curricular designs is a sense of growing student competency. Hence, they can be called competency-based curriculums. Fitting the course into a sequence is less important in these curriculums. Instead, the course should provide challenges that exercise the students' competencies.

When you are teaching in a linear sequenced curriculum, the knowledge base of the course is determined by the course the students took immediately before and the one they will take immediately after yours. Ideally, you read the syllabi from all the relevant courses when you select the knowledge base for your course. By looking at the actual syllabi, you will see what texts were used, what procedures were practiced, and what knowledge was supposed to be acquired. In class, begin with an assessment of where the student is in the curriculum. You need to know how much of the material from the previous class is still active for the students. If you find that it is less than you expect, your schedule has to be flexible enough to allow time to refresh their memories of the material. If that will last longer than a week or so, this will have an effect on the amount of time you can spend progressing through your portion of the curriculum. You ought to bring this up with the chair, not as a challenge to the colleague who taught the previous course, but as an opportunity to think through the expectations of the curriculum. A linear sequenced curriculum can be the most difficult type to teach because of the dependence on the students' prior course experience.

Organizing the Course around Problem Sets

Some courses are organized around solving a particular problem. It may be a classic problem in the discipline offered as an introductory seminar. It may be a way of illustrating theory and method that will be addressed more formally in later classes. It may be a course that introduces the problem focus in the discipline. Finally, it may be a course that is traditionally taught as a text course that you reconfigure as a problem-based course. What all problem-based courses have in common is that the knowledge base is defined by the problem.

Problem-based courses have interesting effects for students' experiences with the knowledge base. On the positive side, students pass through several knowledge areas to solve the problem. This lets them contextualize and recontextualize what they already know as they are gaining more knowledge. On the negative side, knowledge areas tangential to the problem are ignored. Problem-based learning foregoes comprehensiveness in favor of knowledge in use. This is a popular approach in professional education because of the view that the knowledge base is acquired more efficiently and that knowledge is retained for longer periods when comprehensiveness is put aside. The actual research supporting this view shows that there are gains in these areas, but that the gains are modest. Problem-based learning is an alternative to other course designs, but not a magic bullet that works for all students under all conditions.

Problem-based learning can be merely a way of limiting the selection of texts in a course, or it can serve as the design of an entire curriculum. The problem can be well defined, as when students complete problem sets based on their textbook readings, as is often the case in introductory economics courses, or it can be ill defined, as when students research how a hypothetical actor with specific characteristics might have responded in a real historical situation. The less defined the problem, the broader the knowledge that must be assembled to solve it. The process of assembling the knowledge falls to the student. The instructor helps the students manage the various streams of information and questions the quality of the information they collect. The more defined the problem, the narrower the knowledge that must be assembled to solve the problem. More of the process of assembling the information falls to the instructor. The student's role becomes fitting together the textual, procedural, and evaluative pieces supplied by the teacher to solve the problem. We will return to problem-based course design in the discussion of laboratory courses.

Organizing the Course around Specific Experiences

Courses that revolve around laboratory or experiential learning limit the knowledge areas the student will encounter to a specific context. For this reason, such courses are not intended to provide comprehensive knowledge acquisition. Instead, these courses use the experiential context to integrate existing knowledge and develop motivation for acquiring new knowledge. Experiential learning involves three stages in the development of the knowledge base:

→ A setup stage, in which the students learn background or methods for understanding the experience,

→ An on-site stage, where students have the experience, and

→ A reflection stage, in which students think about and attempt to integrate the knowledge gained from the setup and the experience stages.

Serendipity and self-discovery depend on a high degree of openness in the design. Take, for example, the classic field trip to a museum, specialized library, or historical site to provide students with primary artifacts of study. The least effective of these experiences are the ones where students are led before exhibits or targets that are then described and explained by the instructor, docent, or expert. The only difference between this approach and the living textbook style of lecturing is that the students are usually standing during the field experience, making it more difficult for them to take notes. An open approach gives students an itinerary that they can follow on their own or in teams. The itinerary requires that certain pieces of information be found and described. The instructor has chosen targets that will lead students to a defined knowledge base. This approach allows for learning that is more active because it gives the student fewer experts to lean on. The entire class then discusses the collected information.

Many laboratory and experiential learning opportunities, such as internships, study abroad, service learning, or fieldwork aimed at data collection (as in field biology, environmental science, meteorology, archaeology, or ethnography), take place off campus. The principle for these more sophisticated experiences is the same as for field trips, but with one important caveat: the student must be better prepared methodologically to find their own targets. The methodological learning becomes the knowledge base of the course, along with the detailed description of the targets and the contextual and serendipitous learning that has taken place. The instructor should insure that the student has ample opportunity to report and reflect on all of this learning.

Learning Management Software

CHAPTER
31

Almost every school uses some form of course management software (CMS) or learning management software (LMS), and encourages their faculty to use it. Locally produced CMS provides a course website for posting the syllabus and assignments and an email list. The commercial packages purchased for entire campuses or systems include much more flexibility and functionality. They provide several different forms of communication, up-to-date rosters, grade books, calendars, and tools for making the material in the course appear and disappear at the instructor's direction. The most frequently used commercial CMS packages include Blackboard (now incorporating WebCT and Angel Learning), Desire2Learn and CyberExtension. These can be customized to fit the needs of the campus. They are accessed through a campus website or intranet. Three popular packages, Moodle, Dokeos, Ecto and Sakai, are open source and free products that you and students access from the product's website. Web links to these packages where you can learn more about their features are included in the appendix. These do not exhaust the number of companies offering virtual classrooms and electronic learning software, hosting or Web-based class sites. The section on online classrooms will have more to say about these. These packages are the most commonly used for courses that are primarily taught in "bricks and mortar" classrooms. If your university uses a commercial CMS package, they will offer classes in the beginning and advanced use of the product. If you have never used one of these before, take the courses. Your students will thank you.

If you are going to be face to face with the students, why bother with a CMS? There are several reasons: universal access, reduction of photocopy costs, reduction in the costs of reproducing media, efficiency of communication, and ease of grading. Some of these reasons will appeal to new instructors; others will not. These systems were designed for short term corporate learning situations and then expanded to meet the needs of universities. The section on universal access above outlined the history and importance of offering the broadest opportunities for learning to our students. Web-based information is accessible by a much broader range of students than classroom instruction.

Classroom instruction fades fast. Web-based information is repeatable. I have recorded class discussions and embedded the sound file in our course site. Students who were there responded by listening to parts of the discussion again to make sure they followed the points. Putting slide presentations, sound recordings, media clips and documents on the course site from your desk means not having to take a trip to the library to put things or reserve or not photocopying hundreds of pages of material. Permission rights for commercial publications, sound recordings, films and videos require that you prevent students from copying or saving the file to their computers. Universities have what are known as steaming media servers that will let students play the clip, but not save as a file. Putting the links to the library's electronic reserve "shelf" for the course or the university's streaming server is easy and efficient. I send the library or the media office my needs for documents or media and they send me the links to put on the course site.

The emailing function of the course site lets me communicate with individual students, groups or the entire class with a few clicks. They can also email each other. The discussion board lets the students post research information or have a discussion or collaborate on a project without all of them having to be online at the same time. The chat function lets them talk to each other or me when we are online at the same time. Some commercial CMS packages include a function where students can have video images of themselves visible to others when they chat.

All the packages include a grade book. This feature is considered an advanced use of these products. This can be used like a traditional grade book, where the instructor posts grades and the individual students can see their grade development over the term. Or, the grade book can be linked to specific quizzes that are automatically scored. It is possible to set up an entire term's worth of quizzes, have these appear and disappear at appointed days and times, and as the students take the quizzes, they are automatically scored and entered in the grade book. The instructor does not have to look at a single quiz. I don't evaluate students that way, but my colleagues who do say that this function saves them significant amounts of time, both during class and in the office. They have begun to use quizzes more often and have seen a rise in mid-term and final exam grades as a result.

I use these systems in other ways. I have let my syllabi become very elaborate, giving students lots of information about the course policies, supporting materials and explanations of assignments and grading. All handouts and reserve readings are on the course site. I use the discussion board extensively in problem-based laboratory-style courses. I can monitor the student's out-of-class involvement with the project. The students can use the discussion board and chat feature to meet in the teams outside of class without having to be physically present. This makes meeting easier. My use of the CMS is dynamic. For some classes I start with less and add it in as I go along. For other courses, I post the accumulated experience of previous terms. I keep these in document files and post the segments in the CMS as I need them. I've been putting these materials on the Web since 1992. I can't imagine teaching a course without using this tool. My university's CMS system makes that job easier.

PART 8

Setting Your Expectations for Students' Reasoning Skills

Adults continue to develop reasoning skills all their lives. University education challenges people to acquire these skills quicker. In general, the process proceeds from the concrete and certain to the uncertain and abstract, with the student gaining increasing confidence in their ability to support their conclusions with evidence based arguments.

Most students enter college with only basic reasoning skills. Regardless of what they have scored on entrance tests, placement tests, and competency tests, their reasoning founders on the shoals of complexity. Very few of them had a high school curriculum that supported advanced reasoning skills. Those who achieved higher levels of reasoning before college did so because of home schooling, exploratory learning outside the curriculum, or individual teachers who challenged their skills.

The basic reasoning style repeats or paraphrases information from source material to search for a single "correct" solution or answer. The student fills in slots on a grid or makes lists of definitions, elements, and pieces of information. Their active reading, to the extent it occurs at all, is a search for specific words that they believe will point to an ill-defined and unbounded paradigm. They are bringing order to chaos, but it is not an order of their own making. They sift information and select elements that satisfy criteria established by an authority (the book said so). The answers are all in bold type. Success is measured according to a "right or wrong" criterion. Hence, the reasoning is characterized as dualistic and concrete.

Basic reasoning works well for arithmetic, but it fails to recognize the ambiguity and uncertainty of open-ended problems. These beasts do not have a single correct answer. Expert authority on them is fickle. The open-endedness generates confusion and futility. Unambiguous solutions often depend on fallacious argument. Basic reasoners cannot evaluate evidence. They cite textbook or encyclopedic "facts" or definitions inappropriately. They base conclusions on unexamined authoritative viewpoints or what "feels right." Instructors hold students at this level by structuring evaluations around repeating definitions, list elements, descriptions, and calculations. This evaluation strategy is often justified by instructors as necessary to insure that the students control the knowledge base. As we will see, there are better ways to accomplish this.

Students either maintain the level of reasoning they had when they entered college or rise only a single step above where they were when they graduated from high school. When they grow beyond the basic style, the new style has three characteristics: the acceptance of enduring uncertainty; the use of information to parse this uncertainty; and the absence of a single "correct" solution. This is a major improvement over the basic reasoner because of the acknowledgment of enduring uncertainties and multiple perspectives. Unable to rely on the authority of the textbook or teacher, these students begin to reach independent conclusions. They reason by stacking up evidence, while ignoring contradictory information. They commonly confuse evidence with opinion. While multiple perspectives are recognized, they avoid breaking down their warrants. Opinions circulate as the currency of reason. All opinions are equally valid to statements. Therefore, the student discounts any position that contradicts their experience as just another opinion. Experts are another set of opinion holders. Instructors help students move beyond basic reasoning when the challenges they set before the classes focus on exploring uncertainty, on the lack of predictability in outcomes, on the contradictions between experts, on the differing points of view one can hold toward a problem, and on the ranges of solutions that can be applied to a problem. However, if instructors stop there, they hold students back from moving on to the next set of reasoning skills. Only when students can get beyond these opinionated positions can they be said to be reasoning critically.

CHAPTER

32

Characterizing Critical Thinking

When faculty at my university were asked in a workshop to describe critical thinking, they described various behaviors in a student's unprompted response to an argument. These behaviors included:

→ applying and embodying new concepts,

→ the qualification and/or modification of position taking,

→ the identification of methods,

→ conclusions and motivations for research,

→ the distinction of quality or rigor in research,

→ the ability to synthesize information and look for interconnections,

→ the understanding of scholarly standards,

→ the ability to think within a disciplinary tradition,

→ knowing what questions to ask within a research tradition, and

→ recognizing biases in their own and the work of others.

Scholars of critical reasoning pedagogy paraphrase these same observations:

> Critical thinking, as we define it here, means reviewing the ideas we have produced, making a tentative decision about what action will best solve the problem or what belief about the issue is most reasonable, and then evaluating or refining that solution or belief. (Ruggiero 1991)

> [Critical thinking is] . . . an investigation whose purpose is to explore a solution, a phenomenon, question or problem [in order] to arrive at a hypothesis or conclusion that integrates all available information and that can therefore be convincingly justified. In critical thinking, all assumptions are open to question, divergent views are aggressively sought, and the inquiry is not biased in favor of a particular outcome. (Kurfiss 1988, 2)

Critical thinking appears to stress the individual's ability to interpret, evaluate and make informed judgments about the adequacy of arguments, data and conclusions. (Pascarella and Terenzini 1991)

Most formal definitions of critical thinking include the intentional application of rational, higher-order thinking skills such as analysis, synthesis, problem-recognition and problem-solving, inference and evaluation. (Angelo 1995a, 6)

How to Recognize
Critical Thinking

CHAPTER

33

Critical Reasoners Assess the Evidence in Arguments

Somewhere, at some time, someone explained or demonstrated to us how we tell the difference between fact and opinion. Later on, there were different ways of evaluating the validity and reliability of evidence. Perhaps we were lucky enough to have had induction and deduction explained. Or maybe, someone took the time to describe for us the various kinds of fallacies that pertain to evidence, such as the type 1 and type 2 grouping errors. I think about the times when these lessons occurred in my life as a student. Some of them are still happening. The skill in assessing arguments builds over a lifetime of experience. Yet, this is the foundation for all the other elements in critical reasoning. One cannot teach reasoning without a discussion of evidence and the knowledge base for evaluating it and using it.

Critical Reasoners Understand the Standards for Arguments

A well-formed argument is more than just quality of evidence. Paul and Elder (2001) remind us that strong arguments have specific standards. These include clarity, accuracy, precision, relevance, depth, breadth, logic, significance, and fairness. The standards are not arbitrary. They are entailed with reason because they lead to specific outcomes: integrity, humility, fair-mindedness, perseverance, confidence, courage, empathy, and autonomy (2001,12). Argument may begin in rhetoric, but it ends in ethics. If an argument is filled with only confusing or vacuous language, we cannot gauge if any of the other standards are present. Accuracy requires that the audience be provided with the means for independently assessing the truthfulness of the evidence through accessible citations and data sources, and the delineation of potential error. Precision requires that all the relevant details be provided including exacting and delimited definitions of key terms and variables. The standard of relevance connects the argument to the problem in an unambiguous way. It is certainly possible for an argument to be clear, accurate, and precise but irrelevant to the problem at hand. The depth standard refers to the requirement to explore as much of the complexity in a problem as time and resources allow. It fosters intellectual courage and perseverance, the fortitude to follow a problem into unknown areas. The breadth standard requires an evaluation of the problem from alternative points of view. This standard fosters empathy and humility. The logic standard requires that an argument be free of contradiction and fallacy. It fosters confidence. The significance standard requires looking at the problem in its historical context and assessing its importance and centrality to larger issues. This fosters integrity and autonomy. Finally, the standard of fairness requires that the student's self-interest in the outcome be disclosed, especially if that might lead to representing the views of others as inaccurate, incomplete, or inconsequential. This reinforces the development of fair-mindedness.

Critical Reasoners Examine the Underlying Assumptions of Arguments

We have found in research on the teaching of critical thinking at my university that very few university teachers provide undergraduate students with opportunities to develop skills in assessing the warrants or underlying assumptions of an author's claim. In spite of the fact that Toulmin's *The Uses of Argument* (1958) is now over fifty years old, we rarely teach our students that the authority to move from data to claim in arguments is always embedded in cultural rules, legal standards, mathematic truisms or physical laws. We looked at hundreds of assignments, exams, and projects, and fewer than one percent indicated that the students were to pay any attention to the assumptions that guide a position or an argument. There is a good reason for this. The assessment requires an extensive knowledge base within the history of a particular discipline or research tradition. Not only do very few undergraduates have this knowledge, but very few undergraduate programs are designed to provide it. Unless the student has picked up this knowledge independently, we cannot expect the assumptions to be apparent.

When I think of how I learned to identify assumptions, it was primarily through demonstrations of the technique by teachers. They identified the assumptions for me, explained the historical context for the ideas, contrasted those assumptions to others, and showed how the assumptions limited the scope of both the selection of evidence and the parameters of the problem. It was left to me to figure out that one could read the demonstration backward, deducing the assumptions by the limitations in scope. A second thread of learning about assumptions occurred when teachers or classmates made me aware of the assumptions of my own arguments, either in rebuttal in a discussion or in comments on written work. If we want our undergraduates to be able to identify underlying assumptions, then we have to spend more time demonstrating how to do it. We have a better chance of getting the point across as a general skill, rather than a disciplinary one, in the lower division of the curriculum. At that level, the problems and examples involve far less specialized knowledge. Fortunately, many popular and familiar arguments exist that lend themselves to this analysis.

Critical Reasoners Pose Appropriate Questions

In much the same way that the evaluation of assumptions depends on an ever-widening knowledge base, the posing of appropriate questions improves the more one knows about the context of an argument. Still, there are general guidelines for assessing the arguments of others. These can be taught as families of questions that can be posed about the topic of an argument:

→ Is it coherent and focused?

→ Can it be distinguished from related topics?

→ Can it be restated clearly and simply?

→ Is it the same at the end as it was at the beginning?

→ Is it a significant topic or is it trivial?

→ Is it a topic that can be realistically argued, or are significant pieces of required evidence impossible to attain?

Similar families of questions can be assembled for the other elements in an argument: assumptions, point of view, evidence, analytic concepts or key ideas, inferences or interpretations, and implications or consequences (Paul and Elder 2001). As with the search for assumptions, the logical place to develop this knowledge is in the lower division of the curriculum, before the prerogatives of the research tradition narrow the scope of the question.

Critical Reasoners Look for Contradictions in Arguments

The most important question of them all is the internal validity question. In a website devoted to the collection of different kinds of fallacies (Downes 1995), Downes lists thirteen groups of fallacies:

→ fallacies of distraction,

→ appeals to motives in place of support,

→ changing the subject,

→ inductive fallacies,

→ fallacies involving statistical syllogisms,

→ causal fallacies,

→ missing the point,

→ fallacies of ambiguity,

→ category errors,

→ the non sequitur,

→ syllogistic errors,

→ fallacies of definition,

→ fallacies of explanation.

For each, he gives a definition, several examples, and the logician's proof of why the examples are fallacious. Where in our own educational experience did we learn how to identify the internal validity of an argument? As a student, I was fortunate to have a high school teacher who drilled the fallacies of induction and deduction into our heads. When I took rhetoric in college, some of the language-based problems, like definition errors, were emphasized. When I took statistics, I learned another group of fallacies. When I read Downes's list, I found several groups that I knew to look out for but never considered fallacies. At no time did anyone systematically introduce a list of this breadth or explain the underlying system of logical consistencies. Now that we have Downes's list, it is easier to discuss the mechanics of contradictory arguments with students. It also means that we can be more precise and employ a common language when identifying contradictions in student work.

What this discussion hopes to make clear is that your expectations about students' progress as critical reasoners need not be mere lip service. It is possible to set specific goals for skill development, based on your assessment of where the student's skill actually lies. All students can benefit from having scholarly standards spelled out and applied to their work. All students can benefit from more attention to examining underlying assumptions. All students can benefit from spotting the various fallacies, both in their own work and in the work of others. These considerations provide an inexhaustible supply of skills that we can offer them for manipulating their growing knowledge base.

PART 9

Setting Your Expectations for Creativity

The instructor who wants to support creativity in the classroom needs to decide what exactly that means. For many instructors, the difference between an A and a B on an essay will often depend on the student showing some creative spark, a reformulation of existing ideas, an insight into the implications of the ideas that were not foreshadowed in the text or the discussion, a novel format, or an argument that leads to an innovative conclusion. More often than not, creativity comes down to the student telling the instructor something that the instructor does not already know. The implication is that the more specialized the instructor's knowledge, the more easily he or she will be impressed. The teacher who is an interdisciplinary generalist would be much harder to impress. There ought to be a way of understanding the role of creativity in the classroom that does not depend on the instructor's strengths. You might get more creative results when you explicitly describe what you want. Approaches to creativity are not as finely tuned as we might like. While critical thinking is supported and rewarded in classrooms, creativity is systematically undermined. We have farther to go in overcoming the distrust our students harbor to teachers who offer rewards for creativity, but never follow through.

Highly successful teachers incorporate a higher level of creativity into their own classroom practice. In supporting your students' creativity, you are also making room in your classroom to let more of your own innovative impulses shape the experience. Much of the following discussion is as much about you as it is about your students.

The one area of the university where creativity is a core element is, of course, the fine arts. Those disciplines have highly developed techniques for fostering creative performance and evaluating creative products. They also attract students who have been the most resistant to the creativity-stifling practices of elementary and secondary education. This discussion has little to say to instructors in the fine arts. Instead, I would refer you to Elkins's *Why Art Cannot Be Taught* (2001), a work directed specifically at arts students and instructors in higher education. Creativity is as important to students of science, social science, and the humanities, even if the emphasis on critical reasoning often overshadows it. Where else are inspired thesis statements, hypotheses and research designs supposed to come from?

The Cognitive Basis for Creative Thinking

CHAPTER

34

The cognitive scientists who have studied creativity describe at least three different situations in which creativity might be observed. The form and scope of the information processing—and therefore, the nature of the creativity—is different in each. The three situations are real-time creativity (improvisation), multistage creativity (extemporaneity), and paradigm-shifting creativity (Johnson-Laird 1988, 202-19).

► Real-time creativity is time bound. It must take place within specific limits. For this reason, there is not sufficient latitude to develop and test various alternative solutions. The solutions that are generated must meet certain levels of sufficiency. Because the tolerances are so tight, creative performance tends to rely on past experience and what is known, rather than the random generation of ideas.

► Multistage creativity removes the time constraint. Here the performance is underscored by repeated testing of potential candidate solutions. The criteria for evaluating the candidate solutions can permit a wide range of potentialities without regard of the criteria of sufficiency that the final solution must meet. These two situations are related to each other, and Baer (1993) believes they are best understood as points of a continuum, rather than wholly different forms.

▶ Paradigm shifting has received the most attention of all the creative moments because of its implications for understanding genius and discovery. It refers to situations where the creativity results in profound changes in the understanding of the domain under consideration, such that the domain is now understood in a new way.

This highest order of creativity has proven to be the most resistant to investigation because it happens so rarely. It may turn out that higher-order creativity is on the same continuum with multistage and real-time creativity, with genius on one end and everyday, real-time creativity on the other. While this continuum helps us to map creative performance, it does not bring us any closer to understanding the processes involved.

The literature on creativity tends to focus on either the qualities of the creative person, the creative process, or the evaluation of the creative work. I have not been able to find any research on the stages of creative capacity in individuals that parallels the work of scholars on critical thinking skills. Nor have I found much agreement on the operations involved in the creative process. Thus, unlike critical thinking, research on creative thinking has not yet resulted in a staged developmental scheme that would allow us to assess students and to support them in their movement from one level to the next.

How Do You Recognize Creativity When It Occurs?

CHAPTER

35

Amabile defines creative products as socially constructed:

A product or response is creative to the extent that appropriate observers independently agree it is creative. Appropriate observers are those familiar with the domain in which the product was created or the response was articulated. Thus creativity can be regarded as the quality of products and responses judged to be creative by appropriate observers, and it can be regarded as the process by which something so judged is produced. (1996)

She bases this consensual approach on the observation that any other focus—say, on the creative person or the creative process—must ultimately focus on the product. So, she argues, why not just start there. The approach is self-consciously subjective. There is no realistic way of assessing creativity as anything but subjective.

The criteria for even identifying domains of creativity are likewise consensual. They require a historically bound social context. Creativity is something that people can recognize when they are familiar with the domain, even when they are not given a definition of creativity. The creative judgment is the same whether it is applied in the arts or the sciences. Finally, Amabile (1996) assumes that there are degrees of creativity, such that the people judging a product can come to agreement about something being more or less creative than something else.

What exactly do we experience when we encounter creativity? Jackson and Messick believe that there are four aesthetic responses that occur together when we encounter creativity: 1) surprise is the response to unusualness in a product, judged against the norms for such products; 2) satisfaction is the response to the appropriateness in a product, judged within the context of the work; 3) stimulation is the response to transformation in the product, evidence that the product breaks away from the constraints of the situation as typically conceived; and 4) savoring is the response to condensation in a product, the judged summary power or ability of the product to condense a great deal of intellectual or emotional meaning in a concise and elegant way (1965, 309-29, Cited in Amabile 1966, 31). While these factors have not been tested to see if judges actually employ them when left to their own devices, they provide a basis for constructing a rubric for evaluating creative products.

For example, how might the creativity of a thesis statement or guiding hypothesis be judged using these factors? Judging the unusualness of the statement against the norms for such statements is easy. The vast majority of attempts by students to construct thesis statements or guiding hypotheses is predictable, ordinary, and built up out of the most readily graspable relationships. Judging the appropriateness of the product within the context of the work is also readily achieved. We know the elements of the context and whatever solution the student comes up with must work with those elements. When, then, their statements surprise us because they employ relationships that are more remote, the statements themselves suggest an extraordinary reading of the context, or we could not have predicted the statement ourselves, the students are employing what Liedtka has called abductive thinking: logical strings that revolve around what is possible, rather than what is indicative (2004). The students may not be able to prove that something "is" or "must be," but they nevertheless reason that it "may be."

Statements that break away from the constraints of the situation as typically conceived are not beyond our students' reach. This is certainly the case if the students are encouraged to unpack what Jolliffe (1999) calls status quo thinking, the commonsense understandings or readings of the problem, as part of their preparation for formulating the thesis or hypothesis. The extent to which they are successful at doing so, then, feeds our sense of stimulation at this new way of seeing a problem.

The most ambitious part of this creativity rubric lies with judging the summary power of the statement, its ability to condense intellectual meaning in a concise and elegant way. First, the student needs to have firm control of the knowledge base and intellectual history of that knowledge base. Then, the student needs the communication skills to formulate a concise and elegant statement. Finally, the student needs the critical reasoning skills of prioritizing multiple alternatives. Just in terms of these knowledge and skill prerequisites, very few undergraduates could hope to bring us to savor their theses and hypotheses. I would be satisfied with undergraduate creativity if it surprised me and satisfied me. I would be elated with such efforts if they stimulated me as well.

CHAPTER
36

Supporting the Creative Process

Supporting creativity in these contexts predisposes students to take greater interpretive risks and leads to more stimulating discussion-based and seminar-based classrooms. Studios as well as laboratory and experiential learning contexts would be candidates for projects that lend themselves to evaluating student risk-taking. Students have to first learn how to find the opportunities for risk-taking. They must feel competent to evaluate, say, the quantity of the associations they came up with before going public. This means the instructor has to set up a unit in which the evaluation of creativity is the skill set under discussion. Short of this, evaluating student work for creativity sets the instructor up as the cultural arbiter of novel ideas.

Supporting creativity becomes part of the classroom environment. Breaking down the walls around creativity that prior experience in the classroom may have built is a positive goal. Serendipity, similarity, and mediation are modes that lend themselves to exercises designed to maximize student attention to generating associations.

In the case of serendipity, students involved in experiential or laboratory learning environments should be alerted to the importance of accident in what they are about to experience. They should be encouraged to pay particular attention to the unexpected and record such events. Serendipitous elements should be discussed during class sessions. Questions about these accidents generate associations:

→ What other kinds of occurrences do you think could have happened that you did not anticipate?

→ Did this occurrence open up any new possibilities for future occurrences that you might not have anticipated?

→ Looking back on what you thought was going to happen, what could you have taken into account ahead of time that would have made the unexpected event predictable?

In the case of similarity, students should be directed to the creative problems involved in arranging the elements into patterns. Similarity refers to a shift of attention from the elements themselves to the component features of the elements. The kinds of questions you ask even in large, introductory, and highly fact-based classrooms concern the arrangements of elements in sets. The goal is to get the students to reimagine the set according to the similarities and differences among the elements. You should consider the following questions:

→ Are there any possibilities among the arrangement of elements to suggest that there may be missing elements?

→ Are there gaps in the list of distinguishing features that are used to separate the elements from each other?

→ When these missing features are added into the schema, do they generate the possibility for missing elements?

→ Are there alternative arrangements that organize the elements more efficiently?

Efficiency in this context would be domain specific. It might involve either greater specificity (splitting) or greater generalizability (lumping). Supporting creativity in these contexts makes it much easier at higher levels of the curriculum to challenge students to come up with their own hypotheses to test.

One of the best examples of an implementation of supporting creativity and, therefore, higher learning skills through similarity comes from an introductory chemistry class. During the unit on organic chemistry, students were put in pairs and instructed to adopt any organic molecule they could find in the newspapers, magazines, or medicine cabinets. They were then to construct a performance that would educate the rest of the class to the features and properties of the molecule. They would be graded on both the content and the extent to which their presentation "entertained" the instructor. The student teams came up with song parodies, T-shirts, hand jives, dance routines, and poetry, as well as models, posters, diagrams, and the usual components of such demonstrations. Because the evaluation was to be based on creativity, the students first learned the content and then interrogated that content for similarities and differences that could be exaggerated to the point of being entertaining. As a result, a lot of organic chemistry was learned.

In the case of mediation, students identify the existing creativity in their cases or texts by focusing on the metaphoric, metonymic, and symbolic extensions they find there. If you are in a discipline where language figures heavily in the objects of research and/or the products of research, you may have no choice but to support this form of creativity in your classroom. An interpretive hermeneutic is already a part of the disciplinary learning. To support creativity in the lower division of the curriculum, you must overcome the acquired reticence of students to play with language. The emphasis here should be on how language mediates experience. Interpreting the language of cases and texts provides models of what is possible, but to get students to generate novel mediations you must give them conditional prompts. Here are three examples:

→ Metaphoric mediation: if the main character in a novel were a quiz show host, what would the show be called?

→ Metonymic mediation: if the people in the three life histories we just read were all to get the same T-shirt, what would the image on that T-shirt be?

→ Symbolic mediation: add another character to the text that changes the interpretation radically without taking away anything that is already there. How was your decision of what character to add connected to your own world?

Alternatively, the prompt for symbolic mediation can be nonlinguistic and call for a linguistic response. The *New Yorker* magazine has a weekly cartoon caption contest. You could give the students all the same cartoon and ask them to reinterpret the image as if it were connected to the text or case under discussion, supplying the missing caption. Any images or sounds that are sufficiently ambiguous could be used in place of the cartoon.

PART 10

Assessing Student Learning

Assessment is an ongoing process aimed at understanding and improving student learning. It involves making our expectations explicit and public; setting appropriate criteria and high standards for learning quality; systematically gathering, analyzing, and interpreting evidence to determine how well performance matches those expectations and standards; and using the resulting information to document, explain, and improve performance. (Angelo 1995c, 7-9)

The most important tool available for effective teaching is assessment. Anyone can stand in an empty room and teach brilliantly. However, our universities insist that we teach with students present. How do we know that they respond in any way to our efforts? How do we know that learning happens? Assessment provides this feedback and permits us to adjust our methods in a timely manner to meet our students' needs.

Assessment is different from evaluation. Evaluation is the feedback from the instructor to the student about the student's learning. Assessment is the feedback from the student to the instructor about the student's learning. Assessment makes possible a second channel of communication between the instructor and the student about the learning process. Engaged college teaching demands that this second channel be open and active. The old system of "you do your thing, they'll do their thing, and the final exam will sort everything out" does not cut it anymore.

The more you know about the how the students respond to your efforts, the more effective you can be. First, your evaluations improve. Any instructor who does not seize the opportunity to engage the students more fully through assessment may suffer in comparison to those who do. Second, they become better students. The more you know about the variations in your students' learning, the more effectively you can tailor challenges for them as individuals. Third, you become a better teacher. The more feedback you receive as the course unfolds, the easier for you to make midstream adjustments that result in improvements in your practice.

In *Classroom Assessment Techniques: A Handbook for College Teachers* (1994), Angelo and Cross identify the characteristics that set classroom assessment apart from other kinds of communication. It is learner centered. That is, the primary focus of the activity is student learning. It is teacher directed. It respects the independence of the classroom instructor, permitting each one to design assessment tools and strategies that fit specific classrooms, groups of students, and situations. It is mutually beneficial. When students and instructors cooperate in assessment, they absorb more content, motivation improves, and skills are reinforced.

Faculty sharpen their teaching by continually asking themselves three questions: "What are the essential skills and knowledge I am trying to teach?" "How can I find out whether students are learning them?" "How can I help students learn better?" (1994). Ewell (1985) breaks the first two questions down more precisely. He says you should be asking:

→ How do you propose to change the students?

→ What are all the possible behaviors that indicate that such a change might have taken place?

→ What kinds of data can we gather to determine if the change has taken place?

Instructors who continuously seek the answers to these questions simultaneously improve their teaching.

Classroom assessment is formative, rather than summative. Unlike summative evaluation, which must strive to meet several criteria for reliability, validity, and lack of bias, assessment is not graded, is often anonymous, and is usually anecdotal. Its usefulness lies in indexing the students' experience in the class. It is context specific. There is no one-size-fits-all assessment technique.

Assessment is an ongoing process. The best assessment strategy is to do it regularly as part of the students' experience of the classroom. For this reason, assessments tend to be short and quick. I begin assessing in the first or second class to establish a baseline and continue to ask for feedback three or four times a term. In that baseline assessment, I aim specifically at the variation in critical thinking and writing skills in the class. The assessments that occur toward the end of each unit tell me how well I communicated the intended complexity. If there are systemic or glaring patterns with the students' responses, I have time to revise before going on to the next unit. I keep the assessments unobtrusive. Assessments rarely take more than five minutes. They are always written. They are never signed.

Finally, assessment is good teaching practice. Most teachers seek out some kind of feedback from their students as they strive to improve their teaching. Assessment techniques systematize this. Faculty who continuously adjust their approach in response to student feedback will narrow the communication gap between the learned and the learners.

Best Practices in Student Assessment

CHAPTER

37

The American Association for Higher Education has published a statement entitled "Principles of Good Practice for Assessing Student Learning" (Austin, et al. 1998, 189-91). The statement is worth consulting in its entirety. It includes the following points (in italics). I have added commentary on how they apply to the new instructor.

The assessment of student learning begins with educational values. The whole point is to improve teaching. Our values as teachers should drive not only what we assess but how we assess it as well. Under the best of circumstances, assessment and the instructional process should be seamless.

Assessment is most effective when it reflects an understanding of learning as multidimensional, integrated, and revealed in performance over time. If assessment were only about the student's control of the knowledge base, we could accomplish it with an exam. Instead, assessment focuses on knowledge and application, ability and values. Since these change over time, one assessment is not enough to do the job.

Assessment works best when the programs it seeks to improve have clear, explicitly stated purposes. Every course should reflect the intersection of three sets of needs: those of the institution, those of the instructor, and those of the student. Assessment is a process that helps to clarify this intersection of objectives. When these goals are clear, shared, and can be implemented, the course can more fully support the curriculum and the student. It is a better course.

Assessment requires attention to outcomes, but also and equally to the experiences that lead to these outcomes. Where the students end up is important. Unless we know how they got there, we have no hope of improving those outcomes. Assessment helps us to understand how each student moves through the learning challenges of the course and immediately tips us off to the obstacles.

Assessment works best when it is ongoing, not episodic. Assessment must be ongoing and programmatic, reaching students as they move through courses and through curricula.

Assessment fosters wider improvement when representatives from across the educational community are involved. Whether they are physically present or not, you share your classroom with student-life educators, librarians, information technology professionals, administrators, and occasionally, community members. Considering their perspectives as you design your assessments makes the efforts more collaborative and valuable.

Assessment makes a difference when it begins with issues of use and illuminates questions that people really care about. If you care about critical thinking, assess your students' critical thinking. If you care about written communication skills, assess them. If you care about creativity, assess that. If the responses on your assessments motivate you, you will act on the results in constructive ways. If you assess issues that do not move you, you will ignore the results.

Assessment is most likely to lead to improvement when it is part of a larger set of conditions that promote change. Every curriculum has a life cycle. It begins with lots of resources and workshops. We then adjust it to meet the realities of staffing and enrollment. New courses develop and existing ones change. Then, the curriculum outlives its relevance and is replaced. Assessment is more likely to have a dramatic effect on teaching practice at the beginning of this cycle, when classroom strategies are still in flux, than at the end of the cycle. Regardless of where the existing curriculum is in its life cycle, the new instructor is always at the beginning of a cycle and should continuously assess the classroom experience.

Through assessment, educators meet responsibilities to students and to the public. Beyond the contractual responsibility to provide an effective learning experience, there is the professional responsibility to make the wider community better through the education of lifelong learners. Teaching that arrogantly considers itself immune from assessment perpetuates the conditions that undermine students' love of learning. We must continually show evidence that the examined life is a life worth leading. There exists no better evidence than instructors' efforts to examine their lives as teachers through assessment.

Tools for Classroom-Level Assessment

CHAPTER

38

Assessment begins in the same place that course design begins, with an understanding of the curriculum and the position of the course in it. Teaching cannot be assessed in a vacuum. There is no abstract standard of teaching effectiveness that we seek. There is no absolute standard of teaching excellence. All teaching is directed toward immediate and specific goals. It is these goals that provide the criteria for assessing our teaching.

For example, suppose that one of the goals of the first-year course you teach helps students distinguish between fact and opinion. You discuss various texts with them. As students offer their views, you gently challenge them to provide evidence for their position. You summarize the ways that the texts use evidence and how this differs from opinion mongering. The students hear you focus on the difference between fact and opinion in almost every class. Several weeks have elapsed and you want to know whether you have made any headway. You employ a general assessment tool, like GIFT (see chapter 39). The first question specifically asks students to list one or two things the instructor helped them learn. When you look at their responses, you see that a third of the class listed something about the difference between fact and opinion. Another third have focused on the techniques of preparing for the discussion, reading techniques, et cetera, that you use. The final third have focused on the specific content of the texts that you have assigned.

This is a fairly typical distribution for a first-year class relative to this particular goal. You might reasonably ask if you are succeeding when only one-third of the class understands your priorities. The answer is yes for those students and no for the others. The third who are following your priorities are the ones who have responded to the particular technique you are employing. The others have not responded. You need to add additional techniques that challenge the others more directly and more actively without subtracting what you are already doing.

What the assessment has shown you is not that different students respond positively to different approaches. That is an old truth. The assessment has shown you the proportion of students who respond and the proportion who do not. If two-thirds of the students have shared your priorities, one-sixth have focused on the reading techniques, and one-sixth have focused on the content, you would still want to adjust your approach. The assessment has shown you what needs to change and to what extent.

Students who take the time to answer you honestly deserve some feedback. This can take any number of forms. Since assessments are anonymous, you respond to the class as a whole. Take fifteen minutes to report to the students on the major issues that turned up. This can then lead to a discussion about how to improve matters or a brief explanation of an issue that has led to confusion. In a large class, I type up responses and post them on the course website. I do not feel as if I need to address every issue the students raise. I respond to the issues from the larger number of students or ones that I myself feel need more explication. I then ask students to read the response and tell me if it helped them deal with the issues.

You may think that this feedback can end up creating an endless loop with the same issues returning over and over. Yet that rarely happens. The students are interested in moving on, too. When that does happen, it indicates that something is wrong with the way the course is designed. The students may be unprepared to handle the complexity. The material you present may be overly opaque or didactic. Try to find more accessible materials. Consider writing study guides. You may not be communicating effectively enough for the demands of the material. It may be difficult to admit, but we are often called upon to teach material that we ourselves do not completely understand or that we cannot explain fluently. This is particularly true with new instructors. It takes time to learn how to clearly articulate complex ideas. Recognizing this is the first step toward fixing it. The second step is to ask more experienced colleagues how they handle the material.

The exception to anonymous assessments is the baseline assessment of knowledge, writing skills, or critical reasoning skills at the beginning of the term. These will be discussed together with specific teaching techniques in subsequent chapters. Feedback for such individually identified assessments is communicated privately. This baseline assessment is often the most important one of all.

CHAPTER

39

Assessment Essays

Asking students to write something, even if it is just a few sentences, is the commonest form of assessment. The Muddiest Point technique asks students to write a short, anonymous paragraph responding to the question, "What was the 'muddiest' point so far in this session? In other words, what was least clear to you?" (Angelo 1995b). Sometimes, I ask students to think back over several sessions. Frederick Mosteller developed this technique (Mosteller 1989, 10-21). Some issues will not communicate effectively to every student. With this technique, you can get a snapshot of how well the students keep up with the information or discussion. The technique yields different results if it refers to a single session or to several sessions. For a single session, students search their immediate experience for an issue. Under optimal circumstances, they find nothing and say so. More often, they write about highly detailed points where they find small ambiguities. These are often too small to devote time to resolving. When a number of students—more than 20 percent of the class—identify a troublesome issue, revision is needed. For multiple sessions, several themes are likely to emerge. This can be an indication that you move through the material too quickly or that they are not adequately prepared for the discussion.

The Minute Paper technique asks students to write one or two sentences for both of the following questions: "What was the most useful or meaningful thing you learned during this session?" and "What questions remain uppermost in your mind as we end the session?" Like the Muddiest Point Essay, the Minute Paper attempts to elicit the tensions that students may be feeling at the end of class. It assumes that some issues remain unresolved in their minds. The Minute Paper identifies these tensions.

The Group Informal Feedback on Teaching (GIFT) technique ask students to write brief answers to the following: "What are the 1 or 2 specific things your instructor does that help you learn in this course?" "What are the 1 or 2 specific things your instructor does that hinder or interfere with your learning?" and "Please give your instructor 1 or 2 specific, practical suggestions on ways to improve your learning in the course" (Angelo 1995b). This one focuses on what you are doing, rather than the content. It can be instructive, especially if written in the third or fourth week of the course.

Class Feedback Form. This is a one-page handout. Divide the page in half. On the top half print this prompt: "List the major strengths of the course. What is the instructor doing that is helping you to improve your learning? Explain briefly or give an example of each strength." Provide space with numbered rows for students to list four strengths, encouraging them to think through more than one or two strengths. The response space has two headings: "Strengths" and "Explanation/Example." The bottom half of the page includes this prompt: "List changes that could be made in the course to assist you in improving your learning. (Please suggest how these changes could be made.)" Provide additional space with numbered rows to generate more than one or two responses. The response space has two headings: "Changes" and "Ways to Make Changes." This one, too, focuses on what you are doing, rather than the content.

Group Assessment

The Small Group Instructional Diagnosis (SGID) technique gathers information through in-class discussions. This long-standing technique collects student reactions to a class while it is in progress. (Bennett 1987,

100-104; Redmond and Clark 1982, 9-10). Students hear each other reflect on the class, establishing a consensus on what about it is going well and what needs to improve. The procedure starts when the assessor, someone other than the class instructor, holds an initial meeting with the instructor. It proceeds to a twenty to thirty-five minute interview with the class. The assessor then writes up a final report and follows up by detailing points the instructor should discuss with students (Creed 1997).

These are only a small selection of common classroom assessment techniques. Angelo and Cross offer many more in their book (Angelo and Cross 1994). I encourage all new instructors to own a copy and look through it periodically for ideas.

CHAPTER

41

Portfolio Assessment

The portfolio is a collection of student work gathered over the course of the class, the term, the year, or the program. The assessment process underlying the portfolio is that student progress is most easily gauged when representative work from different experiences is read together, rather than separately. Portfolio assessment began in the early 1970s at colleges committed to competency-based education, especially Alverno College and Manhattanville College. Institutional interest in portfolio assessment began in 1988 as a way of documenting student learning outcomes in traditional colleges (Keeton 1988, 4-5). The North Central Association recognizes portfolio assessment as one approach to evaluating student outcomes in program-level assessments (Payne, et al. 1991, 444-50).

> Portfolio assessment is only as good as the clarity and precision of the learning goals assessed. These provide the criteria references for reading the portfolios. Portfolio assessment is labor intensive. Many schools have found that the process of articulating the learning goals alone is worth the effort at portfolio assessment, even if a single portfolio is never read. Deciding what to include in the portfolios is more often a consideration of storage space, the volume

of portfolios that must be assessed, and the number of assessors available. A great deal of useful information can be learned from a small number of items. It is also not necessary to accumulate portfolios for every student. As long as the sample is representative, the information is valuable. Portfolios do not have to be read at the end of the program. They can be assessed at regular intervals. Portfolios tell you how the goals you want the students to achieve are or are not being met over time. When applied to a program or curriculum, portfolios can reveal gaps between the designers' intentions and the classroom execution.

Portfolios provide more detailed information about programs than any other assessment technique currently available. This is both their strength and their weakness. They are a powerful tool for faculty control of the curriculum process. Portfolios promote dialogue between instructors about the teaching process during the goal-setting phase and the analysis phase. Student reviews of their own portfolios stimulate reflection on their learning and aid in acquiring higher critical reasoning skills.

Because portfolio assessment is time consuming, it succeeds only if the faculty and students see that the ends justify the effort. This requires careful planning and adequate resources. Quantitatively oriented researchers find the highly criteria-based assessments suspicious and often question the validity of the admittedly subjective readings and haphazard sample composition. These objections can be met with good research design, but the stylistic differences in research sensibilities are never completely bridged. Portfolios, therefore, represent the largest investment a program or college can make in assessment and offer the highest payout in the end.

PART 11

The Lecture Classroom

This is the first of four parts devoted to specific classroom styles. By separating the styles into lecture, discussion, seminar and laboratory, I am not suggesting that mixtures of styles are not desirable. Many situations call for mixed teaching. However, before you can confidently switch from one style to another, you must know what makes each style work and how to manage the learning situations that arise. I begin with the lecture style because it is the most common form.

What Is a Lecture?

A lecture is a public speech about a topic related to the course. The instructor performs to an audience of students. The lecture has two goals: to inform students of a portion of the knowledge base you expect them to control and to model for them how to make sense of the information. Each lecture should be a self-contained whole. Each has a beginning, middle, and an end. More than merely a talking head, the effective lecturer brings the ideas to life. These are virtuoso moments for the professor—opportunities to highlight an especially original and engaged analysis. At their worst, lectures are living textbooks that continue, sometimes in mid-sentence, from one class to the next. A competently designed lecture can be an effective strategy for college teaching. A weak one drives students to distraction.

There are several different forms of lecture:

- ▶ Expository Form. In this traditional form, the instructor develops a presentation that treats a single topic or problem in detail and with the level of completeness appropriate to the students. Rhetorically, the exposition proceeds from major to minor points. The student's role is to listen, take notes, and remember.

- ▶ Interactive Form. The instructor calls on students to provide the questions that serve as the basis for the instructor's exposition. Rhetorically, it takes the form of organized brainstorming. Students respond to the instructor's call because they have specifically prepared for this form of interaction. The instructor's responses seem to be impromptu and therefore, more lively. In fact, the instructor telegraphs the points of the lecture through the prompts the students use to prepare for the lecture. The instructor connects the responses with examples and counterexamples, all with the aim of exploring a single topic or problem.

- ▶ Hybrid Form. This sort of lecture goes under more common names, such as problem-solving exercise, lecture-demonstration, proof, case method, or story-based exposition. What each of these has in common is that the instructor offers a provocative problem or narrative that piques student interest, such as, "What would happen if . . ." Students engage the problems, actively offering tactics for finding the solution, or passively watching or listening to the instructor model the tactics.

- ▶ Short Form. This is probably the most common form of lecture. It is characterized as an exposition that takes up only a small portion of the class time. It is used to frame the problem that the class will then discuss. Sometimes there is another short integration or summation at the end of the discussion.

CHAPTER

43

Tools for More Effective Lectures

Avoid walking in cold or after the students are already there. You should always get to class early. You must make sure the overhead projectors, video playback, computers, microphones and any other technology you might be using are ready before the class begins. Walk around the room and talk to students as they arrive. This helps you to keep a conversational tone during the lecture when there are many more listeners.

For all lectures, you need to work from notes. No matter how often you have delivered the lectures before, having the notes insures that you will provide the highest level of organization and clarity to the students. Your notes can be an outline, a list of major points, even a tree diagram, depending on what you are trying to communicate. Under no circumstances should you read the notes to the class. Lectures should be extemporaneous. When constructing these notes for the first time, consider using a presentation program that you can project in the lecture hall, but keep the text on the slides to an absolute minimum. Most programs permit you to combine the slide that is projected with notes that only you can see. These update easier than handwritten notes. You will be giving this lecture again.

Preparation

No matter how you choose to record your notes for an expository lecture, be sure to do the following when preparing for a lecture:

→ Write down the technical stuff. Have facts and formulas available on cards. In fact, you should write out anything you want to write on the board ahead of time.

→ Write down the examples. There is nothing more frustrating than to realize you left out an important piece of information. Giving an example is like telling a joke. It's all in the timing.

→ Prepare for the ear, not the eye. This means using short, simple words, personal pronouns, contractions, slang, and other elements of informal diction. Speak in short sentences. Whenever you must string together a complex series of clauses, enumerate them as a list.

→ Use more signposts for transitions and structure than you would when writing.

→ Restate important points several different ways. Summarize as often as possible.

→ In your opening, state the main theme and why students should learn it. You should allow yourself to free-associate when writing this section. You need to find many points of engagement with your audience. There are a lot of different learners out there.

→ Design the lecture in blocks. Writing your notes in presentation software facilitates this.

→ Even if you write out the notes by hand, no section should take longer than ten or fifteen minutes to speak. This is less about the students' attention span and more about their ability to retain the information.

→ You should begin each section by getting their attention. Choose dramatic adjectives.

→ You should always tell them what the section is going to cover. Projecting or handling out an outline is always better than having them guess the organization.

→ You should try to make no more than three points in each section. There will usually be only one point.

→ Vary the pace. If every section has three points, the students will get bored with your rhythm.

→ End every section with a summary. It signals that you are done with this part and going somewhere new.

→ Show, don't tell. There is communication in a demonstration than a description of a demonstration. Actually solving a problem with the tools in question is much better than describing how a problem might be solved.

→ Rehearse. You need to know how long the talk is. Are you going to run out of time before you get to the big finish? Pay particular attention to the opening and closing sections. By speaking out loud, you will discover where the language gets complicated. If you find yourself running out of breath, your sentences are too long.

→ Budget time for questions. You especially want students to ask you to repeat material that was spoken too quickly for them to understand.

Performance

Once you begin the lecture, find ways convey your enthusiasm for the material. If you do not enjoy the material, you cannot expect the students to enjoy it. Here are some additional suggestions:

→ Don't forget to pause! Every ten to fifteen minutes, when you come to a natural break in the lecture, pause for at least a full minute, but no more than two minutes. Tell the students what you are doing and that this is a moment for them to catch up, reflect on what was said, and rest their hand from note taking. Tell them to remain as silent as possible. This one to two minute rest period is called the "pause" method of lecturing. Research has shown that it increases short-term recall of the information (Ruhl 1987, 14-18). When you begin again, start by asking if any questions occurred to them during the pause first, before you begin the section.

→ Keep the tone conversational. Every student should think you are speaking to him or her.

→ Use colorful but respectful language. You cannot talk like a student without reducing your authority. You don't have "street cred."

→ Incorporate anecdotes and stories that connect the information to real people or events.

→ Share your own experiences when they are relevant.

→ Vary your eye contact; try to connect with each student. Pay attention to any patterns that might develop where you find yourself focusing on a set of students or a part of the room more often than others and avoid these patterns.

→ Use movement. This does not mean that you must pace. Some people naturally move when they talk. Others like to stay put. If you pace, change your turning point as often as possible. If you like to stand still, turn your head and use your arms to prove to the students that there is a live human being behind the voice.

→ Bring in objects, even if they have little direct relation to the topic, and move the object around from time to time. Students will pay more attention as they wait to see how the object connects.

153

→ Use facial expressions to show your enthusiasm, surprise, confusion, conviction, or thoughtfulness. Laugh when you make a mistake.

→ Watch the time. If you rehearsed, this will not be a problem, but even well-rehearsed lectures can run too long. Very few lectures will ever run short.

→ If you do begin to run out of time, stop early and summarize, rather than trying to speed up and cram everything in. Next time, choose fewer points.

→ Stay around after the lecture and make notes immediately on the effectiveness of the examples, the clarity of the definitions, and students' questions.

The rise of computer-prepared presentations has added elegance to lecture materials and removed many, but not all, of the technical problems that used to plague slide projectors. If you prepare such presentations, avoid making them text heavy. The presentations should provide the structure of the content but not the content itself. Hand out note pages with facsimiles of the presentation slides and a space for students to take notes. A presentation program like PowerPoint makes producing such note pages very easy. Fewer slides are better than many slides. Pictures are more valuable than words. Charts and figures are more valuable than words. Avoid special effects, like animation and dissolves. They take too much preparation time and can freeze a classroom computer. When the presentation is finished, convert it to a Web page using a program like Camtasia for the PC or Screenflow for the MAC, and put a link to it on your class Web page. This allows students to download it quickly and view it without needing high-end computer technology or special plug-in programs for their browser. These are common problems when we publish presentations on the Web for student use.

At least once a year, have someone videotape you lecturing. These tapes are invaluable for pointing out nervous mannerisms, overused words, and similar features that the students see but the lecturer does not. A videotape is worth several hours of face-to-face mentoring.

What Lecture Formats Can and Cannot Do

Lecturing need not be confined to large classes, although large classes pose special opportunities for lecturers. Lectures are also effective in small classes and serve as a change of pace for discussion-based and even problem-based classrooms. The trick to effective lecturing in all classes is to have students thinking as you are talking, rather than merely writing down what you say. This is known as active lecturing. Providing them with as much of the material you will speak about ahead of time goes a long way toward freeing up time for thinking.

Your challenge is to build in moments when students can switch you off (while you are still talking) to play with the material in their heads before you pull them back. They need an opportunity to write out their solution and then validate their approach with your analysis. The timing of all these activities is crucial to the experience. Lecturers who feel they must fill an hour with facts miss the boat entirely. For learning to take place, there must be a give-and-take of attention between the instructor and the student.

One way to do this is to think of lecture as several self-contained segments, like units in a larger outline. No segment should take longer than ten minutes to present before the focus is turned back to the students. On the lecture handout, they should find a specific prompt for each segment, either to write a question about the segment, talk with a partner about their understanding of the segment, solve a problem related to the segment, or predict the next step. Then, the focus shifts to the instructor again to proceed to the next segment. Not only does this make the lecture experience more engaging for students, it permits students to think along with you.

CHAPTER 45

The Living Textbook Approach

A lecture reinforces students' familiarity with the knowledge base. The instructor articulates the text material, emphasizing and reorganizing it to help students remember the material more effectively. Students take notes, which requires them to hear the material clearly enough to write it down.

How well such a living textbook approach succeeds depends on the skill and creativity of the instructor's rearrangement of the text. Gross-Davis's Tools for Teaching (1993) provides one of the best discussions of this. This is another book that should be on every teacher's bookshelf. She offers far more detail on the method than I can go into here. Some of what she describes is important for understanding the difference between a real lecture and merely reading your own notes to the class. Gross-Davis offers six different ways of organizing the information:

→ *Topical.* The instructor picks a topic and illustrates a range of approaches with examples. For example, an introductory lecture in a psychology course may examine four different approaches to human behavior.

→ *Causal.* The instructor picks a multifaceted process and illustrates how various factors affect the outcomes. For example, a lecture in an economics course might explore the various factors that affect the distribution of wealth.

→ *Sequential.* The instructor describes a chronology or sequence that justifies closer attention to the component events or parts. For example, a lecture in an education course might describe the student's path through a school system from preschool to graduate school.

→ *Symbolic or graphic.* The instructor uses a common graphic or symbolic device over a series of lectures to illustrate shifts in emphasis, progression through a series of topics, or attention to different details in a process. For example, a lecture in a course on the brain might use a transparency of the organ at the start of each lecture, with the instructor drawing onto it the section that will be discussed that day.

→ *Structural.* The instructor uses the same general outline in every lecture to convey information about the elements in a system. A lecturer in physiology, for example, might cover the same topics in the same order for every organ system in the body. Students know the format ahead of time and fill in the blanks as the information is provided.

→ *Problem-solution.* The instructor poses a general problem and then provides examples of how the problem could be solved. In an engineering course, for example, the instructor could offer a series of analyses of structural failure in bridges.

Regardless of which organization you choose, it is important to make your choices known to the students ahead of time.

Developing an Active Lecture Format

CHAPTER

46

Students are passive when listening to your words and writing down notes. The speed with which the information flows permits them to think about what is being said only in fleeting and intermittent ways. Several techniques attempt to carve out active learning time in the lecture hall. Here is a sample of them:

Interactional devices, called clickers, resemble a television remote control. They permit students to send information to a radio receiver connected to the podium computer. The computer collects the information from the students and presets it as a bar chart that can be projected on top of a presentation. The result is instantaneous feedback from the class on the content of the lecture. Several colleagues in the sciences are so enthusiastic about the effect of these devices, they will never teach a class without them. They say that grades improved dramatically once they began to use clickers. Here is how they are used: The instructor presents a ten to fifteen minute lecture. Then, he projects a slide with a multiple choice question about that content. Students use their clickers to select the answer they feel best fits the question. A bar graph of the anonymous responses is projected on the screen. The instructor then discusses both the correct and incorrect answers. In this way, misunderstandings are cleared immediately. They give everyone in the class a voice. Students look forward to the challenge and the change of pace. The clickers cost the student about $30. Universities usually have one brand that is standard across all classes and sold in the bookstore.

Break the students into small groups for focused problems during the hour, even though the shape of many lecture halls makes this challenging. Pestel pairs students with the person next to them and asks them to define a term to each other, pose a "why" or a "how" question to each other or challenge each other to answer questions you posed for them or to recapitulate some point. Misinformation might be reinforced. You can monitor this by selecting a few pairs to report. You are not trying to find the misinformed pairs. Instead, have a few pairs report establishes a common sense norm for all pairs. This is an interesting change-of-pace activity that gives students a break from note taking (Pestel 1990, 4). Other uses of pairs include having students prepare two copies of four or five questions based on readings, a problem set, or a field trip. At the next class, one copy is turned in and the second is used in the pairs, as students alternate asking each other questions from the lists (McKeachie 1986).

A third technique involving pairs is the so-called snowball discussion. It is particularly useful early in the term. You ask a question that is sufficiently concrete that even the least sophisticated student can come up with at least one response. Ask the pairs to generate as many responses as they can in three or four minutes. Then, have each pair combine with another. This quartet combines their lists. Next, have two quartets combine and have the octet produce a combined list. After this, call on the octets to report their list to the audience as a whole. The advantage here is to break up the anonymity of the lecture hall and to show students that they already know something about the field of study. This also sets an expectation of participation for the class (Gross-Davis 1993).

The breakout groups common to professional workshops also work well with large lectures. Divided into sections of twenty or so students, the groups convene in the corners of the room, the hallway, or empty rooms. It is best to give each group a specific task or problem to solve. The groups then report on their discussion when they return. To manage the time for these breakouts and the paired activities, Michaelsen (1983) suggests a 25/5 rule. When 25 percent of the groups have completed the task, the remaining groups get five more minutes to finish.

Techniques for Livelier Lecture Classes

CHAPTER
47

The lecture became the mainstay of university education when class sizes, especially at the introductory level, began to increase. One can try to hold a discussion with three hundred people, but it is hardly satisfying. Large classes will always be a part of the experience, especially in research-oriented universities. All teachers should be prepared to engage large classes in as effective a manner as possible. Make the large classroom a livelier place for learning.

One technique, called scripted cooperation, has students form pairs after listening to a lecture segment. One member of the pair then summarizes the information to the other. The second comments on whether they found the account accurate and complete. If time allows, the partners can share personal experiences that relate to the lecture (O'Donnell 1994, 7-10).

Distribute the teaching assistants around the hall to serve as immediate responders to questions. During question periods, have students direct their questions to the nearest teacher. The shift in focus generates conversation as well as questions. When you pull the focus back to the lectern, the teaching assistants offer examples of the questions asked.

Develop exercises in which students can perform for their peers on a large scale, such as prepared debates scattered through the term or a poster fair based on the research assignment. These performances have students moving around the room.

In the early weeks, invite groups of students to an informal get-together to meet you and the teaching assistants and get to know each other more personally. The more accessible they feel you are, the more readily they will express themselves in class.

Hand out lecture outlines before class, leaving space for students to take notes. Use sidebars to indicate potential exam questions. Project the outline without the questions during the lecture. If you use presentation software for your lecture, you can print out a slide set with space for note taking.

Build demonstrations into the lecture to provide students with different ways of understanding the material. Having concrete objects or people available to demonstrate the principles helps students remember the principles.

Helping Students Listen Effectively to Lectures

CHAPTER

48

Lecture methods work best when students are active listeners. That means they must absorb the context of your talk while remembering the details of your argument. As the details mount, the challenge becomes more difficult. Note taking is usually considered an aid to the juggling act. Researchers describe note taking as an external memory for handling the details (Hartley and Davies 1978, 207-24) and as an opportunity for transforming and elaborating the ideas (Peper and Mayer 1978, 514-22).

Untutored note taking is passive. Students attempt to record what the lecturer is saying without thinking about the ideas. Students rarely receive any tutoring on note taking beyond "write down the important ideas." Such advice counterproduces because students cannot tell what is important unless they are already immersed in the context. Lower-division students, the ones most likely to use lecture formats, are the least capable of discerning this. Giving students an outline supplies this missing context. Thus, passive note taking only benefits students who have some background knowledge (Snow and Peterson 1980).

Students have different styles of note taking, ranging from trying to take down everything to taking no notes at all. Either of these can be effective. The volume of notes is unimportant. The way that students listen is the crucial factor. Active listening means that the students reflect on the information you present. They classify the information as novel or repetitive. They sort between generality and specificity, seeking out contrasts. Students who write nothing down may still be remembering everything that you say. Some students come to active listening on their own. Most students need to be encouraged to do so.

Talk about the differences between the active and passive mode with your students. Build redundancy into your lectures to give them reflection time. Signal the transition to new thoughts consistently. When you distribute the outline of the lecture, include a question at the beginning that you would like them to think about throughout the hour. End with a question that you want them to reflect on in the last two or three minutes of the class and give them time to do so. When you summarize your ideas at the end of the lecture, point out an example or two of how you might have made active connections between them. By modeling active listening, you reinforce their efforts.

The advantage to this approach is that it evens out differences in processing time between students in large classes. The better students usually process information quickly. They can reflect actively on your lecture at almost any speed or density you choose. Average students require more time, if only a matter of a few tenths of a second. Helping them develop active listening skills is one way you can support critical thinking skills in the lecture classroom.

A Note on Computer Distractions: Nobody can deny that computers are a great aid to note taking. They are also controversial. Students who are using the computer may be doing tasks unrelated to the lecture. The controversy has to do with whether the instructor has the responsibility to police the attention of students sitting in their classrooms. There are good arguments on both sides. Those who have banned computers argue that students who text, play video games or edit videos in class are distracting to other students. They are neither participating nor contributing to the learning environment. They feel that the distraction outweighs the benefits. Those who permit computers argue that distracted students passed notes, doodled, and worked on homework long before there were computers. The computers merely give lecturers a target to control behavior that is at its base uncontrollable.

There are several parts of this phenomenon that need to be unpacked. Let us begin with the instructor's responsibility to provide a distraction free classroom. Has the battle with cell phones, pagers and students leaving to attend to the toilet been won? If so, I see little evidence of it. Even my own cell phone goes off occasionally in my classroom. How about the battle with the students sleeping in the back row of the class? My feeling is that the instructor has a responsibility to provide a comfortable learning environment, but to hold us to the standard of distraction-free is probably not realistic.

Is the computer such a weighty distraction that it deserves special attention? Computers in themselves do nothing. What we are really concerned with is our students' attention. Is that part of the contract we make with them? They pay tuition and register for our class. In exchange we provide them with learning environment, access to a knowledge base and skill set, an evaluation of how much they control at the end of the term, and a managed classroom with behavioral surveillance. I do not remember that last part being part of the contract. It seems so much like high school.

Should I care how they spend their time after they have spent their money? The question is a lot like the attendance issue: should I reduce a student's grade if they do not attend class, even if they pass all the assignments? In both cases, we are evaluating behavior that we do not like. We do not like it because it undervalues our efforts. It is a gesture that can be interpreted as the student saying, "I prefer to spend the time doing something else." I will argue that attendance matters at the appropriate point in this book. I will also argue here that attention matters. In fact, it matters so much that I spend time thinking about how to capture and hold it. If I succeed, the computer is no longer the issue. If I fail, the computer is still not the issue. My ability to capture and hold their attention is the issue. There will always be a percentage of students who will resist the best efforts to participate. They are in the classroom for the wrong reasons. If they want to use the time to surf the Web, at least they are not sleeping.

Do we know how many of our students are using the computer for activities that do not support their learning in the class? If those numbers are small and we ban computers, we are guilty of collective punishment, depriving the other students of an efficient means for organizing the information. If the numbers are large, we are deceiving ourselves into thinking we have created an effective learning environment.

Every instructor must decide how students engage the classroom environment. In most classrooms the bulk of the stimulation for learning comes from the instructor's communication with the students. The instructor expends less energy in communicating and can be more inventive when the greatest number of students is attentive. If I could convince myself that it would actually increase attentiveness, I might very well want to ban computers.

CHAPTER

49

Working with Teaching Assistants

Most of us assisted a professor in teaching while we were in graduate school. It was difficult then. Becoming the one who organizes, oversees and mentors others has not become any easier. There is a distinction in effectively communicating with a person as a teaching colleague in your lecture, as a student in your seminar, and as a mentee during staff discussions. You need to keep these roles separate.

The role of the TA is to support your goals for the class. They are in an excellent position to enhance the students' experience if they have a stake in the students' success. The process of working with TAs begins with clarifying your expectations for the class and their contribution to it. Will they summarize assessments and intervene with struggling students? Will they tutor students having difficulty on a drop in basis? Will they be expected to grade exams or read essays? Will they lead discussions? Will they lecture? Will they hold office hours? This should be done before assigning the assistant to the class. This gives everyone the chance to commit to the opportunities in the teacher-assistant-class relationship and not merely stipend.

The next step is for you to assess the skill level of your assistants. Give them a book like this one with specific chapters to read and then have a discussion about how the information might apply to the class you are teaching together. Take a look at a writing sample if you have not had the assistant in class. If they are weak writers, send them to the writing center. If your campus has a course for writing tutors, ask them to take it. Ask them to make a brief presentation of course content to you and the other assistants. Give them supportive, constructive suggestions for how they can improve. Do not expect skill and polish. Most of them have never done this before. You need to know how well they write and speak, and where they need to improve those skills before throwing them into a mentoring situation with even less experienced students. Resist the temptation to work only with the most skilled assistants. The relationship should involve learning appropriate new skills. You should show your commitment to their development by scheduling individual meetings at least twice during the term to see what they have learned about instruction and encourage them to develop further.

Most TAs want to use the opportunity to learn about teaching. The more you explain how and why you are structuring the class a certain way, the more questions they will ask. This process will help you to think through your craft just as it helps them develop theirs. Do not just model the role for them— talk to them about the adjustments you make. Explain why you constructed an exercise or a test the way you did. An informed TA can help you meet your course goals more effectively than an uninformed one. Solicit their advice on how to handle specific issues. Have an exam writing meeting in which they can help word the questions. Invite them to help revise the grading rubric for the exams. They have a complementary expertise because they interact with the students differently. Asking them to work in your classroom without their input limits their professional growth. There should be a staff meeting once a week, in an informal setting, with you actively seeking feedback and advice while sharing plans and thoughts about the course. Finally, give them the opportunity to actually teach, with gentle written criticism from you and a follow-up opportunity. As with any skill, expertise develops through practice in real situations.

The amount of lecturing a TA performs varies with the instructor. For some TAs, a single lecture the entire semester is all they get. Other TAs are expected to deliver entire units of the course. One disturbing trend is for the instructor to make all the decisions regarding texts, schedule, exams and content, and then hand the course over to the TAs to run. This is an abdication of the instructor's responsibilities, and as a chair I would not allow it to proceed. Having TAs in a course is a privilege, not a right. As a privilege, the administration can withdraw it whenever they want. The lecturing relationship between the instructor and the TAs should be collaborative. TAs should have the opportunity to lecture because they must do so to learn that genre of speaking. The students should never be confused about the importance of the instructor's presence in every class. For that reason, I would restrict TAs to lecture for no more that 4/5ths of a class meeting, reserving the final fifth to myself. When the TA is assigned a lecture topic that must be divided across two or more class meetings, I might restrict the lecture time to 3/4ths of each class meeting, using the remaining time to assess student learning of the topic. The advantage is to provide the TA with immediate feedback when they have the opportunity to implement fixes. In this way, I help the TA develop, maintain my presence in the classroom, and insure that student learning proceeds.

If the course is divided into lecture hours and a discussion hour, the TAs are usually responsible for the discussion hours. This provides one of the most direct ways to cultivate the TAs' commitment to the course. This is where the TA interacts with the students directly. This interaction is critical to the TA's and the student's experience of the course. For that reason, the instructor must pay attention to what goes on in the discussion sections. Some best practices for doing so include: weekly meetings to discuss what went on in each section (TAs learning from each other), video taping of a section meeting in the 3rd or 4th week of the term, viewed and discussed only with the instructor and the individual TA (TAs learning from the instructor), a group meeting to review a representative sample of student work from the discussion sections, such as preparatory exercises (TAs learning from the instructor and each other), or periodic assessment of learning in the discussion section, such as Small Group Instructional Diagnosis (see chapter 40) (TAs learning from the other instructors). Each of these offers a different way of reflecting on the TA's experience in the discussion experience while there is still time for technical improvements. On the other hand, having the instructor visit the discussion section to observe may be more distracting than productive. I would avoid it.

For any of these measures to be effective, they must be part of the ground rules for the relationship between the instructor and the TA that are laid out in the initial interview. Some instructors even prepare a Teaching Assistant Syllabus that describes exactly what the expectations for the TA are, how many office ours they are expected to keep, and what kinds of support the instructor will provide.

PART 12

The Discussion Classroom

What is a discussion format? Discussion is first and foremost a conversation with a purpose. Like all conversations, it involves the giving and the taking of attention. The best discussions, like the best conversations, empower everyone to participate. Discussion parts company with conversation when it embraces a pedagogical goal. Conversations are disinterested communication; they ramble endlessly. Discussions begin somewhere and end somewhere. At the very least when the hour is up. A more appropriate end would be when the participants achieve the intended goal. This goal can take any number of forms:

→ to solve a problem

→ to explore an idea

→ to brainstorm a concept

→ to flesh out a domain

→ to analyze a text

→ to edit a draft

→ to reflect on an activity

→ to critique a work

Each examines ideas by taking them apart. It is possible to commit a classroom entirely to discussion. In doing so, the instructor has made a judgment that it best serves the goals of the course and his or her strengths as a teacher. More often, discussion pairs well with other strategies in a complex classroom.

Discussion is not the same as seminar. This may seem counterintuitive since both formats involve students talking about ideas. The differences between the two lie in the role of the instructor. Discussion presumes that students will read a common text, share their interpretations with each other, and reach agreement on a common reading of the text. In place of the text, students might share their learning experiences outside the classroom, their laboratory experiences and their viewing of performances or films. Discussion serves as a bridge between the learning that takes place when the student reads, participates, or views as an individual, and the learning that takes place communally. Discussion works best when closely examining a variety of interpretations is the goal of the class. The instructor is committed to challenging students to differentiate between opinion and evidence. Students unpack a text or an experience through conversation that attempts to uncover the factual support for their positions. The instructor is crucial to this process. The students are not able to ask each other the uncomfortable questions that reveal opinion. This is where the instructor's voice is heard. Discussion and seminar differ on this score. In seminar, regardless of the level of the student, there is sufficient control of a knowledge base for students to identify the difference between fact and opinion on their own. The discussion format excels when students have a common body of knowledge that they are trying to control and a classroom where they can express their separate understandings of that knowledge.

Discussion provides a channel for developing the knowledge base in a way that contrasts sharply with lecture. In lecture, the text and the instructor's reading of the text provide the knowledge base. In discussion, the text provides the knowledge base. The instructor validates the accuracy of that reading as it emerges and identifies areas where the students' readings may be faulty. The instructor insists that statements connect directly to evidence. Discussion cannot function without the instructor as the arbiter of the accuracy of the student's understanding.

Discussion provides students with several advantages. First, it requires students to actively perform the knowledge. Information that is repeated through speaking or writing after being read is more easily recalled later. Discussion is a more powerful approach than short-answer quizzes. Speaking requires coordination of auditory processing with short-term visual memory reading. The transformation helps move the information to long-term memory. This causes the student to reflect as well as recall. The more often the individual student is called upon to actively paraphrase the information, the more rapidly the information moves from short-term to long-term memory (Hartley and Davies 1978, 207-24; Peper and Mayer 1978, 514-22).

The instructor's anecdotes, disciplinary lore, mnemonic devices, debates in the field, and similar oral traditions surrounding the information give students additional handles with which to cross-reference their memories of the material. The instructor's use of tangents may actually help students remember the material, as indeed it helped the instructor remember the material.

A final advantage to discussion lies in the way it supports the acquisition of reasoning skills for lower-division students. Specific prompts requiring critical reasoning can be made the basis for the discussion. Paul and Elder (2001) encourage students to articulate the purpose of the text and to differentiate this from the key questions, the key ideas, the basic assumptions, the evidence used, the main inferences, the implications of the work for the class, and the author's point of view. Using these prompts as the basis of discussion, after giving students a chance to prepare their answers ahead of time, allows the discussion format to support skill acquisition. Students hear how their peers dealt with the prompts. They note how the more successful readings occurred. Over the course of the term, they can practice implementing more critical reading strategies, checking the accuracy and depth of their accomplishments in the discussion. Restatement, evaluation for accuracy, use of multiple channels, and the instructor's comments habituate students to read for structure as well as for content. Discussion that emphasizes the development of critical reading skills need not sacrifice content development.

CHAPTER

50

Discussion Techniques

A well-oiled discussion progresses by juxtaposing perspectives on a text. This creates the teachable moments. It all begins with reading.

Helping Students Prepare for Discussion

Perspective on a text is something that students must work on before class. The preparation can vary depending on your goals. If you want to focus attention on the students' commonsense perspectives on a reading, the instructions you give for preparation will be less directive than if you want to focus on critical reading or points of view far removed from the students' experiences. The scope of the discussion will also shape the instructions you give for discussion. If the discussion will involve the whole class, the instructions will be more concrete and predictable than if you break the class into groups. Finally, if the discussion serves primarily to reinforce the students' control of a body of knowledge, the preparation will involve asking them to become aware of what facts they control.

Preparing for a Critical Discussion

Critical discussions support students' efforts to develop higher reasoning skills. The goal of the critical discussion is to identify as many perspectives on a text or problem as possible so that the discussion can then focus on the arguments for prioritizing one of the perspectives over the others. These discussions lend themselves to courses that prepare students for the demands of later courses. In critical discussions, students offer their reasoning and receive feedback from the instructor and peers. Students prepare by answering specific questions about the text.

You must articulate for yourself what the students should get from the reading. What should they be able to do with what they read? What movement should happen in the discussion? These questions need to asked when you are choosing the texts, not the night before the discussion. Effective classroom discussion depends on the teacher's understanding of students' choices at every step in the class.

Once you understand why you chose the text, you can then offer the students a reading strategy. I am indebted to Chris Anson of North Caroline State University for providing a list of reading strategies and for suggesting how they might be incorporated into the classroom. Almost all of the strategies are good preparations for critical discussions. I offer my understanding of these strategies. I encourage you to find your own ways of using these techniques.

> ► Joining the Conversation. In this strategy, you write out several imaginary responses to the reading before the class, as if they occurred in a real conversation about the work, and share these with the students. For example, you could make up epigram-like quotes from several critics offered during an imagined conversation. As in a real conversation, these should include a range of

responses, from the outrageous and erroneous to the insightful and profound. Include responses that are imprecise and statements unsupported by evidence. After the students read the text, they should turn to the responses you provided and write a brief response to each statement, agreeing or disagreeing, elaborating the point, or pointing out flaws. In the classroom have students discuss why they responded to a particular speaker the way they did. This technique compels students to read the text carefully. Joining the conversation stresses critical reasoning by having the students search out the reasons why a particular statement does not fit their reading. It is an excellent way of introducing a review of logical fallacies by building specific errors into the statements. If the statements include a few outrageous positions, this increases students' motivation to read the text with enthusiasm and purpose.

▶ Situating the Reader. This is a role-playing discussion. You design a simulation in which the student takes on a role and writes a response to the text from the position. In a literary text, the student could be a character in the work. In a history course, the student could be a person from the period who ordinarily would not have a voice in the written history. In a sociology course, the student could respond as a member of a community. In the classroom the students discuss why their "persons" took the position they did. As students hear variations on the reasons, they reflect on how they arrived at their own choices. This technique makes the reading more engaging for students. It gives life to the characters and places the material in a lived experience. It is especially appropriate for discussions where the instructor wants to impress upon the class the variety of perspectives that the text can engender.

▶ Teach It. This is another role-playing strategy. In this case, the student must "teach" the text to a particular audience other than the class. The instructor has the choice of asking the students to teach "up," to teach the material to people who are more familiar with it than they are; to teach "down," to teach the material to people who are less familiar with it than they are; or to teach "across," offering a lesson in some concept to students majoring in another discipline. I have found teaching up to be especially effective for upper-division courses where students acquire new knowledge about a subject matter. I have found teaching down to be more appropriate in lower-division courses. For example, in a physics class, students might prepare a plan to teach gravity to third graders. In an art history class, students might teach forced perspective to their entire family after Thanksgiving dinner. These techniques require students to put complex concepts into their own words. As teachers, we know that one of the best ways to learn something is to teach it. While there may not be time or means for the students to actually teach the material, simulating the teaching through preparatory exercises and then following up with a discussion of how different students approached the problem works just as well. This reinforces critical reasoning as students develop an organizational framework to present the information to others. The fine-tuning of the framework requires the student to systematically revisit their categorizing of the information into levels of generality and specificity. It directly supports skills in prioritizing.

Jolliffe (1999) developed another model where students choose one of the following methods of reading. Three times a week, they write for twenty minutes—preferably doing so immediately after reading the text. The repetition is important to developing the thinking about the texts. The methods are:

► Affective Reading. Students should answer each of the following questions in a paragraph or list: How do I feel about the reading I just finished? What do I think about the reading I just finished? What do I believe about the reading I just finished? What do I know about the reading I just finished? Going through the four questions in order helps students develop a separation between the affective, the reflective, the cognitive, and the evaluative functions of reading the specific texts. Develop a discussion around students' responses in the same order as the questions.

► Paraphrastic Reading. Students should write a summary of the reading, not to exceed half a page. Next, they should select one five-sentence segment (no more, no less) that they think is the most important one in the reading and write an accurate paraphrase of it. Then, they should make a note about why they selected the segment to paraphrase. Develop a discussion around students' responses.

► Dialectic Reading. Students should make three vertical columns on the page of their notebooks. At the top of the leftmost column, they should write, "What question did the text raise?" At the top of the middle column, they should write, "How did the text answer this question?" At the top of the rightmost column, they should write, "How does the answer match my own ideas and experiences?" They then fill in an appropriate response under each column. Develop a discussion around students' responses.

Reading for a Commonsense Discussion

Commonsense discussions validate students' community-based knowledge for the class to examine critically. The goal of the commonsense discussion is to begin the process of substituting universal knowledge (histories of the present, generalized schema, meta-perspectives) for the students' experiential and localized knowledge (experiences of the present, particularized schema, indexed perspectives). The commonsense that the students strive for in this discussion is not that of their home communities, but rather that of the community of scholars. This discussion works well in general education courses. The text serves as the stimulus for students to express community-based ideas. The class is encouraged to look for and identify diversity among the perspectives. The instructor asks questions, taking care to justify the questions and avoiding body language that disrespects or disparages the students' remarks.

The preparation for a commonsense discussion involves situating the students unambiguously in their local communities. Students could be asked to write down how they would explain the readings to their parents, distant relatives, siblings, or friends back at home. Have the students engage a point of view commonly found in their home community. Calling on students randomly insures that they will put some effort into the preparation. The following reading strategies from Chris Anson's unpublished list work well as preparations for commonsense discussions.

► Identifying Prejudgments. Ask students to write informally or free write about a particular course topic before they read about it. Such anticipatory writing helps students to connect their previous knowledge with the new information and prepares them for more candid, critical reading later. For example, in a criminology course, they could be asked to list all the factors they think might lead to police corruption and how those factors might differ between urban and nonurban police forces. This exercise helps students consider prejudgments of a particular topic prior to reading about it. As such, it serves as a stepping-off point for a discussion of the difference between opinion and evidence.

► Reading Logs, Dialogue Journals, and Double-Entry Journals. In a reading journal or log, students write entries each time they finish reading some section of the text. You can provide specific prompts for them to respond to across the double or triple entries, or you can leave the journaling unstructured. Journaling is considered private writing that is not intended for public reading. A dialogue journal, however, is shared. You can set one up electronically through a discussion board, or use sheets of paper that can be exchanged during class. You follow up by asking students to take an idea from their journals and use it to formulate a question for the class. Anytime they formulate questions about what they read, they establish a more critical appreciation of the text, breaking down their impulse to treat texts as concrete knowledge. The discussion proceeds from their questions.

► Finding a Context. Ask students to choose an event or item from the popular press: newspaper story, cartoon, advertisement, etc., that illustrates or connects one concept in the reading. Each student must clearly explain the relevance of the item or event to the reading. When used in commonsense discussions, the technique helps students to directly connect the language of the text to their community experience. After reading the text's discussion of the increasing presence of ideologically identified news programs on cable television, the student brings in a videotape of such a program. After reading Austen's *Pride and Prejudice*, the student brings a photograph of a debutante ball. The technique sends students back to the ways they commonly receive information to look for something not previously noticed. It provides a context for creative problem solving. It gives students an opportunity to apply abstractions in their communities. The in-class follow-up focuses first on suggestions of other places where similar information could be found and, secondly, on how differently the items under discussion are treated in the text and in the community.

► Lenses. Assign students a lens through which they must write about the reading. Lenses are generally interpretive perspectives that help to focus the student's reading and direct attention to certain information. When used in commonsense discussions, associate the lenses with positions in the student's community: How would a newly arrived immigrant from the student's ethnic group respond to this section of the text? How would the student's co-workers at a restaurant think about this character? You follow up by having students compare their interpretations. This technique moves students to multiple perspectives but does so with an eye toward seeing local knowledge not as right or wrong, but as something that reduces uncertainty. Then, bring the students back to the text. Lenses increase interest when students find a connection between their world and the university.

► Web Search. Ask students to search the Web for anything that connects to what they have read. Ask them to print out a copy of the Web page and write up a brief summary of how it connects to the reading. Begin the discussion by having students sort the pages together. Searches that took novel directions or found unexpected associations provide the focus of the conversation: What interests different communities in this information? Why were certain items searched for and not others? Why were certain items not found? This is a more creative exercise than it may initially appear to be. After a few attempts, students realize they have to work harder to find interesting sites with unique relationships to the text. Their problem-solving skills are exercised. The discussion should not turn to a focus on the Web itself. You should take pains to turn the discussion back onto the text at every opportunity, encouraging the students to do so as well.

► Debating Propositions. Before the students read an assignment, give them propositions culled from the critical literature that offer a variety of interpretations on the subject. Ask students to select those they agree and disagree with after they read the text. After making their selections, they should write out a brief response explaining their positions. The back-and-forth movement between text, critical statement, and students' response habituates them to establish their position on the writer's argument. When you follow up in the classroom, ask students to articulate their positions, opening up the opportunity for disagreement.

Reading for a Review Discussion

Review discussions help students memorize and control the knowledge base of the course. The goal of a review discussion is for students to use conversation to rearrange the information into schema they can more easily remember. Moving information from short-term to long-term memory depends on repetition. Review discuss repeat the information several times. In general education or lower-division major courses acquisition of a knowledge base is the dominant goal in the course. The source of knowledge is the text. In the discussion, the students supply the appropriate definitions, distinctions, or relationships in response to specific questions. The instructor or students offer the questions. The discussion helps the instructor identify students' misunderstandings. The following again are taken from Chris Anson's list.

► The Question Box. Ask the students to write anonymous questions about the chapter. The task can be assigned before, during, or after the reading. They deposit their questions in a cardboard box the class before the discussion. You select questions on a transparency, presentation slide, or printed handouts. You ask the class to respond to the questions. This doubles as an assessment technique. It helps you to see how the class reads the material, how carefully their reading unfolded, and who is having difficulty. The technique is useful in review discussions because it focuses the students' learning on the details of the knowledge base.

► Maps, Webs, Trees, and Other Visual Representations. The use of various fill-in-the-blank templates is underutilized in postsecondary education. Yet they provide the fastest and most efficient way to help students learn and retain detailed information sets. The theory here is that specific and general items are not mixed randomly in our heads but are organized in levels of generality and specificity. When these relationships are given graphic representation, they form:

  ▷ maps, if the contrasts are spatial or temporal, such as a plot or an argument,

  ▷ webs, if there are multiple relationships between items on the same level, such as characters or an organizational network,

  ▷ paradigms, if limited contrasting features describe all the relationships between the elements, such as verb conjugations or the periodic chart of the elements,

▷ taxonomies, if the contrasting features are unlimited, such as types of algae or types of democracies, or

▷ trees, if the contrasting features are logical binaries, such as computer programs or kinship systems.

Having students work with a template where some items are filled in and others are left blank can be a very effective preparation for the discussion. You project the blank template on a screen and ask the students to fill in the blanks collectively, stopping whenever there is disagreement over an entry. After reading the material, completing the template on their own, and then again in class, the students will have revisited the relationships between the items three times. This technique encourages students to organize the recall of the information while they are reading.

▶ Teach It. This technique was discussed above. It serves the needs of a review discussion just as well as a critical discussion. For example, after reading a chapter on the Genome Project, the students prepare a lesson for eighth graders studying biology for the first time. After reading about the various criticisms of area studies programs, the students might prepare a paper to deliver on the viability of a new area studies curriculum at a Reinventing Area Studies conference. In both cases, the actual audience can be the class and the follow-up is a question-and-answer session between the "teacher" and the "students." This is a powerful review tool that asks students to translate the material into their own terms and words. It compels the students to organize the information in preparation to communicating it. It works with highly detailed material as well as interpretative material.

Reading for a Small-Group Discussion

In small group discussion, one or more members play the role of the instructor. Choose small groups when the size of the classroom moves beyond the twenty-student range. It gives more students the opportunity to participate. Small-group discussions differ in the scope of the discussion. Participants are usually charged to discuss something quite specific and to do so in a specific amount of time. Small groups usually report to the class as a whole to encourage them to come to closure and reflect on what they have accomplished. While many of the discussion forms already covered can be adapted to small-group form, identifying pre-judgments and creating discussion questions lend themselves particularly well to small groups. In addition, you might consider these forms from Chris Anson's list:

► Discussion Questions. Before class, ask students to prepare a question about the reading and write it out on an index card. Give examples of good questions. Tell students to make sure the questions they come up with follow your model questions in form and complexity. You want divergent questions, i.e. the kind that cannot be answered by a single word.

► Talking Points. Before class, ask each student to write out a position on the material under discussion. The paper should be no longer than one page. It should include one, two, three, or four position points expressed as simple declarative sentences, each developed around a strong action verb. Each point should include several bullet points, each referring to evidence that the student feels best supports the position point. During the discussion, students take turns offering their position points. The other students attempt to refute or modify the position by offering alternative evidence. This technique works particularly well with students who are already advanced in the subject matter, such as upper-division undergraduates and graduate students.

All of these preparatory exercises help students to focus on the relevant issues that you want to raise in the discussion. It is not a matter of choosing one randomly. Usually, one form of preparation fits your goals and the level of skill development of the students better than others. Once you figure out what form will work best, allow the students to accustom themselves to it by repeating it for two weeks. If the results disappoint you, you have probably chosen the wrong form. Try another.

Even when you choose an effective preparation form, the class will tire of it in time. It is a good idea to have at least a second and sometimes even a third form available that serves the same functions as the first. At the first signs of fatigue with the form, introduce a new one. After some weeks, you may be able to return to the initial form. Keeping the preparation fresh and challenging for the students elevates motivation for the discussion.

With this and all other prompts to help students prepare for discussion, the goal is to draw out diverse points of view among the students.

Once those different readings are exposed, the students can use conversation to review the reading, critique it or resolve it to commonsense.

How to Take Notes on a Discussion

During discussions, information comes from all around you. No single person provides a structure for the information. In general, discussions proceed like the rubric for preparation above, starting with terms and concepts, the writer's core idea(s), the questions surrounding the subtopics, and the support for other ideas and positions previously discussed. To take effective notes on a discussion, you might consider the following:

► Using the initials of each speaker, write a brief summary of each major contribution or question. Put a star before the initials if the contribution sets the discussion off in a new direction.

► Keep a running index of the kinds of topics the class discusses and how it relates to your preparation. When definitions and terms come up, put a capital D in the margin. Similarly, when students discuss the thesis, put a T in the margin. Use a Q for questions, and S for comments about support for the thesis. When someone raises a point about the author's biases, use a B. Any system of notation of content will do. Devise your own. If questions or comments occur to you during the discussion, write these down and circle them. If you choose to make a contribution, you will have a way of remembering what you wanted to say.

► In the pauses and as the discussion is winding down (or if it has gone off on a tangent that you are not interested in), try to summarize the discussion so far. Is there anything that confused you or that you do not understand?

Making It Difficult for the Students to Be Unprepared

There are several constructive and supportive (rather than coercive and punitive) techniques for keeping the students prepared. One of the most popular is the admission ticket. This technique has several implementations, and most instructors develop their own nuances. At its base, the technique requires that a student must accomplish some writing task that in turn cannot be accomplished without the student being prepared. In order to sit in the class, the student must present the writing. The admission ticket works best if it is required for every class and students get in the habit of writing them. It is also important that there be a stated attendance policy, which should permit a certain percentage of absences—say, 10 percent of the class meetings. Any absences with or without good excuses beyond that limit would then result in an automatic failure of the course. By establishing a strict attendance rule up front, you give the admission ticket its teeth. The tickets are collected at the beginning of class. Consider students absent if they have not turned in a card.

Instructors exercise their creativity when it comes to what the student puts on the ticket. One version I learned of recently involves specifying that students purchase and use colored cards. Their name and the date go on the top line. Then, at the end of each class, students are given a question about the next reading assignment that they must answer on one side of the 3 x 5 card. Choose the question from the critical reading questions, like the ones discussed in the previous chapter. The cards can be used as assessment devices. A quick read will tell you about the extent of active reading and the understanding of the core issues. A colleague who uses this technique says that it takes less than a minute to scan each card, while recording student attendance. The attendance policy makes it possible for students who are not prepared to have some leeway, while simultaneously motivating them either to commit to consistently being prepared for discussion or to withdraw from the class. The question on the card can also be the lead discussion question of the class, permitting you to call on anyone you want and expect them to have a response.

If the discussion becomes merely a recitation of what people wrote down, the cards can stifle the flow of a good discussion. Another colleague specifies in the syllabus of his literature class exactly what he means by class preparation and makes these actions required for all students. The hook for this technique is the equating of preparation with presence in the class. He states in his syllabus:

> By being present in class, you are affirming that you have done the following preparation:
>
> → You have read the entire text.
> → You have marked passages in the text that you consider important, by underlining, highlighting, or writing in the margins.
> → You have formulated in writing at least one comment on and at least one question about a specific element of the text. We will talk further about marking a text effectively. I expect your comments on and questions about the texts will become more and more substantive as the course proceeds. (Gerry Mulderig, personal communication)

The prepared students determine the direction of discussion. Begin by calling on anyone to pose their question. Students who had similar comments or questions can respond. When the thread is exhausted, calling on a student who has not yet contributed should lead to a different question. Over the course of the term, you should attempt to be evenhanded in how you call on people. By the middle of the term, you may have identified the less active students. Make a special effort to call on them. The technique works because the instructor spends time talking about reading a text to identify the "important" passages, including working through a passage together. You can combine the comment or question with the admission ticket, but because the students know they can be called on at any time and because preparation is required, the admission ticket becomes redundant. If they are not prepared, they are absent.

One of the principle values of classroom teaching is to reward what you value. If you value participation, reward it. This means more than just evaluating participation as part of the final grade. It means valorizing participation in such a way that students get the message early and often. Once you have done this, your responsibility to unprepared students changes. Not being prepared in this classroom becomes the same as not being present at all. Unprepared students absent themselves. There are ways of creating this formally, with admission tickets and similar devices.

Motivational Issues in Discussions

Is there a good reason why students should want to participate in discussion? Requiring participation, handing out rubrics for evaluation, providing study guides, requiring admission tickets, and developing formats are not reasons. They are techniques. Many students do not find it worthwhile to participate in discussion. It makes them vulnerable to criticism. It exposes the superficiality of their understanding to the teacher and their peers. It does not lead to an improved essay or test performance. It feels like a rehash of what they already read in the book. They have to listen to the "talker" in the front row who is always trying to impress the teacher. They have never found out anything in a discussion that helped them understand the text. They do not have anything important to say. They think discussion helps you avoid having to actually teach. Students who believe these sorts of things are not wrong. Their experience has shown them that poorly conducted discussions waste their time. To engage such students, you have to show them that discussion in your classroom is different.

When trying to motivate a reluctant group, remember that discussion is first and foremost a conversation with a purpose. Everyone knows how to converse and what they want from a conversation: socializing, new information, a plan, or reflection on the past. Discussions are different because they begin somewhere and are designed to end when the participants achieve an intended goal. Part of what has turned many students off to discussion is the absence of a goal. They do not want a mere conversation. They want a discussion that sheds light on the knowledge base or skill set of the course. No matter what approach you choose, you must set out at the beginning to convince them that discussions in your classroom will get them closer to their own goals. Once you can get the students to start talking, it becomes easier for them to participate in the future.

These techniques can help you do that:

→ Building community to make participation for everyone as safe and supportive as possible.

→ Using short-term, problem-oriented two person and three person breakout discussions.

→ Presenting a setting for the discussion.

→ Giving every student a stake in outcome, something then can take away.

→ Listing detailed notes of the discussion's progress on the board.

→ Providing a summary statement highlighting the accomplishments of the day's discussion.

Dealing with Silence

CHAPTER

53

Silence is perfectly normal in the classroom. Your initial reaction to silence should be "Wait." Unlike conversation, where silence is a violation of norms, silence in the classroom should best be interpreted as a pause. Waiting gives students time to think. The higher the level of the class, the longer you should wait. In graduate teaching this can be as long as several minutes! If you've waited an appropriate amount of time, acknowledge that it's a difficult question and takes time to think about. This acknowledges that you are not going to let them off the hook and are waiting for an answer. Wait a bit longer. Then rephrase the question. When you finally get a response, resist the temptation to go to another question. They just did all this work, and you only paid attention to the first speaker. Encourage others to speak as well. Avoid the temptation to respond to every student's contribution. If no student chimes in immediately after someone speaks, ask for response. If there is still no response, say something that connects the student's contribution to a previous comment and the student who made it. Ask that student if he or she agrees with the connection. Use your comments to facilitate them talking to each other. If no one responds to the rephrased question, turn the moment into an assessment and have them write out responses anonymously. Or, have them discover a response working in groups of two or three. When you commit to a question, respect the question. Stay with it. If you do this early and often, you establish a pattern in the class that keeps them comfortable with the pauses.

There are as many reasons for dead silence as there are discussion prompts. This is the kind of silence where no one can respond. Dead silence can result when the environment has not been prepared. Are you satisfied that the students are prepared, the conduct for the discussion laid out, the supportive community established, the ice broken, the goals clearly stated, and the format delineated? If not, then you should use the time to do as much of that as you can during that first silent response. If you have put into place much of this infrastructure, then two additional factors may be involved: they are less prepared for your prompt than they thought they would be, or your prompt is at odds with their preparation.

Class preparation is an ongoing challenge. Sometimes competing workloads defeat the students' best efforts. You need to understand these rhythms from the students' point of view and work within them. It is certainly your right to expect that all students will be prepared for every class, but an unexpected silence is often an indication that at this particular point in the term, that expectation was unrealistic.

The prompt itself can be the problem. Some questions are too difficult to begin a discussion. Prompts that call for interpretation or analysis before the facts have been exposed are surefire silencers. When establishing those facts, avoid closed-ended questions. Ask open-ended questions, requiring more than one word answers. Responses that merely repeat facts from the book are boring. Your questions about interpretation or analysis, when you finally pose them, need to be divergent. These are questions with many possible answers. Convergent questions only ask for a conventional response. If you are asking closed-ended, convergent questions, you deserve dead silence.

In general, the prompts for a discussion should proceed from the more concrete to the more abstract. Beginning a discussion with a list gives everyone a chance to warm up to the task and refresh their memories of the text. A projected list provides an index of the evidence as the discussion turns to more abstract matters.

Some instructors respond to silence by talking. Resist this temptation. Off-the-cuff lecturing is ineffective. Substituting your thoughts for theirs only shows students that you are not interested in what they have to say. The instructor dominates most discussions anyway (Brown and Atkins 1988).

Dealing with Talkers

Some students monopolize discussion, responding to every prompt with extended comments intended for the instructor and not for their peers. Some writers on teaching see this as another form of silence (McKeachie 2002). As more Asperger spectrum students, who might not fully embody the conventions of social communication, make their way into college classrooms, managing talkers becomes more important to an effective discussion. Talkers are certainly as much of a concern in discussion as silence.

When you have solved the problem of nonparticipating students, the students who dominate discussion to show that they were prepared will retreat. Starting off each discussion with breakout groups gets everyone more excited about reporting on their findings when the groups reassemble. If the problem persists, raising the question with the class of whether discussion would be more useful if more people took part will give talkative students the clue that they need to monitor the length and frequency of their comments more closely. Putting the talkative student in the role of class reporter, with the task of reporting on the discussion in the last ten minutes of class or videotaping the discussion are time-consuming ways of doing this. The idea is to have the talkative student provide the others with feedback about the class experience. If all else fails, talk to the student outside of class.

Talkative students are often bright and highly motivated. Their verbal performance, however disruptive, may be part of what they need to do to understand the material. They may be bored by the school experience and find in your class an opportunity for excitement and engagement. Giving them feedback about their frequency of contribution helps them understand that they are silencing the other students when they dominate discussion. I was successful in helping one such student get control of her impulse to talk by restricting her to two comments per class. She could choose which two comments she wanted to make, but she could make only two. It took a few class meetings for her to fully control herself, but with positive encouragement, again outside of class, her participation became increasingly attuned to the class.

When students face each other instead of facing you, it is easier for them to engage in discussion. The semicircle is a common device since even the students who are seated farthest away are directly in each other's line of sight. Have the students display name cards so that they can address each other by name. If the chairs do not move, try to position yourself in such a way that students see each other at the same time when they direct their attention to you. If the room uses seminar seating, sit along the long side of the table, not at the head. Research has shown that people tend to talk to the person sitting opposite them, but less so to the people sitting next them. The most centrally located person in the room, the one that the greatest number of people have in their direct line of sight, leads. Left to their own devices, instructors leading discussion tend to sit in the less crowded parts of the room (Beard and Hartley 1984). Reversing these tendencies opens up more opportunities for people to be seen when they talk.

Student-Generated Discussion

CHAPTER

55

One of the earmarks of a well-developed discussion classroom is when the students themselves offer the prompts. These often take the form of questions, text-based prompts. The prompts students offer often get at issues that are of direct concern to students. You should seize every opportunity to let a student question direct the discussion, returning to the student who posed it from time to time to permit him or her to decide when the question has been fully and satisfactorily explored.

If the technology to do so exists at your school, facilitate student-initiated discussion by getting it started electronically before class. This also builds anticipation for the class meeting. Using an electronic discussion board or chat tool, invite students to post their questions about the text and comment on each question. Use these as your initial prompts, asking the students to begin the class discussion by posing the question they had previously described on the discussion board.

Designing a Discussion around Specific Roles

Students fall into different roles in discussions. Not everyone is comfortable playing the role of discussion leader. Some do not like to push themselves forward in public. Others do not like trying to decide when it is time to develop a different direction. There are other roles in discussion that are not as obvious as that of leader. The larger the group, the more likely it is that these other roles will appear.

Some students like to serve as the resource person in a discussion. They always have their hands on the details of the evidence. When they prepare, they do so with a view to providing these details. They are less likely to offer synthesis. Integrating insights are the specialty of the evaluator. These students like to develop the big picture. They have a greater sense of context than their peers, and providing integration is their way of making a contribution. Some students like to play the role of critic, offering various ways of contesting the authority of the author or the validity of the evidence. Some students prefer the role of posing questions. These shapers hold back from participating until the instructor's questions have played out and then offer their issues toward the end of the class. Finally, there will occasionally be the student who is always looking for new approaches and new strategies for dealing with questions. This is the innovator, for whom every discussion is an exercise in creativity. When all of these roles are operating in a group, the discussions are livelier and likely to reach their goals with higher levels of satisfaction. Encouraging students to self-consciously play these roles is as simple a matter as describing them in a handout and suggesting that student try out different approaches until they find the one that feels the most comfortable.

CHAPTER

57

First Aid for Tired Discussions

Some days overwork, weak preparation, difficulty in understanding the text, encroaching illness, and bad weather will combine to produce a discussion that goes nowhere. The rate at which the students offer comments is sluggish. They keep looking at you rather than at each other for prompts. Several thumb through the text looking for inspiration. You try breakout groups and the students talk about everything except the text. There are twenty minutes left in the class. What can you do? Hopefully, you knew where you wanted the class to be by the end of the period. Discussion, after all, is a conversation with a purpose.

My suggestion is to immediately mount a close reading exercise. These can usually kick-start a sluggish discussion. I always begin by having the students move. I ask them to either stand up and stretch or rearrange the seating. This breaks through their lethargy and prepares them to attend to what will follow.

Pick a passage from the text that offers ideas that lead toward your goal. Have students take turns reading sections of the passage—a sentence or two per student will suffice—until the passage is finished. Then, go back to the first student to begin reciting the sentences again. This time, instead of going immediately to the next student, pause and ask the class to paraphrase the sentences. Continue to the next reader, and when that student is finished reading, ask the class to paraphrase those sentences. Proceed in this manner until the passage is completed. You have filled the classroom with student voices. Everyone is familiar with a key passage in the text. You can now pose the questions that will lead to the position on the text you hoped the students would achieve on their own.

Discussions of Controversial Subjects

There are controversies that invade the classroom in every subject. Civil society has opened debate on subjects that were once the province of technical specialists. Literature and the arts have always included dissent as a source of both inspiration and criticism. The social and behavioral sciences have made conflict the basis of their subject matters. Hence, few university classrooms are immune from the discussion of topics that engender strong reactions. Rather than avoiding these issues, the classroom should be the place where divisive issues can be discussed frankly, knowledgeably, and safely. The points offered in the following sections apply to all these issues as well as other kinds of interpersonal conflicts that can occur: challenges to the instructor's authority, race and queer baiting and ad hominem attacks.

Knowledge of the Other and Trust

Our students are not strangers to classroom discussions of difficult issues. Many of the teachers in primary and secondary school have attempted to take on the issues of race, ethnicity, gender, and sexual orientation. Some have opened up discussions of domestic and foreign policy, or faith and reason, ineptly or superficially, in spite of their best intentions. Students have experienced controversy in their secondary schools often enough to understand the pitfalls of dissent and the comfort of silence. Their ethical positions are often that of the naive relativist, a "different strokes for different folks" retreat from confrontation and engagement. Effective discussion of difficult issues has to overcome this experience and this thoughtless relativism. The distinction I am making here is between a relativist position based on a careful assessment of facts leading to a decision that judgment is useless or harmful, and one based on an a priori disengagement from judgment.

To change students' attitudes toward engagement, the classroom must be configured to generate an atmosphere of trust and support.

This environment may take as long as 10 percent of the contact hours at the beginning of the term to achieve. This would be the case where the entire course was devoted to discussion of difficult topics. In less dedicated courses, the amount of time devoted to what we can call community building can be reduced, disappearing entirely in those courses where the goal is the transmission of technical information. Careful attention to community building not only aids in freeing students to discuss difficult issues but also builds a store of goodwill that carries over into other areas of student course interaction, such as motivation and preparation time.

At the beginning of the term, the composition of the class is in flux. Students are shopping for classes, dropping the ones that do not fit their agenda for that term. Other students may simply have made a registration mistake and will disappear after the first class. Students who prioritize vacation over school will arrive after the first few class sessions, expecting that nothing significant has happened. If you were planning to use the first week for assessment and community building, these shifts in the composition of the class will frustrate you and confuse the late-arriving students. The students who have stuck with you from the beginning will form the core of the class and provide enough goodwill to pull in the late ones.

Initial Community Building: Icebreakers

There are as many different ways of starting this process of community building as there are teachers. Which icebreakers you use, sets the tone for the class. Choose an icebreaker that you would enjoy participating in yourself. If you have never found an icebreaker you like, invent one you can like. If you do not like the idea of icebreakers, you may actually not enjoy leading discussions either. The opening up of the classroom during an icebreaker exercise is what the instructor seeks to have happen during discussion. It gives up a certain amount of control, and some instructors find this difficult. Having this conversation with yourself is important. You may find other forms of instruction more comfortable. There is no law that says all instructors must be good at leading discussions.

Since I argued earlier that it is best to begin by giving assessments of the knowledge base or the reasoning skills of the students, it would be helpful to combine this somehow with steps toward community building. In the sciences where demonstrations are possible, this can be done by performing a bit of wizardry at the front of the room and asking the students to discuss in small groups whether the demonstration was science or magic. They then write up their individual positions based on that discussion, providing the assessment.

Bernardo Carducci at Indiana University Southeast has a first class activity that introduces research methodology in the form of a pretest-posttest demonstration of the hypothesis that class participation will kill you. The only material is a sheet of paper crumpled into a ball. This is used to randomly select subjects; the person who catches your tossed paper ball stands and remains standing. The person (with eyes closed) then tosses the ball in any direction, not at anyone in particular. Several tosses will produce a sample of appropriate size for the class. The standing students then come to front of the classroom. The pretest is to determine if the students are alive. After arriving at an operational definition through class discussion, the subjects are evaluated for being alive but not brain-dead (i.e., they are actually thinking and were able to follow directions up to this point). The class then discusses what would be a fair test of "speaking up in class." An obvious test would be giving name, major, class year, and favorite pastime. After the students have spoken up in class, the posttest then assesses if they are still alive, using the same criteria as for the pretest. To move to immediate full-class participation after this demonstration, ask what it would mean if someone had actually died during the demonstration. How might the test have to be modified to account for such occurrences and still produce an acceptable result? This is, of course, a validity measure. At the end, you point out that the nonparticipants who spoke out to help with the definitions and the evaluations did not die either, demonstrating the ecological validity of the hypothesis. Encourage them to test the hypothesis in other classes as well (Bender, et al. 1994).

If you have access to a video recorder, film each student for ten or twenty seconds as they introduce themselves (name, major, class year, and maybe one other short piece of information relevant to class). Using a computer, make stills of the tape, giving you and everyone else in the class a way of learning names more quickly. An alternative with the more common digital camera is to have each student write his or her name on the board and stand in front of it for a digital photograph. These are printed out as a proof sheet and distributed to the students.

Divide the class in half, have each student in group A select a partner from group B to interview for five minutes, finding out as much about the other person as possible. Then, they reverse roles. If there are an odd number of students, the instructor joins in. After ten minutes, two pairs join to make a group of four that will stay together playing different roles over the course of the term. The instructor's partner joins a group as a fifth person. The groups take ten minutes to compare notes on each other, the interviewers providing the information on their partners first. This is one of several "interview" strategies. Another might be to have each student interview the student on his or her right.

Sometimes it is appropriate to combine assessment of the knowledge base with community building by having students develop a testament to their existing understanding of the course information early in the first week. For example, they could bring in images and texts they have found that best illustrate their knowledge of the material and then work collaboratively to create a collage of the material on cardboard trifolds. At the end of the term, you can bring out the posters to show them how far they have come in the control of the information.

Make each student responsible for bringing in a quote from anyone they choose for the second class meeting. Each student reads the quote and explains the reasons for choosing it. The class tries to look for patterns in the selection process that produced the quotes as the number of them increases over the course period.

Understand that you, too, are part of the ice that has to be broken. If you convey respect and civility for the students, you set the pattern for them to display respect and civility to each other. Make a good first impression. Simple things like dressing well and being well groomed, even though they have nothing to do with course content, immediately focus student attention. Your approach to the costuming need not be conventional, but it should be purposeful. I have a colleague in political science who wears a white lab coat to his first class because he says he wants to emphasize the formal, "scientific" qualities of his discipline in the course. Be at least a few minutes early to the first class. Of course, you should avoid being late for any class, but punctuality in these first few weeks sets the tone that you are ready to go as soon as the hour begins— and you expect them to be ready as well. When you are late, you show them disrespect, and they realize it.

Name games have several advantages and disadvantages. The disadvantages are that they are used so often that students tire of them. Also, the focus on names takes time away from other relevant information that is necessary to build trust. The advantage is that everyone can address everyone else by name early in the term, reducing anonymity. The best name games are ones where there is a specific deadline for learning the names and everyone is responsible for helping everyone else learn the names.

Establishing the Rules of Engagement

All students have a basic right to respect and privacy. Classrooms are inappropriate places to engage in therapy, even in its group form. Offering the rules of engagement for students draws a line between the private and the public. Students will have real disputes with each other, just as community members do. These real disputes should be conducted in private, away from the class "jury." If you find that you have students who cannot keep their private animosity from interfering with the class, stop the class. Ask the students to identify the steps that led to the current situation. Then, suggest that they need rules in order to proceed effectively, but you do not intend to set the rules. Instead, you would like them to decide what rules they think will work best. Get them to generate the rules that you then write on the board. Their authorship supported by the class consensus will maintain the rules. They have a real stake in having a civil discussion. Follow up with the most aggressive student(s) outside of class. Help them to understand that they are better able to get their points across with civility than with interruptions, raised voices or attacks.

In-class conflicts should be governed by specific rules. In my syllabi, I lay out these rules and go over them at the beginning of the term. Then, when conflicts occur, I refer students to the fact that rules are in place for dealing with this situation. I begin with a section on how to participate in a discussion, and then a section on conflict. The idea is that if students have participated properly and are taking appropriate notes, few conflicts will occur. When they do occur, preparation and good note taking help students to reconstruct miscommunications and give everyone greater confidence in the group's ability to handle the conflict. The sections look this:

How to Participate in a Discussion

→ Seek the best answers rather than trying to convince other people.
→ Try not to let your previous ideas or prejudices interfere with your freedom to think new thoughts.

→ Speak whenever you wish (if you are not interrupting someone else, of course), even though your ideas may seem incomplete.

→ Practice listening by trying to formulate in your own words the point that the previous speaker made before adding your own contribution.

→ Avoid disrupting the flow of thought by introducing new issues; instead, wait until the present topic reaches its natural end. Then, if you wish to introduce a new topic, warn the group that what you are about to say will address a new topic. Say that you are willing to wait to introduce it until people are finished commenting on the current topic.

→ Stick to the subject and talk briefly.

→ Avoid long stories, anecdotes, or examples.

→ Give encouragement and approval to others.

→ Seek out differences of opinion; they enrich the discussion.

→ Be sympathetic and understanding of other people's views. (Tiberius 1990, 67-68)

Dealing with Conflict During a Discussion

It is OK for people to disagree with each other. Disagreement is an important part of questioning and learning. If a disagreement occurs, everyone should listen carefully and take accurate notes. In order to disagree properly, there are several things that people should keep in mind.

If you disagree with something that someone said, do the following:

→ First, listen respectfully. The other person may have insights that you need to hear. Also the discussion leader may have specifically invited disagreement and the person is offering a disagreement that he or she thought of but does not personally hold. Always focus on the ideas and not the person, even when the idea is offered as a personal opinion.

→ When the person has finished speaking, repeat out loud what you think the person just said.

→ When the other person comments on what you said, think about it for a second. How does his or her comment change the direction of the disagreement?

→ It's possible the other person did not hear you right. Ask the person to repeat back to you what he or she thought you said.

→ Correct any misunderstandings. You need to decide whether the misunderstanding is important enough to continue discussing or if you can move on. If you want to continue, ask if there is anyone else in the class who is having the same disagreement you are. Suggest that there may also be people who are not in disagreement, and invite all of these people to help the two of you better understand each other. (Stocking 1994, 82)

Refereeing the Discussion

Most conflicts that occur in the classroom are the result of miscommunication. The few exceptions to this are conflicts that actually begin outside the classroom. Even students with opposing positions are not necessarily in conflict with each other. Their positions are in conflict. The difference here lies in the emotional investment that one or another student has made to the position they have taken. To open up the discussion to an examination of the position itself, rather than its meaning to the individual, requires that you convince the speakers to reduce that emotional investment. This can be very difficult when the emotional investment is tied to matters of faith, family history, privilege, race, gender, or sexual identity. Insist that description of the position comes before judgment of the position.

The disputants need to carefully describe their positions. Next, the evidence for their positions has to be differentiated from the elements that are opinion-based. Then, the positions have to be described again, this time emphasizing the verifiable elements. Once the elements that are the product of conjecture, prejudice, false assumptions, received opinion, and false information are removed, understanding and judgment have a clear basis. Nevertheless, it is difficult to haul a student who swept up in the emotions of an argument back to the world of reasoned discourse. It helps if you explain what you are trying to do and why you are trying to do it to the class as a whole before you begin. You need to avoid making it seem as if you are interrogating one side while sparing the other side. You also need to avoid making it seem like you have a predetermined outcome that you are seeking. If the class comes to see your actions in either of these lights, you join the dispute, rather than serving as its mediator.

There is a point at which heated discussion flames out of control. When people begin to personalize their arguments either in terms of some perceived personal attack or an overt attack on another, discussion has come to an end. Most of the time when tempers flare out of control, it is the result of unmediated conflicts that have gone on too long. You can avoid these moments by holding students to the three mechanisms for evaluating an argument: clarity ("Do I hear you right?"), verifiability ("How do you know that?"), and validity ("How does this relate to what we are discussing?"). If you interject the need for this kind of close reading of the argument as it develops, you can head off discussions that are about to turn into something else.

CHAPTER

59

The Socratic Form of Discussion

Socratic discussion is a specific form of question asking in which the instructor leads the students from the specific case to the general principle or law. The approach is to first deduce general principles from what the students know and then apply those principles to a succession of increasingly complex cases. For disciplines that require familiarity with general principles or laws, this is an efficient and effective form of discussion. For those where the goal is to develop tactics for problem solving, Socratic technique removes the opportunity for students to find their own path to the goal. The main weakness of the Socratic technique is that only through several repetitions do students learn how to develop the questioning pattern on their own. The questioner has to know beforehand where the questions are leading. This endows the technique with a strong instructor-centered quality.

Several authors have attempted to characterize the Socratic strategy (Boghossian 2002; Brogan and Brogan 1995, 288-96; Elder and Paul 1998, 297-301; Julian 1995, 338-39; Moore and Rudd 2002, 24-25) and to critique it (Mangan 1997, A12-A14). The Socratic strategy generates a discussion out of responses to your questions. The various approaches differ in how many different kinds of questions you ask and whether you ask them in a specific order. The questions are rhetorical tactics that allow the instructor to fine-tune the direction of the discussion toward deriving the general principle. Even if you have chosen not to use a full Socratic technique in your class, some of these tactics apply to other discussions. In general, you follow these steps:

→ Ask about a known case. For example, if I were trying to get a group of students to understand the social construction of roles, I might begin by asking, "Can you think of a situation in which a social role has changed?"

→ Ask for any factors that might be observable in the known case. In my example, I might ask, "Why did women's roles change for many Americans within the last two generations?"

→ Ask for intermediate factors. In my example, I might ask, "Was anything else changing in American life during this time?"

→ Ask for the connection between the why and the what. In my example, I might ask, "Why did working outside the home result in a shift in the way women see their roles?"

→ Ask for prior factors. What are the priorities or processes that appear to be guiding the case. In my example, I might ask, "Why do women want to be employed outside the home?"

→ Ask them to form a general rule. In my example, I might ask, "Do all women want to be employed outside the home?"

→ Pick a counterexample. In my example, I might ask, "Do you think that all of the women who are doing so, chose to work outside the home?"

→ Pick a case with an extreme value. In my example, I might ask, "Why is the number of two-income households increasing as the birthrate is declining?"

→ Ask them to identify the necessary or sufficient factors for an extreme case. In my example, the necessary factors would revolve around the higher availability of low-skill, low-paying jobs, and the sufficient factors would emphasize the high basic cost of living for households before income is taken into account.

→ Pose two cases and probe for differences. In my example, I might ask, "Why are more working-class women than middle-class women working outside the home?"

→ Ask them for a prediction about an unknown case. In my example, I might ask, "If there was a small rural community, where all of the daughters had been raised by mothers who worked at home, what would you predict would be the fate of those women when they got married? Could they continue to imitate their mothers' choices after they had children?"

→ Ask them to trace the consequences. For example, if the students identified the rising cost of living as the primary reason for the increase in women working outside the home, I might ask, "How does this change in household life affect the way women see their role as homemaker?" The discussion then continues by probing the various conflicts and models that are available to women to understand their relationship to the homemaker role, illustrating the process of the social construction of roles.

The value of this form of questioning is its orderliness. When I critique a discussion, either for myself or for colleagues, I find myself relying extensively on this order of questions to determine how logical I was in developing effective prompts for the students. The students become confused and discussion grinds to a halt when the instructor asks a question from the middle of this stack. For the instructor who already has the full background on the case, the chosen question is intriguing. For the students it lacks context. The result is silence. The students can keep up with the logical development of a case when the prompts move painstakingly from question to question. Each question builds on the one before it, permitting students to extend their skills at evidence and argument.

CHAPTER 60

Non-Socratic Forms of Discussion

A non-Socratic discussion is one in which students develop the form the conversation will take. Rather than asking questions, the instructor monitors the discussion, making adjustments as necessary to keep the students on track. Non-Socratic discussions can take a number of different forms. Varying the form within the same class is challenging to students. As comfort with a form grows, it is best to stick with it for the term. Not every form works with every type of class or every group of students. Some of these discussion forms require more experience and preparation than others. If you arbitrarily pick a discussion form before you understand what your students' strengths and limitations are, you may be setting them and yourself up for frustration. The following list of discussion forms comes from William H. Bergquist and Steven R. Phillips (1989, 19-26). I have added comments about how each form fits with different classroom situations.

Group Discussion (Class as a Whole)

→ Definition: Offers the opportunity for pooling of ideas, experience, and knowledge.

→ When Used: Maximizes participation. It is the form used after breakout sessions to share ideas.

→ Preparation and Procedure: Requires preplanning to develop discussion outline. The instructor leads the discussion, guiding the discussion in such a way as to encourage every member to participate. Students enter the discussion with a clearly articulated position on some aspect of the text.

→ Limitation: Only practical with fewer than twenty persons. It tends toward disorganization without careful planning of material to be covered, and it requires preparation from the students.

Buzz Groups (Breakout Groups)

→ Definition: Allows participation by group members through small clusters of participants, followed by discussion within the entire group.

→ When Used: Especially helpful for generating participation from every student. This form is highly adaptable to use with other forms of discussion.

→ Preparation and Procedure: Prepare one or two questions on the subject to give to each group. Divide the members into small clusters of four to six. A student in each group is chosen to record and report pertinent ideas at the close of the session.

→ Limitation: Thought must be given as to the purpose and organization of groups. Without a purpose, the discussion becomes aimless and dispiriting. The discussion prompt should be written on the board. It should be clearly connected to what the students prepared. When the groups are too large or too homogeneous, full participation is thwarted. One way to avoid this is to have the class count off in fives, with all the ones forming a group, then the twos, et cetera.

Panel Discussion

→ Definition: Offers discussion in a conversational manner among a selected group of persons with a leader, in front of an audience that joins in later.

→ When Used: Used to stimulate interest and thinking and to provoke better discussion.

→ Preparation and Procedure: The leader plans with the four to eight members of the panel. The panel discusses informally without any set speeches. The leader then opens the discussion to the entire group and summarizes.

→ Limitation: Can get off topic. The personality of speakers may overshadow content, or a vocal speaker can monopolize program.

Symposium Discussion

→ Definition: Topic is broken into its various phases; each part is presented in a brief, concise speech by an expert or a person well informed on that particular phase.

→ When Used: This form is used when the exploration of specific, well-defined topics is available.

→ Preparation and Procedure: The leader meets with the three or four members of the symposium and plans an outline. Participants are introduced and reports are given, the group directs questions to appropriate symposium members, and the leader summarizes.

→ Limitation: Can get off track. The personality of the speakers may overshadow content, and a vocal speaker can monopolize the program.

Debate Discussion

→ Definition: Presents a pro and con discussion of a controversial issue. The objective is to convince the audience, rather than display skill in attacking the opponent.

→ When Used: Used in discussing a controversial issue on which there are fairly definite opinions in the group on both sides, the intent being to bring these differences out into the open in a friendly manner.

→ Preparation and Procedure: Divide the group into sides of pro and con. Each speaker should be limited to a predetermined time, to be followed by a rebuttal if desired.

→ Limitation: Members are often not objective toward the subject, so the exchange may excite people.

Experience Discussion

→ Definition: Entails a small or large group discussion following a report on the main point of a book, an article, a movie, or a life experience.

→ When Used: Used to present a new point of view or to present issues that will stimulate thought and discussion.

→ Preparation and Procedure: Plan with other participants on how the report is to be presented. Then have an open discussion on pertinent issues and points of view as experienced.

→ Limitation: Participating members may be unable to relate to others or motivate thinking.

Concentric Circle (a.k.a. Birdcage Format)

→ Definition: A small circle of discussants within a larger circle. The inner circle discusses a topic while the role of the outside circle is to listen. The discussion is then reversed.

→ When Used: Used as a technique to stimulate interest and to provoke good discussion. This is especially useful for getting more response from a group that is slow in participating.

→ Preparation and Procedure: The leader and planning group work out questions that will be discussed by the circle and then by the larger circle.

→ Limitation: Much thought and preparation must be given to the questions for discussion. Room and movable chairs are needed.

Reaction Sheet

→ Definition: Discussion revolves around reacting to ideas in the following ways: ideas that you question, ideas that are new to you, or ideas that really "hit home."

→ When Used: Used as a way to get the group to react. Combine this with other methods.

→ Preparation and Procedure: Prepare the topic and reaction sheets. Explain and distribute reaction sheets, instructing the students to write as they listen, watch, or read. Follow up with a group discussion.

→ Limitation: Topics should focus on the most controversial aspects of the readings only.

Phillips 66

→ Definition: A spontaneous method where six people offer their positions on a topic for six minutes apiece.

→ When Used: Used to add spice and variety to methods of discussion.

→ Preparation and Procedure: Define the topic of presentation. Count off six people and allow six minutes for discussion. Allow for whole group discussion as a follow-up. Permit reassignment of six people.

→ Limitation: Use this form flexibly. It places increased pressure on the more passive students in the class.

Reverse Thinking

→ Definition: Students to express their thoughts by thinking in reverse. Reverse thinking asserts the counter-positive position.

For example, a psychology class might be discussing the idea that people get stressed because they work too hard. The reverse idea is that they get stressed because they don't work hard enough.

→ When Used: Used to gain an insight into others' feelings and to see another point of view.

→ Preparation and Procedure: Prepare the topic. Explain to the group the theory of reverse thinking. Combine with other methods.

→ Limitation: This form might be a challenge to group members.

Role-Playing

→ Definition: The spontaneous acting out of a situation or an incident by selected members of the group.

→ When Used: Used as the basis of developing clearer insights into the feelings of people and the forces in a situation.

→ Preparation and Procedure: Choose an appropriate situation or problem. Have the group define the roles and the general characteristics for each player. Participants enact the scene. Students then observe and discuss such things as specific behavior, underlying forces, or emotional reactions.

→ Limitation: Important: the group leader must be skilled at inspiring the students to play their parts seriously, without self-consciousness.

Picture Making

→ Definition: Display of ideas or principles on a topic through simple illustrations made by group members on the blackboard or large chart paper.

→ When Used: Used as a technique to stimulate interest, thinking, and participation.

→ Preparation and Procedure: The leader and members of the planning group select general principles or questions on the topic that would be suitable to illustrate. The leader divides the group into four or five subgroups. Give each subgroup a statement or problem to illustrate. After completing the picture making, each group shows and explains the picture. Follow this by open discussion.

→ Limitation: Instruction must be clear as to the value of picture making, and adequate materials must be available.

Brainstorming

→ Definition: Offers a technique in creative thinking in which group members storm a problem with their brains.

→ When Used: Used to get new ideas and release individual potentialities in thinking up ideas.

→ Preparation: The leader and members of the planning group select suitable problems or questions on the topic selected by the entire group.

→ Procedure: The leader explains to the group the meaning of brainstorming and the following rules: 1.) Criticism is out of bounds. 2.) The more ideas, the better chance of having some good ones. 3.) Freewheeling is welcomed. The wilder the idea, the better. 4.) Hitchhiking is legitimate. If you can improve on someone else's ideas, then so much the better. 5.) The leader rings a bell when one of the above rules is violated. 6.)The recorder lists the ideas. Then, types the list and brings it to the next meeting.

→ Limitation: This form can be utilized as only a part of the class.

CHAPTER

61

Assessing Discussion Outcomes

How do you know if a discussion has succeeded? So often we content ourselves if the issues that we care about have been aired and considered. This position does not take into account the students' stake. What do they get from the discussion? Tests and essays may reveal some of these gains. But because of the time lag between discussion and evaluation, tests and essays are weak tools for assessing discussion. Similarly, end-of-term course evaluations are so far removed from the discussion itself that they provide only superficial measures, at best. If you are willing to prepare an assessment ahead of time, several effective tools are available.

The following evaluation methods are summarized from a classic text on the rhetoric of discussion, by Barnlund and Haiman (1960). Which one you choose to use will depend on your class goals and the amount of time that you want to spend on evaluation. If you have graduate assistants, assigning them the responsibility to assess, while you focus on the role of discussion leader, can be an effective division of labor. Similarly, if you have a discussion hour attached to a lecture that the graduate assistants conduct independently, having them provide periodic assessments of the discussion can help you give them feedback on their performance. All of these require that you think through how you intend to evaluate the discussion before the discussion actually begins.

Postdiscussion Reaction Sheets

Students can fill out reaction sheets immediately after the discussion. The sheets often involve only a few questions where students can register their reaction to what has just transpired. The students fill out the sheets anonymously. Questions might include any or all of the following:

→ How satisfied are you with the conclusions or decisions we just reached about (name of text)?

→ How productive was this discussion for you in terms of learning new ideas about (name of text)?

→ How orderly and systematic was the class in its overall approach to discussing (name of text)?

→ Did the flow of the discussion permit anyone who wanted to contribute to do so?

→ Did the people assigned to be discussion leaders help or hinder the discussion?

→ Did the text became more complicated to interpret or less complicated to interpret through this discussion?

→ Did the class successfully identify the difference between opinion and fact-based position taking in the text?

→ Did students reveal several positions in the discussion?

→ Were there times when the instructor's intervention interfered with the development of the discussion?

Group Observers

One of the discussion roles that you can establish for students is that of observer. Ask these students to pay more specific attention to the process of the discussion than to its content. They are not prevented from participating, but they do take on the extra burden of assessing the discussion as it unfolds. There are usually two of them. The advantage to the students is that it teaches them to observe the structures of discussion. Once they begin to pay attention to these structures, they develop better responses, and discussion in the class as a whole improves. Every student should have a chance to play observer at least once and preferably twice in the course of the term. Some of the forms of discussion (like the debate, panel, or birdcage formats) enable half of the class to be observers. In very small classes, students can play observers as often as the rotation allows. The observers fill out an evaluation sheet as the discussion unfolds and give it to the instructor at the end. Barnlund and Haiman suggest that observers look for more specific kinds of information about the discussion structure, considering any or all of the following questions:

→ Was the problem investigated in a logical and systematic way, considering the topic and the purpose of the class?

→ At what points did digressions occur? How serious were they? Who was responsible for them? How did the group recover?

→ Was an atmosphere of questioning and attention to facts maintained in the discussion? If not, were the lapses serious or were they justified?

→ Was sufficient information brought to bear on the problem or topic? Were facts tested for reliability? Was good use made of the information available?

→ Did members of the group place too little or too much reliance on authorities? If authorities were used, were they adequately evaluated?

→ Was the problem or topic adequately parsed? That is, were its parts identified and explored broadly and deeply enough, or was analysis superficial and oversimplified?

→ Did the group reason logically? Were fallacies identified? Did the group ever resort to prejudice, name-calling, or exhortation as a substitute for thinking?

→ How insightful was the group in finding a wide range of possible solutions or perspectives? Was consideration given to explanations or viewpoints that were unusual or unorthodox?

→ Did the group periodically summarize its conclusions and implications, so that the participants knew what had been covered and what issues remained to be settled?

→ Did the group make use of earlier discussions when considering possible solutions or perspectives?

→ Was a sufficiently persistent effort made to explore, pursue, and attempt to resolve significant conflicts in point of view?

→ Do you think that the final outcome of the discussion reflected the best thinking of which this group was capable? (1960)

PART
13

The Seminar Classroom

What is a seminar? The terms discussion and seminar are often used interchangeably. However, their Latin roots point to very different qualities. The root of "discussion" is to break apart, while that of "seminar" is insemination and germination. The best way to differentiate a seminar from a discussion is to think of a seminar as a laboratory where the method of discovery is conversation. Seminars get their edginess from the existence of something in the room that is unknown. In a seminar, all the participants are simultaneously teachers and students. The seminar participants usually have an independent base of knowledge. They come in knowing something about the unknown. This knowledge differs from student to student because of their separate experiences in life or in a program of study. What they must learn to share is a common method of discovery. Participants in a discussion, on the other hand, share a common base of knowledge, usually a text, and utilize independent methodologies or readings to interpret or analyze the text. The goal of a seminar is to discover new directions for inquiry through the application of this common methodology. Long before there was case-based instruction or problem-based instruction, there were seminars.

We usually think of seminars as the instructional form of choice for graduate education. In these small classrooms, graduate students teach each other under the watchful eye of an experienced professor, honing their analytic skills by testing arguments against the critical acumen of their peers. The seminar atmosphere is for most graduate students the first to test their skills as analysts and interpreters of complex issues. The emphasis is not about acquiring the knowledge base. Rather, the students spend their time subjecting the knowledge base to critical examination, seeking to uncover and exploit its weaknesses.

The spirit of the seminar is egalitarian; contributors are measured by the quality of their contributions, not their academic rank or research experience. Creating a smoothly functioning seminar can be one of the most creative achievements of a college teacher.

Seminars also have the reputation for frontier-style ethics and cut-throat argument styles. One scholar reminisces about his graduate experience as follows:

> A regular (term-time) event, the "idea;" seminar usually brings together 20 or more participants, around a table, under the chairmanship of an experienced teacher and seminar leader. The chairman introduces, and generally gives moral support to, the speaker, while the audience undertake the role of critics, and may, indeed, ask extremely hostile-sounding questions. . . .However, the seminar is not as unfriendly an occasion as it sometimes seems to visitors unused to its conventions. There is an implicit rule that really severe questioning is reserved for speakers who have shown, in the course of their papers, either that they possess the dialectical skill to handle even the most destructive questioning, or on rare occasions, that they are so bumptious and thick skulled that they are unlikely to comprehend the devastating nature of the questioning they receive. . . .The point is that the seminar is a social occasion, a game, an exchange, an ordeal, an initiation. (Gell 199, 1-2)

Such critical seminars are reserved for the latter years of graduate education and professional conferences, not undergraduate or early graduate education. You want to avoid this atmosphere in a seminar if you expect to meet your course objectives.

It is possible to conduct seminars with first year students. Here, instead of a disciplinary knowledge base, the subject matter that they analyze is their life experiences. They do so with an experienced instructor who provides the analytic tools and explains how to use them. All students who enter a university know a great deal about the world. This is not universal knowledge, the knowledge that universities collect and teach. Instead, it is local knowledge, the knowledge that communities—and especially in the context of first year students, high schools—collect and teach.

These students are very likely to have an exquisite knowledge of contemporary popular music. They may even have developed an ear for genre. They could easily participate in a seminar on the problems of defining musical genres. The various models for understanding genre are supplied by the instructor in the first two weeks. The students spend the rest of the term presenting analyses of specific genres, with musical examples brought to class to provide evidence for the argument. The goal is not to increase the students' knowledge of popular music, though this may be an important outcome for some of them. Instead, the goal is to apply preexisting analytic models, each informed by different theoretical perspectives, to data; construct an argument defending the analysis using the data; present the argument orally; and defend its findings against counter-arguments. Is this an important experience for first-year students to have? Many colleges and universities are increasingly convinced that it is. However, when instructors approach first-year seminars as opportunities for knowledge-based instruction, the seminars fail. They transform into discussions and very little skill development occurs. Only when instructors choose the local knowledge that students already possess as the knowledge base for the course do these classes succeed as seminars.

The seminar classroom has four advantages. It empowers students as independent learners. It emphasizes student-centered learning. It generates novel, synthetic, and/or creative ideas within each student. Finally, the emphasis in the classroom favors method over content. The seminar is the only form of instruction in which the content of the course can be controlled as students practice the methods of inquiry. Hence, the emphasis may be on methods, but a significant increase in the students' knowledge base is possible through seminar courses.

Seminars have four disadvantages. Seminars exaggerate the effects of motivation levels among students. Seminars require students to be prepared and remain engaged over the course of the term. Seminars with students in nonprofessional programs may include significant variation in motivation for the required preparation. Those students with low motivation will listen and take up space but do little more in a seminar format, reducing its effectiveness. Seminars reduce the number of clearly defined moments for evaluating student accomplishment. While it is possible to construct a rubric for evaluating the presentation itself, evaluating the dialogue that follows is more difficult. It requires trying to gauge the quality of the critique and counterargument. Seminars require faculty to tutor methods instead of relating content. This is the main reason why new faculty should not teach seminars. Although they are fresh from successfully applying method to a complex research problem in their dissertations, newer faculty have not yet learned how to communicate the nuances of analysis to others. It will take a few more research projects and conference papers before you develop fluency in describing this most complex of intellectual tasks. Finally, seminars require faculty to share responsibility for course outcomes with less experienced students. We are accustomed to taking all the responsibility for student learning. It requires a great deal of confidence in the chosen methodology to sit back and let the process unfold.

This is not to say that the seminar style denies the instructor the possibility to intervene or participate. On the contrary, the instructor who is not participating only acts as a break on interaction. Effective instructor involvement depends on fitting in, rather than standing out. Most students will acquiesce to the instructor at the slightest hint that the instructor wants to control things. Where one sits, how one speaks, how the roles are assigned, and how the evaluations are handled are the key issues for faculty leadership in seminars.

Strategies for Organizing a Seminar

CHAPTER
62

You organize a seminar around a problem. The problem can be theoretical or methodological. A good seminar problem is one that the instructor cannot solve ahead of time but for which the instructor suspects a solution exists. The skill in designing a seminar lies in the instructor's ability to first envision a rich and complex problem and then break the problem down into potential solutions that he or she assigns students to research. To the extent that the problem remains open to reinterpretation as the students' control of the evidence and methods increase, the seminar will be successful. Designs in which the outcome is predictable will revert to discussions and lose the methodological edginess of the seminar atmosphere.

The problem of seminar design is similar to issues in designing a laboratory. Instructors who are attempting to design one for the first time will find the discussion of the laboratory form of instruction helpful. The outcomes in a laboratory are perverse; the same procedures produce a range of results. Only when the procedures are applied precisely and scrupulously do the results come out as intended. Seminar problems can be perverse in the sense that the problem changes as the students learn more about it. These are known as ill-structured problems. The best of these come directly from newspapers. In one famous example of an ill-structured problem, a business school structured its first-year curriculum entirely on the question of whether a well-known investor should buy a specific oil company. The more the students learned about the investor and the oil company, the more complicated the problem became. They were forced to learn accounting, evaluation of management systems, marketing strategies, and financial analysis to make sense of the evidence they were collecting. In the end, they duplicated a first-year, textbook-based curriculum but with higher levels of retention and application.

An example from a seminar I conducted with seniors in an inter-disciplinary international studies program highlights the relationship between the organizing problem and the individual class meeting themes. The problem was a theoretical one: is it possible to construct a definition of radicalism that will apply to all contemporary political conflicts at the state level? Each of the twenty students chose a country or region experiencing a conflict that was portrayed by the press as radical. They spent the term researching and reporting to each other about the background conditions and situation on the ground in each conflict. The presentations were always contextualized through the central question. Each student had to present at least twice in the course of the term. The presentations, including follow-up discussion by peers, lasted from thirty to forty-five minutes. With one week at the beginning to build familiarity with the analytical model, we exhausted the ten-week term and the final exam period. In the end, each student submitted a paper utilizing their own research and building on the research of two other cases offered in the seminar to argue for or against a universal definition of radicalism. This class was successful because each student's contribution was evaluated not by me, but by its usefulness to the seminar's interest in establishing sound evidence for their argument. These criteria for effective presentations created an atmosphere of rising expectations for student work.

CHAPTER 63

The Seminar Process

Great seminar meetings depend on adequate preparation on the part of all the students. However, the student charged with giving the report bears primary responsibility for finding an angle on the material that engages the other members. Since a seminar is about the application of a common methodology to explore material that originates with the student doing the reporting, that engagement has to balance the need to reiterate the crucial elements in the material with analytic knots for the participants to untie. Successful seminar experiences are not merely discussions led by students. They are collaborative efforts at arriving at novel insights through the creative exchange of ideas among informed participants. The successful student report engenders this exchange. Timing is crucial in such a report. The student must get through the presentation as efficiently as possible, without precluding potential questions or excluding opportunities for participation by others. To this end, the following rubric is useful for structuring the presentation. It is based on the Socratic mode of questioning:

> ► Clarification of the Problem. The student begins by relating the particular problem set to the material under examination. Other participants may find other ways of parsing the problem in relation to the material. Take, for example, a seminar on comparative calendrics in archaeology where the problem refers to whether the development and implementation of calendars in various civilizations had common patterns regardless of where the civilization was located. The common methodology is a hypothesis that all calendrical operations were efforts at control of agricultural production from a political center for the purposes of taxation. Each student is charged with reporting on the application of this hypothesis to a specific civilization. All of the students have a basic knowledge of calendrics in every civilization under discussion. The reporting student develops a deeper understanding of the facts needed to clarify the problem.

▶ Fact Finding. This section of the presentation permits the students to identify the important features of their material. This is where the reporting student provides the seminar with additional facts that were not available in the common material. None of the subsequent steps can occur until the crucial facts that set one civilization apart from the others are identified. Other participants participate in fact finding by attempting to develop their own independent search for pertinent facts to introduce at this stage. Participants may disagree on whether the points raised were the most salient, offering other facts and contextualizing insights. The point of this is not to embarrass the reporter with facts he or she missed but rather to keep the research effort as honest and as complete an examination as possible. Since all the students are dependent on the same field reports, the evaluations of these sources are open for dispute. No source is ever perfectly suited to every problem.

▶ Discovery of Possible Causes of the Problem. Soon after the presentation of the facts, the reporting student must state the best available understanding of the necessary and sufficient causes of the problem. In this example, the basis for calendrical development must be shown to lie in the development of a specific form of the state under local agricultural conditions. The details vary with each civilization and rely on the facts evaluated in the previous section.

▶ Evaluation of Alleged Causes of the Problem. Where the previous section was a statement about the application of the hypothesis to the specific region under discussion, this section is the evaluation of the statement. The question for the seminar is whether the hypothetical relationship between calendrics and political control of agriculture is the best explanation of the facts in this case. Since every case will have its ambiguities, reasonable people can be expected to disagree. These disagreements can fall into different categories, which should be spelled out. The dating of the development of the calendar relative to the growth of a state, the variations in growing cycle, the efficiency of agricultural production, and the esoteric nature of the calendrics can all be in dispute

▶ Discovery of Possible Solutions to the Problem. The disagreement developed in the evaluation section provides the basis for discovering nuances or alterations in the basic methodology to more completely account for the facts. In our example, if central control is only one factor in the development of calendrics, what are the others? If central control is not a factor, how else can the seminar explain the development of the calendar?

► Evaluation of Possible Solutions to the Problem. These hypotheses are then tested against the facts, just as the initial hypothesis was. The two sections on new solutions need not occur sequentially. Often, the participants are so well versed in the discriminating facts that the testing can occur simultaneously with the proposal of new ideas.

In a successful seminar report, the entire group has moved to a more complex understanding of factors, dynamics, interrelationships, and outcomes circumscribed by the initial problem. This is the magic of discovery that seminars make possible. By the end of the term, the initial problem transforms into a mere cipher for what is actually a tangle of highly varied contexts, processes, and outcomes that more accurately and realistically describe the research. The participants leave the seminar more fully equipped to creatively and critically engage the research than they were when the term began.

CHAPTER
64

Evaluating Seminar Performance

Most seminars do not require formal evaluation. These are collaborative classrooms that result in collective products. Students can write up individual seminar reports. To the extent that they serve to remind the instructor of that interaction, reports can serve as evaluative instruments. If the student's work was less than competent for the level of the seminar, then that is immediately apparent during the seminar. Sometimes a dazzling report can make up for shyness during the seminar itself. The seminar grade is not about individual achievement in the traditional sense. It is about individual contributions to group achievement during the seminar meeting.

Not all seminars are as research focused as the examples I provided above. Many include a range of problems that are not connected to each other, even though they may employ the same analytic framework. For example, a seminar on the Whitehead and Russell 's *Principia Mathematica* structures itself through the text with the goal of understanding the work. The presentations are more individualistic, and there is less common ground for the participants to provide additional facts or alternative hypotheses.

A poster fair provides an alternative for engaging seminar students, as long as you can find a space to accommodate the size of the class. You will need tables for the posters to stand on. It is unreasonable to put the posters on a slanted desktop or the floor. Make sure that you inform the school bookstore that you will need trifold cardboard displays for the students in the class at least a semester ahead of time. Otherwise, you can usually find them in art supply stores rather than office supply stores. At the time of this writing they averaged between $6 and $12 apiece.

It is important to give clear instructions about what information students should put on the board. Students should be encouraged to be creative in their use of color and the visual presentation of the data. Posters that rely heavily on text should be strongly discouraged. You might even give a percentage limit—say, no more than 40 percent of the board can be covered with text. During the presentation period, students need not stand in front of their own boards. The board should communicate effectively without requiring additional explanation. Instead, students should be assigned to view and record information about a percentage of the total boards, perhaps with randomly assigned board numbers to encourage them to wander over all the exhibits to find their assigned boards. You can evaluate the boards using a check-off rubric that then becomes a percentage of the total grade on the research assignment; the remainder of the grade belongs to the written research report.

PART 14

The Laboratory Classroom

Any classroom learning experience accomplished through partnered, team-based, or joint efforts among students is a laboratory. Any classroom that features collaborative learning as the primary means of instruction can be called a laboratory. These include:

→ temporary breakout groups

→ cooperative learning exercises

→ problem-centered research teams both in and out of science laboratories

→ student groups working through cases (whether these are text based or audiovisual)

→ simulations and games

→ writing groups (whether these are called peer response groups, class responses, or writing circles)

→ reading circles

→ various forms of peer teaching (including learning cells; supplemental instruction; tutoring circles; technique workshops; and learning communities, such as foreign language tables, freshman interest groups, and student group-initiated research projects)

In this part, I want to focus on six common forms of collaborative learning, even though we do not often describe many of these explicitly as laboratory classrooms. They are:

→ scientific laboratory classrooms

→ classrooms that are organized around problem-based learning

→ classrooms that are organized around case-based learning

→ simulations and games in classrooms

→ film, video, and audio case materials in classrooms, and

→ classrooms that employ fieldwork, service learning, experiential learning, and internships.

This does not exhaust the list of possibilities. These are merely the most common forms.

The boundary between collaborative learning and the ordinary sharing of ideas found in discussions and seminars involves the role of the instructor. There are certainly moments in discussion and seminar classrooms when the learning becomes collaborative, moments when the students take sustained control of the conversation. In a collaborative classroom, the instructor designs a course that moves the responsibility for the activities that will result in learning from the instructor to the students themselves. Instead of serving as the font of information and the means for understanding it, the instructor becomes a tutor and a facilitator.

Collaborative learning is currently the most innovative trend within college classrooms. It is important to understand why this departure from traditional instructional authority is happening. As our classrooms grow more diverse, the cultural differences between instructors and students increase. Efforts to diversify the student body outstrip efforts to diversify the faculty. As faculty with ever more specific research agendas transform the curriculum to enable them to teach what interests them, the students lose focus on the big picture. The curriculum fragments. The prevailing college pedagogy has fallen into a routine of lecture and knowledge-based tests that periodically face a crisis of relevancy, while reinforcing student passivity. In the face of this dislocation between pedagogy and practice, retention rates among the must vulnerable segments of the student body drop. Meanwhile, the reward system places a low priority on outstanding or innovative teaching (Smith and MacGregor 1992). Collaborative learning suggests a corrective to these trends. Collaborative classrooms experience higher completion rates, significantly higher student achievement, and a greater sense of excitement about learning. As accreditation agencies require universities to conscientiously measure educational outcomes, collaborative learning has increased.

Schön (1983) has studied how working professionals use their skills to solve problems and expand on their knowledge base, something he calls reflection through action. His observation bears similarity to Dewey's mantra of learning by doing, but also to Kolb's model of experiential learning (1981). Kolb's description of professional learning maps precisely the qualities of collaborative learning in the classroom:

→ an active, constructive process involving the integration of new knowledge with what is already known;

→ a rich context where information comes in many forms and through different people and channels that require attentive monitoring, criteria-based filtering, and prioritizing of tasks;

→ a diversity of perspectives within the professional community about how the problem could be solved;

→ an open communicative environment that permits for informal consultation, meaning making, and feedback; and

→ a social environment complete with differences in organizational power, ambition, and skills.

Collaborative learning motivates students because they sense that the learning is more real, more professional, than routine college pedagogy.

When professors promote reflection through action, students immerse themselves in the "complexity, uncertainty, instability, uniqueness, and value conflicts which are increasingly perceived as central to the world of professional practice" (Schön 1983). This is the basis for student excitement about collaborative learning. This is why instructors are willing to take the risk to decenter their classrooms and task their students with greater responsibility for their own learning. For the new instructor, there is a learning curve to these techniques. The successes experienced the first time out will be balanced with some nagging failures. The following chapters attempt to identify the best practices for the different collaborative classroom contexts.

Collaborative Learning in the Laboratory?

CHAPTER
65

We think of the laboratory as something that belongs to the natural sciences. A laboratory can be any classroom where students develop practices closely identified with the research methods of a discipline. Students collaborate to inform, reinforce, and critique each other's practices. This can occur in any discipline, since disciplines are defined by their methodology as much as by their dominant question. Laboratories can occur at any level of the curriculum. In my thinking about these classrooms, I include several classrooms not ordinarily thought of as laboratories: writing workshops, group work breakouts for problem-based learning, computer-based instruction in geographic information systems, and archival methods courses conducted in archives. When we see these settings as laboratories, we can structure them more effectively. Similarly, when we reinterpret the traditional laboratory as a variety of collaborative learning, we can develop better ways of assessing what goes on there.

In all laboratories, there is a strong emphasis on the development and application of skills. "We learn by doing," Dewey informs us, "after we have reflected on what we have done" (1938). There are several ways to get students to do things in classrooms and several ways to encourage them to reflect on what they did. Research has shown that students performing actions results in greater control of the knowledge base, rather than weakening it (Coppola et al. 1997, 84-94).

Teaching Strategies for Laboratories

The sciences have had the longest experience with laboratories. As the skill base develops, science instructors have found that they can use laboratories for different educational goals. Starting from approaches that merely shift the demonstration of a principle from the lecture hall to the laboratory to experiments that replicate the efforts of research teams at the professional level, laboratory strategies count among the most methodologically sophisticated of all instructional forms. Domin (1999, 543-47) created the following taxonomy of laboratory designs for the teaching of chemistry. However, these methods can be adapted to any discipline.

Expository Method

This is the familiar "cookbook" method of teaching a laboratory. The results are preordained. The instructional approach involves three steps: the setup, the practice, and the review. The instructor presumes that learning takes place when the correct result is attained. As Hofstein and Lunetta (1982, 201-17) have demonstrated, the correct result can be attained for reasons that have nothing to do with whether any learning has taken place. This method has the advantage of being easily mounted with inexperienced students. It has the disadvantage of not having a reliable form of assessment.

Inquiry Method

In this method, there is no predetermined result. Students work with nonstandard samples. As a result, they arrive at separate results through different skill levels and procedures. The review phase asks students to compare the effectiveness of different methods. These are evaluated according to their validity, reliability, and reproducibility. Even the students who are not able to solve the problem learn from those who can during the review phase, increasing the effectiveness of the experience. As exciting as the inquiry method is the first few times it is mounted, there are just so many different procedures and ways of destandardizing the samples. Over time, there is a tendency for inquiry to morph into exposition. A second difficulty lies in keeping the solutions to the experiments secret from one year to the next. The instructor can keep the laboratory fresh and engaging for all students only through constant redesign. Assessment of the learning in this environment is readily available, both for those who solve the problem and for those who do not.

Discovery Method

This is also known as guided inquiry. It differs from the inquiry method because students hypothesize the results ahead of time. The setup phase includes a discussion of the problem that produces these hypotheses and the methods used to falsify them. This is the guided aspect to the method. The students can derive the methods from previous sessions. You can assess at the end of the setup and during the subsequent review phase. The advantage of the method is that it can easily generate a sense of individual student ownership of a particular method. Students find the search for the undetermined result motivating. Students can work individually or in groups.

Teaching Reasoning Skills in the Laboratory

CHAPTER
67

The laboratory environment excels in challenging students' reasoning skills. Through the various problems they encounter, students endure sustained uncertainty, testing multiple perspectives, all the while reassessing their priorities. In the best laboratories, the instructor actively supports and tutors critical reasoning. The following advice on how to be active in the laboratory draws from Coppola, Ege, and Lawton (1997, 84-94). Although written for chemistry labs, it applies to laboratories in all disciplines.

Assess students' skills and set goals that will challenge them. One cannot know where to begin without greater knowledge of who the students are and what their current reasoning skills are like. The method for initial assessment is no different in laboratories than it is in any of the other classrooms. Your challenge from the initial assessment is to establish goals for each student that you can monitor through the term. Ongoing assessment is easier in the laboratory because the reports them-selves reveal reasoning issues both in the way the student analyzes and discusses the results and in the reasons for attaining nonstandard results.

Ask questions that move students to observe and evaluate at higher orders of reasoning. Along with these goals, you should list one or two forms of questioning that specifically challenge the student to develop further. The idea here is that as the student hears the question repeated, he or she will develop more effective strategies for answering it. You can compare these to questions you have established for each student and adjust them to suit the circumstances. If you had initially assessed the student as higher than subsequent performance indicates to be warranted (a common occurrence), you can shift to asking the lower-stage questions.

Build in unknowns for students to explore. The power of the laboratory as a form of instruction is the thrill of discovery. The different approaches build in opportunities for discovery in different ways, the discovery method incorporating the technique most fully. I have found that the best way to create an atmosphere of discovery is to pick a problem that you have never done before. In subtle ways, instructors telegraph the results to students for familiar problems. Choosing an unfamiliar problem reduces this foreshadowing. This same principle holds true for effective seminars. When students have the opportunity to discover features of the material independently of the instructor's knowledge, they gain more confidence in their reasoning skills.

Leave room in the schedule for students to develop their own experimental paths. The essence of the laboratory experience is that student efforts direct the class time. The attempt to orchestrate events is counterproductive. If an experience is so time consuming that it fills the entire period, it should either be redesigned, split up into parts, or scheduled for a special lab period when the students can devote the necessary time to doing it at their own pace. Rushing teams through a procedure is one of the primary reasons why students fail. This does not mean that you can allow students' attention to wander. There is a difference between redirection by asking questions about the procedure and redirection by pointing out that there are only twenty minutes left. Even the most attention challenged students respond when redirected to a problem rather than to a mere task.

Give advanced students more flexibility in the design. Students who are new to the laboratory need to learn procedures. Students with several years of laboratory experience behind them need to be given more responsibility in developing their own procedures. This is essential for the development of reasoning skills, such as considering ways of generating new information when confronted with both the unfamiliar and the familiar.

When students act like professionals, they learn more. With only a few exceptions (first-year composition), laboratory classrooms are part of major curriculums. Students in the major seek out the trappings of the field: the special communication styles and postures that constitute professionalism. Making professionalism one of the components helps to tap these interests and to connect students to the more arduous tasks. I have found that students respond to difficult challenges when these are introduced as the problems faced by professionals. Their practice in the laboratory becomes practice for those roles.

Collaborative Learning in Problem-Based Classrooms

CHAPTER
68

An innovative use of collaboration is the problem-based learning (PBL) method. This method is similar to the inquiry method in natural science laboratories but is applied to problems in the historical, social, commercial, and behavioral sciences. As with the inquiry method, PBL has no predetermined result. Students work with multiple sources that they develop themselves. As a result, they apply different methods and arrive at separate results. The review phase asks students to compare the effectiveness of different methods used. You evaluate these according to their validity, reliability, and reproducibility. Even the students who were not able to solve the problem learn from those who did, increasing the effectiveness of the experience for everyone. PBL often uses study teams, occasioning a class discussion of what makes for effective group work.

PBL is an attractive alternative to discussion and lecture because it offers students some variety in the classroom. Working on a problem over the course of several weeks or even an entire term engages students. It gives them ownership of the learning. It requires them to be more self-regulating in time and distribution of attention. It is the primary way professionals themselves learn. I was originally drawn to PBL when I created a new course for an interdisciplinary program. I wanted a course that would engage students as totally as possible and stand out from other courses and majors. I wanted to give them the opportunity to experience the excitement of discovery often lacking in the social sciences. I attended a workshop, read the readings that were handed out, and began to apply the principles to my course content. I was entering completely new territory in the classroom, and it was exciting for me. I passed this excitement on to the students. Twenty years later, the course continues to be taught the way I initially designed it, even by other instructors.

Be forewarned! PBL requires the instructor to give up significant amounts of class time to the students' group process. This fact plays havoc with the strongly felt responsibility, especially among newer instructors, to control the amount of content the students learn in a course. PBL teaches students to conduct research efficiently and effectively. It teaches them heightened standards of scholarship and pushes them to adapt more sophisticated and professional stances toward learning. It does so through the use of a limited number of specific content domains, but also at the expense of the student's exposure to extensive content domains. PBL in a survey course is a contradiction in terms.

Problem-based learning has its origins in several different areas. It traces its commitment to active learning to John Dewey. It borrows its case-based method from the Harvard Medical School educational practices of the nineteenth century. The ideas about learning the structure of knowledge, rather than a set of facts, belong to the work of Jerome Bruner, as do the method's strengths in developing intuition, "the intellectual technique of arriving at plausible but tentative formulations without going through the analytic steps by which such formulations would be found to be valid or invalid conclusions" (Bruner 1960). Finally, PBL owes its structure to the simulations and games developed in the 1960s around the intersection of mathematical game theory and linear programming. These offered students the opportunity for discovery within the classroom. PBL is different from a game or simulation because the latter usually are programmed by the developer to demonstrate certain principles, in the case of games, or to develop models for known data, in the case of simulations. In PBL, neither the relevant principles nor the scope of the data is known ahead of time.

Problem-based learning is the most student-centered of all of the classroom methodologies. Because it removes the instructor from structuring the learning, it is appropriate to ask whether this is necessarily better than the instructor-centered models. Research shows that PBL is at least as effective as traditional classroom methods. In the case of retention of information, it may even be better. Medical schools use PBL more thoroughly than other schools. PBL's effectiveness was evaluated with medical students, a highly selective group of learners. Nevertheless, these students master content as well as students in traditional medical courses (Aspy et al. 1993, 22-24). PBL students score higher on professional exams and perform more effectively in clinical residency programs than students from traditional classrooms (Mennin et al. 1993, 616-24; Vernon and Blake 1993, 550-63). Students from PBL curricula handled the interface between scientific problem solving and the emotional and social states of the patients better than traditional students (Albanese and Mitchell 1993, 52-81). Bridges and Hallinger (1991) reason that PBL improves test scores because it improves students' comprehension of contexts more effectively and more quickly than traditional techniques. When students acquire knowledge in a specific context, as opposed to decontextualized facts, it is more easily integrated into long-term memory (Mandin et al. 1995, 186-93).

Strategies for Problem-Based Learning in the Laboratory

Before the PBL exercise can be implemented, the instructor must formulate the problem. A good problem is one that changes the more the student learns about it. It is ill-structured, in contrast to well-structured problems and puzzle problems. For example, a well-structured problem requires "the application of a finite number of concepts, rules, and principles being studied to a constrained problem situation" (Jonassen 1997, 65-95). These problems are also called transformation problems (Greeno 1978, 239-70). These problems offer the student a well-defined initial condition, a known goal, and a limited set of logical operations. These are the most commonly encountered problems in textbooks. The student encounters them as an orderly and finite domain of knowledge. Everything needed to solve the problem is in the book. A puzzle problem is a well-structured problem with a single correct answer where all the elements required for the solution are known, no background knowledge is required (i.e., the information on the preceding pages of the textbook is all that is relevant), and the solution requires using logical, algorithmic processes (Kitchener 1983, 222-32). In an ill-structured problem, on the other hand, the solution is "the object of ongoing controversy, even among qualified experts" (Wood et al. 2002, 277-94). Ill-structured problems are situated in and emerge from a specific context, but one or more aspects of the problem situation are not well specified, the problem descriptions are not clear or well defined, or the information needed to solve them is not contained in the problem statement (Chi and Glaser 1985).

Ill-structured problems are encountered in everyday practice. They are typically emergent dilemmas. Their solutions are not predictable or convergent. They may require the integration of several content domains. For example, solutions to problems such as pollution may require components from math, science, political science, and psychology. There may be alternative solutions to such problems. Because they are situated in everyday practice, they are more meaningful to learners. Other writers on ill-structured problems have observed that they:

→ "appear ill-defined because one or more of the problem elements are unknown or not known with any degree of confidence" (Wood 1993, 249-65);

→ "have vaguely defined or unclear goals and unstated constraints" (Voss 1988, 607-22);

→ "possess multiple solutions, solution paths, or no solutions at all" (Kitchener 1983, 222-32);

→ "no consensual agreement on the appropriate solution, possess multiple criteria for evaluating solutions, possess fewer changeable parameters, have no prototypic cases because case elements are differentially important in different contexts and because they interact" (Spiro et al. 1988; Spiro et al. 1987);

→ "present uncertainty about which concepts, rules, and principles are necessary for the solution or how they are organized, possess relationships between concepts, rules, and principles that are inconsistent between cases, offer no general rules or principles for describing or predicting most of the cases, have no explicit means for determining appropriate action, require learners to express personal opinions or beliefs about the problem, so ill-structured problems are uniquely human interpersonal activities" (Meacham and Emont 1989, 7-22).

These researchers all see a clear difference between the well-structured and the ill-structured problem. We never encounter well-structured problems in real life. We only find them in textbooks.

There are several different ways that you can arrive at an ill-structured problem for your class to research. I have had reasonably good luck with real-world simulations. I set up a request from an authority (me) for a position paper by a group of consultants (the students) on a pressing issue. This might include something having to do with social or political policy. One class in the early 1990s wrote a white paper for then President Vaclav Havel of the Czech Republic on whether his country was wise to accept the terms of an International Monetary Fund (IMF) loan at a time when the decision had not yet been made. This exercise took on real-world implications when, in the final week of the class, a group of Czech parliamentarians visiting Chicago had lunch with the students and debated their position with them. The parliamentarians were impressed, the Czech government responded to the loan just as the students had expected they would, and the students had the experience of defending their position to experts. In the humanities, the real-world simulation could be an effort by a philanthropic group to set up a new book, art, or music prize to honor a type of work not already represented by a prize. They ask the class to submit a report outlining the new prize, as well as setting the criteria and the selection factors for the jury.

Related to such real-world simulations is the character-based simulation. The students are asked to write a response to a historical event of life-transforming proportions from the point of view of an individual in a specific situation. The person should not be historically identifiable, but rather one of the anonymous actors in the affected class. The idea is to understand why there might be a variety of ways for the "person" to write the response. The response should be culturally appropriate.

Problems can also be constructed from headlines—the more sensational, the better. Ask the students to research the background on the story. One of my first PBL classes took the conflict in Azerbaijan and Armenia in 1988 from the headlines and researched the possible strategic responses for the Soviet Politburo. Headline-based problems often reveal gaps in the theoretical literature. The class can be set to work developing the arguments and data to fill that gap. I recently asked a group of students to develop an effective definition of radicalism to characterize the extreme positions in any national political arena. Using the team-based research, they were successful.

Applying Problem-Based Learning in the Classroom

CHAPTER 70

How you pose the problem has a lot to do with the effectiveness of the PBL exercise. I took the following rubric for assessing the quality of PBL problems from Coppola and Lawton (1995, 1120-22) (in italics) and added comments on my own experience with these points.

Pose a problem in the form of an understandable question.

Once you have formulated the problem in your mind, you must translate it into a form the students can handle. Always begin with a simple question, such as: Should the Czech Republic accept the terms of an IMF loan? Should there be a national-level endowed prize for graffiti? As a newly emancipated black woman in Kansas in 1866, what do you tell your children about how the federal reconstruction policies will affect their lives? After posing the question, give the students just enough background information to help them frame their research. This includes limiting the geography, language, dates, and form of the response. Most importantly, you need to direct them to the knowledge domains they may have to research to solve the problem. With that last example about the black woman in Kansas, the knowledge domains would include Kansas geography; people's experiences of events before, during, and after the Civil War; the social organization of slavery; the agricultural economics of frontier life; the power relations between freed slaves and former slave owners, veterans of each army, and men and women; and the ideologies of race, frontier, and religion as these shaped everyday life on the prairie. Exactly how you want to tip students' attention toward these topics without actually indicating all this specificity is the art of PBL question formation. I would simply say that they must pay attention to the geography, history, economics, social organization, politics, and worldviews of all the people involved in this woman's life and leave it at that. Then, during the in-class tutoring, I would ask questions that would help the groups find their way more efficiently to the particular domain.

Pose a problem that is too large for a single person to answer alone in the time available.

As I hope is evident from all the examples I have given so far, the scope of the problem ought to be impossibly vast. The whole point is to have a challenge that cannot be met without relatively large investments of time and attention. It is certainly possible to scale down PBL problems to their specifics, but this merely does the discovery portion of the laboratory for the student. It keeps control of the problem in the hands of the instructor. In a student-centered classroom, the students control the direction for learning. The large problem defines an expansive unexplored territory for the students to wander through.

Pose a problem that can be approached from a variety of vantage points and strategies.

Real-world simulation accomplishes this. It becomes more difficult when the problem is an attempt to fill in a theoretical gap or to imitate ordinary classroom processes without the immediate leadership of the instructor. Thus, a reading circle, several students committed to reading and discussing texts together over the course of the term, is an effective discussion technique but does not qualify as problem-based learning. There is no problem. The multiple-perspective qualities and strategic prioritization challenges of PBL are what give it its strength in developing advanced reasoning skills. Reducing the ambiguity of the challenge undermines this strength.

Pose a problem that is open to experimentation.

Students learn from mistakes, just like everyone else. These exercises must offer the opportunity to fail, and these opportunities have to be safe. For that reason, you evaluate the process more heavily than the product. I have found that students follow leads that ultimately prove to be dead-ends. They speak of these blind alleys in their self-evaluations as frustrating but important to the overall experience. One student said that recovering from a wrong strategic decision early on in the process built the team's confidence. If you make the exercise too safe for the students, they will not take risks. PBL demands risk taking.

Organize groups to work on the same problem with opportunities to compare at strategic moments.

Because the problem is so large, the students must collaborate. There are several different ways the collaboration can unfold. Students can post their research on an electronic discussion board for other students to use. Over time, students discover a specialized niche in the problem that they can own. Students can be formed into research groups that strategize the division of research labor, meet to analyze the results, and peer edit each other's reports. I always give groups access to each other's information. Since I, rather than the students, usually choose the groups, making the teams compete against each other only leads to hoarding of sources and a breakdown in the research process. But by giving all groups access to each other's electronic communication or written reports, the class benefits from the total research activity.

The solution to the problem is always more problems, not a specific solution.

If you have chosen a problem that has a single correct answer, you will defeat the students' efforts in a very dramatic way. There is nothing more deflating and demoralizing than for students to get to the end of a demanding effort, only to find that the answer was staring at them all the time. They will feel tricked and abused. When they get to the end of a satisfying problem, on the other hand, they have developed a position that satisfies them, given the available information. They have also found how fragmentary and incomplete that information is. They still have several questions they formulated at the beginning that they have not brought to a satisfactory conclusion. They also have several questions that developed only in the last stages of their efforts. Students who end up in this state of partial satisfaction will have succeeded in the exercise.

You cannot be the expert on the problem.

The less you know about the knowledge base that is most specific to the problem, the better the experience for your students. You should tell them that you are not going to be able to help them on questions of fact, because you do not know the facts. Instead, your expertise comes from having lived in an intellectual environment of enduring uncertainty for several more years than they have. From that perspective, you will help them develop methods to deal with this world. I call this tutoring the method instead of teaching the knowledge.

Assigning Literature in Problem-Based Learning

CHAPTER

71

In PBL, students work in their teams during class meetings. For inexperienced students I have found that a hybrid of the PBL laboratory with the discussion classroom works best. I give over one quarter of the class meetings to the discussion of articles or book chapters that illustrate analytic applications the students can use. By seeding the PBL process with a variety of theoretical approaches, I am able to help the students interpret their research through different lenses, introduce them to literature they would not easily find, provide models of analysis (application of theory to data), and assess the quality of their reading and written summary skills. The theory component in the PBL classroom serves these purposes, and I recommend incorporating a similar component in any PBL laboratories you set up.

I assess summaries of their reading every week. In these summaries, they identify the main idea and the supporting evidence. Their summaries allow me to identify the strength and weakness of individual students. I can then supply them with targeted feedback.

If you choose to assign readings for these purposes, keep the readings short. Students do so much reading in PBL classes that even fifty more pages a week can be onerous. I try to keep the readings to between twenty and forty pages, from at least two and sometimes three different authors, all connected through a theme or theoretical approach.

Framing the Students' Learning in Problem-Based Learning

CHAPTER
72

In PBL, the instructor moves from group to group, listening to, questioning, challenging, encouraging, and supporting the students' efforts. As with previous sections, I will discuss a rubric developed by other practitioners, in this case Wales and Nardi (1982), adding descriptions of my own practices to their points. The rubric comprises statements you make to the students to guide them through the research process on the problem. As a professional scholar, you do these things automatically. They are part of your ordinary practices. Students do not do these things until you teach them to do so. By being open about the process and articulating the steps to them, you help students to mark their progress in uncharted territory.

State the problem and establish a goal that will be pursued in resolving it.

Have students spend the initial hour on the problem, focusing on various ways the problem can be stated. Have them keep track of how different ways of articulating the problem imply different goals. At the end of the session, the group should give a clear statement of what the goal is and how they will know when they achieve it. As this segment ends, you should remind them not to commit to the language they just developed and that the goals may be modified as they learn more about the problem.

Gather information relevant to defining the problem and understanding the elements associated with it.

If the class is to be divided, the second meeting involves putting the students in their groups (cf. chapter 75 below), developing some group-building exercises and setting them to work strategizing their information gathering. Their goal is to figure out how to define the knowledge areas contained in your formulation of the problem. To do that, they must parse the problem, circling all of the relevant nouns that might reveal important information. A list of these areas serves as the agenda for the next few group meetings. Active groups are the most interesting to watch, but they need your attention less at the beginning than the ones having trouble getting started. You can prod them along by asking them what kinds of specialists they might want to consult and what those specialists studied that made them experts. At the end of the meeting, each member of the group should have a specific task he or she needs to accomplish and report on by a specific date and time.

Generate possible solutions.

You should actively encourage hypothesizing about the solution. However, you should also caution students not to attach themselves to the potential hypothesis but rather to treat it skeptically. It is more important for them to think about what evidence would reject the hypothetical solution than it is to generate evidence that would support it. Hypothesizing should begin as the number of reports begins to accumulate on the discussion board. Hypothesizing is one of the ways to generate discussion about the reports that will lead to further questions.

List possible constraints on what can be accomplished as well as factors that may facilitate getting a solution accepted.

Be specific about discussing a hypothesis. To be worthy of research time and reporting, the hypothesis must have identifiable sources of data. There must be few constraints on accessing this data within a reasonable amount of time. The research time of the members cannot already be committed to other lines of development. Too many hypotheses at the same time diffuses group efforts. You should get the students to list all of these factors necessary to give a hypothesis priority, even if that means postponing the decision of whether to pursue the hypothesis until after more data reports.

Choose an initial or possible solution using criteria that an acceptable solution must meet.

The criteria can include tangible and monetary costs and benefits, the likely acceptance of the solution by others, or disciplinary criteria normally applied to such problems. Once the group has decided that there are ready sources of data and the research time available for a particular hypothesis, they should establish criteria for rejecting it. Encourage students to think about the relationship between the hypothesis and a potential solution again. They did this initially when they began to formulate the hypothesis. Now that they are committed to developing evidence around this line of development, they need to have criteria to assess their efforts. You must ask them to consider carefully and formally how they will know if the hypothesis is wrong. They should list as many ways as possible. The members charged with developing the evidence need to keep that list in mind.

Analyze the important factors that must be considered in the development of a detailed solution.

What has to be done, who does it, when should it happen, and where the solution would be used are possible factors to explore. I call this the completeness factor in tutoring. I want to encourage students to be broad in their interpretation of acceptable solutions. This means exploring cross-disciplinary solutions. Students are more comfortable with structural factors and less comfortable with issues of agency. They are happy to develop knowledge of the structural issues because these are the most easily accessible. For that reason, I try to formulate problems that require equal attention to agency and structure. Then, during the tutoring process, as their knowledge of structure begins to increase their comfort level with the problem, I begin to ask more about agency:

- → Who is going to do this?
- → Who is this person?
- → Why them and not someone else?
- → What do they know about the problem?
- → What do they not know?
- → How does their knowledge affect their actions?
- → Where are they in relation to the problem now?
- → Where will they be in relation to the problem after they act?
- → When will they act?
- → What happens if they delay?
- → When they act, will their actions affect others near them, and
- → How will those nearest persons respond?

Most of the answers to these questions will be hypothetical when I first pose them. As the students struggle to develop evidence to test their suppositions about agency, a fuller, more realistic solution becomes possible.

Create a detailed solution.

The solution to a problem is not a single sentence. It is a scenario, a description of a set of factors that are set in motion by certain actions and yield specific outcomes. The scenario can be written as a white paper or policy statement, as a letter to a trusted friend or as a diary entry. Even though the form of the final solution will vary with the problem, the student's self-evaluation should include their reflection on how they used details in formulating their solution.

Evaluate the final solution against the relevant criteria.

As the research process nears its end, encourage the students to describe to you how they applied the criteria to evaluate their hypotheses. They should hear themselves doing this. In the flow of their own internal process, they were evaluating without speaking their thoughts out loud. Articulating helps to make the process concrete to students. Make sure when they do this that they return to their notes describing the criteria. Show your approval of their accomplishments.

Recommend a course of action and ways to evaluate the recommendation.

No research effort is finished without paying attention to what happens next. Depending on the problem, students may want to discuss what the actor would do under different conditions. They may want to propose directions for further research for themselves. They may want to discuss ways of publicizing their results or reporting on their research to others. Allowing them to follow through in this way recognizes their ownership of the process.

To summarize your role in the process, you should expect to tutor the groups in the following features of research:

→ Relating problems to their potential solution,
→ Employing hypotheses to develop a line of evidence,
→ Setting priorities for effort by re-evaluating hypotheses, and
→ Developing further lines of development.

A note on the timing of constructive criticisms: timing is important in introducing these challenges to the students. If you try to do it too fast, they will be overwhelmed. You have to wait for their control of the information to develop before pointing out gaps in the evidence. If you do so too soon, you will overwhelm them, stress will increase, and motivation will lag. Trust the process. Most PBL exercises never reach completion. If students only make partial headway in your class, they will be better equipped to move through the initial stages quicker the next time they face such a problem. I try to do at least two separate problems in a term, rather than one long one. By limiting each problem to a third of the term, I can observe how well they carry over the lessons on research learned from the first project to the second project and still have a third of class time for structuring discussions and housekeeping issues.

A note on note-taking technology: I have found that giving each group an easel with a full easel pad and several colored markers helps them to focus on the details. Someone from each group brings the easel to class from its storage place and returns it there after class. Over the course of the term, the easel pad or text file archives the development of the discussions around the problem, helping the students to see which strategies worked and which ones did not. You should insist on accurate and careful note taking as you move around the groups or as the discussion unfolds within the class as a whole. Technology-rich schools may have electronic mechanisms for accomplishing the same thing, such as:

tablet PC "sketches" of the notes that are then sent in portable document format to the group members, a group blog to which a notetaker posts the features of the discussions wirelessly from the classroom, or a twitter stream with the group's hash code.

A note on reporting technologies: note taking records information developed in class, whereas reporting is a record of information developed outside of class. The technological problem for reporting is the efficient and timely distribution of the information. To be useful, the reports have to be available to everyone at least twenty-four hours before the meeting on the problem. Having printed pages available at a specific location would work if all the students lived on campus. However, this technique discriminates against commuters, who have to make a special trip, often on weekends, to get the material. Email is OK but notoriously affected by server issues, addressing errors, overstuffed post office boxes, and document incompatibility issues. These problems are greatly reduced by using an electronic bulletin board. Almost all schools offer such bulletin boards as part of their course management software, like Blackboard. The advantage of the discussion board is that students can post their report documents, which are then visible to any class member with access to the Web. Students can access the reports anywhere they happen to be: at home, on campus, in a public library, at work, at an Internet café, et cetera. The latest generation of these discussion boards are very easy to use, and even the most technologically challenged students can learn how to use them. The reports do not disappear until the class is archived. Students can refer back to previous reports as the term continues. All the preparation for a group meeting has to take place before class. You should never allow a class or group to spend class time reading handouts or texts to themselves, searching for things to talk about. The only things that students should bring to class are notebooks. Class time should be devoted to strategizing, hypothesizing, and assessing.

Tutoring Group Process in Problem-Based Learning

CHAPTER

73

There is more to your role as tutor than advancing the research agenda. You must also tutor the group process. This begins with various icebreaking and community-building exercises. It does not end there. You must teach students to focus their attention, to organize their discussion, to keep records, and to evaluate their efforts. In short, you tutor them on managing the group process.

Several formal heuristics are available to help you do this. What the heuristics do is give students specific tasks to accomplish and specific questions to ask themselves as they discuss the reports they read the previous evening. I will discuss three of them, although the variations on these heuristics are endless. They are known by their acronyms. The first is FINL, which stands for Facts-Ideas-Info Needed-Learning Needed. The students use the heuristic as follows: One student divides the easel pad page, tablet screen or portion of the blackboard into four columns. At the top of each column, the recorder writes the terms in order: "Facts," "Ideas," "Info Needed," and "Learning Needed." The recorder writes facts, ideas or questions that various members offer after getting the group to agree where it should be put. Evidence for the evaluation of hypotheses is listed under Facts. Before an item can be placed under Facts, the students must answer this question: On what authority do we know this to be a fact? The recorder lists the hypotheses themselves under Ideas. The recorder draws a box under each statement in the Ideas column, to indicate that criteria for evaluating the hypothesis must eventually be added. The box should be big enough to accommodate several legibly written phrases. The recorder lists potential sources of evidence that could possibly be used to evaluate the hypotheses under Info Needed. The recorder draws lines to indicate to which hypotheses in the Ideas column the sources refer. The recorder includes, under Learning Needed, any additional skills that might be required. These should have some sort of annotation explaining how they are relevant. FINL produces a detailed narrative record of the research process. It is not ordinary note taking, and it is not a complete transcript of the discussion. Group members should use the techniques described for taking notes during discussions for their own notes. The recorder is constantly flipping pages back and forth to refer to different stages in the development of an idea. Maintaining the discipline of FINL is very difficult for students encountering PBL for the first time. It is time consuming, exhausting, detailed, and precise, and it requires patience. These are also the heuristic's strength. It is particularly useful for projects completed within a few weeks. You decide how much discipline is appropriate for the class.

Another heuristic, developed by Champagne et al. (1980, 1074-79), is known as POE, for Predict-Observe-Explain. Although not as rigorous as FINL, POE has the virtue of keeping the hypotheses separate from each other. In this heuristic, the recorder divides the easel pad page into three rows. The middle row occupies half the page and the top and bottom rows take a quarter of the page each. The top row is labeled "Predict" (P), the middle "Observe" (O), and the bottom "Explain" (E). As students formulate hypotheses, the recorder writes them in the top row, once the group has agreed on the exact wording. The group develops criteria for evaluating each hypothesis ("How will we know if it is wrong?"), after which the recorder writes it in the Observe space, leaving room to append supporting and falsifying evidence after each criterion. The final row is reserved for the results of testing the hypothesis. As with FINL, POE is not a substitute for students keeping their own records of the flow of the discussion. This technique is particularly effective in complex projects that could generate many lines of development.

A final heuristic is provided by Tien and Rickey (1999, 318) and is referred to as MORE, for Model-Observe-Reflect-Explain. It is similar to POE. Model is synonymous with Predict. Tien and Rickey add Reflect to separate the evaluation criteria from the observations. Otherwise, students employ the heuristic the same way as POE.

Hypotheses are difficult to establish at the beginning of the research effort. Students are still evaluating the problems and strategizing ways of accumulating information. You may want to let students use the easel pad in any way they want until they have several reports to work with and you are ready to push them toward hypothesis development. Then, you can introduce these heuristics.

Whichever heuristic you use, you need to describe it to the students and spend time in the first few class periods reminding them to use it. There will be resistance. The discipline will appear alien and their familiar practices more comforting, especially in the face of a daunting problem. Ask them to indulge you for a few team meetings so they can discover for themselves the advantages in this sort of record keeping.

Managing Team and Group Research Dynamics

CHAPTER

74

Most students come to the PBL classroom with no prior experience in research teams. They have played on sports teams and understand team-work in that context. Research teams are not playing games There is a grade at the end of the term, and the students will have questions about the relationship between team performance and that grade. There are very few classroom situations in which students know the variation in each other's skills, background knowledge, and motivations as much as when working on research teams. Personality conflicts, along with race, gender, and sexuality issues and communication styles, work to under-mine group efforts. You are the only one who sees the larger picture. It is your responsibility to create groups with the highest potential for success and to help students manage conflict when it arises. Fortunately, there is experience that you can draw on to accomplish this.

There are three levels of collaboration in PBL classrooms, informal learning groups, formal learning groups and study teams. Informal learn-ing groups are temporary and their composition has a random quality. These groups form when you tell the class to turn to their two nearest neighbors in order to accomplish a task. When the task is over, the groups dissolve. A student who is uncomfortable with a particular classmate will sit in a different part of the room in the future.

Formal learning groups are more enduring. You paid attention to how they formed. The groups may complete their task in a single class, such as when performing a particular experiment, or they may extend over several weeks, as in a short-term PBL challenge. After the task is finished, the groups dissolve.

Study teams or learning communities are set up to function over a long run, such as an entire term or an entire year. The members support, encourage, and assist each other. They do not dissolve and re-form. For this reason, great care has to be given to how they will form, how they will build trust among their members, and how they will resolve conflicts (Johnson et al. 1991). Study teams are preferred for PBL because their enhanced collaboration leads to more intensive and effective research.

Remove as much anxiety over grading as possible. Explain the objectives of the group process. Tell students that they will not be left to their own devices. You will provide them with a means of getting started, a way of knowing when the task is done, and a method for how to get there. Acknowledge that conflicts over effort will arise. Give students some sense of how they might handle these conflicts. There is discussion of this at the end of this chapter. Describe the difference between grading on process and grading on product. Explain criteria-based grading, how it grades students against a set standard and not against each other. You cannot give the students copies of your grading rubric in this class design because it will include benchmarks for how far each student got in the research process. This would give them too many shortcuts and take away the opportunity to experiment. You must talk about the way the self-evaluation will figure in the final grade.

Realize that students lack group skills because they have no prior experience with active and tolerant listening, supporting each other without patronizing or ego-tripping, and the giving and receiving of constructive criticism. You should choose community-building exercises that help students to practice these skills. Taking time at the beginning of the term to do this properly can result in much more efficient learning, more than making up for the time spent. Just as no sports team can play the game without practicing teamwork, research teams require preparation.

Avoid the pitfalls that make it difficult for groups to succeed. Based on extensive surveys of students, Feichtner and Davis (1992) conclude that the factor that has the greatest impact on whether group work will produce positive or negative student reaction is the degree to which activities and assignments are perceived as being relevant to the content of the course. The instructor controls these perceptions through the way the group work is structured. In particular, they advise the following:

When forming groups, do not allow students to form their own groups or deliberately create homogeneous groups; do not establish groups that are either too small (three or fewer members) or too large (eight or more members); and do not dissolve and reform groups on a frequent basis, such as after each activity or simulation. When formulating grading policies, do not minimize the extent to which group performance affects students' grades; do not limit group work's influence to less than 20 percent of the total grade (or base a very large proportion of the grade (60 percent or more) on a single assignment; and include peer evaluation in the grading. Structure the group assignments so that students cannot easily figure out a way to work independently. Do not have the group work turned in as late as possible in the term; give yourself time to provide feedback while there is still an opportunity to talk about it. When planning group activities and assignment,

+ assign at least two class presentations;
+ assign at least two cases or written reports;
+ avoid group exams; and
+ provide adequate class time for group work.
  (Feichtner and Davis 1992)

On this last point, I usually provide two thirds of the class time per week to group work. I want to see the groups working. For that reason, I ask them not to meet outside of class. This also reduces the problem of group members not being able to attend out-of-class meetings because of schedule conflicts.

Give students the tools to manage conflict. It is not sufficient to tell them to just get over it. You need to give them effective mechanisms for diffusing conflict. For example, offer students a contract that lists the obligations and the deadlines (Connery 1988, 2-4). If students know exactly what will be expected of them, and they have signed on to accept these responsibilities, they are more likely to follow through. Breach of the contract can be sanctioned within the group for minor offenses like a single missed deadline and by the instructor for continuing malfeasance. A sample contract might include some or all of the following parts:

+ Commitment to work as an active member of the team;
+ Agreement to provide assistance, support, and encouragement to group members and other teams in the course;
+ Agreement on meeting deadlines set by the group;
+ Agreement to prepare by reading reports before the group meeting;

→ Agreement to fulfill deadlines by posting reports in an agreed-upon place (e.g., an electronic bulletin board, email, etc.);

→ Agreement to attend all group meetings on time;

→ Agreement to include the following information in the report:

  › how and where the research materials were accessed,

  › a summary (following a rubric) of the research materials,

  › discussion of what was not found, and

  › discussion of the relevance of the material to the immediate issues and long-term issues of the project;

→ Agreement to attend all meetings of the group in class;

→ Agreement to participate in online chats with the group at scheduled times;

→ Agreement to serve as recorder when asked;

→ Agreement to retrieve or return the easels to and from the storage room;

→ Agreement to communicate openly about any problems with the research or the efforts of other group members, either in group meetings or through email, the electronic bulletin board, or a chat session.

These points make the participant aware of what is expected, while outlining solutions to problems that may arise. If you use this contract, you must put it in the syllabus and carefully describe how you will handle sanctions if a student violates the contract. This will also insulate you from a grade challenge if you have to lower a grade or fail a student for a breach of the contract. Knowing that your team members are counting on you to uphold your contract serves as a powerful motivator for students to embrace teamwork (Kohn 1986).

Forming Work Groups in a Collaborative Classroom

There is no ideal group size. Instead, there is an ideal range of five to seven. For PBL exercises of short duration, six is preferred because smaller groups can organize themselves quickly. Participation of the entire group over the short term is better to assure and monitor in groups of six. With teams of five, the work becomes almost unbearable. If one person in a group of five drops out, the remaining four will have great difficulties completing the project. For longer-term PBL exercises, the upper range of seven or eight members works best. These larger teams take more time to organize. They are more difficult to monitor, and it is possible for a student to remain inactive for a longer period. Large teams have more insulation against dropouts. Most importantly with long-term projects, large teams are likely to have a more efficient distribution of tasks, reducing ennui and burnout in the later part of the project. Teams that are formed with nine or more members have serious organizational challenges. Unless the students are experienced in group work, the team will tend to split into smaller internal groups. Large groups need more informal lines of authority. They cannot function without some students becoming leaders in some instances. Finally, the time required to digest reports generated in a very large team is daunting. Fewer reports, read over a shorter period of time and discussed by a smaller group, generate more satisfying experiences with the research.

There is no perfect way to form groups. This having been said, there are ways to minimize the potential problems and to guarantee all the students in the class an equal shot at success. In the most successful group formations, each team will reflect the variation in the skills and knowledge base of the class as a whole. This variation exists on multiple dimensions. Some dimensions, like interpersonal skills, may be out of sync with other dimensions, like analytic skills. The problem for the instructor is deciding which dimensions of the variation to pay attention to and which to ignore. Exacerbating the problem is the timing of group formation. It must take place early in the term, before the instructor has a reasonable understanding of the variation in student abilities.

Group formation based on randomizing the students is susceptible to the distortions that occur when the variations in student skills are magnified by small initial sample sizes. Forming five teams of eight students from a class of forty using some randomizing procedure (such as counting off by fives and then forming into teams based on ones, twos, etc.) will result in the following:

→ One team will perform beyond your expectations.

→ One team will underperform your expectations. This one will include skilled students who then resent the process that forced them to produce results in which they could not take pride.

→ Three teams will meet your expectations.

Randomizing the selection of the teams is the least successful way of forming the teams, though it may be reasonable for informal learning groups that dissolve and re-form more frequently.

Second in order of ineffectiveness is what I call the Playground technique. Here the instructor selects several members of the class to serve as captains. This works best in cohort-based curriculums. The captains select the other members of their teams by calling people out, often with the advice of the members they have already chosen. This technique subordinates the process of randomization to one of social foreknowledge of the class by the captains. This knowledge may be extensive and result in as reasonable a distribution of multidimensional skills as any other technique. If all of the students are strangers to each other, the process is hardly different from counting off.

If the students are relative strangers to each other, have the students produce candidacy statements. These are brief, one-paragraph statements where students respond to this prompt: "If selected for your team, I would bring the following strengths and qualities to our research efforts." With these statements in hand, the instructor could distribute the class members among the teams reflecting the diversity of self-assessments in the statements. This method depends on students having a sense of what they might bring to the team. If they have never been on a research team before, they will not know if they have particular strengths. Their statements, with few exceptions, will read as vague, tentative self-promotions.

Several inventories are available for instructors who are comfortable using them. Most involve the cost of preparing the results. The best known is the Belbin Self-Perception Inventory. It is based on a book by a British psychologist on the success and failure of management teams

(Belbin 1981). At approximately $25 per student, it is also the most expensive solution. There is a version available for people aged sixteen to twenty-three. This one is a bit less expensive and likely to be more meaningful. It is worthwhile to learn about the inventory and especially the characteristics of the roles that people play on collaborative teams from Belbin's website (http://www.belbin.info/).

A less expensive approach, approximate $10 per student, is the Management Team Roles-indicator (MTR-i). Developed by another British psychologist, the MTR-i is based on the Myers-Briggs Type Indicator (Myers 2002). The Myers-Briggs is commonly available and in the public domain. If you do not have a copy, ask around the student services office, career center, or the education school on campus. You can score it yourself. The website has a useful chart that helps you to convert ordinary Myers-Briggs personality types to their group types (http://www.myersbriggs.org). A review of the scale's effectiveness is available (Snyder 2000). If you do use the Myers-Briggs instrument, one study argues that diversifying the groups on the two central dimensions of Intuitive-Sensing and Thinking-Feeling benefits the outcomes (Miller, Trimbur, and Wilkes 1994, 33-44).

The Cognitive Styles Model of Gordon and Morse (1969, 37-49) is based on two dimensions, remote association and differentiation, derived from studies of creativity in organizational behavior. Remote association refers to that aspect of creativity where rapid, nonlinear, and intuitive associations predominate in thinking. Students who score high on this scale and low on differentiation are the problem solvers. Differentiation is a gross measure of multi-perspectival thinking and prioritization habits that permit the students to fix upon and identify discrepancies and gaps in arguments. Students who score high on this scale and low on the remote association scale are the problem finders. Those who score high on both are problem integrators, and those who score low on both scales are problem implementers. For group work in courses with extensive support of creative reasoning as one of its goals, this way of creating mixed groups is worth exploring.

The preceding models all assume that heterogeneity in the initial group composition is a key to effective group functions and student satisfaction. The advantage to these personality inventories is to create as much variety and as little competition for preferred roles as possible. These take time to analyze. A group of balanced personality types alone cannot assure team effectiveness. Nevertheless, if the team must stay together over a long series of exercises, it is worthwhile to make some effort to understand the personality dynamics of student groupings, as long as the cost is not prohibitive.

A final approach to forming groups is the Group Life Model of Bennis and Shepard (1956, 415-57). In their view, any effort to try to build in heterogeneity in study teams is moot because all groups will develop their own tensions and resolutions regardless of the mix of personalities involved. What groups really need is lots of interaction time. This model describes a series of phases that groups go through. Integration and effectiveness grow through common experience. In the first phase, the group is dependent on authority, like the instructor, causing the members to either identify with the authority or reject it. This sets in motion a dynamic of conflict within the group as the dependents and the counter-dependents struggle for control. The phase ends as the group develops its own internal authority structure and the members' roles reintegrate around this new structure. In the second phase, the emphasis shifts to the problems of interdependence and the pitfalls of the intimate knowledge that the members acquire of each other. It begins with a feeling of positive harmony and optimism. There then follows an inevitable disenchantment as ordinary human limitations begin to mount in the face of the research problem. The phase ends with the group developing a tolerance for internal diversity and capability among its members, generating subgroups, stable status hierarchies, and leadership roles. Implementing the Group Life Model requires that the members not be moved around once groups are constituted. The process of developing a strong working relationship takes time (Bennis and Shepard 1956, 415-57). Shuffling groups prevents them from maturing and keeps them dependent on the instructor.

Do the students' previous grades predict how they will contribute to a group? Assuming you have access to the students' GPAs, information instructors should not have access to, you might try to combine students at different levels without, of course, identifying what you are doing. The logic for doing so is that group-building exercises will increase the students' sense of team spirit and the higher-achieving students will help out the weaker ones. The chance of weak students predominating in a group, with the potential for group underachievement, is minimized, as is the potential for concentrating the overachievers in another group. In my experience, the results for this procedure are no different from randomizing the selection. Grades do not measure what we need to know in forming groups.

Finally, you could use your assessment of reasoning skills as your criteria for forming the groups. This removes the ethical challenges of knowing the students' GPAs before the class starts. It avoids the costs and validity issues of the personality profiles. It recognizes an important dimension of variation. The groups formed by seeding the highly skilled among the lesser skilled builds in models of reasoning at the group level. Most importantly, the process is entirely in your hands. As the group processes unfold, you can see the results and modify your future assessment of reasoning. When you use this approach, your group formation decisions should improve over time. The other techniques require you to repeat the same mistakes every time you implement the techniques.

While I would like to say that there is never a good reason for changing the groups after they have started to organize, that would be unrealistic. This is a very short list of good reasons for doing so. Student preference to work with their friends is not one of them. Groups with organizational difficulties should not be altered. Students should be made to confront the organizational issues and work through them, even if this diminishes their satisfaction with the process. If there is open sharing of the findings between the groups, no student will be harmed by participating in an underperforming team. The few occasions in which I moved students around had to do with personality conflicts that persisted in spite of the best efforts of the group to resolve them. On two occasions, the conflict entered the classroom from outside. On another occasion, one student, anxious over the outcome of the project, attempted to monopolize the process and could not be convinced to take a more collaborative stance. The difficulty is to figure out who to move and where to move them. These teams are not a reality show on television, and team members do not have the right to vote one of their members "off the island." That is your responsibility.

Before deciding whom to move, you must decide how to leave the groups in the best possible position after the change. The easiest way to do this is to make a trade with another group. That way, the total sizes of the teams remain the same. If you are using a contract for individual responsibility and the conflict has nothing to do with fulfilling that contract, you can use this information to ease the entrance of the student you chose to move into a new group. If the contract is violated, then the student is subject to whatever sanctions you described in the syllabus, including failing the course. In this case, you do not have to put the student anywhere. The student simply leaves the class. The state of events ought to have progressed to a well-defined stage before you act on any of these strategies. Resist the temptation to intervene early. Give the conflicts at least two or three weeks to resolve.

Dealing with Student Complaints in Group Research

CHAPTER **76**

Students will complain that you are not meeting their classroom expectations because of their lack of experience with group research. Careful attention to their complaints is an important part of enhancing the learning experience. Instead of dismissing these complaints or asserting your authority to construct the classroom any way you wish, consider the strength of commitment to goals and priorities that students describe when they complain. The surveys by Cooper and Associates (1990) inform the following discussion and confirm my own experience in dealing with students in PBL courses over the last twenty years.

Initial complaints are based on students' inexperience with your method. They will argue that they do not like to work in groups. Some may have had bad experiences with groups in high school. They were thrown together and asked to work as a team, with little monitoring and no method. Based on this experience, they will argue that students simply do not work well in groups. They are confident they can do the work on their own, no matter how large the problem. They often beg to be allowed to work at their own pace. You should acknowledge and validate their bad experiences. Explain how your approach is different. Explain the experiences of students in previous classes. If you can convince them that their experience in your class will be different, they will enter the process with open minds. The ones who cannot do so will drop the course.

One commonly heard complaint from students is that no one teaches in a PBL classroom. The students are doing the teaching. This is often linked to the contract between the university and the student that, in return for the student's tuition, the university will supply a subject matter expert who will provide an informed and organized learning experience. In PBL, many students do not see the actions of that expert. These students are at risk for dropping the course. PBL is not very common in college classrooms. It needs to be explained. I have been successful in convincing the skeptical students that in using this approach, I can teach them more subject matter that they will retain, while providing them with real-world research skills. It is useful to say something like this: "This is the way real work is done outside the university. Having experience performing this team-based research gives you an advantage in job interviews." I follow this up with testimony from former students about the value of the PBL class for their current work. Students who are the most skittish about the threat to their education prioritize college as a utilitarian strategy for starting a career. PBL can be connected to that.

Another common complaint is that groups are difficult to organize and manage. This complaint is a plea for a method. Give students a method for discussing the reports. Have students turn in some form of preparation to you after each group meeting. This will show them how seriously you expect them to take the process. Give them a method for dealing with the research. FINL, POE, and MORE help the students to focus on the research issues instead of their internal dynamics. Assure them that the final grade in the course is derived from their individual final report and self-evaluation, not the actions or inactions of the other students. Remind them that they have access to the reports of the other groups. This usually mollifies their insecurity, even as they continue to resent having their class experience so closely connected to other students.

Finally, students complain that they will not be able to cover the breadth of material in a PBL exercise that they do in lecture. When you include group exercises in a course, you take time away from discussing textbook or some other part of the syllabus. While short-term PBL is intended to challenge students' skills as well as the knowledge base, there is a cost in coverage. Students should be reminded of the advantages that come with PBL exercises. When PBL is the primary structuring element in the class, there is no diminution to the breadth and scope of learning. I have seen teams develop control of quantities of information that could not occur in a lecture classroom.

CHAPTER 77

Case-Based Learning Methods

A case is a narrative of an ill-structured problem that is waiting to be resolved. Students collaborate in case-based learning when you present them with a narrative with several possible outcomes and ask them to decide and defend the most likely outcome. Using the analytic models developed in the class, the students work through the facts of the case and decide which outcome best meets the agreed-upon criteria. As with problem-based learning, case-based learning is primarily concerned with developing problem-solving skills using knowledge acquired in the course and in previous courses. Unlike problem-based learning, the students are not expected to add any new information to the case. Cases are often descriptions of actual events, situations and conditions that illustrate the concepts. Sometimes they are fictional cases that permit the instructor to focus student attention more effectively on a small set of relevant factors where a real case might be too complex.

Case-based method teaching began in medicine in the nineteenth century and is used in business, law and medical schools throughout the country today. Beginning in the 1950s, case-based methods were widely adapted in management and marketing courses. In the liberal arts, they are most often found in courses that are related to either medical or legal models, such as clinical psychology, business, and biomedical ethics, and in social science courses dealing with law and legal institutions. I have used case-based method teaching successfully in cultural analysis courses, using the analysis of a specific object as the case that illustrates the method. As students familiarize themselves with the logic of the analysis, they can develop their own case using a different object. The method will work well whenever the goal of the course is for students to acquire analytic competence, rather than knowledge acquisition. The cases are usually too circumscribed to provide a breadth of knowledge.

The classroom environment of case-based teaching is more like that of the discussion classroom than the laboratory. Several authors contextualize the use of cases within the discussion format (Boehrer and Linsky 1990; Frederick 1981, 109-14; Olmstead 1974; Welty 1989, 40-49). I classify it as a laboratory technique because of its emphasis on collaboration for skill acquisition. It hybridizes the laboratory and the discussion classroom. As law and medicine instructors have shown, the non-collaborative, Socratic discussion technique is particularly well suited for drawing students' attention to the analytic possibilities in a case and extending those possibilities to other situations. Other discussion formats can work just as well. Here, I want to focus on case-based teaching that is collaborative.

The more students articulate the facts, diagnosis, and disposition of the case, the better. Lecturing on a case, no matter how exemplary the analysis or how virtuoso the presentation, defeats the pedagogical purpose. Students need to own the cases. All students have to be prepared, and each must have an equal chance of proposing and defending a solution. In a large class, you must break the students into learning groups to solve the case. To get them started, give the groups a Socratic rubric and have them agree on a collective response to each of the questions.

With case-based method teaching, the goal is to acquire analytic skills. The evaluation instrument needs to reflect this. Students should be evaluated on their skills in applying the analytic principles to a new, more complex set of facts. It is always a good idea to withhold the most complex case for the end.

Designing a Case-Based Course

CHAPTER
78

In case-based teaching, students evaluate and prioritize points of view on a decision, sources of evidence, constraining factors, and alternative solutions. Case-based teaching is effective because it provides students with early successes in analysis. As the levels of ambiguity increase, these early successes help the students adjust. If the cases are too simple or too complex, the students become complacent or discouraged. Selecting a series of graded cases is the essential problem in course design. You could write your own cases (Hansen 1987b). You could have the students prepare their own cases (Zeakes 1989, 33-35). You could adapt cases that are published in various collections, especially if you are teaching business, public policy, education, or human services. Lang's book (1986) lists several collections for these subjects. There are websites where students can purchase and download cases that you specify. I have included several of them in the list of Web resources for teaching at the end of the book. There are also journals that publish cases, including:

→ Case Research Journal (http://www.sba.muohio.edu/crj/),

→ The Business Case Journal (http://www.bcj.org/), and

→ Journal of Applied Case Research (http://www.mgt.smsu.edu/swcra).

Consulting these collections is useful if you are going to write your own cases, since they usually include ones that are well tested in the classroom. All good cases have certain characteristics. As identified by both Boehrer and Linsky (1990) and Lang (1986), a good case tells a story, raises thought-provoking issues, has conflicting elements, promotes identification with the core actors, encourages students to take a position, requires a decision, and consists of relevant facts that can all be stated concisely. As with PBL problems, real-life situations add both relevance and finality to the exercise.

CHAPTER
79

How to Teach a Case Laboratory

Organized case-based laboratories work through a series of increasingly complex cases. Beginning cases should have clear solutions before moving to the more ambiguous ones. This gives students early success and builds motivation for the more difficult cases to come. Cases have actors who have interests and differing interpretations of facts. As they act on these perspectives, conflicts arise and must be resolved. The appeal of teaching cases is this opportunity to explore the relationship between motivation and action, action and consequence, and agent and structure.

Preparation

Ask students to prepare for a case discussion by reading the case at least twice before class. If the case had a resolution or a real-life outcome, remove this before giving the case to the students. On the first reading, the students should not be concerned with details. Instead, the students should try to get a sense of the general issue and write it down. On the second reading, the students should identify the points of view of the actors. They should identify the differences between how the actors comment on the case and the actions that have actually occurred. Students should write down alternatives that might have led to different outcomes. This preparation will greatly facilitate discussion (Boehrer and Linsky 1990; Hansen 1987a).

Procedure

Be as consistent as possible in how you want students to discuss the cases. The students need to be able to take notes, and this is facilitated by a consistent structure. The focus of any discussion of a case is always some variation on this question: "What is this a case of?" Team work begins when someone summarize the case. Make sure you have described somewhere what you mean by a summary: the initial action, the facts that resulted from the action, the actor's interpretation of the action, and the ensuing conflict. Hold the student to the rules of the summary and ask the groups to not allow analysis, interpretation, or questions at this point. Their discussion should be interrogatory.

After describing the case, have the teams focus on the implications of the case. Can they develop reasons for the causes of the conflict. Would these lead to conflict in another situation? Ask students to identify the issues that arise from the actors' behaviors. Well chosen cases should keep them busy for an entire class period. They should actively record these comments on the board or projector. As you walk among the groups, be wary of conversations that begin to stall. Prompt the group by asking about consequences of acting. Return to previous points. Offer students opportunities to play roles in the case, either of the actors themselves or of people who are not part of the case but may know the actors or have an interest in the outcome. If the case had a resolution or real-life outcome, tell the students what it was at the conclusion of the discussion. Finish by having them comment on the differences between their suggested outcome and the actual one. If the case has no resolution, finish by making clear that while there is no right answer, some answers are better than others. Have students comment on what criteria the class should use in deciding which of the alternatives they have discussed is the most satisfying. Summarize the key points.

No student should be confused at the end of a case discussion about what they are supposed to take from the case to apply to other cases or other class material. You should assess early and often to insure that students are keeping up with the logical development of the analytic principles. After discussing a third of the cases, it may be too late to identify where confused students lost the thread of the argument.

Simulation and Games

Simulations and games break up passive classrooms and introduce active learning experiences for students. To play the game or enact the simulation, students must strategize, make decisions, and respond to the results, adjusting their strategies. Students know how to play board games, computer games, and sports. The difference with academic games is that the advantage in the game goes to the students who control the greatest amount of information.

There are several well-tested games on the market that use only paper materials, computer interfaces, or some combination of the two. Some faculty prefer to create their own, using materials that are appropriate to the class they are teaching. In some disciplines there are traditions of introducing a specific game into an introductory course to enhance the students' curiosity, challenge, and personal control. Archaeology has its virtual digs and Sid Meyer's Age of Empires. Intercultural communication and cultural anthropology have Bafa Bafa (Anonymous n.d.-a) and Bargna (Anonymous 1989). Sociology has SIMSOC (Gamson 1978) and Starpower (Anonymous n.d.-b). Urban studies has CLUG (Feldt 1978) and SimCity (Anonymous 2003). International relations has Model

UN. American government courses model legislatures. Media studies has What's News? (Gamson 1984). In criminology, a simulation can be devised to model the arrest, trial, and disposition of an offender (Hyman 1981). I have even seen Latin classes create a virtual Rome for students to research and perform. Collections of games and simulations can be found in Abt (1970) and Bratley, Fox, and Schrage (1988) and in the teaching journals of the various disciplines, such as Teaching Sociology, Teaching Political Science, and Journalism Educator. If you would like to design your own simulation, you will find a workable procedure that fits many different classroom situations in chapter 9 of Fuhrmann and Grasha (1983).

Games and simulations run the risk of being either too simple to use in advanced courses or too complex to run effectively in introductory courses. Another problem with any of these games is the logistical one. Some games take several hours to play out, violating the boundaries of the academic hour. If you are pressed for time, Ramsden (1992) describes a procedure for conducting a simulation using email that could work for you. Others require several different sets of game pieces that must be passed out and then collected to keep the game complete. Still others require several hours of preparation time for the instructor. That is why when a discipline hits on the right balance, the game is discussed at professional meetings and taught to graduate students for use in their classes.

Students with little knowledge of the subject benefit from games or simulations, but only when there is considerable academic support and structure (Cronbach and Snow 1977). Introducing a simulation or game out of the box without providing the proper intellectual background will still benefit the top 10 percent of the class but leave almost everyone else with an entertaining diversion, at best. Challenging students to develop their own game converts game playing to problem-based learning.

Film, Video, and Audio Case Materials

CHAPTER

81

Treat audio and visual materials as opportunities for collaborative learning. In many disciplines, teaching with audio recordings or films is as old as the technology itself. Who could imagine an appreciation of music class today without students listening to recorded performances by virtuoso musicians? Films are important case materials in the social sciences, history, and media studies. Interactive distance learning classrooms have now brought real-time conferencing and interviewing at a distance to college classrooms, at least in those schools that have invested in this technology.

Always familiarize yourself with the equipment before the class begins. There is nothing more frustrating than a broken bulb, a quirky CD player, or a faulty video projector. Never show the class something you have not watched. You do not want unpleasant surprises. Also, viewing or listening to the presentation ahead helps you to develop preparation materials for the students. Do not leave the room during the presentation. It is important that students see you participating with them. The idea of showing a film in class while you are at a conference or meeting sends the message that you do not consider the film important. You can learn a lot about what to ask students after the presentation by watching them as they view it.

Students need preparation for viewing or listening to these materials. You should not assume that they will immediately understand the material's relevance to the class. Relate the program to what they already know. Give them a print source on the same topic as the presentation to read before the class. Introduce the musicians or characters and any new terms before the presentation. Develop a list of questions that students should answer as the presentation unfolds. This encourages active viewing and listening.

It is considered a "best practice" in film studies to stop the film, interrupting the visual narrative, and ask the students questions about something that has just happened. This actually helps them to view or listen more critically. It breaks the massaging effects of the images and forces them to engage the experience critically.

257

When choosing presentations for a social science class, you should try to choose materials that reflect different points of view on similar topics. In this context, you can stop the film and ask students to defend a particular side in the unfolding interpretive controversy. Include the material from the film in the questions you use for your evaluations of their performance. If it is not on the test, it is not important.

Never show a film or performance that takes up more than 60 percent of class time. Students need to follow up after the viewing. This is where the collaborative learning takes place. If you want to show a longer film, show it in sections. Even though the film is not finished, students should break out into informal groups to work through the issues that have been presented so far. The groups should remain together until they have seen all the sections of the film. While the groups can busy themselves with working out the concrete details of the film, encourage them to treat the film as a case with implications for interpretation or action in other contexts. Have them play out scenarios that would have resulted in different outcomes. As with all such informal group activity, the various groups should share their reflections with the class.

Fieldwork, Internships, and Service and Experiential Learning

CHAPTER
82

The most intense form of "learning by doing" involves collaborative learning outside the classroom, usually in the context of temporarily visiting a different community. That community may be defined as culturally different, environmentally different, different in its needs, or different in the opportunities for learning that it offers the student. The way that students learn in such contexts is different from the ordinary classroom. Left to their own devices, they engage in a complex series of tests of their growing knowledge to check its validity. Dewey (1938), Lewin (1951), and Piaget (1970) have all attempted to describe how this process differs. Kolb describes the process as follows:

258

> Learning change and growth are seen to be facilitated by an inte-
> grated process that begins with here-and-now experiences followed
> by the collection of data and observations about that experience.
> The data are then analyzed and the conclusions of that analysis are
> fed back to the actors in the experience for their use in the modifi-
> cation of their behavior and choice of new experiences. Learning is
> thus conceived as a four stage cycle. . . . Immediate concrete experi-
> ence is the basis for observation and reflection. These observations
> are assimilated into a "theory" from which new implications for
> action can be deduced. These implications or hypotheses then serve
> as guides in acting to create new experience. (Kolb 1981)

The value of off-campus learning lies in the almost immediate feedback between experience, observation, judgment, and testing. As a result,
field-based learning excels like no other pedagogy in the development
of critical reasoning skills among all levels of learners. The reason it is
not practiced more frequently is because of the logistical difficulties.
Someone, usually, the class instructor has to set up the experience for
the students. Those schools where this kind of laboratory is a common
practice have full-time staff that help set up the courses.

To develop higher level reasoning skills, students need to exercise the
judgment component of reasoning. Ordinary classroom experience does
not mandate judgment. It is an optional way of knowing that we mobilize
only when conflict or crises arise. Most classroom experience falls into
a pattern in which the feedback between observation and experience is
immediate and we expect nothing out of the ordinary to occur. When
unpredictable experiences serve as the channel for learning, the student
must assume that all experiences are extraordinary, requiring reflection
upon the accumulated information, judgment on those reflections, the
formulation of tentative propositions to predict future experience, and
then the testing of the truth of the predictions. Piaget, and more recently
Kolb, have used this active learning-through-experience channel as the
basis for complex and nuanced models of cognitive development. These
theories are structural and yield a variety of considerations that are quite
technical. If you want to learn more about these theories, please consult
the texts, especially Kolb.

CHAPTER 83

Field-Based Learning

Several disciplines use fieldwork as a location for laboratory-style instruction. More and more departments are including internships in their curriculum. Increasingly, colleges include service learning or other forms of experiential learning as part of their degree requirements. Thus, a field classroom can be any location outside of the ordinary classroom buildings. For language learning, it might be a study abroad program. For environmental sciences, it might be a marsh at the edge of the football stadium. For geology, it might require a bus ride to a glacial moraine several miles from campus. For service learning, it might be a cultural center in the heart of an ethnic neighborhood. For a creative nonfiction class, it might be a meeting of the historical preservation commission. For an oral history course, it might be a retirement home. For an internship, it might be the local radio station. Several of the disciplines mentioned even conduct summer field schools whose sole purpose is to permit students to travel greater distances from campus and remain there, undistracted, for longer periods.

All of these are varieties of fieldwork. Learning from fieldwork is at least as complex a pedagogy as problem-based learning and often entails ethical pitfalls as well. If you were trained in field methods, you know what these complexities and pitfalls are. If you were not, your Institutional Review Board (IRB) will be happy to alert you to them. Fieldwork components of classrooms should never be undertaken lightly. Even a simple observational exercise on campus needs to be well thought through before handing it over to students. Research outside the classroom, whether it involves human subjects or the environment, is never impact free. Sending the untrained to provoke and disturb the unwary is the height of pedagogical arrogance. If fieldwork is to be an important part of your curriculum, you must develop it systematically. It is too complicated to be used as an enhancement to a classroom designed around other priorities. To begin, you must be very familiar with the field site and all the people who are going to play a role in the students' experience. No one should be surprised when the students show up. When you do meet the people whose lives revolve around the site, there are several topics of conversation that you must have with them. These include

→ Your understanding of their needs and sensitivities,

→ Their understanding of your learning goals for the students, the products, or outcomes of the students' work that their participation will help generate,

→ What these products of the student's efforts will be used for, and

→ What resources, human and material, the students will need while they are on-site; and who is expected to provide the resources.

All classes with fieldwork components must begin with the ethical considerations of the impact of the research on the environment and people. Students should take the various human subjects training courses that are available on the Internet. On some campuses, the IRB will require the review of all course-based research involving human subjects whether the research leads to publication or not. On other campuses, only research that could potentially be published needs to be reviewed before the research begins. Whatever the IRB wants, you should want your students to understand the ethical responsibilities of a researcher in any laboratory dealing with human subjects. This means having them develop the components of a human subjects protocol even if none is required. Students should write up their own informed consent letters, and these should be good enough to pass an IRB review. Students should plan the organization and control of the research information, including having a disposal plan. For environmental fieldwork, they should understand the various human impacts on environments and write protocols that minimize the impact that results from their research. If animal research in the field is part of the research design, students should be familiar with their university's requirements for the use of animals in research. Ethically informed research is the only research our society can tolerate. The sooner our students learn how to think ethically, the better their research will be.

The primary challenges of field-based research lie in accurately recording and organizing the data. You should teach students a specific method for data recording and control. You should monitor the field notes and data sheets. Hold classroom workshops early in the term to discuss issues of data recording. The data should be copied to electronic formats on a regular basis, and these formats should backed up to insure that no data is lost. Sensitive data, such as tapes and notes from interviews, should be protected from loss and unauthorized access before the interviews begin. As the data accumulates, assign students the task of making catalogues, indexes, and summaries to maintain an effective inventory of the information.

You must consider your students' safety while off campus. As chair, I would get calls from parents when one of our instructors sent a class into a neighborhood the parents had deemed unsafe. Some campuses consider this a pressing enough issue that a standard safety form exists with pertinent information for students. These usually address safety issues while traveling from campus to the site, awareness of the surroundings while at the site, and what the student should do if unsafe, uncomfortable or threatening situations arise. We cannot be everywhere. Students need to develop their street sense and confidence in their ability to handle new situations. Safety conversations bring these teachable moments into focus. Nevertheless, incidents will happen and hopefully no one will be hurt. Knowing that, you need to provide students with the best information on whom to communicate with in case of an emergency. Cell phones have made this a bit easier, but the system you set up should not assume that a cell phone will always be available or working. If this seems like a big task, ask colleagues in departments that do this regularly about the guidance they give students. If you are lucky, a campus task force has already addressed these issues.

CHAPTER

84

Teaching in the Field

A field-based course requires intensive laboratory-style teaching. Your department and college should recognize this by agreeing to cap the size of these courses in the same manner that science labs are capped. In my experience, fifteen to eighteen students is the maximum size; twenty is unworkable. Clearly, this makes the course expensive to incorporate into a curriculum. However, without the support of the institution, this kind of teaching cannot be accomplished. When you compromise on teaching in the field, and large sections will force you to compromise, the risks to the students, the community and the institution increase.

Teaching in the field is accomplished in a manner very similar to problem-based learning. You should concern yourself with both the quality of the data collected and the quality of the analysis. Be as explicit as possible about what you expect each student to do. Ask students to keep a semi-public journal or log of every hour spent in the field and what they did. Give students an explicit prompt every week that they should write about in their journal after their time in the field. Conrad and Hedin use this prompt:

> Describe an incident or situation in which you were not sure what to do or say. What's the first thing you thought to do or say? List three other actions you might have taken (or things you might have said). Which of the above seems best to you now? Why? What do you think is the real problem in the situation? Why do you think it came up? (1990)

At the class meeting every week, students compare these incidents and situations and learn from each other's responses. The prompt is particularly useful because it engages the students' reasoning skills in reflecting on their experiences. In general, students should reflect on as much of their experience as possible. That experience is the text of the course.

Establish a system of site visits and ongoing review. Students should never think that you have abandoned them to face the problem alone. You should be a presence at their field site at least once at the beginning of the term and once in the middle. If this is a logistical problem for you, it is one of your own making. You should design fieldwork so that your presence at the site is not a hardship for you. Talk with the students as a group at the weekly class meeting, but have individual or team meetings every two weeks to discuss their experience. Tailor your support to meet the specific needs of each team or student. As with the intellectual objectives, give each team objectives and have them demonstrate that they tried to meet these objectives at the next meeting.

Finally, field-based research is fraught with peril to your learning goals. Subjects, clients, and those who control access to the site may change their minds about participation. Students may be so intimidated by the tasks as to freeze up or defensively procrastinate. Be prepared with alternatives for students, depending on their degree of complicity in the problem. For those who are blameless, you might scale down the tasks, scope, or activities, redistribute them to other groups, or if time allows, find them another placement. For those who are consistently missing appointments or deadlines or who are acting in a way that embarrasses themselves and the university, do not tolerate these problems indefinitely. Terminate the placement as soon as you recognize the problem. Weak students jeopardize the future of the student placements at the sites.

CHAPTER 85

Evaluating Field-Based Learning

The field-based laboratory does not immediately lend itself to traditional evaluation instruments like tests and expository essays. There may be a final report for certain kinds of fieldwork. However, the report cannot do the entire job of evaluating the student's work. It is never the case that a student receives credit merely for showing up for the requisite number of hours. It is not how much time the student spends, but whether the understanding of the situation has changed because of that time. It is this change in understanding that the student attempts to narrate in some form for evaluation.

Evaluating student work in the field involves triangulating between the experience as seen by the student, the student's experience as seen by others, and the student's reflection on the experience after the fact. The students reflect the experience in the journal that they keep.

The student's experience as seen by others requires you to ask someone who the student will encounter often to serve as an evaluator. Examples of appropriate people to fulfill this role include a supervisor of an internship, a program director on a study abroad program, or an agency officer in a field placement. You need to negotiate this arrangement during the setup phase of the field experience before the student is placed. You need to tell this person exactly what you want him or her to write. Giving them a simple rubric at the beginning and then again during your last site visit helps. In this rubric, do not ask for net assessments of the student's work. That is your job. Ask about attitude, contribution, initiative, growth of understanding, teamwork, communication, and most importantly, how these changed over time. Use this evaluation letter to gain an understanding of the student's level of engagement and whether it grew or waned over the course of the term.

All students engaged in field-based learning should write a reflective essay about their experience. The focus of the reflection will change, depending on the goal of the learning. In service-based learning, the student might reflect on what was learned, how the learning changed the student, and how the student was able to use the learning to begin to effect change in his or her environment. For a study abroad program, the reflection might include what the student learned, how the learning changed the student's thinking, and how the learning helped the student accept membership in the overseas community. The pattern is similar for laboratories, internships, and agency placements: an inventory of the learning, based on the journal or log; a statement about personal growth; and a statement about the student's contribution to the collaborative effort.

If this triangulation approach does not fit your design, you could ask students to demonstrate their learning by writing a tip sheet or user manual for others to use. They could write an essay in which they are critical of the existing literature or journalism about their site. They could produce a presentation or poster in which they attempt to inform others about the reality of the lives of people they encountered during the experience. Whatever form you choose, you are evaluating the fit between the experience itself and the students' understanding of that experience.

Writing Field-Based and Laboratory Reports

CHAPTER
86

Many times we hear people talking about articles written in the IMRaD (Introduction, Materials and methods, Results, Analysis, and Discussion) format. The 'a' is often left in lowercase to indicate that it is an optional section that is included when an experimental procedure must be evaluated as part of the report. Nowadays people also talk about the TAIMRaD format, which is otherwise the same format as IMRaD but includes the Title and Abstract as part of the writer's task. Students should write IMRaD articles in a neutral style with the exception of the Discussion section, where the author's opinions can be brought in to some degree.

Many pieces of academic writing follow the SPSE (Situation, Problem, Solution, and Evaluation) pattern. This pattern has many similarities to the IMRaD format. Information presented in the Situation and Problem sections is similar to that found in the Introduction of an IMRaD format. The Solution contains the Materials and methods section and Results section, while the Evaluation would cover the same material as the Discussion section. The Evaluation will contain more of the personal opinions of the author than an IMRaD article, and in this respect, the format most resembles an essay on the research and less a research report. It prioritizes the writer's point of view. The SPSE pattern is more common in the humanities and social sciences than in the sciences for that reason.

A third format is the DSB (Definition, Solution and Benefits) pattern. Use this report form when students are involved in field-based research involving a client group or agency. Both IMRaD and SPSE have problems communicating to a non-academic reader. They both are written from the writer's point of view and reflect the writer's experience.

While there is good reason to ask students to take on these self-reflective tasks, there comes a point in research where the reader must be taken into account. Mahrer (2000, 162-64) calls this the persuasiveness quality in technical writing, the overt demonstration by the writer of the value, utility, and benefits of the research for the reader. My discussion here is based on his work. DSB is a more advanced format than IMRaD and SPSE because it fore-fronts the relevance of the research for the reader. Definition is not merely an introduction to the scholarly context of the research but is also an explicit statement of a problem to the reader. The reader's interest in the research is brought up immediately, rather than being buried in the results or discussion. The definition section forces the student to think through all the reasons why someone other than the instructor might be interested in the research results. Justifying the work forces the student to put into a larger intellectual context what previously was merely accepted as something the instructor concocted as part of a series of exercises that were supposed to lead the student somewhere.

Writing the definition section calls upon and reinforces much higher levels of reasoning skills. Putting the solution section immediately after the definition instead of a results section or discussion section also increases the value of the writing for the reader. In practice, this section combines the materials and methods section and results section of IMRaD but tailors the materials and methods section to the reader, rather than detailing the chronological actions of the writer in the research. This shift in focus is a crucial component of the solution section. Instead of a discussion or conclusion, the benefits section restates and reinforces the value of the research for the reader in the most direct way possible. A good benefits section must convince readers that they have not wasted their time reading the report because their own understanding or practice can be enhanced as a result of the research. There is no room in this section for speculation. Instead, the writer must show a familiarity with the reader's position and write the benefits of the research with that position in mind.

CHAPTER

87

Evaluating Collaborative Learning

There are three approaches to assigning a grade to collaborative work in the classroom.

You can grade the contributions and end products of the individuals, while assuming that the collaborative process itself is evaluated as part of the value added to individual efforts. Students with less experience in collaboration benefit from using the first approach. This gives them the opportunity to learn the pitfalls and advantages of collaborative learning without risking a fair assessment of their individual efforts in the process. This approach necessitates that the students submit individual reports based on the collaboration. They should reflect on their collaborative learning in a self-assessment. Taking the self-assessment into account in the grading is a form of the combination approach.

You can grade a combination of the individual and group approaches, giving one or the other an initial evaluation and modifying that grade up or down, depending on your evaluation of the other component. As the students' experience with collaboration increases, the combination approach works particularly well. This more highly motivated group of students can reasonably expect that their commitment to a strong process will reward them, even if their individual efforts are merely satisfactory. This approach requires that some effort at group writing or editing be submitted, in addition to some form of a report on individual efforts.

You can grade the collaborative process itself, while discounting the relative contributions of the group members. Students who are the most experienced in collaborative learning benefit more from the second approach. I would use this approach only with advanced graduate students who have substantial research and writing experience or with undergraduates who are part of a cohort that has experienced collaborative projects several times before. The reason to reserve basing evaluation entirely on the collaborative effort is that it requires a level of trust in the group process and a willingness to risk failure in order to be effective. Forcing students with limited collaborative experience into this form of evaluation is cruel and counterproductive. Only the group report is evaluated and all group members take responsibility for the authorship. No effort is made to document or evaluate individual contribution.

Regardless of which approach you use, you must be explicit about what you are grading in the written reports and the process. Some collaborative projects duplicate classic experiments or proofs. The reports come with built-in evaluative criteria. Either the students approached the results you expected them to find or they did not. You can certainly give partial credit for the process. The evaluation is different than it would be in a perverse problem where there were several well-formed solutions and no obvious way of assigning priority between them. Here it becomes more an issue of the rhetoric of the report. How well did the student or group use the evidence acquired and the reasoning produced by the collaborative process to convincingly argue for one solution over another? Criterion-based grading works best with these evaluations.

The collaborative process does not lend itself directly to criterion-based evaluation. There are few benchmarks that groups have to hit. These will be discussed below. The evaluation of the group process itself needs to be a collaboration between the instructor and the group. Self-assessments of the contribution of the member to the group process speak directly to how the process helped the individual work and what he or she learned about collaboration as a result (perhaps what the student would do differently next time), providing valuable insights into what happened when you were not watching and listening. Tell-all peer evaluation is less effective from the instructor's point of view and undermines the trust within the group. You can discover who is doing the work and who is not from observing the group interact over time. The few benchmarks that groups have to hit as they develop include the way they react to tactical dead ends in their research plan, the allocation of members' time to task, the means groups use to resolve conflict between ideas or personalities, whether they stick to the method you have supplied, how they know when they have reached a satisfactory point in the research, and whether they engage in peer editing of drafts as the deadline nears. For advanced groups, an additional benchmark is the organization and execution of the collaborative writing and editing of the final report. Ultimately, the evaluation of group process is one of effective functioning or ineffective functioning. The benchmarks merely help you understand where the group began to get off track.

I generally have several groups operating simultaneously in the classroom. I keep track of where each of them is by asking what each is currently working on as I move from group to group. Most groups that are functioning effectively will hit each of the benchmarks, and I note that on a tally sheet. The groups that are struggling reveal this condition through missing deadlines or reporting that they not working well. I intervene, make suggestions, and occasionally intervene with an adjustment to the group's agenda, if I think it will help them stay on track. By the end of the exercise, the benchmark tally and the self-assessments provide a more than satisfactory picture of the group process.

PART 15

The On-Line Classroom

New technologies have always transformed the university. Consider the effect of the printing press. The new communication technologies will have as profound an impact. We now have elaborate and effective virtual campuses in many of our established schools. These have benefits for admission, retention, program development, faculty development and campus infrastructure. I believe that this development will better educate our students.

As a new instructor you must begin to incorporate communication technology into your teaching practice. This includes mastering at least the basics of course management software, becoming familiar with discussion boards, chat rooms, virtual classrooms, social media, media formats, and the course design features that work best in virtual classrooms. There will always be a market for well-designed on-line classes.

The class that is taught entirely on the Web with no face-to-face interaction is only one kind of on-line class experience. The increasingly common hybrid classes feature some portion of the course in a face-to-face format and some part on-line. In a sense, all courses are hybrid to some extent. When a student is alone with a book and preparing for class, they are experiencing the same sort of interaction that is envisioned by the on-line portion of a hybrid course. Faculty who have learned how to teach on-line discover techniques that they can immediately incorporate into their face-to-face classes.

Before one attempts to design an on-line course, one should have the experience of taking one. That is the best way to learn what to expect. Effective on-line instructors have people-oriented personalities and better than average communication skills. The "Lonely Lecturer" does not thrive on-line. On-line instructors need not be highly technological or dwell on-line twenty-fours a day. Online teaching requires more teaching, rather than less. They need to be organized. Organization is the key element in both student engagement and faculty enthusiasm for the process. The assignments have to be designed with greater elegance than in bricks and mortar classrooms. Expectations need to be clearly communicated. For all these reasons, learning to teach on-line will greatly improve your traditional teaching skills.

As I have with other sorts of classrooms and classroom functions, I recommend owning a copy of Susan Ko and Steve Rosen's book *Teaching Online: A Practical Guide* (Routledge 2008). This book will answer most of your questions about the practical issues surrounding the design and implementation of on-line courses. If your campus has an initiative to develop its on-line courses, there will be instruction available. Take advantage of it. New software and new approaches are always being developed that make on-line teaching easier to develop and more accessible to the student.

Instructor's Considerations for Distance Learning

CHAPTER
88

Distance learning (DL) is any instructional activity designed for instruction mediated by distant communication. Any course that can be taught without communication technologies, with the exception of science laboratories, can be taught on-line. Distance learning is not a new idea or a new technique. Writing technologies in ancient civilizations facilitated the training of religious leaders and accountants. Once the younger trainees were taught to read the symbols, they could access collected wisdom or inventories of resources without someone speaking the text to them. In the early eighteenth century, shorthand teachers sought students through newspaper advertisements who would mail in their lessons weekly (Holmberg 2005, 13). Shorthand was a new writing technology that lent itself to students working independently to practice and master the skill. As postal services grew, so did the possibilities for distance education. The University of London offered the first distance degree program in 1858. The current web-based developments replace the post office communication between instructor and student, but not the pedagogy.

Some professors see the erosion of intellectual property rights over their lecture materials and course designs as threatening academic freedom. The American Association of University Professors (AAUP) has long concerned itself with this issue. Their 1969 Statement on Copyright is explicit about who owns what in the classroom:

> Prevailing academic practice has treated the faculty member as the copyright owner of works that are created independently and at the faculty member's own initiative for traditional academic purposes. Examples include class notes and syllabi; books and articles; works of fiction and nonfiction; poems and dramatic works; musical and choreographic works; pictorial, graphic, and sculptural works; and educational software, commonly known as "courseware." This practice has been followed for the most part, regardless of the physical medium in which these "traditional academic works" appear, that is, whether on paper or in audiovisual or electronic form. . . . This practice should therefore ordinarily apply to the development of courseware for use in programs of distance education. (AAUP 2002)

The Statement applies to faculty who are fulfilling their contracts to teach. This is not considered "work for hire' which always describes a particular scope of the work. Such "work for hire" arrangements are alien to the university, or as the AAUP put it, "Institutional ownership of such work, which gives a college or university the power to edit, revise, and prepare derivative works, and to publish or not to publish, is totally 'inconsistent with fundamental principles of academic freedom,' in the words of the Statement" (AAUP 2002). If you are employed as an ordinary faculty, full-time or part-time in an accredited university, you own the course materials. If part or all of your responsibilities involve DL, you own those course materials, too. That means that you can do anything you like with the materials and academic freedom is preserved. If you are employed on a "work for hire" basis to produce a course packet for a school that does not expect you to teach that packet, merely to produce it, then the school owns the course materials. You sold the materials when you signed the contract.

On the other side of the ledger, many colleagues see this development as creating greater student access and inclusiveness, especially for students with disabilities and commuting issues. You will have time to make up your mind about participating in the online campus at your school. However, at some point in your career, having a course that can be packaged for on-line distribution may become necessary. On-line teaching skills today will expand your employability.

A constant debate in the faculty lunchroom concerns the relative effectiveness of distance vs. face-to-face learning. Bernard and his team conducted a meta-analysis of the comparative distance education (DE) literature published between 1985 and 2002 to try to put this argument to rest. In total, 232 studies containing 688 independent achievement, attitude, and retention outcomes were analyzed. Overall results indicated effect sizes of essentially zero on all three measures and wide variability. This suggests that many applications of DE outperform their classroom counterparts and that many perform more poorly. Dividing achievement outcomes into synchronous and asynchronous forms of DE produced a somewhat different impression. In general, mean achievement effect sizes for synchronous applications favored classroom instruction, while effect sizes for asynchronous applications favored DE. However, significant heterogeneity remained in each subset (Bernard et al. 2004).

Designing a course from on-line teaching is not simply a matter of taking a course you already have and throwing it up on the web. On-line teaching requires a different organization of material. Backward design was introduced in the late 1980s by Grant Wiggins and Jay McTigh, and is part of their larger Understanding by Design framework. Backward design emphasizes assessment as a means of evaluating student capacity to apply newly acquired knowledge in a variety of contexts. Backward design involves three progressive stages. In the first stage you identify the desired results for the students. What enduring understandings do you want your students to develop? In the second stage, you determine what you will accept as evidence that the students have achieved these results. How will your students demonstrate their understanding? In the final stage, you plan learning experiences (projects, readings, research, presentations, lectures, discussions) that offer the students the opportunity to achieve the results. What resources and activities must you give your students to support development of the desired understanding (Wiggins and McTigh 1980)? This procedure is excellent advice for designing any class. For DL classes it is a requirement.

Students want something from a course. It may be knowledge and skills, progress toward a degree, a grade that will raise their average, a better schedule, value for their tuition dollars, or some combination of these. Their success in the class will depend on the degree to which they engage their energy and effort with the experience you design. The engagement will depend on them knowing what they have to do to get what they want. It will also depend on finding this experience interesting and challenging, yet doable because of the built-in support systems. Finally, their engagement with the course will depend on finding the specific experiences relevant to their personal goals and useful to their broader purposes for seeking a degree.

Originating from a grant from the U.S. Department of Education, the Quality Matters project has established the most sophisticated rubric currently available for evaluating the effective of the design of on-line courses. The rubric includes forty specific elements, distributed across eight broad standards. Their website includes a short version of the rubric that you should download and consult when designing your course. The address is available in Web Resources in the back of this book.

I have found that the stumbling block for on-line instructors lies in describing the course objectives for the students. There is a difference between goals and objectives. Goals are statements of ideal or best possible outcomes. They tend to be written in abstract terms with many terms left undefined. Objectives specify concrete results with specific action verbs and identifiable products, behaviors and/or outcomes. If you would like to test your outcomes statements to see how well they satisfy the characteristics of objectives, a website known as the RadioJames Objective Builder will allow you to do so. The address is in Web Resources.

Finally, many faculty worry about the lack of social conventions surrounding communication on the web. They fear students will write uncivil messages, email them at all hours of the day and night, "stalk" other members of the class, and generally create behavioral problems that rarely occur in classrooms. Guidelines for proper behavior in DL, known as netiquette, exist. The address of the most commonly cited guide is in Web Resources. Create a netiquette guide for your class and take time at the beginning to quiz students' knowledge of its rules. Have penalties for students who flagrantly violate the rules. You'll find that it is easier to exclude unruly students from DL classes than ordinary classrooms. Almost every student will play by the rules, once they know what they are.

Student Readiness for Distance Learning

CHAPTER
89

Distance learning is not a solution for every student. DL requires more than access to a computer and a familiarity with how it works. Several universities have excellent on-line tools to help students assess their readiness for this kind of learning. Addresses for several of them are in Web Resources. Each covers essentially the same set of questions with more or less detail. Students ought to have a familiarity with the technologies that will be used to communicate. This means experience with installing new software, using peripheral devices like headsets and cameras, and connecting to the Internet in different environments. The tools also ask students to reflect on their study habits. Are they organized? Are they disciplined enough to work independently? Do they always complete things on time? It asks about lifestyle. Do they have the time to complete the work? Do they have access to the Internet whenever they need it, or is it shared with other people? Do they have a quiet personal space to work in free from distractions? Are they goal-setters? Are they taking the course for a reason, even if it is required? Do they have a preferred learning style that fits with the presentation of materials and learning challenges of DL? Do they have experience collaborating with others to learn? When students fill out these surveys, the tool then provides them with a snapshot of where they will fit or not fit with the learning processes involved in DL. At that point, the students who are not ready for on-line learning can make the choice to pull out, or stay the course. All first-time distance learning students need this moment of self-discovery when they sign up for the course, when they still have time to adjust their schedules.

Structuring Time on Task in Distance Learning

CHAPTER
90

We are accustomed to structuring the time in our ordinary classrooms: ten minutes for introducing the topic, twenty minutes for discussion, ten minutes for in class exercise, etc. Structuring time in an on-line setting is similar, but the intervals are days rather than minutes. Students need hard deadlines for completing every assignment. "By 9:00 PM every Sunday during the course, you will post your summaries of the research your group assigned to you on the discussion board." "Your reaction essays on each of the articles must be posted by 12:00 noon every Thursday." This kind of specificity then allows you to build communication between the students, in the case of collaborative learning, or between the student and you. Your time, too, becomes easier to manage. Effective time structuring also increases the student's ability to organize their time, permitting them to devote more time on task. This, in turn, improves the rigor of the course experience for them. In a hybrid course I have been teaching for many years, there are three specific deadlines every week: a Sunday evening deadline, a Wednesday class time deadline and a Thursday evening deadline. The deadlines establish a rhythm for the students that affects every other class they are taking that term.

Communication Issues in Distance Learning

CHAPTER
91

There are really only two kinds of communication in distance learning, synchronous and asynchronous. These influence everything else that occurs during the course. In synchronous communication, all of the students and the instructor are on-line and in communication with each other at the same time. In asynchronous communication, the students and the instructor are on-line at different times. The differences between these can best be seen in the case of discussion. In a synchronous class, discussion takes the form of chat, a function usually embedded in the course management software in which students type their contributions to the conversation. The typed comments appear in a stream as soon as the student hit's the "enter" key on their computer. Some sophisticated chat functions allow for voice and video, as well as text chat. These come the closest to the ordinary classroom experience of discussion, with the exception that the software can capture the entire experience for students to playback afterwards.

Asynchronous discussion takes the form of a board, analogous to a bulletin board, on which students and the instructor post ideas, comments and reactions. The postings appear as threads, each comment following another in the order they were posted. Anyone at any time can begin a new thread. This form of conversation has been available for two decades, and most people are familiar with it. It follows different rules than the conversational rules that govern chat. First, there is no turn-taking. People post when required to or when they are moved to do so by another's posting. The postings tend to be longer and include more academic text. This is particularly true of discussion boards for collaborating teams. Most importantly, the postings unfold over a much longer period of time. Left to themselves, students post irregularly. Encouraged to post by deadlines, instructor-posted discussion questions and other structuring mechanisms, the postings become more timely and relevant.

For DL courses outside of a course management system, email becomes the most common form of communication. Students mail assignments, questions and comments to the instructor, or each other, and receive replies. This is an early form of DL communication that is always going to be subject to technical errors: full mailboxes that reject new mail, faulty addresses, errant sends, forgotten attachments, and virus infections. Since several web-based, off-campus course management systems are available (see Web Resources), you may find it advantageous to use one, just to avoid email issues.

Managing an On-Line Discussion

Hosting an on-line discussion can be challenging the first time you do it. Depending on your software, it can feel like juggling several balls at once. WIMBA is a live discussion classroom integrated with Blackboard, the most frequently implemented campus-wide course management system. There are others, but they all have similar functionality. In WIMBA, you can have voice interaction simultaneous with text-based chat. There is also a live roster that students and the instructor can use to communicate with each using symbols, such as who is on-line, who is "raising their hand" to enter the queue for speaking, who needs technical help, or who has chosen yes or no in response to the instructor's or classmate's question. I found my first encounter with the hectic flow of information, even with a small class of fifteen to twenty students, disorienting. Adding to my troubles were students who were having technical difficulty with the system. They could not hear or see the video. For all these reasons, it is important for the class to begin their first session in a virtual classroom with the goal of familiarizing themselves with the software. It is also important to enlist the participation of a staff member from the campus office responsible for the software to help out any students who may encounter technical difficulties. That should not be your job. This first step saves a lot of frustration later on. Once everyone is comfortable with what these virtual classrooms can do, they can begin to learn.

If you are using a classroom with capabilities like WIMBA, you must decide how you want to use the different features. The main channel, for example, can be voice. This insures that people must take turns speaking and produces a semblance of a real conversation. These software packages record everything that goes on. You can review the conversation later for quality of participation. If you dedicate the voice channel to meeting the primary discussion goals of the session, the text-based chat can be used for the "back channel". Back channel communication includes notes passed in class, facial expressions directed at a classmate that comment silently on what is taking place, and direct, "aside" comments to the instructor. The back channel in a virtual classroom is often the liveliest part of the whole experience. It is rarely uncivil or hostile, yet it forces students to pay attention to the voice channel. Since the speaker can also see the stream of text comments, they often comment vocally on the comments, connecting the two channels. In this way, on-line discussions are often richer than in-class discussions. As with all forms of discussion, preparation is the key to success. Students should be familiar with the "netiquette" of on-line discussions and your expectations (see Web Resources). They should have something to post before the class that demonstrates their preparation for the discussion. They should be familiar with the software and in a space where they can concentrate without interruption.

If all these elements are in place, managing the discussion becomes a matter of not letting things happen too quickly. Try to establish a rhythm where you take your time responding to back channel comments or questions. Attend to the live roster every few minutes or so, to check the queue or clear the last poll. If the primary channel falls silent, do not rush to fill the void. Use the back channel to encourage more students to step up. The length of these discussions can seem longer than they really are. They are so full of information that they can become exhausting. It is better to have several shorter ones, than a single long one. When you feel the goal is reached, end the session. Remind students that the session will be archived and they can access it whenever they want.

Moderating a Blog or Wiki

Content systems like blogs, wikis and Web-based forums let students develop their own knowledge base, comment on the contributions of others and create meta-structures, also known as tags, to develop greater control over the material. This is also a new channel of communication for the instructor to manage. How much control the moderator exercises over the contribution defines the difference between a blog, a wiki and a forum. A wiki has the least amount of top-down control. The members of the contributing community watch each other and attempt to keep all contributors within certain bounds of civility, veracity, and good taste. Blogs increase control by having a single moderator, usually the instructor in a classroom context, who enforces these standards. In a forum there are usually several "senior" contributors, who decide as a group whether to exclude contributions, comments, or even contributors. Wikis and blogs are more frequently encountered in classroom contexts than forums.

The issues surrounding moderation of wikis and blogs increase as access to these sites increases. Small classes are less of a problem than large classes. Private, access-controlled sites are less of a problem than public sites. It you are faced with moderating a blog or wiki in a large class or a public site, you should set the moderation defaults to review each message before it is posted. The criteria for what to exclude should flow from the objectives for organizing the blog or wiki in the classroom. I could imagine a course on popular culture or deviant sub-cultures that would stretch the community's standards for good taste, but still fulfill the objectives of the wiki. Civility and veracity, however, should never be stretched or violated. The license people feel they enjoy to post inappropriate materials begins with the anonymity of Web-based communication. Registering the users of the blog with their real names circumvents this license to offend or lie. Students will post inappropriate materials in order to direct attention to them. Using real names generates attention at a much higher social cost to the student posting.

Incorporating Social Media in Learning Environments

CHAPTER
92

Social media are to dorm life as distance learning is to in class learning. Technology mediates the relationships. Almost all of the communication features of social media are built into course management software. The difference is that screen that the student sees on a social media site is more personal and customizable than courseware. The oldest of these sites are Friendster and LiveJournal. They still exist but very few college-aged students participate. Facebook is probably the most popular site at the time of this writing. However, like the formerly "most popular" site, My Space, Facebook is losing participants because of its commercialization. Sites that allow students to send short messages to friends, like Twitter, LinkedIn, Friendfeed and Seesmic, are gaining popularity. All of these sites do essentially the same things with slightly different details. Twitter is short messages, like the text messages from a phone, but directed at specific individuals who have chosen to follow the sender's messages. LinkedIn is a professional networking site of interest primarily to graduating and graduate students and technology-related professions. Seesmic uses short video messages instead of text. Friendfeed permits sending messages to multiple social sites at once. Although not thought of as a social medium, blogging is gaining popularity for its social networking. People who follow a specific blogger often leave comments to the posts on a regular basis. Over time, they create a sense of community with each other. Finally, there is the currently most extreme form of social media, Second Life, one of a series of virtual worlds that have evolved over the last twenty years. Second life enables users to communicate with others by having a graphic representation of themselves on screen with representations of the people you are talking to in real time. Several educators have created on-line courses in Second Life. The synchronous chat in the course is performed with the instructor's and students' representations seated in a virtual classroom. All of these refinements add more technological issues to the communication, increasing the student's learning time for dealing with the technology without adding anything new to the on-line learning experience.

What has all this got to do with student learning? After all, if we just want to show our students how well we understand their world, there are more efficient and effective ways to do so. Depending on your student mix, it is entirely possible that only a minority of students are involved in social media. On my campus and several others I know of around the country, the dominant medium for communication is text messaging with cell phones. It does not require a computer. Unless we can find a specific advantage to the students' learning from using social media, I feel we can safely ignore them.

I have experimented with social media in student learning. I have substituted a course management site with an interface that is similar to Facebook in place of my campus's course management software. The goal was to increase the social bonds between students. I have used Twitter in the classroom. The goal was to create a "back channel" of communication that would permit students to comment during the class discussion. Another professor had a similar idea at about the same time and was written up in the Chronicle of Higher Education (Young 2009). In both cases, the primary goal was to enhance the social component in learning. Could I create more effective collaboration on projects? Could I increase involvement in discussion from students who tended to hold back? Neither of these experiments was successful. The Facebook results were no different than the results from traditional means of building collaboration. The

Twitter experience was entertaining, but only the most active students chose to take part in the live blogging during the class. It did not un-mute the reticent portion of the class.

There are many more experiments that social media can inspire. For example, Facebook has several applications that can be added to a students page that add in scholarly research and generate more intellectual engagement outside of class. Applications like Book iRead allow students to share their responses to class readings with friends. Notcentric and Class Notes allow students to take notes on the laptop directly on their Facebook page, automatically sharing them with classmates. JSTORSearch allows students to search, within JSTOR, for archived journal articles from within their Facebook page. My preference would be for them to do so from the library page. It facilitates direct access to the text. The Facebook application only facilitates search. Educators who are interested in experimenting with social media can participate in a national interest group called Classroom 2.0 (http://www.classroom20.com/). They also conduct live workshops in major cities.

There are also applications on Facebook that are destructive to learning. The application DoResearch4me permits the student to submit a thesis statement and your instructions and will return to them several suggestions of sources and directions for completing the assignment. To my mind, this goes far beyond the services of a reference librarian. At least the librarian will teach the student how to achieve the same results on the next project. The application will not. Swaproll allows students to trade textbooks, increasing prices at the campus bookstore. There is a RateMyProfessors plug-in for Facebook. Has anyone ever found a redeeming value to this site? GetHomeworkHelp connects students to tutors and other students who are willing to help them with a class. While this sounds progressive, there is no way for the instructor to monitor the tutoring to insure that it focuses on student learning and not student cheating.

Twitter, on the other hand, has inspired some creative innovations in traditional classroom processes. There is a feature in Twitter called the hash-tag. Any term that is preceded by a hash mark (#) can be searched from the subscriber's home page. One instructor asked students to use a specific hash-tag to organize comments, questions and feedback posted by students to Twitter during or after class. He could then search on the hash-tag and retrieve the comments. These were anonymous only to the extent that the instructor did not recognize the student's Twitter name.

Like all Twitter communication, the comments were limited to 140 characters. The instructor soon found that students needed more space for their comments. The hash-tags can organize short class notes. Because a student can submit a comment to Twitter by texting from a cell phone, the has-tags can be used to share research sources with a team or to note observations during field trips. Students can also receive Twitter messages as text messages on their cell phone, though this may involve a small fee for some. One professor began using Twitter to communicate with students outside of class. He emphasizes anecdotally how the enhanced social communication stimulated learning, but does not provide pre-test/post-test comparison (AcademicDave 2008). No research on the effectiveness of students and instructors following each other on Twitter has been published.

Maintaining the Student-Teacher Relationship in Social Media

If you choose to engage your students in social media, you are changing your relationship with them. Even if you do not provide any personal details about your life, you are changing the time and place in which they communicate with you. You are doing so in a place where they reveal many of the intimate details of their lives: comments from friends about social activities, including embarrassing comments, photographs of social events that reveal relationships with other students, and statements through group affiliations and add-on applications that reveal political and social involvements. Your page may also reveal these features about you. The relationship between a student and teacher is accidental (they did not come to this school because you were there), short-lived (in a few years, they will disappear and you will remain), and contractual (it is based on the delivery of educational services for the length of a term in return for tuition payments). Anything you learn about them or they learn about you in the course of affiliating through social media that is it directly related to the educational services is gratuitous at best and a violation of privacy at worst. With this in mind, use as little information about yourself as you can with students.

I use Facebook primarily for staying in touch with alumni. To that end, it works very well. I try to add current majors in the third or fourth year to make sure I will not forget them when they graduate. I do have personal information on the page, my birthday and my marital status, but no information about religious or political affiliations. All of the groups that appear on the page are either professional- or campus-identified. I use the page to send good wishes on birthdays and alert alumni to campus events. Occasionally, I will chat with current students if they happen to contact me while I have the Facebook page open. I never initiate that chat. This limited use of Facebook works for me. I would not feel comfortable going deeper into its possibilities with my students.

PART 16

Advising in the Classroom

Advising covers all those conversations between students and instructor that indirectly relate to course content. These include:

+ Studentship and study skills,

+ Retention issues, especially among students seeking advice relating to family, finances, and health issues, or social adjustment,

+ Conflicts between the student's personal or community values and the values of the university, and

+ Conflicts between the student's academic goals and the goals of the degree program.

Most formal advising takes place between you and students assigned to you specifically for advising. However, students may often approach you in your course. Effective advising grows out of effective teaching. Best practices in the classroom apply to advising as well. Advisors who take the role seriously find an improvement in their teaching. The two mutually reinforce each other.

You can think of advising as another form of teaching. The difference is that advising engages the faculty and student in a study of local culture and the skill of negotiating it successfully. Professors are the local experts. We must know and understand the rules that govern graduation, general education, declaration of major, the major requirements, course drop and add deadlines for schedules, academic integrity, grade challenges and changes, transfers, and registration. This is no more complicated than reading the college handbook. If your college has a new faculty seminar or workshop, the rules will be covered there. Being the expert on the rules means knowing the hard ones from the soft ones. Soft rules readily grant exceptions for good reasons; hard rules rarely do, even for good reasons.

Advising is a form of teaching in another sense, as well. College is the occasion for young people to practice making decisions that change the course of their lives. I write "practice making decisions" because very few of these decisions are irreversible. Not everyone comes to college prepared for this level of decision-making. Your role as advisor is to show how one goes about making them. This is where your knowledge of the college culture is so crucial. You help find the information they need to effectively evaluate alternatives. You cannot do this if you are in the dark yourself.

Finally, advising is like teaching because professors are not trained in counseling, the dominant disciplinary model for staff academic advisors. They are trained in an academic discipline. As such, faculty approach advising issues with the tools of academics. Literature specialists apply narrative theory to the stories their advisees tell. Sociologists listen for the advisees' appeal to norms that conflict with institutional consensus. Chemists test the advisees' claims in well-crafted experiments. Faculty advise by modeling for students how the discipline solves problems. Staff advisors ask, "What kind of person do you want to be? Faculty advisors ask, " What do you want to learn?"

Most of the time advising revolves around picking classes for the next term. Students visit advisors at registration time, seeking confirmation that they have made optimal choices. Others visit because they are too lazy or disinterested to learn the curriculum and want to be led. You can insist that when students make appointments for advising, they come prepared with partial schedules or at least a list of courses. Avoid the situation where you have to create the schedule for them, looking for specific sections to fit their constraints of work, sports, or commuting preferences. Students who fear making the wrong choices avoid responsibility. Encourage them with the appropriate information about the curriculum. Change the topic of conversation in these sessions from scheduling to decision-making. One way to do this is to encourage the students to seek connections between classes, by topic or method. This builds integration and synergy into a schedule. Another is to direct students' attention to co-curricular activities, like major clubs, research projects, or service activities that can help them see their learning in a larger context.

Diffusing Career Anxiety

The most important of these "larger context" conversations relates the college experience to the career. The outside community instills in our students the need to make that connection. Students have been asked since they were very young what they wanted to be when they grow up. Now, they overflow with anxiety about entering adulthood without a career path. They seek to brand themselves with a major. I help students unpack their anxiety about these connections during advising sessions. I tell them that they are becoming expert learners and not specialists in a particular area. Their employability is related to their learning skills, not what they know about literature or history. I remind them that schools construct curricula around the faculty resources. As such, the major has no intrinsic connection to the knowledge and skill demands of a specific career. After quashing their hopes of there being an easy connection between major and career, I show them how to plan a successful strategy for transitioning from college to a career. Your school's Career Office is your ally. They help students define their interests and develop a list of potential starting points. Encourage the student to begin the process early. I send first-year students to the Career Office for workshops to get them accustomed to using the contacts and resources of the college long before graduation.

Degree Progress Issues in an Era of Restricted Budgets

This edition is being published at a time when public universities are under severe budgetary pressure from their legislatures. Privates, too, have felt the sting as legislatures move to limit support for in-state students. The effect from the student's point of view has been fewer sections of required courses and reduced financial aid support. This, in turn, raised anxiety that the student will not graduate on time, or may have to drop out of school for lack of funds. There is little a course instructor can do to fix the problem. Student anger is appropriate, but it must be directed at the proper actors. The university or college is not doing this to the student. You are just as frustrated by the situation as they are. Your class enrollments are higher. While details vary from state to state, you should encourage students to see themselves as political actors who can make their voices heard through their representatives. While that may not solve their immediate problem, it does empower them to look for solutions. As a practical matter, not all students will graduate in the typical fashion in the next few years. Some will cobble together courses from less expensive schools, finishing their degrees at the schools where they initially matriculated. This may take more than four years to accomplish. That is the way it worked in the 1930s. Try to turn the conversation into a moment when students can see themselves embedded in a history that will unfold in unpredictable ways. Encourage them to look for opportunities they might not otherwise have considered.

Another aspect of this issue has to do with wait lists for students to enroll in a required course. Ordinarily, I would discuss this under administrative issues in the classroom. However, in the present climate it cannot be detached from advising. Any of us can grant permission to over-enroll our classes, even to the point of creating a safety hazard. We rarely do so because it is not in our self-interest to do so. I have often permitted one or two students who were about to graduate into a closed class. At other times, and often in my role as chair, I had to inform students that there was nothing anyone could do and their graduation would have to be delayed until they took the next available section of the class. It was certainly not a conversation I took pleasure in. It points out the problem of agency in student programs. Offering everyone the chance to graduate in four years, regardless of the decisions they make as individuals, was never part of the contract. Going back over the student's history may point out where they took a wrong turn, but does not solve the problem. There should be university, college, or department policies on wait lists. It should not be left entirely to the instructor's discretion.

When wait lists are handled by the course enrollment system, they usually follow a "first come; first serve" principle. The principle works if every student enrolls on the day and time of their appointment. However, even the best-intentioned student can find a hold on their registration, either for good reasons or because of an error. The system is unforgiving. The course is already full. When a seat becomes available, "the student with the highest number of credits goes to the head of the line" or "the student with the greatest number of completed courses in the major goes to the head of the line" are relatively simple rules that build equity among instructors, as well as transparency and fairness between instructors and students. These rules would have to be agreed upon by the entire unit to work well. An instructor can write and apply these rules, too. The important thing is to be scrupulously consistent. Any variation from the rule will make it difficult to apply it the next time the situation arises. When advising in the classroom, you should make students aware of any rules that the unit has adopted.

CHAPTER

95

Supporting Time Management

Successful college students organize time. One cynical professor once told me that in his experience, that is all we really teach them. When underachieving students admit to having difficulty getting the work done, you can have them log their activities to discover patterns of good and bad time management. Angelo and Cross include a seven-day

Productive Study-Time Log that you can use with students who are having trouble organizing their lives (1994). The students keep the log for seven days. Students enter studying, writing, and academic-related activities in thirty-minute blocks. They then indicate where the activity took place and then give a rating on a four-point scale from highly productive to not productive at all. Follow-up questions help students identify not only when they are most productive but also why that is so. Point out how they can plan to complete term-long projects more efficiently.

A recent National Survey of Student Engagement (NSSE) survey discovered that working while going to school begins to reduce overall GPA after twenty hours. This critical tipping point is shrinking. A 1987 study of male college students in the period of 1972-79 found that twenty-five hours of work had no adverse effect on grades, but off-campus work in that amount did affect retention (Ehrenberg and Sherman 1987). Where one works can continue to make a difference. On-campus employment significantly raises engagement, which, in turn, raises grades. Off-campus employment does not raise engagement as dramatically. As a result, off-campus employment distracts students from school for the same number of hours worked. Working more than twenty hours per week can work for some students by helping them develop more efficient time management skills. Such students present themselves by saying they have always worked while going to school and have not seen their grades suffer (Pike et al. 2009).

The most intractable time management issue involves students who must work to support themselves or their families, or care for a young child while going to school. First, make sure that they require a job for tuition and living expenses and not merely for expendable income. Students involved in making high car payments or being able to spend three nights a week in a club need to figure out where their priorities lie. Second, weaker students may have greater economic anxiety than stronger students. The total number of hours and the pay rate should give a clue about this. They may see employment during college as hedging their bets. If college doesn't work out or doesn't create more economic opportunity, then the job experience will keep them employed. A student working off-campus more than 20 hours per week with a GPA in the 2.5 range (4 point scale) should talk about their fears that college may not help them economically. If the need is real and if college rules allow, you might explore reducing the courses per term. Taking five or even six years to complete the degree. Know the rules. Part-time students have a reduced claim on financial aid compared to full-time students. State support for students in private schools also has credit hour minimums and maximums. A higher grade point average is more important for future choices than completing the degree in the traditional four years. Some students will be caught between conflicting priorities.

Understanding Learning Disabilities

CHAPTER

96

Be open to the possibility of a learning disability in underachieving students. Students having difficulty in several different subject areas or who put in the preparation time but are still performing poorly may suffer from a learning disability. It is not your job to diagnose and treat such disabilities. You point the student toward the office in the university where that specialized advice and support is found. Educate yourself about these disabilities. You should know what questions to ask. One website that has extensive resources for you to educate yourself is http://www.ldonline. org/. I can also recommend my university's learning disabilities website http://studentaffairs.depaul.edu/plus/faculty_staff.html. The university's support office can help you figure out what these questions are. Keep the website, street address and phone number of the university support office handy to give to students.

Students who have overcome cognitive disabilities and gone on to become successful writers reflect on the experience in ways similar to this:

> Though I had these problems with languages in high school, I was unaware that they could be attributed to a learning disability. It was not until I went to college that my learning disability was identified.... When I saw a pattern of problems developing in my language courses, I told my parents first. Their initial reaction was to tell me I should work harder and not give up. They instructed me to get a tutor, go to my professor's office hours, and check with the

Academic Skills Center to see what I could do to improve my study habits, memory, and performance on exams. What they did not know was that I had long since done all of these things.... .They, like my teachers, told me that I didn't do well because I didn't work hard enough. The fact that they blamed my difficulties on my supposed lack of hard work troubled me, but I know my parents were caring people and wanted the best for me. I know that they were trying just as hard as I was to sort this out and that my lack of effort was the only reasonable explanation for them. I don't think they meant to be insensitive or to burden me—I just think their lack of knowledge made them less likely to respond as I needed. (Sanders 2001)

The Americans with Disabilities Act requires faculty to make appropriate accommodations for students who have recognized physical and cognitive disabilities. You begin to make these accommodations by putting a statement like this in your syllabus:

Students who may need an accommodation based on the impact of a disability should contact me privately to discuss their specific needs. All discussions will remain confidential. To ensure that you receive the most appropriate reasonable accommodation based on your needs, contact me as early as possible in the quarter (preferably within the first week of class), and make sure that you have contacted the Student Disabilities Office with phone number (or, if a separate one exists at your school, the Cognitive and Attention Disabilities Office with phone number)

You are not obligated to make any accommodations for students who are not registered with the local disability office. Having had accommodations in high school is not enough. Accommodations usually involve more time for tests, taking tests in sound proof rooms, oral testing, sign language interpreters, books on tape and similar changes in classroom routine.

You are never obligated to change the learning goals or course outcomes of a class to accommodate a student. The number and level of difficulty of the readings, the number of tests, drafts of papers, out of class projects, travel to off-campus collections or field sites, or classroom participation must be the same for every student in your class, regardless of physical or cognitive ability. Accommodation does not go that far. You may be asked to help find an alternative way for a disabled student to meet the requirements, but you should never be asked to change or suspend a requirement. If you have designed your class for universal access, this will be even less of an issue.

Helping Students with Life Crisis Issues

CHAPTER

97

Our students deal with pregnancy, crime, drugs, illness, death, victimization, war, and natural disasters. I have had students who did not complete work or attend class for these reasons. If this happens, you need to make decisions about whether the work can be made up. If it cannot, then your role switches to that of advisor. Help the student negotiate with other instructors and the college. Direct the student toward administrative and personal support. You should never advocate for the student with other instructors. It is always better to empower the student to do the talking. Only medical emergencies justify informing another instructor about a student's situation.

Your first response in these situations should be the humane one. Students rarely lie about emotional or medical crises. Students view such problems as stigmatizing. Unless you have evidence that the student may be fabricating, dispense with asking the student for proof. It is the wrong moment to be cynical. Take your cue from the student. Let them weep if they need to. Let them rant their frustration. You offer validation for these feelings. The student needs to get beyond these before they begin to rebalance their relationship with school.

All colleges have policies that permit students to withdraw from classes for medical or personal reasons after the official drop period or even retroactively. You need to know who makes these decisions and what the procedures are. You need to know the address and phone number of the mental health services office on campus. You should follow up with the student to see that they contacted the administrative and clinical experts. Young people are resilient. They bounce back from setbacks to have successful college experiences. Your time and attention during the crisis increases the chances that the resolution of the crisis will benefit the student in the long run.

CHAPTER 98

Helping Underachieving Students

There are several causes for under-achievement. I have already discussed other causes, such as time management, learning disabilities, and personal crisis. There are at least four more reasons: discouragement, under preparedness, lack of motivation and acute reaction. Little can be done for the student with low motivation to succeed. These students are in school at the wrong time in their lives. They would rather be doing something else. When I discover such students I encourage them to do something else for a while. We talk about taking a leave of absence and what the student could do during that time that might be more interesting. You need to know your school's policies on such leaves and when the readmission policies take effect. I also explain about transfer credit for work already completed and adult degree completion programs. I identify as many of the local programs as I can for the student to consider when they are older. I send them to the career center for help with transitioning to a job. I tell them to stay in touch with me and contact me when they are ready to come back to school.

The difference between discouraged students and struggling students is the difference between an acute condition and a chronic one. Discouraged students develop from otherwise competent ones through some change in their support system, self-doubt, or the transition to a new level of education. You can identify them through a change from obvious enthusiasm at the beginning of the term to a pattern of missed classes, papers that reflect marginal effort, and a slacker attitude toward class discussions. You find this in first-term transfer students, students in the first difficult course in the major, and beginning graduate students.

McKeachie cites research that has demonstrated that these students can benefit immediately and dramatically from a conversation with a student who completed the same course in a previous year (McKeachie 2002; Van Overwalle et al. 1989, 75-85; Wilson and Linville 1982, 367-76). As this student describes his or her initial feelings of frustration and self-doubt, the discouraged student realizes that the problem is temporary and not related to a lack of ability that cannot be changed. When the discouragement shows no signs of abating, students risk dropping out or underachieving.

The causes of long-term struggles with grades are often deep seated. Struggling students are identified by weak first-year grades and poor performance on early papers or quizzes. As a general rule, you should have conversation with any student who has significantly underperformed on an early evaluation. These students can be overwhelmed by the level of skill that is being demanded of them. They may have competing demands on their time that greatly reduce their opportunity to study. They may be in the midst of familial or personal crises.

Most of these issues are beyond the means of a class instructor to remedy. You can, however, serve as a resource for encouraging the student to seek the right kind of help. To that end, you should know what these resources are. At the very least, you should have the phone numbers and campus addresses of the mental health center, the dean of students, the financial aid counselor who works with continuing students, the writing and reading skills center, the learning disabilities office, and campus ministry. Whatever your recommendation, you should follow up with such students within a week to insure that they have begun the process of rescuing themselves.

The final possible stumbling block among otherwise motivated students involves acute reactions: emotionally based reactions that interfere with the student's performance. The best known of these is test anxiety. When a test is given, some students fear the outcome so much that they cannot perform. Another is a crisis of self-esteem. For reasons that even the student may not be able to identify, suddenly he or she cannot meet the demands of the class. Still another is an acute depression after completing a project that consumes a substantial amount of time and attention. This acute depression can disable the student so that he or she cannot finish the term.

These are mental health issues. It is important that you recognize them as such and help the student to see them in that light. While you have no basis for diagnosing or solving their problem, you can provide information for the professional support on campus. More importantly, you can validate that they indeed have a problem. If you have had a similar problem, now is the time to share that with the student. When students begin to understand that such acute reactions can happen to anyone, especially to people under stress, they will make that appointment with the counseling office. Some schools hold group sessions for discussing and overcoming test anxiety because that reaction is so common. Find out what resources exist for handling acute reactions and be prepared to help students understand that there is no stigma attached to seeking help for such problems.

Dealing with Angry, Aggressive, or Bullying Students

CHAPTER
99

Students challenge your authority when they are openly hostile to you over a position you take in class, over a grade you give, or in response to your effort to move the discussion. Some students automatically discount the authority of the teacher if the teacher is a woman, has an accent, is racially different from the majority of the class, has a non-assertive demeanor, or is physically small. This behavior can be covert as well as overt. The first indication you have that a student covertly undervalues your authority in the classroom is often the course evaluation. Several studies focus on the effect of stereotyping on course evaluations, notably conducted by untenured faculty (Anderson and Miller 1997, 216-19; Hendrix 1998, 738-63; Johnson 1994, 409-19). Bullies exist at all ages and include both genders. They can make the classroom an uncomfortable environment for both students and teachers. You must deal openly and directly with such hostility.

Challenges to authority are rarely about you personally. The student relates to you as a stereotype. Faculty can diffuse this by scheduling fifteen to twenty minute office appointments with students who show aggressive signs. Establishing a personal connection with these students makes it more difficult for them to relate to you as a caricature.

As difficult as it may be, ignoring an open challenge to your authority is the worst approach you can take. This is followed in order of wrong-headedness with attacking the student right back. The best way to diffuse anger and aggression is to listen to student. Anger is often a mask for fear. If you respond to the fear instead of the anger, you can diffuse it. Always allow the student a way to gracefully retreat from the confrontation. In the social sciences and humanities it is often possible to make the emerging hostility the example of whatever you want the class to discuss.

If the anger arises over what appears to be an emotional reaction to a topic being discussed, summarize what was said about the subject before the outburst. Conclude the summary by saying, "You seem really angry about this. Does anyone else feel this way?" Solicit peer pressure to hold the angry student in check. Allow the student the opportunity to resolve the problem being addressed in an alternate way. The student may not be able to offer solutions and will sometimes undermine his or her own position. Do not position yourself in opposition to the angry student by defending the position that was upsetting in the first place. The exception to this is that you should never accept the premise or underlying assumption of the angry student's argument if it is false or prejudicial (e.g., you might respond to an antigay slur by saying, "If by 'faggot' you mean homosexual . . .").

Sometimes students are angry for good reasons. They are not getting the educational experience they thought they were promised. You need to deal with that. When they are angry for the wrong reasons, you need to diffuse their emotion by letting them vent so that you can bring them back to the discussion at hand. Recognizing that their anger comes from a frustrated effort to engage the class is an important step for you. Even though it is upsetting to be interrupted or have your agenda for the class meeting derailed, you need to acknowledge the possibility that the student could be partially right. McKeachie (2002) suggests three different approaches at this point. First, you can restate your position, acknowledging that you are not perfect and that not everyone will agree with the position you take. However, you are responsible for making these judgments as best you can and you have done so. Second, you can address the issue to the class and engage them in a discussion. Have other students summarize the argument as they see it. This runs the risk that you or the student may lose the support of the class, but the class may help shed light on the disagreement. Finally, you can take a moment to reflect on the student's argument, admit the possibility that you were wrong, and state that you will take the time to reconsider your position and report back to the class at the next meeting. This has the advantage of delaying the discussion until tempers have cooled, and it gains you a reputation for fairness. In all three approaches, listen to what the student is saying and avoid being overly defensive.

For students who are stubbornly fixated on a particular grade, do not offer to have another faculty member read the paper or test. This just puts your colleague in an awkward position. Remind the student that the school has a grade challenge procedure that you would encourage them to use if they disagree with your decision. You should know what the first step in the procedure is and tell the student that you will be happy to supply whatever documentation the review requires. You can trust the grade challenge procedure. In my experience, fewer than ten percent of all grade challenges are reviewed in the student's favor.

CHAPTER
100

Dealing with Flattery

Be wary of students who approach you with flattering remarks. They will not know that you are the best teacher they ever had until long after they leave school. Some may be insecure about their own learning and looking to establish a personal relationship with a teacher that can be advantageous to them. They may be looking for special favors, extensions on papers, better evaluations, or help in negotiating a problem with another teacher. The real danger with such students is that they lead you to doubt the sincerity of other students. We all yearn for positive feedback from our students. Some students really do need special considerations with deadlines. The best approach is to take students' comments with a grain of salt and afford all students the benefit of the doubt that they are always forthright about their situations, at least until they reveal themselves otherwise.

Dealing with Emotional Reactions to Sensitive Topics

CHAPTER 101

Unpacking accepted truths is our reason for existing. Many students are unaware of this when they enter, coming, as many do, from homogeneous communities where the "truth" is never questioned. We discuss topics our students consider sensitive all the time. The university is the one place in society where we examine sensitive topics and dangerous ideas. Whether the topic is group differences in intelligence, the existence of race, animal experimentation, birth control and abortion, UFOs, conspiracy theories, radical ideologies, nationalism and patriotism, literature that portrays child abuse, art that addresses taboo subjects, music that forces us to listen hard, or the decision to drop the atomic bomb on Japan, some students will have strong reactions. The challenge is to seize the teachable moment that conflict and emotional reactions engender.

Emotionally charged topics polarize the class. When emotions rise, students get nervous that nothing will be accomplished that day. If you remain calm in the heat of the conflict, it will be easier for the students to regain control. Your behavior will send the appropriate cues to the class about how it should interpret what is going on. Take the time to collect yourself. There is nothing wrong with allowing everything to go silent for a moment or two; as long as you show that you are comfortable with it. Even if you have been attacked personally, do not take it personally. The attack was against your authority to raise the topic, not your person. Turn your thoughts to the needs of the students and their feelings at this moment. If the attack was against you as a member of a group, remember that the group's interests are better served by enhancing people's understanding in general rather than tearing into this one student. These hurtful comments are never original. Remind yourself of what the student's position represents in the classroom and in the larger world.

The teachable moment begins when both sides of an issue start to really listen to each other. Sometimes this requires a cooling-off period. Ending class early so that you can prepare the opposing students to listen to each other more carefully during the next class can be an effective tactic. It also gives the students a chance to catch their breath, collect evidence, and return with better prepared arguments (Warren 2002). Here are some additional strategies from the Derek Bok Center at Harvard:

→ Ask students to step back and think about what the heated exchange has taught them about the topic.

→ Ask students to think about (or write about) how their reactions to the exchange mirror the subject itself.

→ Ask students to write a short five-minute essay in which they state their position on the exchange.

→ Go around the room and ask each student who has spoken (and others who wish to speak) to restate their position and the reasoning behind it.

→ List all of the positions and reasons on the board. Use the passion of the speakers to talk about the differences in the kinds and levels of discourse: who is comfortable with emotion and who is not; who favors personalizing material and who prefers to keep it abstract, whether or not there are community-based styles that underlie these differences.

→ Use the passion of the speakers to look at how group dynamics work— who speaks and who does not, who allies with whom, who plays what role—and to think about how the group wants to work. (Bok Center 2002)

It takes great skill on your part, not to mention a high comfort level with conflict, to decide how and when to stop the emotional charge of a discussion or whether to use it to explore the discussion at hand.

Some students are simply not ready to listen to the other side. They find it too threatening or too painful. These students need extra time to adapt their reaction from one of emotion to one of reason. The place to hold this conversation is in your office, not the classroom. You should also expect that the discussion will last for some time, so plan accordingly. You need to validate their feelings at the onset, or they will not listen to you. You need to talk about your challenges when you first came to university. Then, when you have them listening, you need to explain the special role of the university in society. While this discussion of the topic may lead away from the position the students hold, no discussions in a university are ever closed. As new evidence becomes available, any argument can be reexamined. Explain why the topic is important to the goals of the class. Ask the student if he or she thinks that evidence is an important part of determining how we should act in the world and, if so, what we should do with evidence that contradicts the beliefs and opinions of the majority or a vocal minority. If they are still upset at having their beliefs challenged, help them identify a faculty member who participates in a community where the student's perspective is commonly supported. A conversation with that faculty member might help them sort out their feelings, while providing them with the evidence they need to assert their position through reason rather than emotion. If no one on the faculty can be found, ask the student to consider researching the evidence of their position in the library, giving them some search strategies to help them begin.

PART 17

Effective Evaluation of Student Achievement

Grading establishes categories to evaluate students. Grading does not begin with assigning a letter grade to a student in a grade roster. Rather, that is the final stage in a complex process. As Walvoord and Anderson rightly point out, grading involves identifying the most valuable learning in a course, constructing exams and assignments that will test that learning, setting standards and criteria, guiding students' learning, and implementing changes in teaching that are based on information from the grading process. They urge faculty to abandon false hopes that grading can be easy, uncomplicated, uncontested, or one-dimensional (1998).

Only by going through the process of understanding exactly what you put into the course can you begin to evaluate what the students got out of it. Grading is as much a judgment about you as it is about them. This is not to say that if they all did well, you did well. They might have done well either because the course was pitched lower than their reasoning level or because you motivated them to reach beyond their normal level performance. Even after several years of course development, the ordinary variation in student skills filtered through the random processes of registration will produce specific groups of students for whom the class does not work. You can only know the difference if you are mindful of this possibility and have a well-defined sense of what is being measured by your grades. Grading specifically to the needs of a course serves the needs of that course independently of the variation of the students who register in a particular term.

People study the relation of grades to adult achievement more than any other feature of higher education. These studies are important because they help us as teachers to put the grades we give students in a realistic context. One meta-analysis (Cohen 1984) employed common measures of adult achievement, including supervisor's job performance ratings (in 50 studies), income (in 34 studies), promotions (in 14 studies), graduate degrees (in 23 studies), etc. The results show a very small positive relationship between grades and achievement: less than 4% of the variance in adult achievement is predicted by GPA. Another meta-analysis (Samson, Grave, Weinstien, and Walberg 1984) reported that less than 2.5% of the variance in measures of occupational performance can be predicted by academic grades. The authors concluded that "the overall variance accounted for makes grades or test scores nearly useless in predicting occupational effectiveness and satisfaction. Educators, employers, students, and research workers need to think again about what is taught, learned, and measured."

We commonly believe that the course grades we assign are both useful and lasting measures of academic achievement. Milton, Pollio, and Eison (1986) surveyed 850 faculty across 23 campuses in the U.S. and found that 83% believed that a students' grades or grade point average were "excellent" or "good" measures of academic achievement. Further, 34% of the faculty felt that the difference in "knowledge" (i.e., achievement, learning, performance) represented by one student who made an A in a given class and a second student who made a C in that same class would last five years or more.

Compare this confidence in the vitality of grades to that of business recruiters, who focus less on the GPA's of job applicants than faculty and students imagine (Eison 1988). When 450 college recruiters rated the relative importance of 15 different pieces of information about job candidates on a seven point scale, the single most important piece of information was "students' personality" (60% of the respondents rated this item six or seven); overall GPA and grades in major courses were rated of lesser importance (33% and 52% of the respondents rated these items six or seven, respectively) (Milton et al. 1986). These recruiters see grades differently than professors. On the other hand, we try to ignore personality. For me there is no more compelling evidence that grades and adult achievement are apples and oranges.

Still, grades matter in our community. Even when we admit that the 32 to 48 grades that constitute a bachelor's GPA involved wildly divergent criteria, we still believe that students who consistently impress us should be differentiated from those who impress occasionally and those who do not impress at all. Were this to make sense only in the context of the academic community, it would still be valuable.

Establishing Fair and Effective Grading Policies

CHAPTER
102

Grading can serve a number of purposes. The first is the ordinary evaluation of the student's work in a manner that is valid, fair, and trustworthy. The second purpose is to communicate a particular message to the student and also to future employers, graduate schools, the military, and fellowship agencies. Because of its potential emotional charge, the grade may be the most important communication between the instructor and the student. Grades serve the purpose of motivating students to study. This is true not just in your class but in the student's entire collegiate career. Grades that reward effort act as an incentive for the student to continue putting forth the effort. Grades that thwart effort act as a disincentive. Finally, grades mark transitions between segments of the course or between the end of the course and the beginning of the next term. Grades bring closure and help students and instructors focus their efforts. (Walvoord and Anderson 1998)

The university may have already defined the grade categories for you. If so, you'll probably find the distinctions too general to be useful. "A is for excellent work" does not help us to differentiate the excellent from the very good. To say that we know it when we see it reveals laziness. After so many years of learning to make discriminating judgments about the works of other scholars, describing analytic criteria for our students' work ought to be a piece of cake. We do it infrequently because it is time consuming and uncomfortable. As Walvoord and Anderson make clear in that quote, grading entails evaluating our own contribution to the students' performance.

General guidelines about your grading would define, for example, the difference between an A and a B on essays as a principle for all the classes you teach (e.g., the A paper will address as many counter-arguments as possible while the B paper will not, all other features of the essay being equal). You would still need to provide specific criteria for a particular essay (e.g., the excellent paper will showcase the quality of the student's own reflection on the question). Several rubrics are available to help you decide for yourself how you will distinguish between these marks. You must make these distinctions at some level of precision, both for yourself and for your students. You can always make adjustments later if the grade for a particular essay needs to be raised to help keep the student motivated or lowered because of poor proofreading or missing pieces.

Even after going through this exercise, we need to acknowledge that grading can never be an objective process. No matter how many numbers we put between the student and ourselves, our judgments are written all over the grades we give students. Some may object that by giving multiple-choice exams and avoiding the subjective reading of essays, the instructor's judgments can be made to disappear. This ignores the judgments that go into the selection of the questions, the construction of the alternative answers, and the residual ambiguity that exists in language. The so-called objective test merely forefronts the instructor's judgments; it does not dispense with them. We also need to acknowledge that reasonable people can disagree reasonably over the appropriate grade for a student. If you have never experienced a group grading session, you should. It is heartwarming how consistently experienced teachers evaluate student work. It is also remarkable how frequently they disagree. If the high levels of agreements are to be celebrated as evidence of the existence of common standards, then the disagreements must be taken as signs that such standards are never complete. When you are grading on your own, imagine how the residual disagreement among co-graders evaluating the same work might affect the outcomes for specific individuals. It is a sobering thought.

Finally, we need to understand the importance of grades for students. As much as we have chosen the life of the mind and the joy of learning, it is folly to believe that all of our students have the same motivation. Whether we like it or not, students view our grades as judgments about their personal and social worth, as well as intellectual achievement. We did not invent the stratified social arrangements they inhabit, but our grades reproduce these arrangements inadvertently. Hence, every instance of grading is dependent on the context of the course, the experience of the instructor and socially constructed categories of grades the instructor is employing.

Walvoord and Anderson's *Effective Grading* (1998), which should be on every teacher's bookshelf, offers twelve principles for managing the grading process that every instructor should take to heart. My discussion of the principles here is necessarily brief. For a fuller discussion, consult chapter 2 of *Effective Grading*. First, appreciate the complexity of grading and use it as a tool for learning. Grades have taken on different forms and meanings throughout the history of U.S. higher education (Milton et al. 1986). They must continue to evolve. Grades mean different things to different students even in the same classroom (Guba and Lincoln 1989). No one-size-fits-all system of grades will ever work in this context. In Walvoord and Anderson's view (1998), the greatest good is served when grades fulfill the needs of all the participants in the process and are used to bring about useful change. To this end, they see skills in listening, negotiation, cultural understanding, and empathy—the same effort to understand the variation in students who register for a class that I have consistently urged on you—as strengthening the process of evaluation.

Second, substitute judgment for objectivity. You must accept responsibility for rendering your best judgments about the quality of student work. This is the most difficult aspect of teaching. Your ability to do so will grow over time. At the beginning, you protect yourself by being as transparent about the process as you can. You and students should know what criteria you will use before the assignment begins. Share your criteria and your experiences with other faculty.

The third principle directs you to distribute your time effectively. Do not obsess over the grading process. Spend enough time to form an opinion, make the judgment, add some comments about why this judgment is appropriate, and move on. Reviewing your efforts and second-guessing yourself will not improve the quality of your grading. It is always going to be a messy process.

Fourth, be open to change. I know my grading has become more precise and assured as I have gotten older. I remember passing through phases when I was more generous and other times when I was stingy. I like the reputation that I have among students that I give few As. I didn't always have that reputation. I know that when I am dealing with first-year students, I think of the grades differently than when I am dealing with a mixed age class of majors or a homogeneous senior capstone seminar. The differences in skill level require that I use the grades differently.

The fifth principle asks you to listen and observe. It is the meaning that the students attach to the grade that will have the biggest impact on their future learning. The grade may mean something immediately important to a student. This will take the form of a hasty conference in your office or a series of anxious remarks over time. Perhaps a father is going to withhold tuition support unless the student's grades rise at the end of the term. Maybe the student is on the verge of dropping out from frustration over low grades. Is this student tired of the pressure that comes from always being given A's? Grades are judgments couched in local meanings. The better you are at understanding those local meanings, the more effective your grading (1998).

Sixth, communicate and collaborate with students. Students want fairness and help more than anything else. Certainly, you make their lives easier in the short run if you simply hand them A's. But they are capable of seeing beyond the immediate and realize that they need your honesty more than your generosity. When you explain the criteria you use in evaluating, you make your students collaborators with you in the evaluation process. When you are explicit about the standards for a particular grade, the post-evaluation conversation can focus on why specific features were absent or why a particular issue was not addressed. This level of specificity helps students to learn more effectively.

The seventh principle integrates grading with other classroom processes. At the very least, you should be able to write your criteria for evaluating everything you assign and for class participation. In doing so, you reveal your values about learning. The practice of writing out your criteria also forces you to look at the amount and complexity of the material you assign. If students do all the work you expect, will your evaluations capture this? If students find the workload overwhelming, how will this be reflected in your grades? The evaluation component serves as a check on how well you have achieved the balance between the knowledge base and the skill set.

Eighth, seize the teachable moment. College students undergo rapid physical, social, and intellectual change. When a student has an emotional reaction to a grade, perhaps leaving the class in tears after receiving your judgment, you must stay focused. What do you want the student to understand at this moment? What do you want to communicate about the values of your classroom, your profession, and your institution? Be prepared because what you say can change the student's attitude for a significant amount of time (1998).

The ninth principle makes student learning the primary goal of evaluation. In prioritizing the various audiences for your judgment, such as other students, a future employer, or a graduate school, put the student first. A grade that is lower than what the student needs, offered with support and understanding, is always preferable to trying to second-guess the invisible audiences. Astin (Austin 1996, 123-34) describes three "conditions of excellence" based on hundreds of studies of college students. These include the student's involvement in learning, the level of expectations in the classroom, and the quality of the assessment and feedback of student performance. Putting the student first in your approach to evaluation reinforces all three of these conditions. Grading is also implicated in all seven of Chickering and Gamson's principles of good practice in college teaching (1987, 3-7).

Closely aligned with these sentiments is the tenth principle: be a teacher first and a gatekeeper second. The role of gatekeeper comes at the end of the process, not at the beginning or the middle. Being a teacher first means that the goal of the classroom should never be gatekeeping—it should be change and growth. Far too many colleagues see one or another course in the major as the grade that really matters for the student to take the next step. For that reason, they make the course inscrutably difficult in the mistaken belief that they insure high performances in the future among those who pass. These colleagues abdicate their responsibility as teachers to those students. They show no faith in the students' ability to change. This attitude interferes with helping students learn. It produces highly flawed evaluations. It may sometimes be necessary for students to engage complex and sophisticated material. In such cases the instructor should remain optimistic that every student will succeed.

Eleventh, encourage learning-centered motivation for students to succeed in the course. It is a truism that without strong motivation, new learning, as well as breaking old habits, is severely inhibited. Research by Milton, Pollio, and Eison (1986) has shown that the negative effects of grades on motivation derive from the attitude students hold toward grades, rather than the grades themselves. Students believe that they lack the power to affect what happens to them. They may be convinced that hard work is not rewarded, especially if it does not result in a right answer. They may hold that success in school depends on luck or that failure results from circumstances beyond their control. I have found in my own practice that when students understand the criteria through which grades are derived ahead of time, and when my feedback to them provides a detailed narrative about how their performance matched the criteria, these attitudes begin to fall away and motivation to succeed increases.

The twelfth and final principle emphasizes student involvement in the grading process. According to Pascarella and Terenzini (1991), involvement is the key to unlocking effective student learning at all levels. Give them a chance to discuss the grading criteria. Give them opportunities to read each other's work, either informally with students of their own choosing or formally with their names removed. If you do provide a set of model papers for students to look at and compare to their own work, provide representative papers from all grading levels. The advantage of openness is the increase in motivation it provides to the students in general. They learn from the model papers and the flawed papers alike. If this method of student involvement does not appeal to you, seek another. Building student involvement into every aspect of your classroom practice is the faster way to increase learning among your students.

CHAPTER

103

Grading Practices to Avoid

Walvoord and Anderson (1998) make the point that grading on a curve introduces dynamics that are harmful to learning and I agree. I never grade on a curve. This practice involves allocating a certain percentage of the class to each grade—say, 15 percent get A's, 35 percent B's, 35 percent C's, and 15 percent D's. Walvoord and Anderson list six features of this practice that either are logically flawed or introduce attitudes that are antithetical to learning.

In the first place, grades are not a limited commodity dispensed by the teacher. They are indexes of the performance of individual students according to criteria of achievement of learning. There is no a priori reason why all students should not get A's or why all students should not get F's.

Second, when high grades are meted out as a limited good, it introduces competition among the students that could very well lead to active suppression of learning by some students at the hands of others. This includes absconding with or defacing library books, sabotage of group efforts, the seeding of false information about upcoming tests, plagiarism, and stealing of notebooks. You want students to collaborate in learning. Limited numbers of A's sends the opposite message. If I can prevent you from doing better than I do on a test, I get the better grade, regardless of the quality of my work.

Third, learning is not a statistically distributed feature. Learning in a specific context, like your class, depends less on social background and more on motivational factors. These factors will vary from class to class, even among the best prepared students.

Fourth, a classroom is not a random sample of the population at large. It was determined by the registration lottery, a process that sorts students according to criteria the must bias the sample and undermine all assumptions of a normal distribution. Hence, the distribution of grades on a curve can only be arbitrary.

Fifth, this practice forces the instructor to be a slave to a formula that ignores actual student achievement in favor of some theoretical distribution. This provides the teacher with a false sense of insulation from student complaints.

Finally, curved grades are usually grades that lower the standard for a certain percentage of students. If you set a standard and students do not reach it, there is something wrong either with the standard or with the methods you employed for teaching the material.

You want to set standards that represent what students need to know and what they can achieve, given the hours available and the variety of goals you have set for them. Curving the grading may protect that particular class from your errors in setting these standards, but it does not solve the underlying problem. It also leads to grade inflation, the subject of the next chapter. In sum, when faced with student demands or a department practice to grade on a curve, do not do it.

CHAPTER 104

Combating Grade Inflation

Many instructors claim that the administration's concern with grade inflation motivates them to grade on a curve. Some argue that the average grade in the United States used to be a C. Today it is somewhere between a B- and a B. It is unclear what this means, and there have been no definitive studies on the issue. An older argument held that antiwar professors gave higher grades to students to help them avoid failure and subsequent draft into the army during the Vietnam conflict. After the war, the practices became the norm. For this reason, grade inflation rallied the troops in the Culture Wars. People attribute grade inflation to the widespread use of curved or motivational grading, the practice of giving higher than appropriate grades to sustain the students' motivation to learn. Still another canard one hears is that instructors' lack of standards make it too easy for students to get good grades. For those on the other side of the argument, the change in the national average reflects better-prepared students, more effective classroom teaching and textbooks, a greater amount of information flowing through society, higher literacy advantages that were not available to previous generations, and changes in the standards for grading that encourage greater student participation with a concomitant rise in motivation and learning. Political attitudes about the benefits of meritocratic education, diversity, affirmative action, and cosmopolitanism strongly influence this debate.

The concern expressed by administrators has less to do with the culture wars and more to do with an overall concern for the perception. Thus, an instructor whose students earn the same number of C's as A's in an introductory course but all A's in a senior seminar is less likely to be called into the chair's office for a conversation about grading than one whose introductory students all earn A's. It is not that such a situation is impossible. Rather, it is unlikely that introductory students would consistently perform at that level. If I were the chair, the conversation would be about why the instructor thinks the class was so successful, what goals were set, what evaluation criteria were established, what assessments were made, and what evaluations were administered. If any of these pieces were missing, then we could talk about how their absence may have affected the overall grade profile. If everything was in place, we could talk about the standards in relation to standards set by instructors in other sections of the same course, to see if any adjustments might be necessary. It could be possible that this instructor was lucky enough to have exceptionally motivated students enroll in the section disproportionately to other sections. But that should only happen once or twice in a career.

Students in advanced courses contribute disproportionately to the perception of grade inflation, especially when it is averaged across curricula and across institutions. Since the 1970s, students have enjoyed a dramatic increase in the number of available majors. This means that they can select ways of finishing their degrees through subject matters for which they have a high motivation for success. Previously, students were caught up in finishing degrees in subject matters that barely interested them. The process distributes highly motivated students disproportionately to the upper-division courses. There are still going to be the few students who do not do well. However, the wider distribution of grades that we often encounter in the lower division is unlikely to occur in the upper division today.

This discussion is not an argument for complacency about grade inflation. On the contrary, it is vitally important that all instructors pay considerable attention to their grade distributions. It is one of the best ways of assessing an instructor's overall design of the course. That final distribution is a sort of final grade for the instructor as well as for the student. Faculty who ignore an unexpected distribution do so at their peril. You know these students best. Only you can determine whether the distribution was the result of standards that were too low or too high, a class roster that was disproportionately motivated or unmotivated, or evaluation standards that were too easy or too hard. If everyone were to do a similar analysis, there would be no argument about grade inflation.

CHAPTER 105

Criterion-Based Grading

All grading is criterion based. Articulating these criteria, to yourself and your students, determines whether the grading is effective or ineffective. According to Walvoord and Anderson (1998), when grading is effective, it uses the instructor's time efficiently. It is consistent and fair. The expectations are easily explained to students. The grades show what you are trying to teach. The grades identify relationships between knowledge and skills. The grades help students know what they should aim to accomplish. Students can evaluate their own and each other's work. Providing the criteria saves the instructor from explaining grades after the fact. It helps students give each other constructive feedback on drafts. It helps team teachers and teaching assistants grade consistently across sections. It helps instructors in sequenced courses communicate about standards and competencies. Finally, criteria-based grading can help departments and institutions assess their programs more effectively.

I urge you to read Walvoord and Anderson because the brief summary of the technique I provide here is intended only to whet your appetite. Their book provides many discipline and classroom specific examples. It also provides much more detail on the technical points. Criteria-based grading uses a technique known as Primary Trait Analysis (PTA). It was developed to score essays on the National Assessment of Educational Progress, an exam administered across the country over several decades to measure changes in educational standards (Lloyd-Jones 1977). Before you can evaluate the student's performance, you need to first identify the list of traits or factors that will be evaluated. These are directly related to the knowledge categories and skill sets that you have made the core goals of the course. Your list of traits should be worded as nouns or noun phrases. The number of traits does not matter. It is more important that you are satisfied that the traits you choose reflect the goals you have set for the course. You then create a scale for scoring student performance. Scales from two to five points are common. More than that, the scale becomes unwieldy. If, for example, you choose a four-point scale, each of the four points corresponds to the student's control over the knowledge or skill trait. These should be descriptive statements.

Following is an adaptation of a five-point scale developed by the Writing Program at my institution that I sometimes use for evaluating essays in my lower-division classes:

Grade of A. For a detailed narrative that extensively and accurately uses the concepts, theories, and ideas from the readings, lectures, discussions, interviews, and other research materials to make sense of the research problem. The narrative adequately states and defends a point of view and answers most counter-arguments and counterexamples suggested by class discussion, reading assignments (specific arguments and authors are mentioned by name in the commentary), and the common sense of students and scholars. The essay is very well written, consisting of coherent and logical organization, clear and precise use of language, and very few technical errors in spelling and grammar.

Grade of B. For an occasionally vague or imprecise narrative that frequently and accurately uses the concepts, theories, and ideas from the readings, lectures, discussions, interviews, and other research materials to make sense of the research problem. The narrative states a point of view that is supported by clear arguments and factual evidence. Counter-arguments and counter-examples might be mentioned but are not adequately answered. Other weaknesses may include factual evidence that is incorrect, missing, or not specific; linking points of view that are either unclear or missing; and counter-arguments and counter-examples that are not clearly stated. The narrative may employ a "straw man" argument. The essay is well written, with only occasional imprecise or ambiguous phrases or sentences and occasional but still infrequent technical errors.

Grade of C. For a narrative that states a point of view but where supporting arguments and factual evidence are missing, incorrect, irrelevant, anachronistic, or opinion-based; not sufficiently specific; and/or all or partly obscured by errors in language and usage. The narrative is vague or imprecise more often than it is detailed and descriptive; it offers few applications of concepts, theories, or ideas from lectures, readings, interviews, and other research materials; it includes several instances of misapplication or misunderstanding of concepts, theories, or ideas; and it exhibits only an acceptable level of writing. In the upper range of this grade, the narrative states a point of view that is supported by clear arguments and factual evidence, but counter-arguments and counterexamples are not mentioned or answered.

Grade of D. For a narrative that is generally vague, indicating inadequate participation in the course material and research or inadequate effort invested in the writing process. The narrative exhibits sloppy writing, and either no application of concepts, theories, or ideas from the course materials or frequent errors in their application. The narrative simply lists, narrates, or describes data that include factual errors. There is little or no attempt to frame a point of view for the writer.

Grade of F. For a narrative that is so general it could have been written without the student having been enrolled in the class. The narrative exhibits seriously deficient writing, contains so many errors in applying concepts as to indicate a lack of comprehension of the subject matter, or completely ignores the questions asked. The narrative is incomprehensible due to errors in language or usage, contains serious factual errors, and/or is plagiarized.

As students' writing improves, I adjust these criteria. Upper-division students are less likely to exhibit the kinds of weaknesses described in the C and D scores. I add course-specific skill issues in the middle range and begin to add professional communication standards to the upper range.

In offering this scale, I am not trying to argue for a standard in all classes at all institutions. You need to work through your own scales for the classes and students you teach. In practice, having these scores described this way makes grading more effective. First, I can put these descriptions in the syllabus and discuss them with students. I want to make sure they understand what a counter-argument, counter-example, and straw man argument mean. Because I want the highest participation possible, I encourage them to bring up any features they think are missing. I try to find ways of incorporating their concerns. Then, when I am actually grading, I can get to the judgment score quicker because I am reading the essay for specific traits. As a result, my grades are more consistent from essay to essay and from class to class. When I return the essays with the grades, I can add comments that help the students understand their essays relative to the criteria. This helps me communicate with the students about what they need to improve in their learning and writing. When I have the same students in several classes, as is the case with majors, they familiarize themselves with the criteria so well that they incorporate the standards into their writing. As I grade their work over time, having consistent criteria permits me to discuss their long-term development as learners.

Walvoord and Anderson discuss several important considerations in developing PTA scales. Overly general trait descriptions introduce more traits that need to be defined. Commonly, trait descriptions improve over time, becoming more precise and detailed. I found that when I applied the grading rubric described earlier to some papers, they were scored lower than I would have scored them without the rubric. The rubric tends to focus on the quality of the argument. All of us are susceptible to evaluating a well-styled piece of writing high, even if the argument is mediocre. I had to decide if I wanted to include stylistic qualities in the scale that would lift a paper with a level 2 argument to a level 3. I decided that for the purpose of the course I taught, that would not be a good idea. Instead, I added comments that supported the stylistic qualities, while reinforcing the need to develop a stronger argument. When you find that you give students a grade that is different from what you might otherwise have given them and you are not satisfied with these scale-based grades, you probably need to reexamine the scale. Some measurable trait that you consider important is likely to be missing.

There is a tendency to want to express the traits as descriptions of actions or commands. These descriptions are less useful because they tend to be binary, generating a two-level, pass-fail scale. The student either did or did not perform what was expected. Converting these descriptions to noun phrases permits you greater latitude in assigning degrees of accomplishment to the performance of the task.

The relationship between the trait descriptions in the scales can be additive-subtractive or qualitative. In the additive-subtractive relationship, the increase in levels either adds traits to or subtracts traits from the previous level. Thus, moving from level 4 to level 5, the student must do everything at level 4 plus an additional feature (additive). Or, moving from level 5 to level 4, the student must do everything in level 5 except one feature (subtractive). The essay grading rubric I described earlier is an example of additive-subtractive relationships in scale building. Scales that are built on qualitative relationships use different skills.

A qualitative rubric lists specific criteria, such as clarity, accuracy, precision, etc. and then indicates a set of standards for each. For example, if you decide to have a set of three standards for each criterion, for clarity the standards might read as follows:

- → Low Range: Student makes points, but these are confusing. There is no effort to elaborate, to express the same point in other ways, or to give an illustration or an example of the point.
- → Mid Range: Student makes points that are not confusing because s/he elaborates, expresses the same point in other ways, gives an illustration or an example of the point, but not consistently or effectively.
- → High Range: Student makes points that are not confusing because s/he elaborates, expresses the same point in other ways, gives an illustration or an example of the point, consistently and effectively.

Student writing that is consistently evaluated in the low range receives the lowest grades. Mixed low and mid range standards earn a low grade. Predominantly mid range standards rate a mid range grade. Those students who consistently score in the high range get the A's. Each of these approaches has its own strengths, depending on the assignment or assessment goals.

Another issue involves the words "correct," "appropriate," and "adequate." Left by themselves, these words in trait descriptions do not communicate effectively to students. You can make them more precise by including a modifying phrase that indicates what class of responses would be incorrect, inappropriate, or inadequate in the lower levels of the scale. Thus, when the students read the entire scale's trait descriptions, the range of correct-incorrect, adequate-inadequate, and appropriate-inappropriate responses are described.

PTA scales lend themselves to every sort of assessment or evaluation setting. They work with written and oral narratives and arguments. They are adaptable to experiential and collaborative activities. They can be devised for creative work, portfolios, theses, and dissertations. PTA scales even work with multiple-choice tests. The questions are grouped according to a scale based on their level of complexity. Students are graded not merely on how many questions they get right but on the level of difficulty of each correct question. In short, PTA can accommodate all evaluation situations. Walvoord and Anderson's book (1998) has many examples of successful PTA scales in these different contexts.

Asking Appropriate Questions for Evaluation

Throughout this book, I have attempted to consistently apply Wolcott and Lynch's adaptation of King and Kitchener's reflective judgment model in various classroom environments. The strength of this model becomes even clearer when it comes to evaluating the students' critical thinking skills. There are ways of asking questions that are so challenging as to frustrate the student. Other ways are so simple as to stifle their motivation to learn. Effective evaluation of student performance begins with asking the appropriate questions. As with every other part of the teaching experience at this level, you cannot prejudge anything about the students sitting in front of you. The questions you choose cannot be the ones you wish the students could answer. Instead, they must be the ones that lie just a bit beyond the level of reasoning the students display during the class. This leads to the untenable situation of creating individual tests, tests for subgroups at different levels, or complex tests with several sections or differing cognitive complexity, each weighted differently. It is no wonder that the conventional wisdom on testing has assumed a one-size-fits-all approach.

There is a way out of this quandary, and it is a systematic solution. If the new instructor has already assessed the reasoning levels of students in the classroom, you can individualize the expectations in the feedback that you provide. Speak directly to the student's learning issues, offering suggestions of what he or she might work on for the next assignment, in addition to your ordinary evaluative comments. The assessment orients you to construct the appropriate opportunities for the students to engage the material. The evaluation can concern itself with a net assessment of what the student has done with the opportunities. Choose a level of questioning that challenges the majority of students, even if it overly challenges the bottom 20 percent and leaves the upper 20 percent off the hook. The advantage to this strategy is that it provides the greatest good for the greatest number. Support the bottom and top 20 percents through other assignments. Do not expect one test to serve as the perfect evaluation for everyone.

The following sections rely on the task prompts Wolcott and Lynch devised to help students gain mastery over higher levels of cognition(2001). They provide a telling model of how you can create gradations in evaluation over time to capture the students' development. Using them as evaluative prompts does not preclude also using them as exercises. By all means, use them as exercise prompts, too!

Basic Performance: Knowledge and Skills

This is the lowest level of cognitive function one is likely to encounter in a college classroom. The level of reasoning here is equivalent to Wolcott and Lynch's level-0 skill pattern. We make a mistake when we assume that we find students at this level only in schools with open admission policies. Even highly selective schools are likely to have students at this skill level because admission criteria are not attuned to sorting applicants based on differences in critical reasoning. I have found that some students are able to do well on standardized tests and high school courses with these low reasoning skills. The proportion of students with these skills can vary from class to class. The features of this level include repeating or paraphrasing information from textbooks or notes, looking for a single "correct" solution, computing a correct answer, or connecting the logical dots in an unambiguous argument. They seek the minimum required to pass the test. To begin to move these students to the next level of reasoning, we need to challenge them with questions that involve departing from the text, the algorithm, or problem sets and begin to introduce the idea of enduring uncertainty. Some appropriate questions for this kind of student include (in order of increasing enduring uncertainty):

→ Calculate x, where x is a pattern students have seen before but with new values.

→ Define x, where x is a pattern students have seen before but with new qualities.

→ Define x in your own words, where x is a pattern students have seen before but with new qualities.

→ List the elements in the set x, where x is a set that is related to one students have seen before but contains different elements.

→ Describe x, where x is a quality that is related to one students have seen before but contains different features.

→ List the pieces of information contained in x, where x is a specific narrative, paragraph, or text.

→ Recite the arguments about x, where these arguments are explicitly provided in the textbook or notes.

The transition in the questions is a gentle one. The question has the comfortable form, but the predicates are increasingly abstract. They start with the substitution of novel values and qualities into a familiar pattern and proceed to questions requiring greater departures from what is immediately available. The questions also avoid asking the student to take a position. If you want students to use their own words, you should phrase this very carefully. You need to indicate that the appropriate response is a paraphrase of existing material and not the student's opinion.

Identify the Problem, Relevant Information, and Uncertainties

This is still a relatively low level cognitive complexity. Students in general education and lower-division courses in most schools should be carefully assessed to determine if this is not the most appropriate evaluation strategy for them. The features of this level of reasoning are Wolcott and Lynch's level-1 performance pattern. The primary issue for these students is how to build their comfort with uncertainty. In evaluating their achievements in this respect, they should be asked to identify the problems and information relevant to the problems as precisely as possible. In this identification of the problems, the key to higher levels of achievement lies in students' ability to articulate the reasons for continuing uncertainty and the absence of a single "correct" solution. The following prompts move the students from identifying the relevant information to articulating the enduring uncertainties in the text:

→ Identify the main idea, thesis statement, or governing hypothesis in a text and list the evidence that supports it.

→ Explain why even an expert about x can't predict with certainty what will happen when y occurs.

→ Explain why x can't be known with certainty.

→ Identify aspects of x in which uncertainty is a major factor.

→ Create a list of information that might be useful in thinking about x.

→ Consult experts and explore literature or other resources to create a list of issues related to x.

→ Create a list of different points of view related to x.

→ Identify a range of possible solutions to x.

→ Sort pieces of information to identify reasons and evidence that support a given solution.

The list moves from the most concrete task, identifying the main point and supporting evidence, to the more difficult tasks of listing different points of view and ranges of solutions.

Explore Interpretations and Connections

Beginning with Wolcott and Lynch's level-2 skill patterns, we begin to work with established critical reasoners. Students at this level are the ones who can begin to do more serious work. They are the ones who dominate lower-division classes, but stand out as having exceptional skills. Ordinarily, this is the skill level I expect to see in upper-division and entry-level graduate classes. Most of the students who graduate are reasoning somewhere between level 1 and 2 (King and Kitchener 1994). Students at level 2 are already reasoning beyond the average.

The primary issue for students at this level is how to interpret information. This requires them to identify and control their own biases and opinions. It requires them to seek out the assumptions that underlie an argument, an especially difficult task for students who do not already have a broad knowledge base. It directs them to examine arguments associated with alternative points of view. Finally, the interpretative tasks ask them to organize information that meaningfully encompasses the complexities of the problem. The following prompts bring the students from a mapping of the existing argument to an evaluation of alternative arguments:

→ Discuss the strengths and weaknesses of a particular piece of evidence related to x.

→ Interpret and discuss the quality of evidence related to x.

→ Interpret and evaluate the quality of the same body of evidence related to x from different points of view.

→ Compare and contrast the arguments related to two or more solutions to x.

→ Identify and discuss the implications of assumptions and preferences related to one or more points of view about x.

→ Identify and discuss the implications of your own experiences and preferences for how you think about x.

→ Develop one or more ways to organize information and analyses to help you think more thoroughly about x.

The sequence in the prompts increases the students' awareness of the importance of the alternative perspectives on a problem as the term progresses. The term begins with an emphasis on evaluation. Can the students at the beginning of the term apply standards to the texts? The term continues by offering several rhetorical variations on the problem of narrating multiple perspectives. The end-of-the-term prompt demands that the problem itself is jettisoned in favor of a discussion of general methodology.

Prioritize Alternatives and Communicate Conclusions

This describes a high level of critical reasoning. Even at the upper division, this level of thinking may characterize selected individuals but rarely characterizes a class as a whole. The features of this level are at the transition point between Wolcott and Lynch's level-3 skill patterns. This kind of reasoning is sensitive to context and knowledge base. For that reason, there can be a sizable amount of backsliding among otherwise advanced reasoners in new learning environments. Do not assume that graduate students who are adept at these skills in one of the subfields of your discipline are equally adept in all of them. The primary issue for students at this level is how to adapt arguments effectively to particular contexts and audiences. The following prompts push students to develop and use general principles to develop priorities among competing solutions and to adjust these priorities to communicate with different audiences and in different settings:

→ Prepare and defend a solution to x.

→ Identify which issues you weight more heavily than other issues in arriving at your conclusion about x.

→ Explain how you prioritize issues in reaching a solution to x.

→ Describe how the solution to x might change, given different priorities on important issues.

→ Explain how you would respond to arguments that support other reasonable solutions to x.

→ Identify the most important needs of the audience for communicating your recommendation about x.

→ Explain how you design your report, memo, or presentation on x to effectively communicate to your audience.

→ Describe how you would communicate differently about x in different settings.

The prompts bring the students through a process of increasing contextualization and nuance in the formulation of argument and evidence. At the beginning of the term, the evaluative prompts return the students to the problems of multiple perspectives. Through the term, a variety of mounted challenges ask the students to adjust, first to alternative arguments and then to alternative audiences. By the end of the term, the evaluation directly addresses the context sensitivity of arguments as a methodology.

Integrate, Monitor, and Refine Strategies for Readdressing the Problem

This highest level of cognitive complexity corresponds to Wolcott and Lynch's level-4 reasoning. I have observed this level of reasoning among advanced graduate students, professional academics and researchers, and executive administrators. Reserve these evaluative prompts for students engaged in independent learning tasks and comprehensive exams. All of the tasks assume a high level of control over subject matter, interpretation, and context. The last few prompts might even remind you of the questions at your own dissertation defense. Acknowledging and explaining the limitations of their solutions and strategies challenges students at this level. The prompts put a premium on the monitoring of the processes of data collection and analysis with a view toward early and appropriate modification. The prompts encourage habits of flexibility and inventiveness. More importantly, they encourage the students to see the process of independent learning as having its own inner dynamic, one that does not always lead where we hope it will and one that offers only time-bounded solutions. The following prompts place a high value on humility when facing important research:

→ Describe the limitations of your proposed solution to x.

→ Explain the implications of limitations to your proposed solution to x.

→ Describe conditions under which you would reconsider your solution to x.

→ Explain how conditions might change in the future, resulting in a possible change in the most reasonable solution to x.

→ Develop strategies for generating new information about x.

→ Establish a plan for monitoring the performance of your recommended solution to x.

→ Establish a plan for addressing the problem strategically over time.

These prompts make evaluation possible in contexts where the student generates most of the content of the work being evaluated. The early prompts demonstrate the student's control over research design, while the subsequent prompts ask for greater levels of refinement. The final prompts demand disciplinary knowledge and professional-level agenda setting.

CHAPTER

107

The Test

The test tells the instructor what each student has managed to integrate through class experience and outside learning. We design tests for summative evaluation. They measure what students can recall and manipulate at a specific point in the process. Tests take many different forms. Find the appropriate form for the learning goals you have set. If you have designed a course around problem solving, the test should require students to solve problems. If you have designed a course around the basic vocabulary of the discipline, the test should evaluate students' control of those concepts. If you have designed a course around critical reading of core texts, the test should evaluate students' critical reading skills. One test does not fit all classes. Tests that attempt to evaluate achievement on multiple goals, such as control of concepts and problem solving, are certainly feasible but should reflect the actual emphasis of the class.

CHAPTER

108

Timed vs. Untimed Tests

The practice of requiring test takers to complete a test within a specific time period dates to Yerkes's administration of IQ tests to army recruits in 1917. With thousands of recruits to test and rooms large enough to hold only fifty at a time, he had no choice but to use a time limit. These and other compromises he made to establish a baseline scale for intelligence testing have undermined the legitimacy of timed tests ever since (Gould 1981). Previously, students were given whatever period of time they needed to complete tests or until it was apparent to the proctor that the student was unable to finish. This older approach to the duration of tests survives today in master's and doctoral written comprehensive exams and in the tradition of assigning take-home essays as exams. Many experienced instructors believe that if the students know the material, they ought to be able to complete the test in the allotted time. They argue that timed tests measure students' grasp of course content because the instructors design the test for those time limits. These assertions miss the point that timed tests unnecessarily stress students. After searching for the evidence, I have not found a double-blind test result that timed tests evaluate control over the course material better than untimed ones.

Some instructors will defend timed tests as more accurate exhibits of student knowledge because the students must rely on what they can recall. Take-home tests, they argue, are less accurate because the students can consult the text as long as they like, distorting the measurement of their recall. Even an open-book exam in a timed classroom environment is a more realistic challenge, the proponents argue, because the time limits restrict students to checking the accuracy of their memories rather than looking up information they never controlled. It is true that professionals can keep stores of information in their heads, mostly because they periodically rehearse and refresh it. How many scholars can write an article without consulting a source for an accurate quote? If students have the opportunity to engage the knowledge base actively and the assessments carried out during the process indicate their participation in the process, timed exams are unnecessary distortions in evaluation. More importantly, testing takes up classroom time better spent in a learning activity.

Partial vs. Comprehensive Testing

There are different ways of scheduling the evaluations in a course. Partial testing is commonly known as quizzes, evaluations that focus on small parts of the materials. Comprehensive testing, like mid-term and final exams, focuses on the recall of large amounts of course material. How you schedule them depends on your learning goals for the students. Reading an introductory textbook is different from the same amount of time reading a civilization-generating epic. Evaluating that reading must occur at different intervals: more frequently for the textbook, more comprehensively for the epic. Evaluating control over a knowledge base is different from evaluating control over skills. Frequent and repetitive assessment of the student's control of information establishes a pattern of evaluations. If the students know that the same kinds of material from the weekly quizzes will show up again on the midterm and final comprehensive exams, they put more time into the material. No matter what approach you decide to use, the pattern of evaluation communicates what you consider the most important course outcomes.

There is a very fine line between partial evaluations and assessments. Before instructors became accustomed to assessing student learning, the periodic quizzes served notice to instructor and student alike about the effectiveness of the learning. The use of a grade and lack of anonymity on a quiz sets it apart from assessment. Quiz grades shape the final grade.

Some students find this a perfectly reasonable motivator. Other students see this as a system stacked against them, and they give up. Removing grades from quizzes allows the assessment function to dominate.

Some instructors think that the material a student must control to succeed in the course requires comprehensive exams, especially if they schedule the tests only at midterm and end of term. There are at least two responses to this position. First, the students do not know specifically what will be on the exam. They will study as if everything could be on the exam, if encouraged to do so and if supported in that studying with the appropriate tools and instructor feedback. Second, the midterm and final are conventions that you can easily dismiss. Very few colleges or departments insist that all evaluations conform to the same schedule. However, many colleges require that some sort of evaluation be given during the scheduled final exam period. This is an issue of fairness. Faculty who schedule their final evaluation for the last regular class meeting are shortchanging students by one contact hour and undermining their colleagues who do schedule during the finals period. However, no college that I know of requires the final evaluation to take the form of a test.

You should schedule comprehensive evaluations at intervals that make sense for the material that you are trying to cover. If there are natural divisions within the textbook, place your comprehensive exams there, even if that means irregular spaces between the exams. You should schedule evaluations to coincide with the end of each monograph or collection of articles. Hold the last evaluation during the final exam period and call it a final exam, even if it relates only to the last unit of the course.

Comprehensiveness has two different meanings. It means a strong inclusive quality such that all that ought to be included in a set is, in fact, there. It also means a thorough understanding of a subject in its specifics. (We reserve the related word "apprehension" for the thorough understanding of subjects in their generality.) These two different meanings of comprehension can be in conflict with each other in evaluation. The students' ability to fill a set with all of its appropriate members while excluding any nonconforming items is different from demonstrating their understanding of the specifics of a subject through problem solving. Which comprehensiveness are you really seeking? If it is the former, what is it you expect the students to do with the set when they are finished with it? Will it apply in future classes? Is it an end in itself? This is a passive form of comprehension that is easily forgotten once the test is over. If the comprehensiveness you seek lies with understanding, does this have to be demonstrated all at once as the culmination of learning? Is it better to have students demonstrate their understanding developmentally and in stages? This is an active form of comprehension. It should be possible to construct evaluations that communicate to students that we value this sort of comprehension.

My own feeling is that comprehensive midterm and final exams in a course are professional-level evaluations that serve no useful purposes at the undergraduate level, even in courses that emphasize control of a knowledge base. It is too easy to give students the erroneous impression that passing such an exam means that they control the information, when they have never had the opportunity to actively use the information, outside of the test. Ask a class to recall material they studied during the previous term. They greet your question with stunned silence. Retention of the information is problematic with comprehensive evaluations. Even in those courses where the instructor has designed a syllabus around the students' growing understanding of a single complex principle or a set of related principles, and the outcome of the course depends on their demonstrating their control of this central idea, the comprehensive exam is misleading and counterproductive. The student will go deeper into the subject if there are more opportunities for comments from the instructor, rather than reserving that response until the end of the course.

Oral vs. Written Exams

CHAPTER
110

Oral examinations have an older history than written examinations. However, outside of graduate comprehensives, dissertation defenses, seminar presentations, and laboratory practica, they have disappeared from university classrooms in North America. The pedagogical theory behind oral exams was to challenge the students' recall of the knowledge base. Students asked specific questions about the information in the course were expected to immediately and accurately recall the important details and distinctions. Faculty evaluated poise and speed of recall as much accuracy and detail. This time consuming style of exam still persists in some European systems. In North America, written exam forms, such as essay, true-false, multiple choice, and short answer dominate.

The oral examination of the skill set remains in graduate comprehensive orals, oral defense of the dissertation, the seminar presentation, and the laboratory practicum. In the seminar presentation, the student performs orally for several minutes, laying out an argument, organizing and presenting the evidence, and drawing the appropriate conclusions. In a laboratory practicum, the student states the problem, describes the procedures that were followed, presents the results and the analysis, and discusses the outcomes in a competent manner. Certain traditional laboratory courses in the sciences may still use the practicum as a test of detailed knowledge. When I studied comparative anatomy in the late 1960s, the professor would examine our dissection skills by having us identify various features on our specimen. The exam took less than two minutes, since he had thirty students to work through in one hour.

This last detail points out why the oral exam declined as a viable method of evaluation. It is too time consuming. My European colleagues tell me that the increased enrollments in universities have made the examination system unwieldy. The written exam permits hundreds of students to be examined simultaneously. The oral exam persists in situations where the number of students is small, such as the doctoral program, the laboratory, and the seminar.

The oral and written exams emphasize different aspects of the learning process. You can think of it as analogous to the differences between being able to read and write a foreign language and being able to speak that language. It is certainly difficult to learn all the vocabulary, syntax, grammar, social codes, and idioms that constitute the written form of a language. Acquiring them engages a different part of our cognition than the spoken form of the language. The spoken language has all of the features of learning the written form plus two others: the almost simultaneous translation of thought into speech and the overcoming of the social stigma of speaking incorrectly or in the manner of a child. Students face the same differences when they sit for an examination. In addition to grasping the knowledge base, they must also recall and perform that knowledge almost simultaneously, while attempting to speak the social code of the instructor. That means using the technical terms precisely, getting the idioms correct, and not sounding like the scholarly equivalent of a child. At the doctoral level, the form of the exam makes sense. The candidate has had plenty of practice absorbing the language codes and performing scholarly speech before their own classes. At the undergraduate level, the opportunities for oral practice are limited. No matter how well you describe the various components of the seminar presentation for students, they will only perform well if they are already accustomed to making presentations in some other context. This does not mean that you should avoid oral examinations. It means that if oral performance is a core part of the discipline, opportunities to practice must be built into the major curriculum. By the time students get to seminar-style classes, they should be accustomed to speaking the language.

CHAPTER
111

The Presentation

Presentation combines written performance, oral performance, and sometimes design to demonstrate learning and reasoning. The combination allows students to use multiple channels of communication. Presentations also permit students to teach and learn from each other, building the competence of a learning community. Presentations abound in seminars, where they find their most embedded expression. Presentations are easily adaptable to all levels and styles of classrooms. If planned carefully enough, they can be seeded throughout the term to break the rhythm of discussion or lecture. Presentations appear less frequently because their performance consumes time. It is rare for each student to need less than fifteen minutes; twenty or thirty minutes is more often the norm. In a class of twenty students, this amounts to as much as ten hours of class time. Still, there are ways of making presentations more time effective without reducing their value.

There are several different types of presentations. These are defined by the nature of the inputs and the type of performance. The seminar-style presentation is a research report employing several different sources to lay out a problem, resolve a contradiction, or test a hypothesis. The difference between a seminar-style presentation and a seminar presentation proper lies in the absence of the coherent methodological context of the seminar. Seminar-style presentations tend to be performed by individual students, rather than pairs or teams, and they involve a written report and sometimes handouts. These are distributed ahead of time and read by the class before the presentation begins. The presentation itself is an outline or a summary of the written report. The presenters hope to generate discussion. This discussion is sometimes assigned to a specific individual, who prepares a second report (based on the first report), to provide a critique that will engender discussion. In a common variation on the seminar-style presentation, the writer of the initial report distributes it, but does not present it orally. Instead, the discussant (who prepared the second report) presents his or her report orally and leads a discussion in which the initial presenter is a participant. I have seen this work very well at the graduate level. Undergraduates may be too timid for the potential conflicts unless ample community building has taken place beforehand.

Another common form of presentation focuses on a single book, chapter, or journal article. The presenter is asked to summarize the main argument, list the most important pieces of evidence in support of the argument, highlight any apparent gaps or fallacies in the argument, and develop a series of questions about the argument for further discussion. The presenter should make this available to the class in a handout. Instructors vary as to whether the class reads the same article or the presenter brings independent material to the class. These presentations are shorter than the seminar-style presentation. As part of the activities of the classroom over the week, the presentation can occupy the last fifteen minutes of a class or the entire class on Friday, with each student getting fifteen minutes to make a presentation and lead a discussion. This can be an efficient way to add a collection of classic or contemporary treatments of the material to the students' experience.

A third variety of presentation is the professional-style presentation. This style is appropriate when a model from the professional world can be described and modeled for the class. This might be a pitch for a sales plan or film script, a paper presentation at a scientific conference, a report to clients of the results of an investigation, or a simulation of teaching a unit to younger students. There are as many forms of these as there are professions. The conventions of professional-style presentations vary. You should teach what you know. The students are not really learning a professional skill. They lack the context for making the kinds of judgments that constitute the "skill" of these presentations. Instead, they are using the simulation of the presentation to practice making oral arguments.

A fourth variety of presentation is the debate style. Here two to six students develop strong arguments on two sides of a proposition. They then perform the debate for the class. The class keeps careful notes of the points each side makes and how well each point was refuted. In the end, the class votes to decide which side made the most points. There are some technical issues in setting up good debates. If you want to use the form and you yourself are not an experienced debater, you might want to consult Bean's extended discussion of how to do it (Bean 1996). Debates can be effective for highlighting the fine-grained nature of evidence, for exposing the degree of uncertainty around commonly accepted propositions, and for involving students in deeper levels of research. Like all simulations, these debates are time consuming. Their payoff for the students lies in the centrality of the proposition under debate to the course goals as a whole. There is also the logistic issue of finding enough critical topics and time to allow every student the chance to be a debater.

The final form of presentation is the persuasive speech. Here a single student presents one side of a debate without rebuttal. The students are given a rubric of what they must include, and the class scores them for the presence of an argument broken down into its component parts, the confirming and disconfirming evidence for the argument, the main arguments against interpreting the supporting evidence as confirming, and the implications of the argument for the class. The persuasive speech requires that a considerable amount of class time be invested in teaching the rhetorical principles that underlie persuasion, the variety of fallacious arguments and how to identify them (Downes 1995), and how to evaluate the source of evidence. Persuasive speeches also take substantial time to deliver, score, and critique, sometimes as much as twenty minutes per student. As a result, this form of presentation is rarely found outside of specialized classes. Instructors should look for ways to use persuasive speeches more often. Oral persuasiveness reinforces written persuasiveness and leads to much more compelling essays.

The importance of presentations in general, and the reason why you should consider building them into the classes you teach where they can be most easily implemented, is that they give students an understanding of the differences between written and oral communication. This not only helps students build a separation between formal and informal tone in their writing, it makes them more conscious of the different requirements of their audience. Students must listen actively in order to score the presentations. The advantages tend to flow from the oral to the literary because our students are so much more accustomed to being persuaded by texts.

Just as the students take the presentation apart to score it, your evaluation of the presentation should follow the same pattern. Presenters should not have to worry that they must do one thing to satisfy their student audience and another to satisfy you. The difference between your score and the scores of their classmates is that you are providing formative as well as summative evaluation. That is, you are taking research process, source quality, and the degree of difficulty of the chosen topic into account, while the classmates score the formal aspects of the argument. You should be explicit about these differences; provide both the student rubric and your own in the syllabus or assignment sheet. It is also important for you to make your judgments and write comments as soon after the presentation as possible. Much of the subtlety of your experience with the presentation will be lost the longer you wait.

CHAPTER

112

The Essay

I cannot separate the evaluation of writing from the evaluation of thinking. For me, the essay is the place where everything comes together: the knowledge base, the critical thinking skills, and the communication skills. I never use the essay as a substitute for a test of knowledge. To me, that is like using a hammer as a doorstop. I usually assign an essay every three weeks in a typical term, in addition to the final essay. I admit this is a lot of writing. I tie the questions I want the students to explore to the critical issues in the readings they do immediately preceding the essay. The essays help me integrate the various pieces of the course, provide the students with time to reflect on the ideas, and push them to pose questions and explore solutions on their own. The essay is my preferred form of evaluation.

It is actually counterproductive to ask students to choose the topic they will write about. What they should be choosing to write about is a problem or question. We advance students' thinking skills and avoid many of the immature writing forms when we steer them away from thinking topically about their writing. This means that instead of asking students to discuss the symbolism of Ahab's fixation on the whale in Moby Dick, you provide students with two conflicting readings from the critical literature and ask them to figure out which is the more persuasive reading of the text. Instead of asking students to explain the relationship between poverty and unemployment, you provide the contrasting position of the liberals and the conservatives and ask students to determine which position is best supported by the available evidence. These are very large problems, and I am using them as illustrations of the difference between the traditional way of assigning essays ("Discuss . . ." or "Explain . . .") and a problem-centered or question-based approach. You want to stimulate students to look for a position in a conversation.

After they decide on the problem or question, insist that students use a thesis structure. Create learning tasks that are directly supportive of the students becoming comfortable posing and answering their own questions. Take the POE method from problem-based learning. The students prepare prewriting exercises listing several predictions, make several observations, and collect evidence about the predictions, and then write up discussions of the tested predictions. Review these on a non-graded basis. Only after they complete this prewriting exercise do the students begin drafting their response to the problem.

You need to build adequate time into the essay writing assignment for all of these steps to unfold. I usually provide at least thirty minutes every other Friday for students to work through the prewriting assignments or hold peer-editing sessions for their essays. I ask them to staple all of the prewriting material and earlier drafts to the final draft. This helps me, as well as the students, discover the process that produced the draft. With all this time devoted to the writing, I can be quite demanding when reading the essays. If the rhetorical structure does not hold, if the evidentiary support is insufficient, or if counter-arguments were not addressed, the student can be marked down and asked to rewrite and resubmit for a better grade.

There is a difference between an essay that is written for summative evaluation and an essay that is written as the basis for developing critical thinking skills. The students write them under different conditions, and the instructor reads them with different knowledge of the students' efforts. The form can be exactly the same: a five-paragraph theme, a discussion of several stipulated texts or topics, an analytic summary of a single work, a literature review, a journal article that argues a position based on new evidence (at the graduate level), creative nonfiction that builds a novel structure around evidence to better communicate its qualities, or an editorial that argues a position based on analysis of existing evidence.

The choice of what qualities to evaluate in the essay should be consistent with both the goals of the course and your understanding of the students' needs for feedback. First- and second-year students and ESL students need more feedback on writing mechanics than advanced students. Nevertheless, it is a waste of time to line edit summative essays. If students do not have the opportunity to rewrite, your editing is ignored. Only when students must take your edits into account do they begin to adjust their ears to "hear" the difference between the spoken language and the written language. If improving their writing is important to you, use formative assignments that give them the opportunity for revision and choose a different form of summative evaluation. All students need feedback on the rhetorical quality of their writing. Does the student have a strong, well-articulated position? Did the student provide sufficient high-quality evidence to support that position? Did the student recognize and discuss the alternative positions? How detailed and stringent you want to be in evaluating these qualities depends on the students' level and their progress through the discipline. All students need feedback on style. Was the essay engaging or burdensome? Did the student have a sense of audience? Was there a strong voice?

Two of the biggest pitfalls in grading summative essays include the search for a "right" answer and the grade based on a "global" reading. There is a difference between asking students to demonstrate accurate knowledge of a subject matter. Questions that begin with verbs like arrange, define, list, name, and order leave little room for interpretation and should not be part of the prompt for a summative. If you want to evaluate knowledge, use a test. Essay prompts should focus on application, synthesis comprehension, analysis, and evaluation of ideas. As such, they leave room for the students to arrange the thoughts and emphases in their argument to satisfy their own sense of completeness and appropriateness. There is no one way to do this well. Every time I think I have found the essay that best resolves the fullest dimensions of the prompt, somewhere in the next few papers I will inevitably find another paper of equal quality that took a different approach entirely. It is fairer to the students to set up your rubric for evaluating their essays in such a manner that there are several ways to do well.

I am not sure what the global reading is actually evaluating. I suspect it is more style than rhetoric or content. A global reading is an attempt to give a grade without articulating the criteria that underlie the grade. The only positive reason to practice global reading at all is to be able to get to those criteria quickly. When I am teaching a course for the first time, I am trying out essay prompts and have not fully articulated my rubric beyond the specificity of content that each prompt creates. I use global reading as a way of helping me set up my rubrics for scoring the essays. I globally read five or six essays drawn haphazardly from the pile. I then try to discover the criteria that emerged as I think about the differences between them. When I read the next five or six essays, this time drawn from the pile in order, I self-consciously apply the criteria. When the criteria do not describe the strengths and weaknesses sufficiently, I add more or modify the descriptions of the ones I have. While global reading may appear to save time, it is actually slower than criterion-based scoring. It also introduces inconsistencies into the grading process, makes the grade less defensible to the student, and gives you less control over the evaluation process than you should have.

The Research Project

The research paper or term paper is one of the most engaging assignments we can offer our students, especially those who are well established in the major curriculum. Whether the final product is a written report, a poster presentation, or some combination of the two, you should approach this form of evaluation with care. For the research project to be effective, students need to embrace the opportunity to research the answer to a problem, preferably one they devise on their own. These projects are often corrupted by the high school habit of turning the research paper into a cut-and-paste assignment. A research project should never be described by the instructor or the student as a report that is "all about" something. Aside from the intellectual arrogance of the approach, such a project reinforces the lowest levels of critical thinking by directing the student to search out fully formed answers that are out there waiting to be gathered. McKeachie demonstrates the long-term effects of this approach when he describes the alternatives faced by the undergraduate assigned a research paper as follows:

→ Buy one or borrow one from a friend or fraternity or sorority file.

→ Find one or several books in the library that cover the material. Copy out relevant passages with varying degrees of paraphrasing and turn it in.

→ Review the relevant resources and, using powers of analysis and integration, develop a paper that poses and solves a problem using secondary data, while revealing connections with the course material. (McKeachie 1986)

Most teachers expect their to students adopt the third alternative. Few of us, however, have evolved techniques for eliminating the first two. Cohen and Spencer (1993, 219-30) complain that student papers in economics are "mediocre, regurgitative and uninspired." Even teachers in literary subjects often say that same thing. The responsibility for guiding students to effective term papers lies with us. We create projects in major courses in which we assume that the first-year composition course was sufficient to teach students how to write longer reports—we are inevitably disappointed. We end up grading the omissions in our curriculum.

Each discipline will have its own take on what constitutes research. These can range from the most positivist natural science and social science approaches involving the falsification of null hypotheses to the most hermeneutical exposition of literary or philosophical texts. From the students' point of view, the experience is the same regardless of the final form of the report. Bean (1996) characterizes the problem as one of rekindling a sense of wonder in the student. We must find ways of advocating curiosity in our students. The first step, according to Cohen and Spencer (1993, 219-30), is to assign a project that requires students to argue a position or solve a problem, rather than describe a condition. By going back to assignments around true problems, students remain sufficiently engaged and will avoid most of the pitfalls that plague vacuous term papers.

Be aware that different disciplines support different levels of originality. The website Turnitin (http://turnitin.com/static/index.html) generates an originality index for a body of text that you submit. It is used primarily to identify plagiarism. Over the years, experience with this website by my colleagues demonstrates that the sciences will have a lower index than the humanities. This does not mean that science students cheat more than English majors. It means that the nature of science writing is more likely to employ the words of other authors within the text than literary criticism. Science is collaborative and its writing reflects that. Literary criticism is individualistic and glorifies the lone intellectual. Its style reflects that. You need to understand the level of originality that is appropriate for your discipline. Tell the students what it is. Then let them test their text against the index on Turnitin before they turn it in to you. You'll get research papers that are closer to your expectations than you would otherwise.

You should evaluate term papers in stages. If students must submit a prospectus that lets you see the research problem and an annotated bibliography that lets you see their sources well ahead of the paper itself, the opportunities for engagement increase and the temptations of plagiarism are removed. These preliminary writings do not interfere with the summative use of the term paper evaluation. Whether you grade the prospectus and annotated bibliography depends on the course goals and the mix of assignments you already have in the course. These prewriting exercises permit you to tutor the research process: designing an inquiry, accessing and evaluating sources, using sources as evidence, analyzing the evidence in light of the emerging argument, and structuring of the argument in the written form most appropriate for the discipline. The grading of the term paper, then, grows directly from these criteria.

CHAPTER

114

The Group Writing Project

The section on the collaborative classroom provided some guidelines for constructing problems. It also discussed the problems and patterns in written reports produced by groups as opposed to individuals. Once you have decided how the mix of collaboration and individual effort can best meet the goals of your classroom, you will still face a stack of papers. You should treat these as term papers and research reports. As with term papers, requiring students to turn in some preliminary steps ahead of time reduces the temptation for plagiarism.

Collaborative reports present a separate set of problems. You need to decide whether you want to try to evaluate individual effort within the report or to assign the same grade to all the collaborators. There are good reasons to take different strategies in different situations. If you assigned a collaborative report to groups that were experienced in collaborative research, you should not hesitate to assign a single grade to the group. This is especially true if this is not the first collaborative report they have written.

If they are experienced collaborators, your task is to extend the cooperative research patterns to the report writing. As with initial cooperative research efforts, something can go wrong. Cooperative writing stretches many students beyond their comfort zone. Hopefully, you will have discussed how to write collectively in the class and shared your own experiences. You need to be flexible in your grading. You want to reward students who have succeeded but not unduly punish the groups that fail. In failed groups, the collaborative research efforts may have succeeded, but either the report will be written by one member or the members will each write different sections, though not in time for collective editing to have the report speak with one voice. Students with these issues are usually advanced in the subject or graduate students. It may be worth the effort to encourage them to submit a second draft and have a conference with them about group editing procedures. If a time extension is not possible, then the fairest thing to do is recognize the efforts separately in addition to giving a hypothetical group grade. It is important to offer these students the most specific guidance about the weaknesses in the draft and encourage them to avoid these pitfalls in future efforts. However, as a group and as individuals, their grades should be lower than those of the successful groups.

CHAPTER
115

Evaluating Group Work

I have provided a rubric from San Diego State University of how you might go about evaluating collaborative work. The rubric works well in most circumstances, especially if students are familiar with it ahead of time. This rubric focuses on observable behaviors. I have found the self-evaluation tells me important information about non-observable behaviors in evaluating group work. I always ask students to write me a letter in which they answer four questions:

→ What were the most important research findings in the process of developing your report, and which group member contributed those findings?

→ What do you consider to be your most valuable contribution to the group effort?

→ What did you learn about the research process through this project that you did not realize before?

→ What will you do differently the next time you are involved in a collaborative research project?

Notice that the students are only asked to talk about the other members of the group in positive terms. In my instructions, I tell them that I do not want them to use the self-evaluation to criticize the efforts of others. While some students who slacked off in the research process will attempt to inflate their efforts through the self-evaluation, when the letters are read as a group, who did what becomes readily apparent. Also, you should already have a pretty good idea of who did what from your time with the groups, by noticing who contributed what to the electronic bulletin board or the group conversations and, in the extreme, by listening to the complaints of the highly motivated student who is stuck in a dysfunctional group. Note also that students are not asked to give themselves a letter grade for their efforts, though some will do so as part of their narrative. These can be ignored, although I have found that for most students, the grades are accurate estimations of their perceived level of effort.

Your skill in evaluating the actual product of collaborative research will improve over time. Initially, you will tend to focus on the relative elegance of the report and the proximity of the conclusions to those you have reached yourself. As you read through several sets of these self-evaluations, you will begin to perceive the different levels of creativity in the research strategy, effective use of uncommon or unexpected sources, the quality of the evidence and argument used to reach a conclusion, and the individuality of the conclusion for the group effort. The relative value of the conclusion will be less important. This is because the process of exploration in collaborative research is generally higher than that for term papers. Students in high-functioning groups push each other to uncover evidence in novel and insightful ways. This is one of the reasons why teachers look for opportunities to build this kind of classroom whenever the possibility presents itself.

PART 18

Administrative Issues in the Classroom

As an officer of the university, you are responsible for insuring that the rules and procedures that provide the highest level of fairness to all students are followed. You are also in a position to advocate for students who need to be exempted from these rules. How you balance these two roles constitutes the administrative function of the professor.

CHAPTER

116

Academic Integrity

Academic institutions are communities that reduce conflict through the administration of both law and custom. Universities construct legal and quasi-legal frameworks to govern the contractual relationships between students and the institution. The scholarly community operates in a world of custom where closely held values of openness and the free flow of ideas are possible because of the obligation of all members to acknowledge the origin and genealogy of ideas. Instructors are university officers. You must respond to any infringements of this custom. This response can take the form of helping the student interpret the rules, demanding a change in behavior on the part of the student, reporting infringements to the appropriate office of the university, or in extreme situations, calling the security office. Instructors are also scholars. You must respond to violations of the scholarly responsibility. Your response can take the following forms: discussion of the canons and standards of academic integrity in every class; notifying students that certain behaviors could be violations if viewed in a certain light; impeaching student work that is in clear violation; reporting and submitting evidence of violations to the appropriate office of the university; or failing student violators. No one who chose an academic career did so to take on a policing role. On the other hand, we do not have police on campus (security aside) because the officers of the university do educate students to the rules and enforce them when violated. The alternative to such active enforcement is an academic world in which no one would like to work.

Every university should have an academic integrity policy. The policy covers both students and faculty. It defines the custom of acknowledging the origin of ideas in our work and describes the various levels of sanction for plagiarism. It defines the custom of representing as our own work that which is truly our own and describes the various levels of sanctions for representing others' ideas as our own. You must familiarize yourself with your university's policy. Unfortunately, you will encounter both plagiarism and dishonesty in your classroom. When you do, how you respond, what evidence you collect, how you establish the facts of the situation, and how you decide to proceed will determine the immediate academic future of the students involved. If you make a mistake, you could find yourself undermining university policy, alienating colleagues, and making yourself liable for a lawsuit. The key to protecting yourself is to know the policies and know how to establish the facts of a situation. Some of the questions you will want to ask your colleagues are as follows:

→ In which classes are students informed of the academic integrity policy, their responsibilities to cite the authors whose ideas they use and the penalties for submitting papers they did not write?

→ Who has responsibility to impose the different levels of sanction in cases of violation of academic integrity?

→ Is there a central office that keeps track of the cases of violation and identifies serial offenders?

→ If so, what are the opinions of other instructors about the functioning of this office? Do instructors submit their minor infractions, or do they wait for really egregious cases before sending them on?

The effective implementation of any academic policy is education.

Academic integrity is a complex subject, and most faculty would have difficulty articulating in the abstract some of the more subtle ways in which students will trip up, such as confusing common knowledge with specialized knowledge or obscuring the contributions of legitimate collaboration. Partly, this is result of not understanding how students incorporate the challenges that instructors impose on them. An excellent study by Nathan (2005) has provided strong ethnographic evidence that most students succumb to plagiarism as the result of conflicts between priorities in their lives. While this does not excuse such behavior, it does help us to understand the slow, steady rise in the number of incidents. The increasing number of international students and first generation immigrants from parts of the world that may treat intellectual property quite differently from North American schools complicates the picture even further.

Students have not gotten a consistent message about academic integrity in high school, especially with regard to the appropriate use of source material. Issues that are ambiguous and open to interpretation at the university level are dealt with mechanically in high school, as in the rule that common knowledge is anything you can find stated in an encyclopedia. Fortunately, there are several excellent websites where some of our colleagues have struggled successfully to articulate these distinctions for students. You should be familiar with their content and use them as part of remedial exercises for those students who are at risk of violating your school's policy. In Web References later in this book, I've included some websites from schools that have parsed to complexity for students. You do your students an enduring service if you give them the opportunity to familiarize themselves with these sites, as well as your own university's academic integrity policies.

What do you do when the unfortunate case does come to your attention? If you have prepared properly, you will have a section in your syllabus in which you say that the university's academic integrity policy will be strictly enforced, giving students the chapter or page numbers in the student handbook or the website address where the policy can be found. You will have stated that it is the students' responsibility to cite everything on every assignment, if they want to avoid being accused unfairly of violating the policy. If this is too broad for you, modify it, but be explicit about what level of citation you expect. You will have also kept the in-class assessment of student reasoning skills that you collected in the first or second week of class to help you gauge the diversity of student learners. If you have prepared appropriately, it will be easier for you to get the student to admit wrongdoing and take responsibility for the confusion. What you want to avoid is a situation where students can say that a reasonable interpretation of your statements (or silence) in class or on the syllabus opened the door for their actions.

The five most common cases of academic dishonesty you will see are cheating on tests, faulty citation, misrepresentation of originality, a purloined paper, or an attempt to hide collaboration. Cheating can include having unauthorized access to the test before it is administered, possessing notes during a closed-book test, having someone else take the test in the student's place, copying answers or receiving help from another student, and giving assistance to another student. Students are subtle in the ways they bring information into tests. While fewer instructors are committed to closed-book, in-class tests, the sort most vulnerable to cheating, the students still seek advantages. If closed-book testing is going to be part of your classroom practice, there are ways you can stymie cheaters. The more the students' grade depends on their performance on only one or two tests, and the more those tests, in turn, revolve around control of a detailed knowledge, the more incentive the weaker students have to cheat. It is much more difficult to control a greater amount of knowledge (necessary when the term consists of only one or two tests) as opposed to a smaller amount when tests are given more frequently. . We remove this incentive when we give students more frequent evaluations—for example, weekly tests where they can demonstrate their control over a week's worth of material, rather than six weeks' worth of material. Midterm and final exams can then be in the form of take-home essays. These are not immune to cheating, but this cheating is somewhat easier to catch.

Faulty citations are a common first-year mistake. When seniors make this mistake, it is a grave infraction of scholarly practice. You recognize the faulty citation because of your familiarity with the evidence. In using a faulty citation, the student represents someone else's idea as his or her own. You need to find the missing citations and confront the student with the evidence. Nine times out of ten the student is clueless about how to cite properly. The tenth time, the student is being consciously duplicitous in the hope of receiving a higher grade. In any event, this becomes a teachable moment. My approach with less experienced students is to combine an appropriate lowering of the grade (not an automatic failure) with a remedial exercise in citation and reference. This is sufficient to get the point across to the student that this is one area where ignorance or duplicity will not be tolerated. With more experienced students, the violation is an automatic failure in the assignment.

Misrepresentation of originality differs from faulty citation because the student is using the borrowed idea as the thesis, controlling idea, or analytic model without attribution. This is a stronger violation of academic integrity because the originality becomes part of the global evaluation of the quality of the work. This is not merely an act of omission, forgetting to cite a reference in evidence. This is actively appropriating an aura of quality and passing it off as one's own. This is stealing a higher grade. You need to find the missing citations and confront the student with the evidence. Ignorance of this violation among experienced students is less of an excuse than it was for faulty citation. At the least, I give the student a failing grade in the course and pass the evidence on to the appropriate office of the university. I also require the student to complete (as a prerequisite for not failing the course) a remedial exercise in which the student becomes better acquainted both with the academic integrity policy and the process of developing innovative organizations for discussing existing ideas.

The purchased research paper is currently the most common form of gross violation of academic integrity. Purchased term papers will come to your attention because of features that jump out at you as you read:

- → the topic will be slightly off from what was assigned;
- → specific information that was asked for in the assignment is missing;
- → specific sources that were asked for in the assignment are missing; or
- → the paper's diction is an unlikely one for a particular student (when compared with the student's in-class writing).

We are getting to the point where we must take the students' readiness to buy these research papers into account when we devise our assignments. There are far too many websites where these papers can be purchased. Since each must offer the student the chance to see what they are buying first, the websites are vulnerable to search engines specifically designed to find specific strings of words. One popular instrument that some universities make available to their faculty is Turnitin (http://www.turnitin.com/static/home.html). The Google search engine and similar natural language engines will look for long strings of words and are often successful in finding the website the student used to purchase the paper.

Some universities have purchased proprietary software that keeps track of the various websites that sell research papers and can search within them to find strings of words.

When you have evidence that a student has turned in a purchased paper, you should confront him or her with the same paper taken from the Web. The sanction in such cases should be the most extreme sanction the instructor can impose on his or her own. This usually is limited to failure in the course. The evidence should also be passed on to the appropriate university office. Students buy these papers to save time and effort. In doing so, they mock the seriousness of scholarship and insult the intelligence of their instructors. Most important of all, they shortchange themselves by substituting their purchasing power for that confrontation with ideas that underlies the sustained research effort.

Regardless of the extenuating circumstances, such students do not belong in a university community. Even though you do not have the power to dismiss them, you can see to it that they will not receive any recognition from your class. If this seems harsh, consider the alternative. You give them an F on the paper and they receive a final grade of a D in the course. The course counts toward graduation. Such students have come one step closer to finishing their degree but with less effort than their peers. Additionally, others have learned from these students' experience and may be emboldened to buy a research paper themselves. You then end up confronting the same situation in future classes. Failing these students in your class deprives them of these marginal advantages and slows down the growth of such behavior in our community.

The attempt to hide collaboration can take several forms. The most common is when someone other than the student edits a paper. The student then turns in the paper as if the language is entirely his or her own. There is nothing wrong with seeking editorial help. Academics do it all the time. The violation of academic integrity occurs when it is not acknowledged. Writing centers train their tutors to avoid providing any writing to their clients. However, changes in wording can slip in through conversation about the piece. More frequently, a roommate or friend edits the paper. You recognize the violation when the quality of the paper far exceeds the quality of in-class writing on the assessment exercises. You might discuss the responsibilities of collaboration when going over the assignments section of the syllabus at the beginning of the term. This is a good time to talk about how one learns to be a better writer from an editor. You might encourage students to compare their original with the edited version, to make sure they understand why the editor made changes. If the students do not understand something, then they should talk to the editor about it. If you have not discussed it up to this time, then the fairest thing to do is to advise students to acknowledge the help in future papers. If you have discussed it, then you certainly should confront the student with the evidence, lower the grade, and make certain the student understands that the sanction is because the editing was not acknowledged, not because the paper was edited by someone else.

More pernicious than not acknowledging the help of an editor is not acknowledging the collaboration with someone on the development of the paper or in the writing of the paper. In laboratory-type classrooms, students are collaborating all the time. If you have been explicit in the syllabus about what the collaboration is intended to accomplish, you can state that any collaboration beyond what you expect must be acknowledged. The acknowledgment must describe as precisely as possible the contributions of the collaborators to the final product, even if that product is turned in as the work of a single individual. You recognize the collaboration because of a similarity between the works of two or more students in the class. This can begin quite innocuously. Students often form study groups and share outlines of material. The outlines are incorporated into the final products word for word rather than through paraphrase, and the final product ends up looking identical to products submitted by the others in the group. My practice in this case is to confront the students with the evidence and fail the papers with the unacknowledged collaboration. I make sure the students understand that it is the lack of acknowledgment that is being sanctioned, not the collaboration. I then require them to complete an exercise on paraphrasing that helps them to understand how to work with shared outlines in the future.

Other forms of undisclosed collaboration are more difficult to identify. A roommate who helps by brainstorming a paper with the student, a conversation with another faculty member in the department, or a consultation with a reference librarian that goes beyond the identification of sources are all collaborative contexts that are much harder to identify. These collaborations fall into the gray area in scholarly production. The professional might willingly acknowledge the help of colleagues, but students are burdened with what they believe to be your expectation that they produce papers wholly on their own. This assumption is also at the base of the impulse to hide citations as well. You should address these assumptions. Students should enter every research assignment prepared to keep track of all of the conversations that influence the development of their thinking. Not all of these have to be acknowledged, of course. This awareness of the social basis for intellectual creativity is an end in itself, sensitizing students to the process of critical reasoning as they reject some suggestions while exploring others.

Consider the student who turns in an identical, original paper in two different classes. This appears to be common in many universities. This is similar to the professional practice of publishing the same article in two different journals. It is harder to detect because the paper may fulfill the assignment in both classes. The practice needs to be distinguished from a situation in which the student submits two different interpretations of the same data or text. That might actually be desirable, if it were disclosed. What makes submitting duplicate papers unethical is the undisclosed collaboration between two instructors, each of whom contributed to the paper by creating a classroom context that fostered the thinking. Their collaboration is invisible to each other and cannot be evaluated. Instead, the paper is represented as originating entirely within a single class.

Some collaboration assignments are intended to produce a group product. Graduate students must have this experience. It is part of their professional preparation. I do not recommend this for undergraduates unless they have worked together as a collaborating cohort over a series of terms. Some programs are structured around close, cohort- or team-based learning activities. The students learn how to work together effectively and build on each other's separate strengths as researchers and writers. To ask students who have not had this experience to produce a group project in a single term is unfair. It presumes an equal level of motivation and intellectual maturity that rarely exists in the undergraduate classroom. The probable outcomes are that one person writes substantial portions of the product or that the individual contributions are not integrated. You would generate more effective statements if the students submitted individual reports based on the collaborative research. Collaborative group projects afford the less motivated students the opportunity to hide behind the work of others. To make it more difficult for them to do so, I require students to include a self-evaluation with every group report. This self-evaluation usually reveals a truthful profile of the experience of the different members of the group.

This discussion does not exhaust the variety of academic integrity issues you can face in the classroom. It merely addresses the most common forms. Some of the others that you should be aware of include falsification or sabotage of data, destruction or misuse of the university's academic resources (library books, computers, lab equipment, etc.), alteration or falsification of academic records, or direct forms of misconduct in the academic context, such as bribery, physical intimidation, harassment, or libel. When faced with these rarer, more unsettling forms of breaches of community norms, seek consultation with your chair and the officers of the university, who are likely more experienced in handling them. There are issues of evidence and record keeping in these instances that are quite complicated. The sooner you bring in the experts, the better for everyone concerned.

CHAPTER
117

Student Contractual Issues

When students register for a course, it sets up a contract between the university and the student. The student pays tuition, and the university provides the educational service. As an officer of the university, you (among others) are the one responsible for providing that service to those students with a valid contract. You are also responsible for withholding services from students without a valid contract. The faculty handbook will lay out exactly what the contract requires of you. Your responsibilities can include, but are not limited to,

- → providing a syllabus that outlines the conditions for the student to successfully complete the class,
- → being present at the scheduled class meetings,
- → responding to student assignments in a timely and effective manner,
- → giving feedback to students at regular intervals concerning their progress in the class, and
- → compiling a summary evaluation of their performance within the period of time stipulated by the university.

In addition, you must not move the class to a different room without informing the students and the college. You cannot cancel large portions of the class meetings without prior approval from the chair. All of your classes have to meet certain minimal requirements for length in order to qualify for their allotted credit hours. You cannot rearrange the class meeting times without the agreement of the students and without informing the chair.

The students to whom you owe these services are the ones whose names are on the class roster. The roster includes the names of the students who show up on the first day and continue to show up through the term, as well as the names of the students who never show up. The class may also have students who show up but whose names are not on the roster. Depending on your school's registration system, the roster may need to be updated at the end of the "add" period and at the various deadlines for the "drop" periods. The final roster, often called the grade sheet, reflects those students to whom you must provide a grade. If that includes students who have never been in class, you need to know what your school's policy is toward no-shows. Sometimes a grade of M, for missing, is entered. In other schools, a special grade that indicates an administrative failure, rather than an earned failure, is available.

Under no circumstances should such students be automatically given an incomplete grade. The incomplete grade has specific policies for its use in every school and these can differ. It ought to be given only when the student requests it before the grading period is finished. Faculty should never extend an incomplete grade to a student who has not asked for it. The incomplete can bind the student to certain obligations to have the grade changed within a specific period of time or it becomes an F. For students who have done all the work in the course but do not show up for the final exam or never hand in the final paper, it is often kinder to compute the grade with the missing work treated as an F and generate a final grade of C or D than it is to give an incomplete.

If an undergraduate student does approach you for an incomplete, you have every right to say no. I always say no when the issue is the student's mismanagement of time. I warn students in my syllabus that the management of time is a requirement of the course. If the student needs a few extra weeks to overcome difficulties that were not of his or her own making, I am willing to grant an incomplete. Even in these cases, the student and I write a contract in which the student agrees to complete the work by a certain date, and we specify exactly what work needs to be completed.

Incomplete grades at the graduate level are more complicated. At the graduate level the kind of learning that takes place does not often fit reasonably into the academic schedule. This can result in requests for incompletes. At one end of these requests are the students who are at risk of leaving the program. They cannot keep up with the work or are so intimidated by the level of reasoning that is being demanded that their confidence is shot. At the other end are students who are highly competent, having been working assiduously, but who have tackled a problem that no one could have completed within a single term. Somewhere in the middle of this continuum is the procrastinator. This student may be capable of brilliant work but can never turn it in on time. How you handle each of these situations, as well as the shades of experience between them, has to do with the atmosphere of your program. Is it intent on moving students through quickly? If so, you should reserve the incomplete grades for the highly competent and cut the others loose. Is your program one where students take forever to finish and everyone involved is resigned to that? If so, hand out the incomplete grades to all but the riskiest cases. The issue of incomplete grades in the program would make an interesting subject for a faculty meeting. This may be one of the few ways for you to gauge the range of sentiment among your colleagues.

There is another kind of course that results in an incomplete grade. This is the course where the student was never expected to finish the work and receive the grade within the grading period. This might include courses where students register for credit for thesis research and writing, field research, or study abroad. Some schools give a special grade that does not entail the bureaucratic restrictions of an incomplete grade. If your program has such courses, make sure you understand how they are graded. Even if you are not teaching them, you may need to explain them to your advisees.

Extra-Credit Registrations

Most students register for the typical number of credit hours with each course they take: three semester hours or four quarter hours, depending on the length of the term. In some schools, students may register for extra credit under special circumstances. In a summer school, for example, where the university anticipates that students from other schools will be enrolling, students may have the opportunity to register for credit for a course that will transfer more efficiently back to their school. This is especially problematic for students from semester-based schools taking summer courses in a quarter-based school. The four quarter hours fall just short of a full three semester hours when transferred. To remedy this, quarter-based summer schools offer students the option to register for four and a half quarter hours, which translates into a full three semester hours. What do you as the instructor do with the extra ninth of an hour? The school will usually describe the option to the student as entailing an extra bit of work. This, of course, also means extra work for you. Check with your chair about the established practice for the department.

Labs sometimes carry extra-credit registrations. This often means that faculty workloads are computed in fractions to insure equity for those supervising laboratory-based classes. It also means that such registrations require more effort. Lab work must be assessed and evaluated differently from work in the regular classroom. Preparation time can more than double, if the department does not provide a laboratory assistant. In labs that are field based, establishing cooperation with external agencies, site visits, and reporting add to the instructor's involvement in the class. Nevertheless, these are among the most exciting, professionalizing, and engaging experiences students can have—and they are the reason that many of them came to university in the first place. Working with students in these types of classes is well worth the extra effort, as long as that effort is recognized by the administration.

Auditors

A different kind of contractual relationship is established with auditors. This used to occur more frequently than it does now, but auditors may still turn up from time to time. These students are paying less tuition or no tuition for the opportunity to sit in class and merely listen. In some schools, they pay full tuition. They are not assessed. They are not evaluated. They are not graded. You do not even have to call on them if they raise their hands. Those among my advisees who have proposed auditing a class tell me that it lets them learn about new subject matters or attend the lectures of a visiting professor during terms when their class schedule is already full. You will know that a student has auditor status from the initial class roster. It is a good idea to question auditors outside of class about their motivation. Often a student is auditing for the wrong reasons, such as previewing a course before taking it for credit to insure a higher grade, and should be fully registered. Solving this problem early reduces bureaucratic strain on everyone. For students who are auditing for good reasons, such as a narrow but otherwise exclusive interest in a portion of the subject matter, you might discuss what your expectations are. You adjust your expectations, depending on the auditor's reasons. A grandmother who wants to know more about what her granddaughter is majoring in at another school will interact differently with the class than a student from the engineering school taking an advanced Renaissance art history class to prepare for a vacation in Italy. If the auditor can play a role in the class, you may have helped create an enthusiastic and active participant.

A step closer to fuller participation is afforded by the pass-fail option. Students can contract to be awarded a grade of either pass or fail in the course rather than a letter grade. They pay full tuition for the course. There is usually a deadline each term for students who are eligible to make this choice. The logic of this option for the students is that they can take a course for credit without having to pay very much attention to your evaluation of their work. Students think that this somehow frees them to learn without stress. The information about who might be taking your course under this option is withheld from you in most schools until you receive your final grade roster, so as not to prejudice your periodic evaluation of the student. In other words, only the students know that your evaluations are irrelevant to their final grade. Such pass-fail registrations are usually restricted in several ways. Students may need to accumulate a certain number of credit hours before they can request this option. Certain segments of the curriculum, like the major or core courses in the general education program, may be off-limits for the option.

Repeaters

Occasionally, students repeating the class will show up. Some schools allow students who repeat and earn a higher grade to have the previous grade dropped from the computation of their grade point average. These students want to improve their performance over the previous try. They pay full tuition for the opportunity. When you identify repeating students in your class, you should have a conversation with them about their previous experience. Ask them what they hope to accomplish this second time. Ask them not to tell you what their previous grade was. Regardless of whether it was a B or a D, that knowledge cannot help but influence your evaluation. Instead, you should ask them what they believe has changed that will permit them to earn a higher grade. While you should not try to make their path more difficult than you would for students taking the course the first time, you can suggest that the repeaters might want to take on new challenges, such as serving as the first discussion leader or making the first presentation to the class.

You have some choices in how you evaluate repeaters. If you intend to evaluate these students in light of their having previous exposure to the material, you should tell them this ahead of time and explain exactly how they can succeed under these conditions. Otherwise, you should tell them that you will evaluate them according to the criteria you apply to every other student.

Completers

Very rarely, you will be asked to clean up a registration mess that was created by the misjudgments of others. Some students believe that they can register for classes one term and actually take them another term. This works in two ways. Some students register for a class normally, but do not complete a substantial portion of the class. They negotiate an incomplete grade with an instructor who will not be teaching that course for some time. This is usually contrary to almost every university's policy on registrations, but some of these students find compliant faculty members. These students end up in your class with a letter asking that they be permitted to take the class even though they are not on the roster. They want the grade they earn from you to be sent to the original professor to fulfill their incomplete course. The other approach is for students to audit a class either officially for no tuition or unofficially with the connivance of a faculty member. They turn up registered in your class with a letter from the faculty member saying they have already completed the course and that you should turn in the following grade for them.

These situations test the ethics of even the best teachers. This fraud gives some students financial or academic advantages that other students do not enjoy. The students who take the first approach may be doing so to maximize their limited tuition resources. They are certainly not alone in suffering the temporary poverty of the student years. If the university wanted to let students register for courses in one term and take them in another term, they would advertise that fact. But universities would incur tremendous costs in having underused classrooms alternating with over-crowded ones if they did so. How you respond in this situation depends on your calculation of what is best for all your students, not just the completer. The second situation is more clear cut. Your colleague has other options available if he or she wants to help the student in this way. Colleges often let students undertake required courses as independent studies. You might tell the student that your colleague is responsible for seeing that a grade is entered. Recommend that the student register for an independent study under your colleague with the same course title as the required course. Then, have a conversation with the chair about completers and the college's approach to these issues. It may be that this colleague does provide this option to students often and is seen by students as a soft touch on registra-tion issues. In any event, be wary of letters from colleagues attesting to the student having completed the work for your course. If they are not forger-ies, they may still be fraudulent.

CHAPTER
118

Independent Studies

Most of us benefited from one-on-one courses when we were graduate students. We could explore a specialized literature with an interested pro-fessional to build a knowledge base for our research. Independent studies will always function that way in graduate programs, especially at the doc-toral level. They are one of the reasons that faculty in graduate programs have such small teaching loads. For faculty with normal teaching loads, independent studies are rarely compensated. Some schools may have a system where every seven to twenty such registrations constitute a course equivalent, but for most of us, independent studies are contributed service. When should you agree to take on a student, especially an undergraduate or first-year graduate student, and when should you decline? I have seen many new teachers accept independent studies only to complain after the fact that it had been a mistake. On the other hand, some of the best learning experiences I have had as a professional have occurred one-on-one with talented students exploring a literature that was new to both of us. What makes the difference between these situations is your assessment of the students' learning skills.

It is not enough to be highly motivated to read the books. Independent studies place an extra burden on the learning skills of students. Students are motivated to take on independent studies because of curiosity about a subject matter that is not offered as part of the regular curriculum. You have no obligation to offer this subject matter, on which you may or may not be knowledgeable. You gain no tangible benefit from doing so. There are two key questions to whether this interaction is worth your time: Where will it lead the student when it is completed? And does the student have the reasoning skills to learn independently using literature of the complexity entailed in the chosen topic? When I discuss potential independent studies with students, I listen for them to describe a series of experiences they are willing to undertake, beginning with some previous experience and continuing through the independent study to other experiences, of which they have some clear vision. I liken the images they generate to a row of dominos. Some of the dominos have already fallen. The rest are likely to fall. The one domino in question is the independent study. Another way of thinking about this is the overdetermination test that is often applied to grant proposals: do the students' preparation and future goals constitute an existing organic whole that will only be reinforced and strengthened by the independent study? As a general rule, these will be students in the upper division of the major or interdisciplinary program, most often in the third or fourth year, who are professionally oriented and proactive in seeking out extracurricular learning. In almost all of the independent studies I have participated in recently, the students were preparing to write fellowship proposals or graduate admission essays.

Even average undergraduate students can sometimes develop strong, overdetermined scenarios in support of their request for an independent study. As difficult as it might be for them to accept, such students are better off waiting until graduate school to pursue their interests. Students with well-developed level-2 reasoning skills, the level in which students are comfortable juggling multiple perspectives and are well on their way to learning how to prioritize, are the lowest level of reasoners to adequately take on independent learning tasks. You can have the student write out an assessment before making up your mind. I suggest you take a long quote from a prominent figure in the discipline and ask the student to write something on the quote. You will be able to tell the level almost immediately from the student's essay if this is someone with whom you can learn.

When you have found a student who has the motivation and the skill to undertake an independent study, you should negotiate a learning contract. I try to keep a general-purpose syllabus for independent studies, which I can print out whenever the occasion arises, that explains the learning contract to the student, as well as how the student will be evaluated. The learning contract consists of three parts.

The first part describes the goals of the independent study. These can be straightforward (e.g., to read all the literature published in the last four years on forensic botany), or they can be more general (e.g., to explore contemporary approaches to producing Brecht's plays).

The second part lists all of the readings and/or experiences that the student will undertake. The student, working with the catalogues and databases, as well as with suggestions from the instructor, should generate the list. The list should be of reasonable length for the time of the project, and the reading level should be within the student's grasp. Much of the instructor's input during class meetings provides the intellectual context for the readings, and therefore, the student should be encouraged to read professional-level texts and journals.

The third part describes how the student will demonstrate learning to the instructor. At a minimum, the student should prepare a presentation on the readings for each meeting.

In addition, the student might prepare an integrative essay, a funding proposal, a review article, or a manifesto. This section also describes how often the student and instructor will meet. Depending on the reading load, this could be one hour per week or two hours every other week. The duration of the project is also negotiable. There is one good reason for most projects to last a single term. Students deserve the opportunity to bring a complex independent learning project to completion within a time frame with which they are familiar. It establishes good independent work expectations and affords them an early success. Under some circumstances, such as for topics dealing with hard-to-access materials, the project could last several weeks longer.

CHAPTER
119

Makeup Policies and Exams

Even under the most stringent of attendance policies, some students will have appropriate excuses for missing an exam or a paper. To protect students from overzealous instructors, colleges establish policies of makeup exams. These usually take the decision of when and where the exam will be given out of the hands of the instructor. The instructor still gets to decide in most cases whether a makeup exam is warranted. You should be aware of any policies your college has established about makeup exams. The chair is usually your best source of information on this.

You also need to realize that in some departments there is a lot of contention about the academic role of the department assistant or secretary. Some departments take the position that showing films, proctoring exams, and giving makeups are part of the assistant's responsibility. Other departments take the opposite position, excluding the assistant from involvement with any academic functions. Do not assume that the practices of your graduate program are the same everywhere. Staff members often view new faculty as arrogant because they adapt far too slowly to the norms of interaction in the department. You should have a conversation with the chair as early as possible about what the department staff does and does not do for individual faculty.

CHAPTER
120

Grade Challenges

Students have the opportunity to challenge a grade that was falsely computed or unfairly attributed. The policies describing the grounds for such a challenge and the procedures for doing so can usually be found in both the faculty and student handbooks. You need to understand these policies both to avoid common errors that could reverse your own grades and also to advise your students when they have potential reversible grades from other instructors. Universities limit the grounds for reversing grades to two fundamental areas: errors by the instructor in the technical application of the criteria and procedures stated in the syllabus for determining the grade and prejudice on the part of the instructor toward the student.

Colleges vary in how they administer grade challenges. In some, there is a single board made up of faculty from different disciplines. In others, the committees represent all natural science professors or all humanities professors. There is often a student representative to the committee as well. There are limitations on how much time the student has to file a challenge. The procedures of the committees can also vary. For some, the last thing they would ever consider doing would be to second-guess an instructor on the grade on an individual assignment. The burden of proof is with the student. He or she must show that instructor misapplied the criteria or evidence of prejudice. The instructor responds in writing to the student's challenge. There is a lot of variation among colleges as to whether the instructor, the student, both of them, or neither of them can be present for the hearing. Since most students challenge grades because they expected to do better yet do not have evidence that satisfies these grounds, the vast majority of challenges are not supported.

I have served on grade challenge committees for twenty years. In those few instances where we supported the student, the reason always lay with incomplete, ambiguous, and/or contradictory statements in the syllabus or in class about how the student's grade would be calculated. If you explicitly state these facts of life in your syllabus, you need not fear having your grades reversed by challenges on this ground.

Prejudice is even harder to prove, although it does happen. Prejudice need not be social prejudice. Faculty are too wary of identity politics to reveal their biases in class. The student-instructor interaction is sometimes susceptible to ordinary personality conflicts. To the extent that instructors allow their personal feelings about student personalities to influence grading, that grade could be considered prejudicial. Students do not have access to the pattern of grading, unless the instructor posts the grades. If all the grades are available, students might be tempted to challenge on the basis of a prejudicial pattern, asserting that the instructor disproportionately grades men lower than women or sophomores lower than seniors. This argument shifts the burden of proof to the instructor, who must show that the pattern does not exist or that the pattern is misleading. Finally, prejudice can be found in class procedures that the student believes are especially harsh. An attendance policy that has no flexibility for absences that were beyond the control of the student, a final paper format policy that was sufficiently ambiguous in the syllabus that students could not figure out what style to use, or a class participation grade whose components are never stated in the syllabus are all examples of successful challenges for prejudicial procedures. When a challenge is successful, the committee determines what changes to make in the grade and sends through the appropriate forms. The student and the faculty member are informed and the matter is closed.

PART 19

Evaluating the Instructor

Teachers have been evaluated by their supervisors since schools began (Walden 1909). In the United States, the efforts to understand teaching effectiveness in universities and colleges began at the turn of the twentieth century. There were six studies on college teaching in the form of peer evaluations between 1900 and 1913 (Morsch and Wilder 1954). Evaluations took the form of asking students to respond to survey questions in several colleges beginning in the 1920s (Marsh 1987, 253-388). All of us have had the experience of sitting through classes with especially effective teachers and some spectacularly ineffective ones. Students are concerned with effective teaching because they want to be in classrooms where learning is going on. They want to have the choice of whether to learn or not. If the teaching is ineffective, that choice has already been made for them. Instructors monitor evaluation because they want fair and effective feedback to help them improve or at least to give them an early warning of problems that might interfere with their annual raises, tenure, or promotion. The institutional concern with evaluation stems from the desire among schools to offer their students the most effective teaching across the curriculum. This means that the administration must seek out information about each classroom experience. But what are the administrators supposed to be looking for? What are the qualities of effective teaching? Is it something the teacher does (behavioral approach)? Or is it something the students do in response to the teacher (systemic approach)? In order to learn something valid from the information, everyone has to be convinced that it reveals the relevant parts of the experience, asks the right questions about it, and understands what the answers are really saying. This is where the controversy in teaching evaluation lies. We know good teaching when we see it. However, we can see it in a wide variety of behavioral styles, classroom formats and student responses. Trying to establish one instrument that can be sensitive to these variations is very difficult indeed.

Student-Based Evaluation

CHAPTER

121

There are several different ways to evaluate teaching that give instructors the feedback they need, while providing students with a sense of having significantly contributed to the improvement of teaching at their institution, and offering the institution information it can use to make personnel and mentoring decisions. The typical method is for a department, school, or university to construct a survey instrument administered at the end of the term. The survey asks students to rate components of the instructor's teaching on a scale. The ratings are then averaged, and the report is provided to the instructor after the grades have been turned in. Sometimes that instrument contains one or two questions that are asked of every teacher in the university and several more that pertain only to teachers in that college, and still another section contains questions particular to that department. Many departments also include open-ended questions that permit the students to construct a short narrative of their experience in the class and provide some degree of qualitative feedback.

There are issues associated with using surveys of this kind. The first issue is one of representation. The students who fill out such a survey are the ones who are present on the day the instructor decides to administer the survey. If the entire class, rather than just this subset, were polled, the results might vary significantly. Some colleges have experimented with putting the survey online and requiring the students to fill it out before they can see the grade they received in the course. Forcing students to provide opinions strikes some observers as introducing a new bias into the result.

The second issue is one of validity. In order for the questions about teaching to be answered correctly, they have to concern behaviors and practices that students understand as being part of effective teaching. If there are sections of the survey that ask questions the students do not think are relevant, or if the students do not see questions about behaviors they do believe are relevant, their judgment of the instrument will influence their judgment of the instructor. Research has shown that students will make up their minds about an instructor in the first thirty seconds of contact and these same judgments will turn up as the evaluations at the end of the term (Ambady and Rosenthal 1993, 431-41; Erdle et al. 1985, 394-407; Marsh and Dunkin 1992, 143-233). The form of the survey instrument, then, has a crucial function refocusing students' attention on the experience of the course and away from their evaluation of the instructor's personal qualities. They should inform students of the behaviors that they consider to be the hallmarks of effectiveness. There is agreement about only a small number of these in the literature, as I will discuss a bit later. If we cannot agree on what the specifics of effective teaching are (external validity), how can we construct an instrument that will eventually yield valid results in a particular classroom?

The third issue is reliability. When students are evaluating their experience of the course, they could be combining the aspects of the experience that the instructor was responsible for with those aspects that they the students are responsible for. Thus, if a student is having a bad term, social relationships may not be going well. Other classes may have proved too time consuming, and their grades may therefore be suffering. The instructor in the course under evaluation was innovative and challenging, and that was the last thing the student wanted that term. There are potentially other forms of bias. In a meta-analysis of the teaching evaluation research, Pritchard et al. (1994) found that there are features of the classroom that are believed to bias teaching evaluations but do not, features that cause bias by increasing ratings, and features that may cause bias but where the results are so mixed that further research is required. These are summarized as follows.

→ Do Not Cause Bias: Instructor gender; Student age; Student gender; Student level (e.g., freshman, sophomore, etc.); Student personality; Time during the term when ratings were done; Time of day when ratings were done.

→ Cause Bias (increase ratings): Lack of anonymity of raters; Instructor's presence during ratings; Telling students ratings will be used for personnel decisions

→ Results Unclear: Student interest in the course; Instructor age and teaching experience; Class size; Course level; Academic field of the course; Grades in the course. (Pritchard et al. 1994)

There are several surprises in these findings. We often assume that some students evaluate women instructors lower. However, four studies of the influence of gender on evaluation results show no significant relationship (Brandenburg et al. 1984, 67-78; Brown 1976, 573-78; Marsh 1987, 253-388; McKeachie 1979, 384-97). The three features that do cause bias are not logically related to the classroom experience. They are extraneous factors that enter the classroom only at the time of the evaluation. The most interesting group of features are the ones for which the results are not clear. These are features that could introduce bias into the ratings of an instructor. They are all logically related to the experience of the classroom. This means they could be sources of legitimate influence in student ratings. However, they are also features over which the instructor has either no control or limited control (grades). As a result, when students evaluate the class through an over-reliance on their experience with these factors, bias can be introduced into the result.

Assuming your institution has wrestled with these issues and arrived at some level of comfort with the survey instrument, administration procedures, and reporting practices, you should familiarize yourself with the survey as soon as you start teaching. Do not wait until after the first administration of the evaluation. You need to figure out ahead of time how you can use the instrument for real feedback on your teaching. Can the survey tell you what went right and what went wrong during the term?

Certain behaviors are common to effective teaching. If the behaviors are present, the teaching is effective. If they are absent, there is need for improvement. In their review of the literature on teaching evaluations, Pritchard et al. identified sixteen such behaviors based on four different sources of information: studies of surveys of administrators, instructors, and students; summaries of previous researchers on teaching; theories of effective teaching; and statistically identified factors. The behaviors he identified were:

→ Organization

→ Group or individual rapport

→ Clarity

→ Enthusiasm

- → Communication
- → Flexibility
- → Preparation
- → Impact of the course
- → Stimulation of curiosity and motivation to learn
- → Favorable attitude toward students
- → Fairness in grades and exams
- → Encouragement of independent thinking
- → Assignment of appropriate workload
- → Progressive attitude
- → Knowledge of subject
- → Atmosphere conducive to learning. (Pritchard et al. 1994)

The results show a good deal of overlap between many of these behaviors, as well as some interesting divergences. The idea of comparing these different sources of information points up how much effective teaching is the product of a discourse among educators, administrators, and students, rather than an objective set of observed activities. The behaviors are not discrete. Many are broad categories that might subsume others. For example, clarity and communication are clearly related, although the former usually refers to a public speaking style and the latter to a private one. There are only three behaviors that occur in all four sources: organization, communication, and fairness. Organization refers to the logistics of the classroom, getting the required information into the hands of the students in a manner that does not handicap them in any way, and communicating a sense of being on top of things. Students need the course to be well thought out. They want to see the method that generated the challenges you have set for them. Communication usually refers to questions of access and affability in the evaluation forms and reports. Students need an approachable instructor, who is open to discussing their issues. Fairness usually refers to operating without bias or favoritism in the classroom process or in evaluation. Each of these is certainly a component of a well-functioning classroom. Are they sufficient to describe effective teaching? I think not. Rather, they are the sort of minimal conditions that make effective teaching possible. If a significant number of your students are reporting that they have issues with your organization, communication, and fairness, you need to pay attention, figure out what is wrong and fix it.

Three out of the four sources cite an additional six behaviors. They are rapport, clarity, enthusiasm, flexibility, encouragement of independent thinking and the level of the assigned workload. Rapport refers to the friendliness, public openness and good-naturedness of the instructor. Students want a connection to their teachers. They recognize that it will be different according to the differences of age, gender, and experience. Faculty who make it clear that they are not interested in any connection with students that isn't directly related to the material create a less effective learning environment. Clarity is a quality of effectiveness of the instructor's communication style, specifically that the essential information is conveyed in an understandable fashion. Rapport is also related to communication. Rapport refers to openness, but unlike communication, it is created in the classroom, rather than privately. Enthusiasm refers to the level of energy the instructor generates around the topics of the course. For the students, this is a measure of how much the instructor wants to be in the class teaching these subjects. Flexibility describes the instructor's willingness to express doubt, indecision, or error, without appearing stiff or defensive. A flexible instructor is desirable because the behavior does not trivialize the role of the students. It creates room for the students to participate in shaping the classroom experience, even if only to a small degree. Level of assigned workload refers to the instructor's understanding of the complexity of the students' lives. A teacher who is oblivious to the workloads of students' other classes, the importance of the learning that takes place outside of classrooms, and, in some schools, the necessity of the students' work hours to their continued progress toward the degree may assign unfair amounts of work. Effective teachers assign work that takes these outside factors into account and still meets their learning goals.

What to Do About "Bad" Evaluations

CHAPTER

122

New instructors commonly receive unflattering evaluations within their first two years of teaching, even if they had previous experience as teaching assistants or visiting faculty at another school. A "bad" evaluation is one where the students score the components of the instructor's teaching consistently and significantly below the department or college average. For the new instructor, this can be unsettling. While such evaluations need to be taken seriously, their significance should not be overblown. It is an extremely rare occurrence when an instructor's career has ever been destroyed by a year of lukewarm evaluations. What personnel committees look for is how the instructor responds to such feedback. If the pattern of weak teaching holds over a number of years, that is cause for concern. If the evaluations show steady improvement after a rocky start, that is as it should be. Any instructor, regardless of experience, can receive weak evaluations. I still get the occasional weak evaluation if I try to do something in the classroom that my students are not ready for or if I am so distracted by research or administration that I cannot give the class the attention it deserves. We all want our efforts to be viewed as valuable by our students. Even after tenure, weak evaluations sting.

There are several reasons why new instructors are particularly susceptible to bad evaluations. First, as I have emphasized throughout this book, there is a natural variation in the level of heterogeneity among students in classes. Just as this challenges the instructor throughout the term, it also challenges the instructor at the time of the course evaluation. Some students bring negative attitudes to class that poison the well, making it difficult for others to have a positive experience. The vagaries of registration may result in classes where the number of students with low motivation or low skill levels shapes the atmosphere in such a way that active learning is rejected. When the instructor does not then deliver an effective teacher-centered classroom experience, the students retaliate with weak evaluations. New instructors are more likely to suffer in these situations than their established colleagues. Their lack of experience prevents them from recognizing the underlying weaknesses in the students and adjusting accordingly. This is not an argument that blames bad evaluations on weak students who just didn't "get it." The evaluations in these situations are valid. They give accurate pictures of the learning that did not take place, and the adjustments that were not made.

Second, different schools have different classroom expectations. These often have to do with very slight discrepancies in workloads, rhythms of discussion, forms of evaluation, levels of energy, and communication styles. Taken singly, these elements do not add up to very much. Taken as a set, they lead to student discomfort with the classroom. Because the students experience a broad range of classrooms, they are the experts in this local knowledge. Thus, no single set of expectations can be communicated to the new instructor by the chair. The students must communicate it. They provide the clues for socializing the new instructor through course evaluations. The evaluations improve when the instructor adjusts the course design within the range of student expectations.

Third, students respond to instructor's personalities, personal qualities and attractiveness on evaluations rather than teaching effectiveness. As noted above, students make up their minds about the instructor in the first thirty minutes of the class. This is known as "primacy effect." It is a common and well-studied phenomenon in many social interactions. Primacy effect converts first impressions into lasting judgements. Thus, negative results may have nothing to do with teaching effectiveness. This possibility needs to be brought to the attention of the department if the instructor considers himself/herself vulnerable to these prejudicial evaluations. I provided references to studies of this issue previously and a simple search can yield even more. The instructor who is the victim of prejudice can find support for that claim and mechanisms to generate hard evidence of its existence in the classroom.

Finally, the inability to effectively communicate the complexity of the concepts of the course is the most common reason for bad evaluations from students. We teach ideas that took us years to comprehend. The tendency to view the classroom as a performance stage where we can show what we know and how well we know it is strongest among recent graduates of our professional programs. Learning to communicate complexity takes a lot of practice. It is not a matter of dumbing down the formulas and shortcuts that worked well in graduate seminars. You certainly have significant depth of knowledge or your dissertation would never have been accepted. It is the breadth of knowledge that is lacking.

This involves the myriad contexts in which the core concepts of your discipline can be found, the analogies to common experience that help students grapple with the complexity, and the images and memory tools that help them hold the different pieces of the concept accurately and actively in their minds. Bain holds that the best teachers know their discipline inside and out (2004). I learned more about my discipline in the first five years of teaching than I did in eight years of graduate school. As hard as it may be for young scholars to accept, they still have a great deal to learn about how to communicate their discipline to nonspecialist audiences. The students are not there to be a fawning audience to your learning. They are there to learn for themselves.

If you are the recipient of a bad evaluation, it is in your best interest to analyze the basis for the students' responses. If none of the four reasons for bad evaluations just described apply in your case, look for further clues to the students' concerns in their open-ended responses. You should not hide weak evaluations from your mentor or from colleagues who have shown themselves to be helpful. They may help you see things in the evaluation that you might have missed. You should always write a response to the evaluation and include it in filings for personnel review. Avoid blaming the students in your response. Do not accept analyses from colleagues that blame the students. It is more professional to accept the students' responses as valid at some level. In your response, describe what you intend to do in future classes to try to address the students' concerns. If the evaluations improve, and they almost always do, you can then say that you made a successful adjustment to the classroom.

CHAPTER

123

Peer-Based Evaluation

Peer evaluation usually involves one or more of your colleagues who familiarize themselves with your courses and may visit one or more of your class sessions. Often they write a formal report on your approach to teaching. Peer evaluation serves several important purposes. First, it builds community within the department. The more your colleagues know your teaching, the greater their sense of how your classes fit with their own. As you visit other classes as the evaluator, you will experience this, too. Over time, everyone gains more confidence in the ability of the department to deliver its curriculum. Second, peer evaluation improves teaching. Most peer evaluation formats are formative, rather than summative. That is, they provide feedback to you about what works and what is not working in your classroom. These visits can uncover issues about which you may not be aware or give you a chance to discuss issues that you have not yet figured out how to resolve. Third, these evaluations provide a different kind of feedback than that provided by students. The peer evaluator will pay attention to content in ways the students cannot. For this reason, peer evaluation generates important feedback for teachers. For all these reasons, you should embrace peer evaluation opportunities.

You should always meet with your evaluator before the class visit. It is very rare for the instructor not to know when the colleague will arrive. Any visit by a colleague will create a nontypical class. For that reason, the surprise factor loses its saliency quickly. When you meet with the evaluator, explain the syllabus and class design. It is especially important for the colleague to know where the class will be when he or she visits. If the colleague has taught the same class, you can discuss together where your approaches may overlap and where they may contrast. If the colleague is not familiar with the course content, you can use the occasion to discuss how it fits into the department's learning goals or disciplinary traditions. This is also the time to discuss the questions you would like the colleague to consider about your class design choices. The more open and revealing you can be, the more effective the evaluation will be for improving your teaching.

During the class visit, introduce the evaluator to the class. Students will want to know the identity of the stranger in the room and the reason for his or her visit. Seeing that the school cares enough about the classroom to engage in peer evaluation, an apparently time-consuming and complex process, students will have greater faith in the quality of the education at their institution. Evaluators take notes during the class. I always write down how many students are participating, how the topic of conversation shifts, and any patterns that emerge in the flow of the class. Departments usually develop rubrics to help guide the evaluator's note taking. Expect the colleague to engage students in the class in conversation afterward. It is part of the process. I always ask one or two students sitting around me if the class was typical or atypical.

After the class, do not expect immediate feedback. Give the evalua-tor time to digest the experience. In the role of evaluator, I always wait at least three or four hours but never more than a week to get back to the instructor to discuss the class. I share the patterns I observed, and we discuss what is positive or problematic about them. After that, I submit my formal report.

The formal report should not depart from the items we discuss. For that reason, you should have kept notes on what you talked about with the evaluator. The report always emphasizes the positive aspects of the classroom. Positive feedback is more helpful than a list of complaints and suggestions for improvement. When there are issues, I will have already discussed them with the instructor. I describe the issues as accurately as possible and what the instructor and I discussed to best deal with the issues. This is important for future evaluators. They will have access to the report and will come to class prepared to see how well the instructor's strategy has worked.

A Final Word

Teaching is the most exciting part of my career. The various details and situations I have described in this book help me recall specific situations in which I first encountered a challenge and the people who helped me resolve it. Teaching is a team effort. No one should ever have to learn to do it alone.

The most important way that you can enhance your teaching is to talk about your experiences with other teachers. Students are not so different from class to class or school to school that your colleagues have not encountered similar situations. Talking helps everyone discover more effective approaches and techniques.

Finally, you haven't really succeeded as a teacher until your students become independent learners. It may not happen in your class, but you contributed to the process in some concrete way. This is what the effort is all about. Giving them the answer holds them where they are for another day. Showing them how they can find the answers on their own moves them toward life-long learning.

Web Resources

Updates on Changes in Copyright Law

http://www.unc.edu/~unclng/public-d.htm

Stephen's Guide to the Logical Fallacies. Electronic document.
http://www.datanation.com/fallacies/index.html.

Sources for Course Management Software Packages

BlackBoard
http://www.blackboard.com/

Desire2Learn
http://www.desire2learn.com/

CyberExtension
http://www.rightreasontech.com/Managed_Learning_Environment/
     CyberExtension.php

Moodle
http://moddle.org

Sakai
http://sakaiproject.org

Dokeos
http://www.dokeos.com/

Sources for Cases

CasePlace
http://www.caseplace.org/

iCase
http://www i-case.com/

Electronic Hallway
http://www.hallway.org/journal

Pearson Custom Publishinghttp://www.pearsoncustom.com/

Irwin/McGraw Hill PRIMUS
http://www.mhhe.com/catalogs/cust_serv/

Sources for Students with Physical or Cognitive Disabilities

Learning Disabilities Online
http://www.ldonline.org

DePaul University's PLuS Program
http://studentaffairs.depaul.edu/plus/faculty_staff.html

Sources for Academic Integrity Education

Dartmouth
http://www.dartmouth.edu/~writing/sources/

New York University
http://ls.nyu.edu/page/ls.academicintegrity

Northwestern
http://www.northwestern.edu/uacc/plagiar.html

Princeton
http://www.princeton.edu/pr/pub/integrity/08/intro/

Support for On-line Course Development
Quality Matters
http://www.qualitymatters.org/Rubric.htm

RadioJames Objective Builder
http://www.radiojames.com/ObjectivesBuilder/

Netiquette Guidelines
http://www.dtcc.edu/cs/rfc1855.html

Student Readiness for Distance Learning

University System of Georgia
http://alt.usg.edu/sort/

Penn State University
http://ets.tlt.psu.edu/learningdesign/assessment/onlinecontent/
online_readiness

Ball State University
http://www.thenicc.edu/courses/teachnology/online_survey_scale.htm

Rubrics for Collaboration and Discussion in Online or Traditional Classrooms

San Diego State University, The Cabrillo Tidepool Study
http://edweb.sdsu.edu/triton/tidepoolunit/Rubrics/collrubric.html

Worcester Polytechnic Institute
http://www.wpi.edu/Academics/ATC/Collaboratory/Idea/
        gradingdiscussions.html

References

AAUP (American Association of University Professors). 2002. Intellectual Property and the AAUP. Last access: 8/30/2009. http://aaup.org/AAUP/pubsres/academe/2002/SO/Feat/Smit.ht

Abt, C. 1970. *Serious Games.* Washington, DC: University Press of America.

AcademicDave (pseudo.). 2008. Twitter for Academia. Last access: 8/30/2009. http://academhack.outsidethetext.com/home/2008/twitter-for-academia/

Albanese, M., and S. Mitchell. 1993. Problem-Based Learning: A Review of the Literature on Its Outcomes and Implementation Issues. *Academic Medicine* 68:52–81.

Amabile, T. M. 1996. *Creativity in Context: Update to the Social Psychology of Creativity.* Boulder, CO: Westview Press.

Ambady, N, and R. Rosenthal. 1993. Half a Minute: Predicting Teacher Evaluation from Thin Slices of Nonverbal Behavior and Physical Attractiveness. *Journal of Personality and Social Psychology* 64:431-441.

Americans with Disabilities Act of 1990. 42 U.S.C.A. § 12101 *et seq.*

Anderson, Kristi, and E. Miller. 1997. Gender and Student Evaluations of Teaching. *PS: Political Science and Politics* 12:216-219.

Angelo, T. A. 1995a. Classroom Assessment for Critical Thinking. *Teaching of Psychology* 22(1):6.

———. 1995b A Classroom Assessor's Dozen: Fourteen General Findings from Research That Can Help Us Understand and Improve Teaching, Learning and Assessment. The 1995 Assessment Conference in Indianapolis, IN. American Association for Higher Education.

———. 1995c Reassessing (and Defining) Assessment. *The AAHE Bulletin* 48:7–9.

Angelo, T. A., and K. P. Cross. 1994. *Classroom Assessment Techniques: A Handbook for College Teachers.* San Francisco: Jossey-Bass.

Anonymous. 1989. *Bargna: A Simulation of Cultural Clashes.* Yarmouth, ME: Intercultural Press.

———. 1999. Policies and Procedures—School of Education, Vol. 2003: New York University School of Education.

———. 2003. SimCity 4. *Electronic Arts.* http://www.ea.com/home/home. jsp

———. n.d.-a Bafa Bafa. Available from SIMILIE II. P.O. Box 1023, LaJolla CA 92037

———. n.d.-b Starpower. Available from SIMILIE II. P.O. Box 1023, LaJolla CA 92037

Aspy, D.N., C. B. Aspy, and P.M. Quimby. 1993. What doctors can teach teachers about problem-based learning. *Educational Leadership* 50:22-24.

Association of American Colleges. 1985. Integrity in the College Curriculum: A Report to the Academic Community. Washington, DC: Association of American Colleges.

Astin, A. 1998. Principles of Good Practice for Assessing Student Learning. In *Effective Grading: A Tool for Learning and Assessment.* B. Walvoord and V. J. Anderson, eds. Pp. 189–191. San Francisco: Jossey-Bass.

Austin, A. W., et al. 1996. Involvement in Learning Revisited: Lessons We Have Learned. *Journal of College Student Development* 37(2):123–134.

Bain, K.. 2004. *What the Best College Teachers Do.* Cambridge, Mass.: Harvard University Press.

Barnlund, D. C., and F. S. Haiman. 1960. *The Dynamics of Discussion.* Boston: Houghton Mifflin.

Baxter-Magolda, M. B. 1992. *Knowing and Reasoning in College: Gender-Related Patterns in Students' Intellectual Development.* San Francisco: Jossey-Bass.

Bean, J. C. 1996. *Engaging Ideas: The Professor's Guide to Integrating Writing, Critical Thinking, and Active Learning in the Classroom.* San Francisco: Jossey-Bass Publishers.

Beard, R. M. and J. Hartley. 1984. *Teaching and Learning in Higher Education.* New York: Harper & Row.

Becker, H. S., B. Geer, and E. C. Hughes. 1968. *Making the Grade: The Academic Side of College Life*. New York: Wiley.

Belbin, M. 1981. *Management Teams: Why They Succeed or Fail*. London: Butterworth Heinemann.

Belenky, M. F., et al. 1986. *Women's Ways of Knowing: The Development of Self, Voice and Mind*. New York: Basic Books.

Bender, E., et al. 1994. *Quick Hits: Successful Strategies by Award Winning Teachers*. Bloomington: Indiana University Press.

Bennett, W. E. 1987. Small Group Instructional Diagnosis: A Dialogic Approach to Instructional Improvement for Tenured Faculty. *Journal of Staff, Program and Organizational Development* 5:100–104.

Bennett, W. J. 1984. To Reclaim a Legacy: A Report on the Humanities in Higher Education. Washington, DC: National Endowment for the Humanities.

Bennis, W. G., and H. A. Shepard. 1956. A Theory of Group Development. *Human Relations* 9:415-457.

Bergquist, W. H., and S. R. Phillips. 1989. Classroom Structures Which Encourage Student Participation. In *Classroom Communication: Collected Readings for Effective Discussion and Questioning*. R. A. Neff and M. Weimer, eds. Pp. 19–26. Madison, WI: Magna Productions, Inc.

Bernard, R.M., et al. 2004. How does distance education compare with classroom instruction? A meta-analysis of the empirical literature. *Review of Educational Research* 74(3):379.

Biggs, J. 1999. What the Student Does: Teaching for Enhanced Learning. *Higher Education Research and Development* 18(1):57–75.

Bloom, B. S., et al. 1956. *Taxonomy of Educational Objectives, Vol. 1: Cognitive Domain*. New York: Longman Green.

Boehrer, J., and M. Linsky. 1990. Teaching with Cases: Learning to Question. In The Changing Face of College Teaching. M. D. Svinicki, ed. *New Directions for Teaching and Learning, no. 42*. San Francisco: Jossey-Bass.

Boghossian, Peter. 2002. Socratic Pedagogy, Race, and Power. *Education Policy Analysis Archives* 10(3).

Bok Center, The. 2002. Encouraging Students in a Racially Diverse Classroom, Vol. 2003: Derek Bok Center for Teaching and Learning, Office of Race Relations and Minority Affairs at Harvard University.

Bourdieu, P. 1984. *Distinction: A Social Critique of the Judgment of Taste.* Cambridge, MA: Harvard University Press.

Bowe, F.G. 2000. *Universal Design in Education: Teaching non-traditional students.* Westport: CT: Bergen and Garvey.

Boyer, E. L. 1987. *College: The Undergraduate Experience in America.* New York: Harper & Row.

Brandenburg, D. C., J. A. Slindle, and E. E. Batista. 1984. Student Ratings in Instruction: Validity and Normative Interpretations. *Journal of Research in Higher Education* 7:67–78.

Bratley, P., B. L. Fox, and L. E. Schrage. 1988. *A Guide to Simulations.* New York: Springer-Verlag.

Brethower, D. 1977. Research in Learning Behavior: Some Implications for College Teaching. In *Teaching in Higher Education.* S. Scholl and S. Inglis, eds. Columbus: Ohio Board of Regents.

Bridges, E. M., and P. Hallinger. 1991. Problem-Based Learning in Medical and Managerial Education. Paper presented for the Cognition and School Leadership Conference of the National Center for Educational Leadership and the Ontario Institute for Studies in Education, Nashville. September 26-27, 1991.

Brogan, Bernard R., and W. A. Brogan. 1995. The Socratic Questioner: Teaching and Learning in the Dialogical Classroom. *Educational Forum* 59(3):288-96.

Brotherton J, and G. Abowd. 2004. Lessons Learned From eClass: Assessing Automated Capture and Access in the Classroom. *ACM Transactions on Computer-Human Interaction* 11(2), 122. Last access: 01.16.2007. http://portal.acm.org/citation.cfm?id=1005362

Brown, D. L. 1976. Faculty Ratings and Student Grades: A University-Wide Multiple Regression Analysis. *Journal of Educational Psychology* 68:573–578.

Brown, G., and M. Atkins. 1988. *Effective Teaching in Higher Education*. London: Methuen.

Bruner, Jerome. 1960. *The Process of Education*. Cambridge, MA: Harvard University Press.

Burgstahler, S.E. 2008a.Universal Design in Higher Education. In *Universal Design in Higher Education: From Principles to Practice*. S.E. Burgstahler and R.C. Cory, eds. Pp. 3-20. Cambridge, MA: Harvard University Press.

Burgstahler, S.E. 2008b. Universal Design for Instruction: From principles to practice. In *Universal Design in Higher Education: From Principles to Practice*. S.E. Burgstahler and R.C. Cory, eds. Pp. 23-44. Cambridge, MA: Harvard University Press.

Cantor, L. M., M. J. Peterson, and A. G. Brzycki. 2002. Academic Integrity at Princeton. Office of the Dean of the College.

Center for Universal Design. 1997. *About UD*. Raleigh: North Carolina State University. Accessed August 27, 2009, from http://www.design. ncsu.edu/cud/about_ud/about_ud.htm

Champagne, A. B., et al. 1980. Factors Influencing the Learning of Classical Mechanics. *American Journal of Physics* 48:1074–1079.

Chi, M. T. H., and R. Glaser. 1985. Problem Solving Ability. In *Humanabilities: An Information Processing Approach*. R. J. Sternberg, ed. New York: W. H. Freeman.

Chickering, A. W. 1969. *Education and Identity*. San Francisco: Jossey-Bass.

Chickering, A. W., and Z. F. Gamson. 1987. Seven Principles for Good Practice in Undergraduate Education. *American Association for Higher Education Bulletin* 39(7):3–7.

Chickering, A. W., and Associates. 1981. *The Modern American College: Responding to the New Realities of Diverse Students and a Changing Society*. San Francisco: Jossey-Bass.

Cohen, A. J., and J. Spencer. 1993. Using Writing Across the Curriculum in Economics: Is Taking the Plunge Worth It? *Journal of Economic Education* 23:219–230.

Cohen, P. A. 1981 Student Ratings of Instruction and Student Achievement: A Meta-analysis of Multi-section Validity Scores. *Review of Educational Research* 51:281–309.

———. 1984 College grades and adult achievement: A research synthesis. *Research in Higher Education* 20(3): 281-293.

Connery, B. A. 1988. Group Work and Collaborative Writing. *Teaching at Davis* 14:2–4.

Conrad, D., and D. Hedin. 1990. Learning from Service: Experience Is the Best Teacher, or Is It? In *Combining Service and Learning: A Resource Book for Community and Public Service*. J. C. Kendall and Associates, eds. Vol. 1. Raleigh, NC: National Society for Internships and Experiential Education.

Cooper, J. L., and Associates. 1990. *Cooperative Learning and College Instruction*. Long Beach: California State University, Institute for Teaching and Learning.

Coppola, B. P., S. N. Ege, and R. G. Lawton. 1997. The University of Michigan Undergraduate Chemistry Curriculum: 2. Instructional Strategies and Assessments. *Journal of Chemical Education* 74:84–94.

Coppola, B. P., and R. G. Lawton. 1995. "Who Has the Same Substance That I Have?" A Blueprint for Collaborative Learning Activities. *Journal of Chemical Education* 72:1120– 1122.

Creed, T. 1997. Small Group Instructional Diagnosis, Vol. 2003: The National Teaching & Learning Forum.

Cronbach, L., and R. E. Snow. 1977. *Aptitudes and Instructional Methods: A Handbook for Research on Interaction*. New York: Irvington.

Cross, K. P. 1986. Taking Teaching Seriously. Paper presented to the Annual Meeting of the American Association for Higher Education (Washington, DC, March 11, 1986). Pp. 15.

Dewey, J. 1938. *Experience and Education.* New York: Collier Books.

Domin, D. S. 1999. A Review of Laboratory Inspection Styles. *Journal of Chemical Education* 76:543–547.

Downes, S. 1995. *Stephen's Guide to the Logical Fallacies.* Electronic document, http://www.datanation.com/fallacies/index.html.

Education, Study Group on the Conditions of Excellence in American Higher 1984 Involvement in Learning: Realizing the potential of American Higher Education. Washington, D.C: U.S. Department of Education.

Ehrenberg, R. G. and D. R. Sherman. 1987. Employment While in College, Academic Achievement, and Postcollege Outcomes: A Summary of Results. *Journal of Human Resources* 22(1): 1-23.

Eison, J. 1988. "How can I get into graduate school, and what do I do if I want a job?" In *Is psychology for them? A guide to undergraduate advising.* P. Woods, ed. Washington, DC: American Psychological Association. Pp. 91-95.

Elder, L., and R. Paul. 1998. The Role of Socratic Questioning in Thinking, Teaching, and Learning. *Clearing House* 75(5):297-301.

Elkins, J. 2001. *Why Art Cannot Be Taught.* Urbana and Chicago: University of Illinois Press.

Erdle, S., H. Murray, and J. P. Rushton. 1985. Personality, Classroom Behavior and Student Ratings of College Teaching Effectiveness: A Path Analysis. *Journal of Educational Psychology* 77:394-407.

Ewell, P. T. 1985. *Assessing Educational Outcomes.* San Francisco: Jossey-Bass.

Feichtner, S. B., and E. A. Davis. 1992. *Why Some Groups Fail. In Collaborative Learning: A Sourcebook for Higher Education*. A. Goodsell, M. Maher, V. Tinto, and Associates, eds. University Park: Pennsylvania State University, National Center for Postsecondary Teaching, Learning and Assessment.

Feldman, K. A. 1976. The Superior College Teacher from the Students' View. *Research in Higher Education* 5:243–288.

Feldman, K. A., and T. M. Newcomb. 1969. *The Impact of College on Students*. San Francisco: Jossey-Bass.

Feldt, A. 1978. *CLUG: Community Land Use Game*. New York: Free Press.

Fischer, K. W. 1980. A Theory of Cognitive Development: The Control and Construction of Hierarchies of Skills. *Psychological Review* 87:477–531.

Fischer, K. W., and T. R. Bidell. 1998. Dynamic Development in Psychological Structures in Action and Thought. In *Handbook of Child Psychology, vol. 1: Theoretical Models of Human Development*. 5th edition. R. M. Learner and W. Damon, eds. Pp. 467– 561. New York: Wiley.

Frederick, P. 1981. The Dreaded Discussion: Ten Ways to Start. *Improving College and University Teaching* 29:109–114.

Fuhrmann, B. S. and A. F. Grasha. 1983. *A Practical Handbook for College Teachers*. Boston: Little, Brown and Company.

Gamson, W. A. 1978. *SIMSOC: Simulated Society*. New York: Free Press.

———. 1984. *What's News? A Game Simulation of TV News*. New York: Free Press.

Gamson, Z. R. 1991. A Brief History of the Seven Principles for Good Practice Undergraduate Education. In *Applying the Seven Principles for Good Practice in Undergraduate Education*. A. W. Chickering and Z. F. Gamson, eds. Pp. 5–12. San Francisco: Jossey-Bass.

Gardner, H. 1993. *Multiple Intelligences. The Theory in Practice*. New York: Basic Books.

Gell, A.. 1999. *The Art of Anthropology: Essays and Diagrams*. London and New Brunswick, NJ: The Athlone Press

Gordon, G., and E. Morse. 1969. Creative Potential and Organizational Structure. *Journal of the Academy of Management*37–49.

Gould, S. J. 1981. *The Mismeasure of Man*. New York: W. W. Norton and Company.

Greeno, J. 1978. Natures of Problem-Solving Abilities. In *Handbook of Learning and Cognitive Processes*. W. Estes, ed. Pp. 239–270. Hillsdale, NJ: Lawrence Erlbaum Associates.

Gross-Davis, B. 1993. *Tools for Teaching*. San Francisco: Jossey-Bass.

Guba, E. G., and Y. S. Lincoln. 1989. *Fourth Generation Evaluation*. Newberry Park, CA: Sage.

Hansen, A. J. 1987a. Reflections of a Case Writer: Writing Teaching Cases. In *Teaching and the Case Method*. C. R. Christensen and A. J. Hansen, eds. Boston: Harvard Business School.

———. 1987b. Suggestions for Seminar Participants. In *Teaching and the Case Method*. C. R. Christensen and A. J. Hansen, eds. Boston: Harvard Business School.

Harley D., et al. 2003. "Costs, Culture, and Complexity: An Analysis of Technology Enhancements in a Large Lecture Course at UC Berkeley." Full report available online at: last access: 8/30/2009 http://cshe.berkeley.edu/publications/docs/cost_culture_and_complexity.pdf

Hartley, J., and I. K. Davies. 1978. Note-Taking: A Critical Review. *Programmed Learning and Educational Technology* 15:207–224.

Hassiotou, F., and P. Finnegan. 2009. Effect of lecture recording on lecture attendance and student performance in science. In *Centre for the Advancement of Teaching and Learning: University of Western Australia*. Last access 8/30/2009. Last update: 5/14/2009 http://www.catl.uwa.edu.au/page/157160

Heath, D. W. 1968. *Growing Up in College: Liberal Education and Maturity*. San Francisco: Jossey-Bass.

Hendrix, K. G. 1998. Student Perceptions of the Influence of Race on Professor Credibility. *Journal of Black Studies* 28:738-763.

Hofstein, A., and V. N. Lunetta. 1982. The Role of the Laboratory in Science Teaching: Neglected Aspects of Research. *Review of Educational Research* 52:201–17.

Holmberg. 2005. The evolution, principles and practices of distance learning. Bibliotheks- und Informationsystem der Universität Oldenburg. Last accessed: 8/30/2009. http://www.c3l.uni-oldenburg.de/publiktionen/volume11.pdf

Howe, N., and W. Strauss. 2000. *Millennials Rising: The Next Generation*. New York: Vintage Books.

Hyman, R. T. 1981. *Using Simulation Games in the College Classroom*. Manhattan, KS: Kansas State University, Center for Faculty Evaluation and Development.

Jackson, P., and S. Messick. 1965. The Person, the Product and the Response: Conceptual Problems in the Assessment of Creativity. *Journal of Personality* 33:309–329.

Johnson, C. 1994. Participatory Rhetoric and the Teacher as Racial/Gendered Subject. *College English* 56:409-419.

Johnson, D. W., R. T. Johnson, and K. A. Smith. 1991. *Cooperative Learning: Increasing College Faculty Instructional Productivity*. Washington, DC: George Washington University, School of Education and Human Development.

Johnson-Laird, P. N. 1988. Freedom and Constraint in Creativity. In *The Nature of Creativity*. R. J. Sternberg, ed. Pp. 202–219. Cambridge, England: Cambridge University Press.

Jolliffe, David A. 1999. *Inquiry and Genre: Writing to Learn in College*. Boston: Allyn & Bacon.

Katchadourian, H. A., and J. Boli. 1985. *Careerism and Intellectualism Among College Students: Patterns of Academic and Career Choice in the Undergraduate Years*. San Francisco: Jossey-Bass.

Katz, J., and Associates. 1968. *No Time for Youth: Growth and Constraint in College Students.* San Francisco: Jossey-Bass.

Keeton, M. 1988. Thoughts on Documenting an Institution's Educational Outcomes. *CAEL News* 4–5.

King, P. M., and K. Kitchener. 1994. *Developing Reflective Judgment: Understanding and Promoting Intellectual Growth and Critical Thinking in Adolescents and Adults.* San Francisco: Jossey-Bass.

Kitchener, K. S. 1983. Cognition, Meta Cognition, and Epistemic Cognition: A Three-Level Model of Cognitive Processing. *Human Development* 26:222–233.

Knefelkamp, L., C. Widick, and C. E. Parker, eds. 1978. *Applying New Developmental Findings.* San Francisco: Jossey-Bass.

Kohn, A. 1986. *No Contest: The Case Against Competition.* Boston: Houghton Mifflin.

Kolb, D. A. 1981. *Experiential Learning: Experience as the Source of Learning and Development.* Englewood Cliffs, NJ: Prentice-Hall.

Kremer, R. L., and S. Culbert. 1998. Sources: Their Use and Acknowledgement: Dartmouth College.

Kurfiss, J. G. 1988. *Critical Thinking: Theory, Research, Practice, and Possibilities.* Washington, DC: Association for the Study of Higher Education.

Lakoff, G., and M. Johnson. 1980. *Metaphors We Live By.* Chicago: University of Chicago Press.

Lang, C. 1986. *Case Method Teaching in the Community Colleges.* Newton, MA: Education Development Center.

Lewin, K. 1951. *Field Theory in Social Sciences.* New York: Harper & Row.

Liedtka, J.M. 2004. Design Thinking: The role of hypothesis generation and testing. In *Managing as Designing.* R. Boland and F. Collopy, eds. Palo Alto, CA: Stanford Business Books. Pp. 188-197.

Lloyd-Jones, R. 1977. Primary Trait Scoring. In *Evaluating Writing: Describing, Measuring, Judging.* C. Cooper and L. Odell, eds. Urbana, IL: National Council of Teachers of English.

Lynch, C. L. , and S. K. Wolcott. 2001. *Helping Students Develop Critical Thinking Skills.* Manhattan, KS: IDEA Center.

Mahrer, K. D. 2000. The DSB Method—Persuasiveness Writing Made Simpler. *The Leading Edge* 162–164.

Mandin, H., P. Harasym, and M. Watanabe. 1995. Developing a "Clinical Presentation" Curriculum at the University of Calgary. *Academic Medicine* 70:186–193.

Mangan, Katherine S. 1997. Lani Guinier Starts Campaign To Curb Use of the Socratic Method. *Chronicle of Higher Education* 43(31):A12-A14.

Marsh, H. W. 1984. Students' Evaluation of Teaching: Dimensionality, Reliability, Validity, Potential Biases, and Utility. *Journal of Educational Psychology* 76:707–754.

———. 1987. Students' Evaluation of University Teaching: Research Findings, Methodological Issues, and Directions for Future Research. *International Journal of Education Research* 11:253–388.

Martin, E., and M. Balla. 1991. An Expanding Awareness: How Lecturers Change Their Understanding of Teaching. *Research and Development in Higher Education* 13:298–304.

McGuire,J.M., S.S.Scott, and S.F. Shaw . 2003. Universal design for instruction: The paradigm, its principles, and products for enhancing educational access. *Journal of Post-secondary Education and Disability* 17(1): 11-21.

McKeachie, Wilbert J. 1979. Student Ratings of Faculty: A Reprise. *Academe: Bulletin of the AAUP* 65:384–397.

———. 1986. *Teaching Tips.* 8th edition. Lexington, MA: Heath.

McKeachie, W. J., et al. 1986. *Teaching and Learning in the College Classroom: A Review of the Research Literature.* Ann Arbor: National Center for Research to Improve Post-Secondary Education, University of Michigan.

McKeachie, W. J., et al. 2002. *McKeachie's Teaching Tips: Strategies, Research, and Theory for College and University Teachers.* Boston: Houghton Mifflin.

McLeish, J. 1968. *The Lecture Method.* Cambridge, England: Cambridge Institute of Education.

Meacham, J. A., and N. C. Emont. 1989. The Interpersonal Basis of Everyday Problem Solving. In *Everyday Problem Solving: Theory and Applications.* J. D. Sinnott, ed. Pp. 7– 22. New York: Praeger.

Mennin, S. P., et al. 1993. Performances on the NBME I, II, and III by Medical Students in the Problem-Based Learning and Conventional Tracks at the University of New Mexico. *Academic Medicine* 68: 616–624.

Michaelsen, L. 1983. Team Learning in Large Classes. In *Learning in Groups, New Directions in Teaching and Learning, No. 14.* C. Bouten and R.Y. Garth, eds. San Francisco: Jossey-Bass.

Miller, J. E., J. Trimbur, and J. M. Wilkes. 1994. Group Dynamics: Understanding the Success and Failure in Collaborative Learning. In *Collaborative Learning: Underlying Processes and Effective Techniques.* K. Bosworth and S. J. Hamilton, eds. Pp. 33–44. San Francisco: Jossey-Bass.

Milton, O., H. R. Pollio, and J. A. Eison. 1986. *Making Sense of College Grades.* San Francisco: Jossey-Bass.

Morsch, J. E., and E. W. Wilder. 1954. *Identifying the Effective Instructor: A Review of Quantitative Studies, 1900–1952.* San Antonio, TX: Air Force Personnel and Training Research Center, Lackland AFB.

Moore, L., and R. Rudd. 2002. Using Socratic Questioning in the Classroom. *Agricultural Education Magazine* 75(3):24-25.

Mosteller, F. 1989. The "Muddiest Point in the Lecture" as a Feedback Device. *On Teaching and Learning* 3:10–21.

Myers, S. P. 2002. Belbin/MTR-i Team Roles—MBTI Comparison. Electronic Source: http://www.teamtechnology.co.uk/belbin.html, March 2005.

Nathan, R.. 2005. *My Freshman Year: What a Professor Learned by Becoming a Student.* Ithica, NY: Cornell University Press.

National Commission on Excellence in Education. 1983. *A Nation at Risk: The Imperative for Educational Reform.* U.S. Department of Education.

Newcomb, T. M., et al. 1967. *Persistence and Change: Bennington College and Its Students After Twenty-Five Years.* New York: Wiley.

Newman, F. 1985. *Higher Education and the American Resurgence.* Princeton, NJ: Carnegie Foundation for the Advancement of Teaching.

O'Donnell, A. M. 1994. Facilitating scripted cooperation through the use of knowledge Maps. *Cooperative Learning and College Teaching* 4(2):7-10.

Olmstead, J. A. 1974. *Small-Group Instruction: Theory and Practice.* Alexandria, VA: Human Resources Research Organization.

Parker, C. E., and J. A. Schmidt. 1982. Effects of College Experience. In *Encyclopedia of Educational Research.* H. E. Mitzel, ed. New York: Free Press.

Pascarella, E. T., and P. T. Terenzini. 1991. *How College Affects Students: Findings and Insights from Twenty Years of Research.* San Francisco: Jossey-Bass.

Paul, R., and L. Elder. 2001. *The Miniature Guide to Critical Thinking Concepts and Tools.* Dillon Beach, CA: Foundation for Critical Thinking.

Payne, D. E., F. N. Vowell, and L. C. Black. 1991. Assessment Approaches in Evaluation Processes. *North Central Association Quarterly* 66:444–450.

Peper, R. J., and R. E. Mayer. 1978. Note-Taking as a Generative Activity. *Journal of Educational Psychology* 70(4):514–522.

Perry, W. G., Jr. 1970. *Forms of Intellectual and Ethical Development in the College Years.* New York: Holt, Rinehart, & Winston.

Pestel, B. C. 1990. Students 'Participate' with Each Other. *Teaching Professor* 4(5):4.

Piaget, J. 1970. *Genetic Epistemology*. New York: Columbia University Press.

Pike, G. R., G.D. Kuh, and R. Massa-McKinley. 2009. First-Year Students' Employment, Engagement, and Academic Achievement: Untangling the Relationship Between Work and Grades. *NASPA Journal* 45(4), 560-582.

Pritchard, R. D., et al. 1994. *Helping Teachers Teach Well: A New System for Measuring and Improving Teaching Effectiveness in Higher Education*. San Francisco: The New Lexington Press.

Prosser, M., and K. Trigwell. 1998. *Teaching for Learning in Higher Education*. Buckingham: Open University Press.

Ramsden, P. 1992. *Learning to Teach in Higher Education*. New York: Routledge.

Redmond, M. V., and D. J. Clark. 1982. A Practical Approach to Improving Teaching. *AAHE Bulletin* 1:9–10.

Richardson, R. C., E. C. Fisk, and M. A. Okun. 1983. *Literacy in the Open-Access College*. San Francisco: Jossey-Bass.

Ruggiero, V. R. 1991. *The Art of Thinking: A Guide to Critical and Creative Thought*. New York: Harper Collins College Publishers.

Ruhl, Kathy L. 1987. Using the Pause Procedure to Enhance Lecture Recall. *Teacher Education and Special Education* 10(1):14-18.

Said, E. 1978. *Orientalism*. New York: Vintage Books.

Samson, G., et al. 1984. Academic and occupational performance: A quantitative synthesis. *American Educational Research Journal* 21(2):311-321.

Samuelowicz, K. 1987. Learning Problems of Overseas Students: Two Sides to the Story. *Higher Education Research and Development* 6:121–134.

Samuelowicz, K., and J. Bain. 1992. Conceptions of Teaching Held by Teachers. *Higher Education* 24:93–112.

Sanford, N., ed. 1962. *The American College.* New York: Wiley.

Sanders, M. 2001. Trusting my Strengths. In Rodis, P., A. Garrod, and M.L. Boscardin. *Learning Disabilities and Life Stories.* New York: Allyn & Bacon.

Schön, D. 1983. *The Reflective Practitioner: How Professionals Think in Action.* New York: Basic Books.

Shuell, T. J. 1986. Cognitive Conceptions of Learning. *Review of Educational Research* 56:411–436.

Smith, B. L., and J. T. MacGregor. 1992. What Is Collaborative Learning? In *Collaborative Learning: A Sourcebook.* A. Goodsell, M. Maher, and V. Tinto, eds. University Park: Pennsylvania State University, National Center for Postsecondary Teaching, Learning and Assessment.

Smith, J. 2002. *How to Avoid Plagiarism, Vol. 2003.* Northwestern University.

Snow, R. E., and P. L. Peterson. 1980. Recognizing Differences in Student Attitudes. *New Directions in Teaching and Learning* Vol. 2.

Snyder, P. D. 2000. Management Team Roles-indicator (MTR-i), CPSY6001 Tests and Measurements, Seton Hall University, November, 2000. Electronic Source: http://patx2.home.mindspring.com/MTRiReview.html, March 2005.

Sorcinelli, A. D. 1991. Research Findings on the Seven Principles. In *Applying the Seven Principles for Good Practice in Undergraduate Education.* A. W. Chickering and Z. F. Gamson, eds. Pp. 13–26. San Francisco: Jossey-Bass.

Spiro, R. J., et al. 1987. Knowledge Acquisition for Application: Cognitive Flexibility and Transfer in Complex Content Domains. In *Executive Control Processes.* B. C. Britton, ed. Hillsdale, NJ: Lawrence Erlbaum Associates.

———. 1988. *Cognitive Flexibility Theory: Advanced Knowledge Acquisition in Ill-Structured Domains*. Champaign, IL: University of Illinois, Center for the Study of Reading.

Stocking, H. 1994. *Feedback or Criticism?* Bloomington: Indiana University Press.

Study Group on the Conditions of Excellence in American Higher Education. 1984. *Involvement in Learning: Realizing the Potential of American Higher Education*. Washington, DC: U.S. Department of Education.

Tiberius, R. G. 1990. *Small Group Teaching: A Trouble-Shooting Guide*. Toronto: Ontario Institute for Studies in Education Press.

Tien, L. T., and D. Rickey. 1999. The MORE Thinking Frame: Guiding Students' Thinking in the Laboratory. *Journal of College Science Teaching* 28(5):318.

Toulmin, S. 1958. *The Uses of Argument*. Cambridge: Cambridge University Press.

Traphagan, T. 2005. "Class Lecture Webcasting, Fall 2004 and Spring 2005: A Case Study." Report from the Division of Instructional Innovation and Assessment at the University of Texas at Austin. Last access: 8/30/2009 http://www.utexas.edu/academic/diia/research/reports/

Van Overwalle, E., K. Segebarth, and M. Goldchstein. 1989. Improving Performance of Freshmen Through Attributional Testimonies from Fellow Students. *British Journal of Educational Psychology* 59:75–85.

Veenstra, M. V. J., and J. J. Elshout. 1995. Differential Effects of Instructional Support on Learning in Simulation Environments. *Instructional Science* 22:363–383.

Vernon, D. T., and R. L. Blake. 1993. Does Problem-Based Learning Work? A Meta-analysis of Evaluative Research. *Academic Medicine* 68:550–563.

Voss, J. F. 1988. Learning and Transfer in Subject-Matter Learning: A Problem Solving Model. *International Journal of Educational Research* 11:607–622.

Walden, J. W. H. 1909. *Universities in Ancient Greece.* New York: Scribner.

Wales, C. E., and A. Nardi. 1982. Teaching Decision-Making with Guided Design. In Idea Paper No. 9. Kansas State University, Center for Faculty Evaluation and Development.

Walvoord, B., and V. J. Anderson. 1998. *Effective Grading: A Tool for Learning and Assessment.* San Francisco: Jossey-Bass.

Warren, L. 2002. *Managing Hot Moments in the Classroom, Vol. 2003.* Derek Bok Center, Harvard University. Electronic Source: http://bok-center.harvard.edu/docs/hotmoments.html. March 2005.

Welty, W. M. 1989. Discussion Method Teaching. *Change* 21:40–49.

Whitkin, H. A., and C. A. Moore. 1975. *Field-Dependent and Field-Independent Cognitive Styles and Their Educational Implications.* Princeton, NJ: Educational Testing Service.

Wiggins, G., and J. McTighe. 2005. *Understanding by Design*, 2nd ed. Upper Saddle River, NJ: Prentice Hall, Inc.

Wilson, R. C., et al. 1975. *College Professors and Their Impact upon Students.* New York: Wiley.

Wilson, T. D., and P. W. Linville. 1982. Improving the Academic Performance of College Freshman: Attribution Therapy Revisited. *Journal of Personality and Social Psychology* 42:367–376.

Winter, D. G., D. C. McClelland, and A. J. Stewart. 1981. *A New Case for the Liberal Arts: Assessing Institutional Goals and Student Development.* San Francisco: Jossey-Bass.

Wolcott, S. K., and C. L. Lynch. 1997. Critical Thinking in the Accounting Classroom: A Reflective Judgment Developmental Process Perspective. *Accounting Education: A Journal of Theory, Practice and Research* 2(1):59–78.

———. 2001. Assignment Templates . Electronic Source: http://www. wolcottlynch.com/index_files/Assignment Templates_030627.pdf . March, 2005

Wolcott, S. K., C. L. Lynch, and G. E. Huber. 2001. *Overview of Steps for Better Thinking Performance Patterns.* Electronic Source: http:// www.wolcottlynch.com/index_files/Overview of Performance Patterns_030828.pdf. Last access: 8/30/2009.

Wood, P. K. 1993. Inquiring Systems and Problem Structures: Implications for Cognitive Development. *Human Development* 26:249–265.

Wood, P. K., K. Kitchener, and L. Jensen. 2002. Considerations in the Design and Evaluation of a Paper-and-Pencil Measure of Epistemic Cognition. In *Personal Epistemology: The Psychology of Beliefs About Knowledge and Knowing.* B. K. Hofer and P. K. Pintrich, eds. Pp. 277–294. Mahwah, NJ: Lawrence Erlbaum Associates.

Young, J. 2009. Professor Encourages Students to Pass Notes During Class -- via Twitter. *Chronicle of Higher Education* September 13, 2009. Last access 8/30/2009. http://chronicle.com/blogPost/ Professor-Encourages-Students/4619

Zeakes, S. J. 1989. Case Studies in Biology. *College Teaching* 37:33–35.

About the Author

Robert Rotenberg has a doctorate in anthropology from the University of Massachusetts. He has taught university-level classes for more than thirty years, at Hampshire College, the University of Massachusetts/Amherst, the University of Rhode Island/Kingston, and DePaul University in Chicago, where he was named a Vincent de Paul Professor for Distinguished Teaching. For more than twenty years he has mentored dozens of faculty. He has served on teaching improvement task forces, conducted workshops on teaching effectiveness and assessment, and given conference papers on the relationship between teaching and curriculum development. He is currently College Coordinator of Faculty Advising for DePaul's College of Liberal Arts and Science. His previous books include *Time and Order in Metropolitan Vienna: A Seizure of Schedules*, *The Cultural Meaning of Urban Space*, co-edited with Gary McDonogh, and *Landscape and Power in Vienna*.